the years of work leading to
this book — I trust the
friendship will continue long
after the book is forgotten.
With love and thanks,

Ruth Mays Abely

7/12/04

ROYAL HISTORICAL SOCIETY

STUDIES IN HISTORY

New Series

1659: THE CRISIS OF
THE COMMONWEALTH

TO MY PARENTS RICHARD AND DIANE MAYERS

The Great Seal of 1659, reproduced from George Vertue, *Medals, coins, great seals and other works of Thomas Simon*, London 1780 [BL item 603.i.29], plate xxiv. *By permission of the British Library*

1659: THE CRISIS OF
THE COMMONWEALTH

Ruth E. Mayers

THE ROYAL HISTORICAL SOCIETY
THE BOYDELL PRESS

First published 2004

A Royal Historical Society publication
Published by The Boydell Press
an imprint of Boydell & Brewer Ltd
PO Box 9, Woodbridge, Suffolk IP12 3DF, UK
and of Boydell & Brewer Inc.
668 Mt Hope Avenue, Rochester, NY 14620, USA
website: www.boydellandbrewer.com

ISBN 0 86193 268 4

ISSN 0269-2244

A catalogue record for this book is available
from the British Library

Library of Congress Cataloging-in-Publication Data
Mayers, Ruth E. (Ruth Elisabeth), 1972–
  1659 : the crisis of the commonwealth / Ruth E. Mayers.
    p. cm. – (Royal Historical Society studies in history. New series,
  ISSN 0269-2244)
Includes bibliographical references and index.
ISBN 0-86193-268-4 (hardback : alk. paper)
1. Great Britain – History – Commonwealth and Protectorate,
1649–1660. 2. Great Britain. Parliament – History – 17th century.
I. Title. II. Series.
DA425.M39 2004
320.941'09'032 – dc22   2004002288

This book is printed on acid-free paper

Printed in Great Britain by
Antony Rowe Ltd, Chippenham, Wiltshire

Contents

Publication of this volume was aided by a grant from the Scouloudi Foundation, in association with the Institute of Historical Research. It was further assisted by a generous grant from Washington University, St Louis, Missouri.

Acknowledgements

Although research and writing are essentially solitary activities, they would be impossible without assistance from others. I am indebted to the several libraries and record offices that allowed me access to their collections, and to the senior historians who read earlier versions of the manuscript and offered comments. Especial thanks are due to my adviser at Washington University, Professor Derek Hirst, and, supremely, to Richard and Diane Mayers, my parents, whose patient support enabled me to complete the project. This book is for them, with grateful love.

Ruth E. Mayers
July 2002

Abbreviations

A&O	*Acts and ordinances of the Interregnum*, ed. C. H. Firth and R. S. Rait, London 1911
BL	British Library
Bodl. Lib.	Bodleian Library, Oxford
Burton	*The diary of Thomas Burton Esq.*, ed. J. T. Rutt, London 1828
CCJ	Common Council Journal, 41
Clarke	*The Clarke papers: selections from the papers of Sir William Clarke*, ed. C. H. Firth (Camden n.s. lxi, lxii, 1894–1901)
CLRO	Corporation of London Record Office
CPWM	*Complete prose works of John Milton*, VII: *1659–1660*, ed. R. W. Ayers, New Haven, Conn. 1980
CSP	*State papers collected by Edward earl of Clarendon, commencing from the year 1621*, ed. R. Scrope and T. Monkhouse, Oxford 1767–86
CSPD	*Calendar of state papers, domestic series 1658–9, 1659*, ed. M. A. E. Green, London 1867–95
CSPVen.	*Calendar of state papers . . . relating to English affairs . . . in the archives . . . of Venice*, xxxii (1659–1661), ed. A. B. Hinds, London 1931
DRO	Derbyshire Record Office, Matlock
DWL	Dr Williams' Library, London
ESRO	East Sussex Record Office, Lewes
FHL	Friends House Library, London
FSL	Folger Shakespeare Library, Yale
GRO	Gloucestershire Record Office, Gloucester
Guizot, *Histoire*	F. Guizot, *Histoire du protectorat de Richard Cromwell et du retablissement des Stuart*, Paris 1856, appendices (correspondence of Ambassador Bordeaux)
HJ	*Historical Journal*
HMC	Historical Manuscripts Commission
Journal	*Journals of the House of Commons*, vii, London 1802
KRO	Kent Record Office, Maidstone
Nicholas	*The Nicholas papers*, ed. G. F. Warner, iv (Camden 3rd ser. xxxi, 1920)
Occurrences	*Occurrences from Forraigne Parts also a Particular Advice*
PI	*The Publick Intelligencer*
Politicus	*Mercurius Politicus*
Post	*The Weekly Post*
PRO	Public Record Office
Rep.	Repertory of the court of aldermen, CLRO
Scout	*The Faithful* [from July *National*, then *Loyall*] *Scout*

TSP	A *collection of the state papers of John Thurloe*, ed. J. T. Birch, London 1742
WCO	Worcester College, Oxford
WI	*The Weekly INTELLIGENCER*
WRO	Wiltshire Record Office, Trowbridge

All contemporary correspondence cited was written in 1659, and all contemporary works were published at London in this year unless otherwise stated.

Introduction:
Recovering the Republic of 1659

On Saturday, 7 May 1659, approximately fifty members of the Long Parliament reassembled at Westminster, by invitation of the very Army that had expelled them six years earlier.[1] Restoration of this familiar authority, achieved by intensive public lobbying and private negotiations between officers and leading MPs, ended the fortnight of indecision following the effective collapse of Richard Cromwell's Protectorate. The speed and size of the transformation impressed observers of all political persuasions. A French correspondent expressed astonishment 'that such a stupendous alteration could happen without trouble'; Richard's secretary of state, John Thurloe, deplored the 'great and unexpected Change', while Cavalier squire William Lawrence exclaimed that 'a small time may give birth to many great Revolutions' – a sentiment shared by the godly Major Nehemiah Bourne, who reported general 'wonderment' at the 'suddaine manifestation' of providence in this 'late great Revolution . . . of the whole Civil Government . . . from monarkie to a free state and Commonwealth'.[2] For contemporaries, Parliament's return thus seemed an event of immense, even revolutionary significance, signalling the reversal of recent conservative trends, and the restoration of the unicameral Republic of 1653.[3]

That Republic found itself the welcomed focus of considerable expectations. Bourne's confidence that 'very great things' were 'upon the wheele' was far from unique. The Protector's fall had unleashed intense excitement and creativity, that found expression, not only in the sudden host of ephemeral pamphlets which poured from the liberated presses, but in the reappearance of competing newsbooks, displayed and discussed in the numerous new coffee-shops, which were themselves becoming important centres of political

---

[1] Fifty is the estimate of one Royalist, writing on 12 May: Bodl. Lib., MS Clarendon 60, fo. 541. The problematic lists of William Prynne and Arthur Annesley, who by different routes reached a total of forty-two, are considered in chs 2 and 3 below.
[2] French letter, 12 May, MS Clarendon 60, fos 529–30; John Thurloe to William Lockhart, 5 May, ibid. fo. 483; William Lawrence to Isaac Lawrence, 30 May, in *The pyramid and the urn: the life in letters of a Restoration squire: William Lawrence of Shurdington, 1636–97*, ed. Iona Sinclair, Stroud 1994, 149; Nehemiah Bourne, 20 May, *Clarke papers*, iii. 214, 209, 216.
[3] Despite its imperfect, transitional nature, this government may accurately be described as a 'republic', the Latinate form of 'commonwealth', Parliament's official English name for the 'free state without single person, king or house of peers': following contemporary practice, these titles will therefore be used interchangeably.

culture.[4] To all those dissatisfied with the Cromwells the revolution opened a 'door of hope'.[5] Men whose ignominious departure in 1653 had been largely unlamented were now hailed as the 'Renowned Parliament', 'the Good Old Parliament', the 'famous, memorable and successful Long Parliament', God's 'chosen instruments'.[6] Not only the sensationalist press but eminent intellectuals such as John Milton joined the general 'demonstrations of joy',[7] advertising this government's past achievements as firm forerunners of the blessings to be anticipated from its present tenure.[8] A multitude of pamphleteers eager to influence its debates shared Milton's hope that an assembly formerly so favoured by providence would proceed to establish a lasting Commonwealth that would safeguard liberty, and complete the reformation of law and religion. Never had the Republic's prospects looked brighter: not even the nominated assembly of saints had received such widespread endorsements. Compared with the hesitancy and overt hostility surrounding the Commonwealth's initial creation in 1649, the enthusiasm of a well-affected minority for its reinstatement was promising indeed.

While acknowledging that 1659 was 'republicanism's *annus mirabilis*', yielding the 'richest outpouring of republican theory', historians have tended to divorce ideology from practice, and so dismiss contemporary confidence as intrinsically ill-founded.[9] Thus Blair Worden and Jonathan Scott have,

---

[4] *Clarke papers*, iii. 217. The massive expansion of the pamphlet literature is evident from the catalogue of tracts collected by London bookseller George Thomason, who now resumed purchasing at a rate unequalled since 1648/9. 1659 saw a sudden acceleration in the growth of coffee houses: seven more opened in London alone. Thanks to John Aubrey, the most famous remains that in which the Rota debated Harrington's theories. On the political significance of coffee houses see Steven Pincus, 'Coffee politicians does create – coffeehouses and Restoration political-culture', *Journal of Modern History* lxvii (1995), 807–34, and Stephen B. Dobranski, ' "Where men of differing judgements croud": Milton and the culture of the coffee houses', *Seventeenth Century* ix (1994), 35–56.

[5] Capt. Robert Stafford to Adam Baynes 15 May, BL, MS Add. 21425, fo. 50. More famously, the Army had expressed thanksgiving for 'this door of hope again opened towards the obtaining a consummation of those things so much breathed after by the good people' in the officers' *Humble PETITION . . . to the Parliament* of 12 May, 3.

[6] Examples of the use of each of these titles include the *Scout*, no. 1, 22–9 Apr., 6; *The Humble REMONSTRANCE Of the Non-Commission Officers and Private Soldiers of Major General GOFFS Regiment (so called) of Foot*, 2; *Scout*, no. 2, 29 Apr.–6 May, 16; and *A Publick PLEA Opposed to A Private Proposal*, 1.

[7] This phrase described the reaction of Monck and his officers in Scotland in a letter reprinted in *Politicus*, no. 568, 19–26 May, 456. Bourne similarly reported that Parliament sat 'to the reioyseing of the generality of honest harts': *Clarke papers*, iii. 214. In the autumn Milton recalled that he had been 'overjoyed' to hear of Parliament's return: *CPWM* vii. 24.

[8] Milton expressed his confidence in *Considerations Touching The Likeliest Means to Remove Hirelings out of the Church*, the preface to which addressed the members as those 'whose magnanimous councels first opened and unbound the age from a double bondage under prelatical and regal tyrannie', and urged them, as the 'authors, asserters and now recoverers of our libertie', to heed the 'just petition' of the well-affected against tithes: *CPWM* vii. 274–5.

[9] P. Zagorin, *A history of political thought in the English Revolution*, London 1954, 155;

2

respectively, seen Parliament's recall as indicative of the 'barrenness of the army's political posture', and the 'poverty of the practical political imagination' – judgements taking for granted the members' incapacity to deliver the constructive solutions that many, including the officers, expected.[10] Commenting on the 'great commotion in the London press' inspired by Parliament's return 'with *what appeared to be* a commitment to reform', Ronald Hutton implies that this appearance was constructed by 'government supporters' who portrayed 'the regime as a promoter of liberty and honest administration' when actual reform was, in fact, improbable, since MPs in the past had 'not been prepared to produce any fundamental . . . reformation'. Godfrey Davies, correctly observing that the diversity of the schemes propounded by the pamphleteers precluded the satisfaction of all, concluded that the 'optimism which inspired the drafters of a new constitution rested upon no solid basis'.[11] In a more sophisticated examination of the pamphlet literature, Austin Woolrych concedes that it was 'no small triumph to succeed in identifying the good old cause with the good old Parliament', but regards the high hopes for that Parliament's future as cynical manipulation by power-seeking 'republican propagandists', or a 'web of fantasy' spun by 'millenarian enthusiasts' whose immersion in emotive prophetic language had completely blinded them to political realities. Milton's confidence Woolrych ascribes to the ignorance born of increasing retirement 'to more congenial tasks than politics'.[12] The shadow of the Commonwealth's eventual demise lies heavily upon all these interpretations: because this Parliament did not survive to enact the 'good things' desired by its supporters, it seems reasonable to conclude that it could never have done so, and hence interpret the expectations of the spring and summer as unrealistic dreams or empty propaganda.

Denial of the Republic's prospects and significance has a lengthy pedigree. From the moment of its reappearance, a few bold monarchists publicly denigrated the 'casheered House of Commons', and sought to subvert it by all possible means. Ridicule proved more effective than armed resistance: the Royalists' greatest coup, facilitated by the second interruption that autumn, and vastly reinforced by the Stuarts' advent, was to label this Parliament 'the Rump', so reducing its rule to a repulsive absurdity.[13] Nothing more clearly

J. Scott, 'The English republican imagination', in J. S. Morrill (ed.), *Revolution and Restoration*, London 1992, 35–54 at p. 51.

[10] A. B. Worden, 'Harrington's *Oceana*: origins and aftermath, 1651–1660', in D. Wootton (ed.), *Republicanism, liberty and commercial society, 1649–1776*, Stanford 1994, 134; Scott, 'English republican imagination', 51.

[11] R. Hutton, *The Restoration: a political history of England and Wales, 1658–1667*, Oxford 1986, 47, 45, 42; G. Davies, *The Restoration of Charles II, 1658–1660*, San Marino 1955, 92.

[12] A. H. Woolrych, 'Introduction' to *CPWM* vii. 67, 24, 69, 96.

[13] [Arthur Annesley], *ENGLAND'S CONFUSION OR A True and Impartial Relation of the late Traverses of State in England* (collected by Thomason on 30 May), 22. This was the first publication to refer to Parliament as 'the Rumpe'; though also used in Royalist correspondence, this epithet rarely occurs in print until the late autumn.

illustrates the success of their campaign to consign the Commonwealth to the historical rubbish-heap than the persistent use of this scatological sobriquet in supposedly neutral academic writing. Recent scholarship has, however, done much to counter contemporary disinformation. Since Worden's invaluable study, dispelling the charges levelled against Parliament at its first interruption, our knowledge of the early Republic's institutions, ethos and politics has been further enhanced by the work of Sean Kelsey, Sarah Barber and Steven Pincus.[14] The spotlight of historical scrutiny has also illuminated the origins and development of republicanism as an intellectual, literary and cultural phenomenon. David Norbrook's brilliant analysis expressly challenges the post-Restoration 'process of erasure', and affirms the 'potential creativity' amidst the chaos, while Nigel Smith goes so far as to imagine the Republic's 'triumph and survival'.[15] Yet the Commonwealth of 1659, in which republican aspirations and practice most closely converged, has remained the 'eve of the Restoration', receiving occasional tributes to its importance, but comparatively little attention in its own right.[16]

Relative neglect of the restored Republic reflects not only lingering partisan prejudice, but a real historiographic problem. 1659 saw unprecedented political instability – four regimes ruled in the space of less than nine months.[17] The multifarious schemes for the future, and the intricate arguments between their proponents can easily mystify the modern reader, and obscure the fact that substantial change was deemed possible by both its advocates and opponents. Events themselves were equally complex, and moved with bewildering rapidity: the abundant evidence suggests that Parlia-

---

[14] A. B. Worden, *The Rump Parliament, 1648–1653*, Cambridge 1974; Sean Kelsey, *Inventing a republic: the political culture of the English Commonwealth, 1649–1653*, Manchester 1997; S. Barber, *Regicide and republicanism: politics and ethics in the English Revolution, 1646–1659*, Edinburgh 1998; S. Pincus, *Protestantism and patriotism: ideologies and the making of English foreign policy, 1650–1668*, Cambridge 1996.

[15] D. Norbrook, *Writing the English Republic: poetry, rhetoric and politics, 1627–1660*, Cambridge 1999, 3, 18; N. Smith, 'Popular republicanism in the 1650s: John Streater's "heroic mechanics" ', in D. Armitage, A. Himy and Q. R. D. Skinner (eds), *Milton and republicanism*, Cambridge 1995, 137–55 at p. 137.

[16] Both Norbrook and Smith obtrude this phrase as a synonym for 1659 in contexts where its connotations of republican twilight and monarchical resurgence are inappropriate. For examples see Smith, 'Popular republicanism', 138, and Norbrook, *Writing*, 6. Norbrook does devote a section of his penultimate chapter (pp. 396–407) to 'the republican revival' of 1659. Worden, who includes a brief discussion in 'Oceana: origins', 132–8, affirmed the restored Commonwealth's importance by excluding it from his earlier work, on the grounds that it would be 'unsatisfactory and misleading' to reduce it to 'an addendum, the mere rump', of 'the earlier Rump': *Rump Parliament*, 17.

[17] The four regimes in office between April and December 1659 were the Protectorate, Parliament, the Council of Officers/Committee of Safety, and Parliament. The only possible precedent is 1653, when the same period saw the successive rule of Parliament, Council of Officers, Nominated Assembly and Protectorate. However, army unity under Oliver Cromwell ensured that this year was characterised by relative calm despite the changes.

ment's fortunes sometimes fluctuated almost daily. Given the undoubted difficulty of constructing a comprehensive and coherent picture, it is hardly surprising that textbooks tend to pass hastily over this 'extraordinarily complicated' period, despite its centrality in British history.[18] More sophisticated accounts frequently resolve the apparent confusion by isolating an inexorable progression towards the ultimate outcome.[19] Thus Godfrey Davies, though attempting to compose a 'history of England' from 1658 to 1660, announced the Restoration as his 'theme' at the outset, and assumed that it was only a matter of time before the 'large class' alienated by the 'work of reformation' arrived at the 'point of revolt' for the king. Ronald Hutton, taking a similar title but discussing a much longer period, is primarily interested in the transformation of 'the political and religious world of the Protectorate . . . into that of the Restoration monarchy'. The result, in each case, is a detailed but selective narrative in which the republican revival is reduced to one short episode in the broader development.[20]

Though it mirrors their refusal to concede any potential to the Republic, Woolrych's approach affords some interesting contrasts with that of Hutton or of Davies. In this version, the vital turning point at which the Restoration became 'inevitable' was the fall of Richard Cromwell, whose Protectorate was 'widely enough accepted . . . to be vulnerable only to force'. By yielding to the agitation for the 'Good Old Cause', the Army abandoned rational thought for an emotional 'parrot-cry'. Richard's rejection was a 'work of pure destruction', whereby the Army exchanged a 'government which preserved some at least of the freedoms they valued' for the 'political bankruptcy' of 'the Rump', whose members had 'learnt nothing' from their former expulsion, and lacked the 'foresight and statesmanship' necessary to consolidate the propaganda triumph that had restored them to power. Parliament's incompetence was manifest, not only in the divisions that brought deadlock to its constitutional debates, but in the 'series of foolish provocations' with which it alienated the Army. The result was a smouldering crisis, whose eruption into open conflict was deferred only by the Royalist menace of the summer.[21]

---

18 Worden, *Rump Parliament*, 17. A good example of the problems this period presents to textbooks is A. H. Woolrych, *England without a king, 1649–1660*, London 1983, which devotes less than 3 of its 45 pages to the last year of the Commonwealth, on the grounds that the speed of events prohibits the mention of more than a 'few salient developments' (p. 44).

19 This solution is not confined to the detailed narratives. Scott too dismisses 1659 as 'a year of constitutional confusion leading inexorably to Restoration': 'English republican imagination', 51.

20 Davies, *Restoration*, vii. 96; Hutton, *Restoration*, 1. Davies devotes five of his seventeen chapters to the eight months between Richard's fall and Parliament's second restoration; Hutton gives only two chapters to the same period.

21 A. H. Woolrych, 'The Good Old Cause and the fall of the Protectorate', *Cambridge Historical Journal* xiii (1957), 133–67 at pp. 133, 160; 'Introduction', 100–2; and *England without a king*, 44–5.

The bleak portrait of the Republic's last months painted by these historians is not without merit. Parliament did face considerable problems, and these had a part to play in the crisis that resulted in the catastrophic dissolution of October. The memory of the 'short and scandalous night of interruption', as Milton and other republicans[22] termed the Protectorate, added tensions to relations with the Army, and exacerbated divisions within and without the House.[23] Though these divisions, together with the diversity of the blueprints for reform, increased the difficulty of devising a settlement, the necessary preoccupation with urgent security measures was an even more serious obstacle to constitutional progress. Parliament was threatened by the hostility of its old enemies, the Royalists and Presbyterians, and its unpopularity with everyone outside the narrow constituency of the 'well-affected' was enhanced by the high taxes necessary to offset the legacy of insufficient revenue and growing debt left by the Cromwells.

Yet these difficulties, though serious, were not automatically fatal. To assume the contrary, and deduce from the eventual disaster that the republicans were 'doomed' to defeat, is to entertain an ahistorical determinism.[24] Such hindsight produces a one-dimensional picture that ignores or dismisses conflicting evidence. Parliament possessed significant advantages, that included, but were not confined to, the 'potential for rapid, ruthless and effective government' acknowledged by Hutton.[25] Its members had, however reluctantly, introduced fundamental changes, and weathered great storms in the past: not all the praises heaped upon them were hyperbolical. Nor was this assembly incapable of fulfilling at least some of its supporters' hopes for the creation of a permanent republic. Though it is easy to magnify divisions by citing hostile sources eager to present the least rumour of discord as proof of an imminent rupture between Parliament and Army, this method overlooks the important, and far from futile, efforts on both sides to reconcile past differences and establish a working relationship. Opponents who prophesied failure from the first were not necessarily more, and in some cases decidedly less, politically informed than their many contemporaries who were either unsure or convinced that the Commonwealth could succeed. Milton's employment on state business might be diminishing, but he remained close to the corridors of power, with friends in high places who kept him apprised of

---

[22] I use the term 'republican' in two senses, distinguishable by the context – broadly, to denote all those prepared to support or serve the Republic, whether principled enthusiasts or pragmatists who preferred limited monarchy, and, more narrowly, to indicate the smaller number who developed and/or defended ideas for shaping a future kingless state and society. Many, including Milton, match both definitions.

[23] Milton, *Considerations*, 274; *Publick plea*, title. The latter pamphlet urged Parliament to dismiss all civil and military officers who had supported Cromwell's 'tyranny'. Many of these, of course, were members themselves.

[24] Davies frequently uses the expression 'doomed' in this connection: for examples see *Restoration*, 116, 121.

[25] Hutton, *Restoration*, 42.

6

developments there.[26] So important was contingency, and so far from predict-able the Republic's fate, that even some Royalists in London feared that it would establish itself.[27]

The scant attention paid by existing histories to these signs of republican strength, and the fluidity of the moment, indicates the need for an alternative approach to the restored Commonwealth. Having first examined the sources of its adverse reputation, this book analyses the Republic's activities themati-cally. Successive chapters explore Parliament's domestic priorities, internal dynamics and relations with the Army, the City of London and the English and Welsh provinces. Foreign policy and the challenge of ruling Scotland, Ireland and the colonies receive separate discussion, as does the positive political identity projected by republican print, ceremonial and iconography. In each case, a functioning regime had clearly been established – there was no paralysis or sclerosis. Rather, Parliament for several months contended with remarkable success against considerable odds. Capable of both effective administrative action and coalition-building, formulating and pursuing British and European policies, the Commonwealth attracted support from soldiers and civilians in City and country. Among this following, republi-canism of various kinds remained a vital energising force; the 'vision of the New Jerusalem' had neither faded, as Woolrych asserts, nor become the exclusive preserve of the Quakers, as Hutton suggests.[28] The final chapters investigate the turning of the tide against the Republic in the autumn and winter. Parliament's second expulsion left irreconcilable divisions among its former adherents, whose conflicts in turn prevented the establishment of a stable alternative authority. The resultant slide towards anarchy and civil war provoked a strong conservative reaction amongst the previously passive majority of the population, and this, together with the breakdown of Army unity and the inclinations of General Monck, made a reversion to monarchy virtually certain. Until October, however, the Republic's failure was far from foreordained. Viewed without the distorting lens of hindsight, the crisis of the Commonwealth in 1659 emerges as a major turning point in Britain's history.

[26] Milton's continued contacts are manifest in his unpublished 'Letter to a Friend Concerning the Ruptures of the Commonwealth' of 20 Oct. (*CPW* vii. 324–5), which alluded to the 'sad and serious discourse' between Milton and a 'friend', possibly Bradshaw, who was deep in republican counsels, and now urged Milton to write another pamphlet.
[27] For examples of Royalists who feared that the Republic, if unassailed, might soon become indestructible see the letters to Nicholas from Edward Massey (3 May), Col. Gervase Holles (25 May) and 'Miles' (17 June), *Nicholas papers*, 126, 142, 157.
[28] Woolrych, 'Introduction', 69; Hutton, *Restoration*, 121–2.

1

Identity Denied:
The Case Against the Republic

> The Interest of the late Kings Sonne is cryed up and promoted daily, upon pretence that there will be nothing but Confusion and Tyranny, until he come to govern; and that such as declare for a Commonwealth are for Anarchy . . . and can never agree amongst themselves: HUMBLE PETITION of Divers Well-affected Persons, July 1659.

> Had the members of the Rump been disinterested framers of a new constitution, and not . . . ambitious seekers for some scheme that would perpetuate themselves in authority, they could not have satisfied their adherents: Davies, Restoration, 90.

Dispassionate assessment, never easy, becomes doubly difficult for the historian approaching a moment like 1659, where hindsight reinforces intense partisan prejudice. The epigraphs that head this chapter exemplify the powerful, and enduring, impact of contemporary hostility to the Republic. One comes from loyal supporters who urged Parliament to disprove the Royalist contention that internal divisions made the creation of a viable Commonwealth impossible. Though these petitioners had their own axe to grind, in the form of a Harringtonian settlement, they exaggerated neither the prominence nor the pernicious potential of inimical propaganda. The godly republican John Rogers, no friend to Harrington, found it necessary, in the same month, to compose a massive treatise confuting 'the Grand Designs' of those Presbyterian latter-day 'Gunpowder plotters', William Prynne and Richard Baxter, to 'conclude the Commonwealth . . . but a firme Nihil, or a meer Nothing without a foundation'.[1] Much more than a tactical ploy by conservatives[2] eager to undermine the regime, this conclusion represented the genuine belief of those blinded by detestation of the Republic to any

---

1   THE HUMBLE PETITION Of Divers Well-affected Persons, Delivered The 6th day of July 1659 To the SUPREME AUTHORITY, The PARLIAMENT, 5; John Rogers, Diapolitieia. A Christian Concertation With Mr.Prin, Mr.Baxter, Mr.Harrington, for the True Cause of the COMMONWEALTH, preface.
2   Although Conal Condren and others have condemned classifying individuals on a scale from 'conservative' to 'radical' as anachronistic and potentially misleading, since all sides claimed 'the mantle of authentic conservation' (Condren, 'Radicals, conservatives and moderates in early modern political thought: a case of Sandwich Islands syndrome?', Journal of Political Thought x [1989], 525–42 at p. 536), this vocabulary can usefully denote polarities of principle and practical recommendation, whatever their rhetorical dress. In

possibility except its downfall. The zeal and imagination with which such individuals communicated that conviction in print and in person not only seriously threatened Parliament at the time, but have exercised a profound influence upon its posthumous reputation ever since.

It is no surprise that Royalist historians from Clarendon onwards depicted the Republic as an illegitimate government, the collapse of which was only a matter of time. That Godfrey Davies, writing nearly three hundred years later, shared their confident assumption that MPs neither could nor would have produced a satisfactory settlement, is more remarkable. His verdict is far from unique. Contemporary protestations to the contrary notwithstanding, the image of the restored Commonwealth as a government incapable of surmounting disorders due to insuperable divisions among self-interested leaders has persisted with little alteration since its enemies first created it. Though twentieth-century historians have seldom simply taken such propaganda at face value, they have none the less, consciously and unconsciously, allowed hostile sources to shape their interpretations at key points. This is partly because Parliament's second expulsion lent apparent verisimilitude to, and found a convenient explanation in, the testimony of those who so much desired and so frequently predicted it. Yet hindsight alone cannot explain it. To understand the historiographic ascendancy of the negative image, it is necessary to examine, first the plausibility of the case against the Republic to contemporaries, then the process whereby it has gained scholarly acceptance.

Unlike the actual conspiracies that it was designed to support, the polemic against Parliament in 1659 has been relatively neglected by modern scholars.[3] Since Royalists consistently advocated the return of the Stuart monarchy throughout the Interregnum, their arguments tend to be considered familiar, and less interesting than the multitude of novel and exciting radical schemes. It is, however, an error to suppose that the reactionary menace was uniform. The Cromwells had tried, with some success, to reconcile former Royalist and Presbyterian opponents, and to restrain the expression of subversive opinions. The return of the hated Republic swept away all that had been achieved by these efforts, provoking a massive conservative backlash. Irreconcilables who had lain low under the Protectorate were now rejoined by many who had accepted Richard, but found the radicalism associated with the Commonwealth intolerable. The collapse of censorship in the last weeks of Protectoral rule cleared the way for an outpouring of

1659 radical/conservative thus closely corresponds to the republican/monarchist dichotomy.

[3] A partial exception to this neglect is Elizabeth Skerpan, who analyses the mechanisms of Royalist discourse in 1659–60 from a (often historically misinformed) literary standpoint in *The rhetoric of politics in the English Revolution, 1642–60*, Columbia 1992. The classic account of the conspiracies is D. Underdown, *Royalist conspiracy in England, 1649–1660*, New Haven 1960.

anti-republican polemic unparalleled since 1649.[4] Though the Stuart restoration was the dominant theme of these pamphlets, the chorus of disapproval
was also swollen by disappointed Cromwellians advocating Richard's return.
Contemporaries of all viewpoints acknowledged the importance of this
propaganda. Royalists congratulated themselves on the acquisition of
Prynne's indefatigable pen; republicans inside and outside Parliament
anxiously called for the reimposition of strict censorship. Meanwhile the
Venetian ambassador repeatedly reported the free circulation of treasonable
pamphlets as proof that this Republic would not last long enough to need
recognition from his government.[5] Such rare unanimity suggests that the
arguments and methods of these pamphlets merit serious historical consideration: how potent was their threat to the regime's credibility at home and
abroad?

Contrary to the hopes of the first republicans, who had endeavoured to
silence its detractors with cogent refutations, this Parliament's return
prompted the revival of all the arguments that had been advanced against its
authority ten years earlier. Central to the monarchist case remained the
condemnation of the regicide and revolution, upon which the Republic's
claim to legitimacy still rested. Royalist and Presbyterian detestation of these
events had lost nothing of its force during the interval. William Prynne, with
typical vehemence, denounced the 'whorish forheads, brows of brass, hearts
of steel and consciences seared with a hot iron' of those who justified the
'Transcendent Treason' of the king's trial and execution. The legislation
whereby the Commons had established a republic and assumed the 'Supreme
Authority' was intrinsically invalid: not only did it invade the prerogatives
and lack the consent of king and lords, but it was enacted by a usurping
minority whose expulsion of 'the Majority . . . made it no legal *House*'. By no
stretch of the imagination could the people be said to have entrusted these
members with power to change the ancient constitution: at the time of the
elections in 1640, as another writer observed, it was unthinkable that 'the
People' had 'intended . . . turning out the House of Lords, equal to themselves
in lawful Power . . . turning out one half of themselves, deposing the King to
whom all had sworn Allegiance'. At the moment when the people's representatives became guilty of these crimes, exceeding the bounds set by 'Reason,
Religion, the Peace of the Nation, the Fundamentals of settled government',
they forfeited their authority. By proclaiming 'Reason and the Fundamentals'
as the limits determining the power of all parliaments, it was easy to dismiss

4   Compared to the radicals, conservatives were slow to profit from the new opportunities.
In April and May Thomason collected only 11 conservative tracts. The real upsurge
occurred in June, during which Thomason gathered 23 pamphlets, an increase coinciding
with new and ambitious schemes for a nationwide rising.
5   'Miles' to Nicholas, 17 June, *Nicholas papers*, 157; bill to prevent publication of scandals
and false rumors, *Journal*, 725; council order to 'suppress sedditious and libellous bookes and
pamphletts', Bodl. Lib., MS Rawlinson C79, fo. 70; *CSPVen.*, 24, 29–30, 38–9, 59–60.

11

the law against the involuntary dissolution of the Long Parliament as 'void in its Creation', and hence no bar to the customary cessation of legitimate parliamentary authority on the death of the king.[6]

The experience of effective dissolution from 1653 to 1659 immeasurably strengthened the argument that the revolution of 1649 had destroyed the Long Parliament's just authority. Whilst the remnant of that body retained actual power, its claim to respect and obedience had the support of powerful theological and practical arguments, capable of swaying many who deplored the contravention of the ancient constitution. In April 1653 these assets vanished immediately. It was, of course, the Cromwellians who most eagerly defended the dismissal of the Long Parliament, and insisted that there was now 'no lawful power . . . but the Protector and the Army'. If popular sanction conferred legitimacy, then Richard, recognised by the 'freest Parliament chosen in ten years', and local addresses subscribed by 'four or five hundred thousand hands', had a very strong claim. As he had done nothing since to forfeit their allegiance, the officers who abandoned him were castigated for abolishing 'the free choice and election of the people', contrary to their oaths and even the 'greatest testimonies of the soldiers good will'.[7] But the Stuarts' open supporters were not above invoking these events to confirm the Republic's fundamental illegitimacy. The Royalist author of A WORD to Purpose: Or, A Parthian Dart fuelled his condemnation of Parliament by reproducing several arguments commonly used to justify the Protector: the validity of the 'agreement subsequent of the People', expressed by their election of new representatives, the readiness of some MPs themselves to sit in these assemblies, the judicial pronouncement that 'a Parliament discontinued is dissolved'.[8] Whatever their preferred alternative, all the Commonwealth's critics concurred in citing its unpopularity in 1653 as proof that the people had countermanded any authority once delegated. Thus Prynne maintained that the members had been expelled 'to the general joy and contentment of all three Nations', as a government 'worse than the worst of all our Kings', while the Parthian dart's writer professed that he 'never heard one man speak concerning it, but heartily rejoiced, that the yoak was taken off their necks'. Though such statements naturally suppress the protests that were made, the

---

[6] William Prynne, The RE-PUBLICANS and others spurious Good Old Cause, briefly and truly Anatomized, 9, 2; A WORD to Purpose: Or, A Parthian dart, 3–4.

[7] TRUTH Seeks no CORNERS: or, Seven Cases of Conscience Humbly presented to the Army and Parliament, 5; Let me Speake too? Or, Eleven QUERIES Humbly Proposed to the Officers . . . Concerning The late Alteration of Government, 3; A Pair of SPECTACLES For this Purblinde NATION with which They may see the Army and Parliament like Simeon & Levi Brethren in Iniquity walk hand in hand together, 1, 2.

[8] Parthian dart, 9–10, 5. Cromwellians did not necessarily oppose the Stuarts. One writer represented both 'Carolus Rex' and 'Protector Richard' as 'Standards of righteousness' threatened by a 'lawless Arbitrary Power': Spectacles, 5.

general passivity did, indeed, expose the hollowness of Parliament's claim to power derived from the people.[9]

The dissolution, in fact, offered visible proof that Parliament's power had depended solely upon the Army. As the republicans themselves condemned the military interruption of civil government, reactionaries could point to a glaring inconsistency: if all such interventions of the Army were intrinsically illegitimate, then so too must be the purge of 1648 that had produced this assembly. Cromwellians therefore reasoned that these MPs, having once justified the Army's authority, should now submit to its subsequent creation, the Protectorate.[10] Presbyterians, however, maintained that the officers' declaration inviting the members to return should logically be extended to include all those who had been secluded. On this basis, Prynne, Annesley and others sought to re-enter the House, admonishing the guards at the door that their repentance, if genuine, should be 'universal, not partial', and asserting their 'own and the Peoples right of having their Representatives freed from force and admitted'.[11] The attempted invasion, though thwarted, was far from being the 'interlude of comedy' that Woolrych depicts.[12] Skilfully publicised in newsbooks and pamphlets, this incident accelerated the transformation of the secluded members' cause into a common conservative rallying cry that seriously embarrassed Parliament. It also illustrates the new and constructive possibilities opened to monarchist critics by the changed conditions: the Presbyterians' active endeavours to subvert the restored assembly contrast with their relative passivity in 1649, when their leaders were either imprisoned or else remained aloof, insisting that the Parliament had been dissolved.[13]

But the detrimental consequences of the Cromwellian dissolution extended beyond Parliament's theoretical legitimacy to afflict its reputation. As Prynne gleefully recalled, the Army itself had denounced its masters as a 'CORRUPT PARTY carrying on their own ends, to perpetuate themselves . . .

9 Prynne, Re-publicans, 3; Parthian dart, 9.
10 Thus the author of Truth seeks no corners insisted (pp. 2–3) that Parliament approved the Army's 'dissolving or incapacitating their Brethren . . . although they were the major . . . part' in 1648 and that 'if the Armies authority was good which they exercised upon their brethren . . . it must needs be good also upon themselves'.
11 William Prynne, A true and perfect Narrative of what was done, spoken by and between Mr Prynne, the . . . secluded Members, the Army Officers and those now sitting . . . with the true Reasons . . . inducing Mr Prynne . . . to press for entry, 6–7; [Annesley], England's confusion, 15.
12 Woolrych, 'Introduction', 71.
13 Prynne himself appreciated this contrast, noting that many considered him an 'Apostate from his former principles' for seeking entry to a parliament he 'publickly printed to be dissolved above 10 years since': Narrative, 16. Besides the detailed accounts in England's confusion and Prynne's two pamphlets – the lengthy Narrative, and the briefer Loyalty Banished: Or ENGLAND in MOURNING – the attempt of the secluded MPs on the House was widely reported, though with a negative gloss, in the non-official newsbooks: see, for examples, Scout, no. 6, 27 May–3 June, and Post, no. 6, 7–14 June.

never answering the ends which God, his People and the whole Nation expected'. The Army critique of the members' ungodliness and self-interestedness in 1653 supplied substantial ammunition for the assault on their integrity in 1659: hostile writers took pains to remind readers that the Parliament had been justly rewarded for 'self-seeking and notorious crimes and miscarriages'. Even ostensibly reasonable pamphlets accused MPs of intending to 'continue themselves in absolute power'; the more vituperative denounced them as 'a Juncto of Tyrants, whose Design is nought else, but to enrich themselves by the publique ruine'.[14] Royalist satirists were particularly adept at harnessing the scandals surrounding a few individuals to suggest the hypocrisy of the rest; Presbyterians, too, sought to render the members ridiculous by appending disparaging epithets to their names.[15] This once formidable Parliament's humiliation at the hands of its own general lent greater plausibility to monarchists' jeers at the resurrection of 'this *Rumpe* of a casheered House of Commons', 'this carcase of a Parliament, dead many years ago, conjured up from its ashes and rotteness by the omnipotence of the Army'.[16]

Such opprobrious titles highlighted not only the illegitimacy but also the insignificance of a republic dependent on the soldiers. Royalists undermined the exalted status ascribed to MPs by portraying them as the officers' puppets. Deliberately parodying republican rhetoric, one writer affirmed that 'our old renowned Heroes' were most fit 'to defray the publick debts, wipe off old scores, make clean the Rooms for new-Comers, and do some other drudgeries for the Army'. Celebrated leaders were thus reduced to 'a few hackney drudges', an 'incompetent and inconsiderable number of seeming Legislators', whose claim to represent the people was 'so thin that a sober person would be ashamed to own it'.[17] Statistics were frequently invoked to support this judgement. Hostile estimates of the number in the House ranged from thirty, in the case of those especially eager, however implausibly, to assert the parallel with the Athenian tyrants, to eighty, from the few more anxious to appear accurate; the commonest figure was between forty and fifty. These totals were, of course, contrasted unfavourably with the five hundred required for a full

---

[14] Prynne, *Re-publicans*, 3; [Annesley], *England's confusion*, 20–1; *The Interest of England stated: or A faithful . . . Account of the Aims of all Parties . . . Offering an Expedient? to the bringing solid, lasting Peace*, 4; *A Friendly LETTER of ADVICE To the SOULDIERS*, 6.

[15] Royalist satires to this effect include *University QUERIES*; *BIBLIOTHECA MILITUM: Or the SOULDIERS Publick LIBRARY*; and *PAUL'S CHURCHYARD. Libri Theologici, Politici, Historici, Nundinuis Pualinis una cum Templo prostant venales Done into English for the Assembly of Divines. . . .* For Presbyterian lists see [Annesley], *England's confusion*, 10–11, 16; Prynne, *Narrative*, 34–5.

[16] [Annesley], *England's confusion*, 22; *Interest of England*, 7.

[17] *The Unhappy Marks-man: or, Twenty three QUERIES Offered To the CONSIDERATION of the PEOPLE*, 5; [Annesley], *England's confusion*, 9; *Vox vere ANGLORUM: or Englands Loud Cry for their KING*, 5; *Interest of England*, 8.

[18] For examples of the various estimates see *Truth seeks no corners*, 1–2; *Vox*, 5; *Spectacles*, 7; and *Let me speake*, 5. The greatest manipulator of statistics was William Prynne, who

Parliament, or the two to three hundred excluded since 1648.[18] The members' position, as an undoubted minority of the Long Parliament was, indeed, unenviable – though not unprecedented[19] – and their derogators naturally made the most of it. Historians, however, have sometimes been almost as ready as contemporary critics to discount this government's claim to be representative. Hutton, for example, dismisses the 'purged Parliament' as a 'handful of men', and makes indiscriminate use of partisan sources, such as Prynne's list, that have crept into the official record.[20] Thus conservative contempt for the insignificant numbers present in the House has succeeded, where charges of moral turpitude and political corruption have not, in shaping modern historical assessments.[21]

The case for the Republic's illegitimacy and insignificance was not, of course, primarily a matter of constitutional theory or statistics. It was designed to support seditious conclusions, which were clearly spelt out to readers.[22] At best, the *Parthian dart* contended, a people who 'doubt the grounds of the Supream Authority' should yield only 'passive submission'. At worst, the attacks of Prynne and others on the 'usurped Authority of the pretended *LONG PARLIAMENT*' openly incited subjects to civil disobedience or active rebellion.[23] Such resistance was rendered doubly attractive by a second line of reasoning, which held that the Republic was not only

published the longest lists of secluded and sitting members in his *Conscientous, Serious THEOLOGICAL And LEGAL QUAERES, Propounded to the twice-dissipated, self-created Anti-Parliamentary Westminster Juncto*, 45–8. This pamphlet only appeared after the second expulsion, and could therefore afford to concede the generous total of 91 members present at some point. Prynne's list of surviving MPs, though incomplete, was reproduced in *Old Parliamentary History* xxi. 375–6, and hence has attained canonical status for some historians, especially Hutton.

19 Attendance in the 1640s had sometimes, for example during the summer of 1642, fallen to similarly low levels, a fact conveniently forgotten by those exclaiming against numerical thinness.

20 Hutton, *Restoration*, 42, 44, 305. The failure to recognise the figure of 91 MPs as Prynne's results in confusion and inaccuracy. Hutton interprets it as a comprehensive list of those surviving and eligible to sit, then suggests that only the 78 who appeared on 14 May ever sat, and that the remaining 13 were 'written off by those who did'. This is quite wrong. Prynne certainly included no MP unless his presence in the House at some point were incontestable, and in almost every case the *Journal* contains confirmation. Davies, however, uses the more cautious, though still imperfect, estimate of the nineteenth-century biographer of Milton, David Masson, and hence provides less prejudiced totals: *Restoration*, 96–7.

21 For the exoneration of MPs from these charges, at least insofar as they concern their first tenure of power, see Worden, *Rump Parliament*, esp. ch. v.

22 Hence Skerpan's assertion (*Rhetoric*, 171) that Royalist discourse, by demanding assent not analysis, 'absolved the audience of the burden of active participation in . . . contemporary politics' seems mistaken. Rousing readers to active opposition was a major aim, and stimulating 'correct' understanding of the issues at stake a significant method.

23 *Parthian dart*, 11; William Prynne [?], *MOLA ASINARIA: Or, The Unreasonable and Insupportable BURTHEN now press'd upon . . . this groaning NATION: By the headless Head, and unruly Rulers, that usurp upon the Liberties and Privileges of the oppressed People*, title, 6.

illegitimate but also inexpedient. This argument was, indeed, the logical corollary of the first: a revolution that contravened both the divine order and the English constitution could not fail to produce an alien, monstrous, and utterly unrighteous government. As one Royalist proclaimed, there could be 'no more phantastical, insolent and bestial Government . . . than that of an ill-ordered Commonwealth, of a free tumultuous State'. Anti-parliamentary propaganda, whether Royalist or Cromwellian, worked by opposing a stark choice between monarchy, the government 'most safe, most for the ease and appeal of the Oppressed, most Honourable . . . most Heaven-like and most Consentaneous to an English heart' and the Republic, compounded of '*Oligarchy, Anarchy, Tyranny, Oppression, Libertinism, Marshal-Government and all kinds of Heresies*'. In this world of polar opposites, no common ground between the two forms could be conceded: the contest between King and Commonwealth was portrayed as an extension of that between good and evil, in which the ultimate defeat of the latter was certain.[24]

The imminent demise of 'our Eutopian free State' was therefore a central theme of conservative polemic. Monarchists derisively christened Harrington 'his *Utopian Excellency*', and insisted that England's true interest lay in the 'restitution of our *Hereditary King and Kingly Government*, not an *Utopian Republike*'.[25] The repeated allusions to utopia were obviously intended to imply that republican hopes were intrinsically unrealistic: the Commonwealth's adherents wilfully rejected the only 'proper and natural' government for an impossible ideal of their imagination. Such folly was frequently ascribed to lunacy, lethargy or bewitchment. One attempt to dispel the 'Chymera of setling a Free State' observed that 'fond people dream of freedom, and a free state . . . as long as their inchanters have prevalency over their weak brains', while another warned inactive Londoners that 'whereas you are sooth'd and fool'd with the opinion and expectation of a free State, you are so far from ever being so, that you will find under that specious name is hid . . . a boundlesse liberty to enslave and ruine you'. To arouse such careless or deluded individuals, reactionaries repeatedly found it necessary to assert the selfish and fraudulent character of republican pretences. Thus Prynne's call to restore Charles Stuart denounced the rhetoric of 'Liberty, Conscience, a glorious Nation, The *Good Old Cause*' as the 'Machiavilian Tricks and political Cheats' of those who had advanced their own 'Interest by

---

24 A Seasonable ADVERTISEMENT To the People of England. Whether a Monarchy, or Free State, be better; in this juncture of time, 3; Timely Advice, from the Major part of the old Souldiers in the ARMY, To all the rest of our fellow Souldiers, wherein is held forth the Politically intended Destruction of the whole Souldiery By our new Masters, 3–4; Prynne, Re-publicans, 1.
25 Vox, 8, 1; AN ANSWER To A PROPOSITION In order to the proposing of A Commonwealth or Democracy. Proposed by friends to the Commonwealth by Mr. Harringtons consent, title; William Prynne, A Brief Necessary VINDICATION Of the Old and New SECLUDED MEMBERS, from Calumnies; And of the Fundamental Rights, Liberties . . . Interest of the . . . Parliaments, People of England, from the late avowed Subversions, 1. Of John Rogers 2. Of M: Nedham, subtitle.

villainy'. A Cromwellian critique maintained that republicans, like Roman Catholics, were capable of any equivocation to deceive credulous followers: 'they term all things by contrariety, light darkness . . . calling our greatest thraldomes liberty'.[26]

Counter-revolutionaries' anxiety to expose republican promises as disingenuous is itself testimony to their appeal. One Royalist paid unwitting tribute to this attraction when he observed that he would himself vote for a 'Free State' that protected property from 'unjust Taxations', and restored 'antient Rights and Liberties' encroached on by 'illegal Power', though he hastened to add that the rhetoric actually masked designs for anarchy or military dictatorship: 'every one shall be free to do that which is good in his own eyes, or . . . what he hath power enough to do or . . . what the Army will suffer us to take, enjoy or have'. Another similarly warned that the republicans intended only a 'free Commonwealth of wealth, Ambition, luxury, power and Revenge against whom they please'.[27] The Republic's positive image was, however, so strong that its opponents could not hope to conquer merely by pronouncing it false. Considerable attention therefore was paid to the presentation of 'proofs' referring readers to their own authoritative 'experience'. Thus an appeal to revolt for Richard Cromwell's restoration deplored the constant 'pretence of the Religion and the Liberties . . . of the people, when dayly Experience shewes us that nothing less is intended', and contended that 'every Man can clearly discern the Face of Fallacies in the Glasse of his own Woes, and that we are headlong running to Confusion'. Cavaliers lamented that the republicans' 'so much talkt of and so often promised *liberty*' had 'prov'd nothing but Reall and almost intolerable Slavery; their *plenty* has been turned into Miserable *poverty*; and their *Peace* into endlesse Troubles'. This bleak picture of the present Commonwealth contrasted with the idealised memory of 'Monarchy', the government 'Experimentally found most congruous and sutable to the Genius of this People'. Even Prynne introduced his lengthy denunciations of republican policies as the 'infallible, experimental, sensible evidence' that kingship was the 'true publike interest'.[28]

The objectivity of experience was, of course, an illusion carefully fostered by conservatives, who constructed Parliament's actual problems and policies so as to commend their negative concept of the Republic. Thus the temporary absence of settlement was twisted into proof that a Commonwealth could never be anything but a 'heap of confusion, disorder and incertainties'. Debates amongst republicans were presented as the outward manifestations of incurable divisions that precluded all possibility of agreement. Prynne, for

---

26 *Vox*, 5, 11; THE LONDONERS LAST WARNING, 4; [Prynne], *Mola asinaria*, 2, 6; *Truth seeks no corners*, 4.
27 *Parthian dart*, 13; ENGLANDS REMEMBRANCES, 12.
28 *Timely advice*, 2, ENGLANDS SETTLEMENT, *upon the Two solid foundations of The Peoples Civil and Religious LIBERTIES*, 1; *Friendly letter*, 6; Prynne, *Vindication*, 49–50.

example, ridiculed republican ideas as intrinsically fantastic and altogether irreconcilable:

> The Commonwealth is a mere Chaos . . . without form and void . . . the chief Sticlers for it being much divided both in their debates, judgments and affections. Some would have it to be an Aristocracy, others a Democracy, many a Theocracy . . . Many are for a Roman, some for an Athenian, others for a Lacedemonian, not a few for a Venetian, another partie for a Helvetian or Dutch Commonwealth. Some for a vast body with two heads, others for a head with two bodies, a third sort for a body without any head, printing against each others models with much eagerness.[29]

Prynne here exaggerated republican divisions by representing the various ideological influences on the proposed constitutions as a multitude of distinct and conflicting parties, and ignoring the large areas of common ground: the ideas of Harrington alone had both classical and Venetian antecedents. It is equally significant that, despite the allusion to theocracy, Prynne neglected to mention the substantial influence of Scripture upon some republican models. Elsewhere, he explicitly denied that any 'pattern' for a Commonwealth could be found in Scripture: those who rejected the monarchy enjoined by that sacred authority must necessarily admire the ungodly example of the 'Old Heathen, bloudie Romans', so much given to changing their governments, or else the 'old seditious Grecians' who had 'caused endless wars and tumults' until subdued by foreign conquerors. But the portrait of republican differences also excluded any arbiter with authority to resolve the disagreements. Instead, monarchists insisted that the selfish ambitions of contending republicans must prevent their submission to any proposed settlement. The author of the *Parthian dart* spoke for many advocates of a single person when he observed that 'the Parliament and Army cannot agree', since 'all would be Governours, and the hearts of most . . . are stuffed with excessive pride and can never subject themselves . . . if all be Governors, there are no Governors'. In such ways, the real tensions amongst the Parliament's adherents were exploited by their enemies to dismiss republicanism itself as essentially anarchical, and hence impossible.[30]

The partisan depiction of internal divisions was, however, only one of many ways to 'prove' republican hopes vain. More common was the manipulation of material grievances. Republicans promised that a free state would bring prosperity; their opponents used pre-existing economic problems to insinuate that the actual consequence could only be the growth of poverty. Typical was the Royalist who not only accused the Parliament of excessive and inequitable taxation – 'vast sums . . . so frequently and violently exacted . . . from all sorts, and some . . . who want it for bread to feed their Families' – but blamed it for the 'deadness of trade and all other chearful and usual ways

---

[29] *Truth seeks no corners*, preface; Prynne, *Vindication*, 56.
[30] Prynne, *Narrative*, 93; *Parthian dart*, 11.

to advance livelihood'. Prynne pronounced the Commonwealth 'a prodigious, All devouring, unsatiable Monster', evidencing its voraciousness by listing the multiplication of taxes: in addition to excise, this government 'since its new revival hath raised a whole years tax upon our exhausted purses in Three Months . . . and then imposed no less than one hundred thousand pounds each Month'. By dwelling on the magnitude of the Parliament's fiscal exactions, reactionaries not only exploited the perennial unpopularity of taxes, but portrayed that unpopularity as proof that the Republic could never attain the goodwill of its citizens for its survival.[31]

Even more damaging than the assault on the taxes themselves were the motives ascribed to the men that imposed them. Conservatives naturally refused to admit pleas of necessity or the public good. Taxation, in their view, was not only 'needless' and 'intollerable', but symptomatic of a more sinister design to enslave the people by means of the Army that it supported. In July, Royalists dismissed rumours of the rising they were at that moment planning as the inventions of tyrannical rulers to justify the 'insufferable burden laid upon the Nation' by military expenditure.[32] No alleviation of that burden could be expected from the corrupt Republic, whose governors were portrayed as 'New Aegyptian Tax-masters', without compassion for their subjects' sufferings, or as ambitious parasites eager to 'perpetuate themselves a Multitude of Princes, Feeding upon the Ruines of the People'. Contrasted with seventy costly tyrants 'hungry as Hawkes' was, in a reversal of a common republican argument, the inexpensive and benign supremacy of a single person, who would require public support only for his own family, and would have an 'Interest to preserve his People, to enrich his Dominions'. Here monarchists again invoked the blissful memory of the past, comparing republican taxes unfavourably with controversial royal levies such as ship money: one Royalist asserted that since 1643 there had been 'scarce a Month but the Nation have submitted to as great, if not a greater exhausting of Treasure'. With characteristic exaggeration, Prynne announced that the Commonwealth had been 'more expensive, oppressive, wasteful . . . than all our Kings since the Norman Conquest . . . only to make us greater slaves to our late Mercenary Army, Servants & Fellow Subjects than ever we were to our beheaded King'. In equating increased taxes with the growth of slavery and oppression, counter-revolutionaries sought to awaken readers to the practical hazards of the illegitimate Republic: since the Parliament had no lawful

---

31 Vox, 11; Prynne, Vindication, 58.
32 Friendly letter, 6. Tracts denying the necessity for taxes include Several New Cheats brought to Publique View; or the Good Old Cause Turn'd to a NEW CHEAT, 3, and One SHEET, Or, if you will A Winding Sheet for the Good Old Cause, 5.
33 Prynne, Concordia Discors, or the Dissonant Harmony of sacred publique oaths . . . lately taken by many Time-Serving Saints, 38; Timely advice, 2; Let me speake, 5; Friendly letter, 7; A DECLARATION Of the Christian-Free-Born Subjects of the once Flourishing Kingdom of ENGLAND, 15; Prynne, Vindication, 59.

power to tax, there was no restraint on its greed, and hence no security for property.[33]

Parliament's indisputable tax increases were, indeed, a godsend to those eager to foster discontent with its government, and disbelief in its integrity. But there was no shortage of additional 'evidence' for the republicans' supposed design to enslave the nation: the invasion of taxpayers' property was just one of many 'proofs' that traditional society was in peril. Thus Prynne blamed the Republic's arbitrariness as much as its fiscal greed for the 'impoverishment, destruction of most of the antient Nobility, Gentry, Corporations'; a more restrained Cavalier deplored the plight of every social stratum – 'the Nobility degraded . . . the ancient Gentry slighted, the Merchants and Commons by decay of Trade and . . . extraordinary Taxes, impoverished and exhausted'. The rationale behind such charges was clear: the monstrous Commonwealth that had abolished the ancient hierarchy of king and lords must necessarily oppose the rights and interests of the surviving gentry and nobility. Royalists sneered at the humble origins of some republicans, and deliberately fuelled fears of social levelling by falsely alleging that this was the Parliament's intention. One verse satire proclaimed:

> we have a people now
> Blew apron blades, men that know how . . .
> Each man's another Machivell
> to keep the Gentry under.

By denouncing the members as 'a spawn sprung from a dunghill birth', or, less impolitely, as those who had rejected 'that Station where God hath placed them by their Birth right' to usurp an 'absolute power . . . over their Brethren and Fellow Subjects', reactionaries affirmed that republican government was in revolt against the natural order, and hence entitled to neither respect nor obedience. Subjects who were equal, if not superior, to their supposed rulers, were quite justified in overthrowing them. Thus the actual rising of Sir George Booth was defended as an attempt of the legitimate elite to rescue themselves and the nation from 'this Babylonish captivity and tyrannical yoke of bondage . . . exercised by . . . our inferiors', while the Parliament's proceedings against the rebels were billed as proof of their design to destroy the gentry.[34] So prevalent was such propaganda that the Venetian resident easily convinced himself that the Republic, as a government of 'base and vile folk' who defied the interest of 'the grandees and middle classes', could not possibly endure.[35]

Subversion of the social order was, in the monarchists' opinion, only one

---

[34] Prynne, *Vindication*, 50; *Englands settlement*, 2; *ENGLAND'S CHANGELING . . . A clear Discovery of the New Cheat of the Thing called the Good Old Cause*, 5; *Vox*, 3; *Several new cheats*, 3. Royalist accounts of Booth repeatedly emphasised the quality of his supporters.
[35] CSPVen., 30. Giavarina also described (p. 69) the arrests following the rising as intended to destroy 'all the nobility of the realm'.

aspect of the wider republican design to 'introduce Democracy, Independency, Parity and leave neither King, Church, Lord nor Gentleman'. It was no coincidence that the destruction of the political hierarchy was so closely associated with that of the national Church whose doctrine had defended the ancient government. Despite their differences on the proper constitution of that Church, Presbyterians and Royalists concurred in condemning the Commonwealth as the natural enemy of the Protestant religion. Even a Cromwellian critic could attack republicans as 'a malignant party . . . working to . . . subvert the being of the true Protestants, and therein to bereave us of all our hopes of reformation or future peace or happiness to this Church'. Such accusations were substantiated by a highly coloured interpretation of Parliament's religious policies. Thus the effective toleration of dissenting Protestant groups was portrayed as a deliberate refusal to maintain order and protect the people from dangerous heresies: indeed, to the more extreme writers, republican rebelliousness was explicable only by the assumption that they were themselves heretics or crypto-Catholics. Prynne attributed the growth of 'all sorts of Blasphemies, Heresies, Errors . . . prophaness, contempt . . . of Gods word' to the Parliament's malign example, and complained that its members had been not protectors but the 'Step-Fathers and Plunderers of the Church', helping themselves to ecclesiastical revenues and encouraging sectarian attacks on the clergy.[36] The outpouring of tracts against tithes and a compulsory national ministry afforded ample apparent justification for these charges. Even though it never implemented these demands, Parliament's readiness to contemplate reforms, and refusal to discountenance all radical petitions, sufficed to damn it.[37] Still worse for Parliament was the construction put on its willingness to accept sectarian offers to raise volunteer forces or serve in the new militia during the emergency of the rising. Conservative pamphleteers and preachers exploited this ostensible confirmation of the suspected plot to whip up popular hysteria against Quakers, Baptists and Fifth Monarchists, and urge genuine Protestants to rise first in self-defence. Thus one tract exhorted Londoners to join Booth on the grounds that 'Sectaries govern . . . Heresies are armed against you . . . and will suddenly take possession of your lives and Fortunes'; another broadsheet warned that the Fifth Monarchists were 'Arm'd, Officer'd and every way in a Readiness . . . to surprise and suppress the Army, to Fire the City, and to Massacre all considerable People'. The harm that such misrepresentations could do in areas less closely patrolled than London is illustrated by the success of Presbyterian minister Henry Newcome's colleague Mr Stockport, who much assisted the

---

[36] Prynne, *Re-publicans*, 14; *Spectacles*, 7; Prynne, *Vindication*, 53.
[37] See, for example, Prynne's *Ten Considerable Quaeries concerning TITHES, The Present Petitioners and Petitions for their total Abolition . . . excitedÿ by disguised Jesuits . . . to . . . extirpate our Protestant Ministers, Church, Religion*, in which he complained (p. 1.) that the petitioners should have been punished for faction, schism and sedition, instead of being 'thanked, encouraged, as zealous, conscientous, well affected persons'.

onset of Booth's rebellion in Cheshire by sermons 'to invite the people to arms on the score of the Quakers being up'. Captured rebels confessed that Lancashire preachers had been equally busy, redeploying such texts as 'Curse ye Meroz', formerly used against the Cavaliers, to affirm 'that Religion was in dainger' from 'Quakers and those who would destroy ye Ministry' and exhort 'all men for to take up armes as for Gods own Cause'.[38]

Ominous as their incitements to insurrection were, the monarchists' endeavour to foment divisions within the republican camp constituted a still graver menace. This was the explicit policy of Charles Stuart's lord chancellor in exile, Edward Hyde, who instructed resident Royalists to 'make all the friends you can in the Parliament to pursue those counsels which may provoke the Army' and *vice versa*. A second dissolution would deprive the Commonwealth of credibility abroad, and stimulate advantageous confusion at home.[39] To encourage distrust of the Army, predictions abounded that an ambitious senior officer would soon re-enact the role played by Oliver Cromwell in 1653. Some extreme republican tracts pressing Parliament to magnify its authority, punish ex-Cromwellians and severely repress the least signs of discontent among the soldiery may well have had Cavalier authors, since there is a suspicious resemblance to letters the latter composed in the style of commonwealthsmen.[40] But counter-revolutionaries concentrated most attention on the task of alienating the Army, which had the power to impose an alternative government. Thus the assault on the Republic's illegitimacy and oppression was frequently accompanied by appeals to the soldiers to liberate themselves and the people from such contemptible masters, and restore the rightful ruler.[41] Only by so doing, monarchists maintained, could

---

38 *Londoners*, 4; *An Alarum to the City and Souldiery* (broadsheet); *The autobiography of Henry Newcome*, ed. R. Parkinson (Chetham Society xxvi, 1852), 109; 'Confession of Thomas Greenhalgh of Brandleshome, Lancashire', 20 Sept., MS Clarendon 64, fo. 339. Lancashire was one of the few regions where the Presbyterian classical structure had taken root.

39 Edward Hyde to Viscount Mordaunt, 4 June, CSP iii. 481.

40 Such counterfeit republican publications include *The Army Mastered, OR GREAT BRITTAINS JOY: Briefly Presented to those true Patriots . . . now assembled in Parliament*, a broadsheet which recommended 'destroying the Interest' of an Army likened to 'hardbiting . . . Lyons', and a pamphlet collected by Thomason under the title *Ambitious TYRANNY*, but also published as *IRELANDS Ambition taxed, The PARLIAMENTS Authority vindicated*. Extravagant assertions of parliamentary prerogative and gratuitous insults to the Army culminate in the hope that MPs would subdue the Army in Ireland 'with as much ease and honour as you have their fellow creatures in England, whose hands . . . you have so tyed behind their backs that they shall never be able . . . to lift them up agst the face of your authoritie': *Ambitious tyranny*, 6. This closely parallels Hyde's counsel, written in the assumed character of a republican, to Parliament to do 'exemplary justice upon those who offered that barbarous violence to them, and thereby dishonoured Parliaments and secure themselves for the future from the like ignominious affronts': MS Clarendon 60, fo. 548.

41 See, for examples, *Truth seeks no corners*, 4–5; *England's confusion*, 21; *Friendly letter*, 6; and *The SOVLDIERS Alarum Bell, To awaken all such Who are lull'd asleep in the supposed security of a Parliamentary Conventicle . . .*, 6.

the Army fulfil its original engagements to promote 'Religion . . . the Laws, the liberty of the Subject, the priviledge of Parliament, and the safety of the KING'. Presbyterians skilfully redefined the influential radical concept of the 'Good Old Cause' so as to benefit the Stuarts; Cromwellians naturally stressed the importance of keeping oaths to the Protector.[42]

In seeking to arouse Army discontent, conservatives displayed their habitual skill in magnifying grievances and misrepresenting Parliament's policies. Thus the actual problem of providing overdue pay was exacerbated by mendacious assertions that the Parliament, despite extorting 'farre greater summs . . . than would satisfie all our Arrears' had deliberately made 'small provision', leaving soldiers and their families to 'beg, starve and perish'. Besides recommending the rank and file to compare their poverty with the sumptuous 'Wealth and something like Honour' enjoyed by the members, Royalists promised that King Charles would relieve their necessities. Cromwellians, with greater plausibility, recalled the late Protector Oliver's care for his men, and exploited the strong residual loyalty to his memory, instancing the 'many undue Reflections, Calumnies and unchristian scoffes cast upon' him by republicans as signs of the 'baseness and vanity of their minds, with their dunghil spirits'.[43] Far from esteeming the Army, the Parliament that despised its most famous general must be plotting to avenge itself by humiliating the officers and excluding them from power. To make this version of Parliament's motives more credible, supporters of a single person not only did their utmost to maximise resentment of genuine anxieties arising from the Indemnity Act, and the reissue of commissions by the Speaker, but invented grievances. Thus they depicted the new militia as an attempt to supplant the regular Army, and announced, without a shred of evidence, that MPs intended to disband the latter or send it to Jamaica. It is arguable that this propaganda, designed as it was to increase mutual suspicions to the point of shattering the fragile accord between the Parliament and the Army, was even more deadly to the Republic than the direct appeals for a popular uprising.[44]

The reactionary challenge to the Commonwealth was therefore a problem of the first magnitude. Parliament faced a comprehensive indictment of its policies, based on a coherent theory that not only denied its legitimacy and predicted its downfall, but advertised the perfections of a familiar alternative, whether King or Protector. Nor was argument confined to the theoretical

---

[42] *Friendly letter*, 3. For the Presbyterian redefinition of the Good Old Cause see especially William Prynne, *The true Good Old Cause rightly stated, and the False un-cased*, and *Republicans*. Annesley offers a similar reconstruction in *England's confusion*, though he also criticises the Army for abandoning Richard. For the Cromwellian critique see *Spectacles*, its milder version *Let me speake*, and *Truth seeks no corners*.

[43] *Souldiers alarum*, 4; *Timely advice*, 2; *Friendly letter*, 5, 7–8; *Souldiers alarum*, 5.

[44] See, for examples, *Souldiers alarum*, 4; *Interest of England*, 7; *Truth seeks no corners*, 4; *Timely advice*, 4; and *Friendly letter*, 4, 6.

realm: this black legend was devised and propagated in close conjunction with the most ambitious conspiracy of the decade. Moreover, the persuasiveness of the anti-republican cause was much enhanced by the diverse genres and tactics employed in presenting it.[45] Straightforward invective and scurrilous satire, triumphal prophecy and allegorical romance reinforced and sometimes merged with ostensibly neutral or moderate analyses, which approached the intelligent reader in the name of reason, history, law and 'naturall Logick'.[46] Even convinced republicans were courted, their most cherished principles applauded yet redirected to diametrically opposed ends. Thus Prynne redefined self-denial, a duty much prized by godly patriots, so as to require the surrender of 'usurped power'. Another, less vehemently hostile, writer besought 'all honest disinterested Commonwealthsmen' not to read with 'prejudicate Opinions' against the 'distracting names' of 'King' or 'Lords' but to consider 'the things themselves' and hence concur in the national consensus that the ancient constitution represented the authentic public good.[47] In such ways, advocates of single-person rule reached out to the widest possible reading public. Amidst the general uncertainty that attended the absence of settlement, such polemic threatened to destabilise the infant Republic altogether, both by fomenting popular disrespect and disobedience, and by inflaming internal tensions. The alarm of contemporary commonwealthsmen concerning it was consequently entirely justified.

But counter-revolutionary rhetoric has sabotaged Parliament's subsequent reputation still more successfully than its actual government. In 1659 there was, at least, debate, featuring lively rebuttals of hostile arguments and vindications of the Commonwealth. Historians have, however, tended to ignore this positive, though undoubtedly partisan evidence, and perpetuate, in its essentials, the negative image so zealously propagated by the Republic's

---

[45] Skerpan provides interesting analysis of some of these methods, such as Richard Brathwait's romance *Panthalia*, but her rigid distinction between 'rhetorical tracts' offering specific arguments and 'philosophical tracts' providing general principles is less helpful, since it overlooks the substantial overlap between these categories in many tracts, and insufficiently recognises the variety of genres, leaving no place, for such as Arise Evans's prescriptive prophecy, *A Rule from Heaven, OR, VVholsom COUNSEL To A Distracted STATE.*

[46] *England ANATOMIZED: Her Disease discovered, and the Remedy prescribed*, 5. This pamphlet, purporting to originate from within the regime, exemplifies the blending of styles – the 'light of reason' not only exposes the Republic's flaws but licenses vigorous abuse of its rulers. A more dispassionately logical route to the same conclusion was taken by *Three PROPOSITIONS from the CASE of our Three Nations: Viz. I. That Monarchie . . . is the best way of Government . . . Ergo, neither Parliamentarie nor Militarie Government is best. II That it is very dangerous . . . to change the antient Government . . . Ergo, till our antient Government be resumed . . ., the Nation lieth exposed to many dangers . . . III. That Hereditarie Succession is the onely way for preservation of Peace in Nations . . . Ergo, till the Stuarts return Princes . . . no hope of Peace.*

[47] Prynne, *Vindication*, 56; William Bray, *A BRIEF ADMONITION of Some of the Inconveniences Of all the three most Famous GOVERNMENTS known to the World: With their Comparisons together*, 1, 5.

critics. This is due not to simple credulity, but to a real problem with the sources. Printed propaganda, whatever its political stance, is seldom considered reliable; instead, historians prefer the less consciously biased evidence found in correspondence or journals. Disinterested sources, unfortunately, do not exist: monarchists' manuscripts were permeated by exactly the same assumptions that governed the printed tracts. Given the presupposition that the Commonwealth was ungodly and anarchic, it was both reasonable and desirable to anticipate its downfall. It is therefore hardly surprising that the correspondence of these individuals interpreted all events in the light of this expectation, magnifying the least indications of difference between the Parliament and Army into harbingers of a second dissolution, and diagnosing the mildest symptoms of popular discontent as proof that a successful rebellion was imminent. This faith in Parliament's approaching demise was also shared by foreigners ill-disposed towards it. For example, the Venetian resident, Francesco Giavarina, whose reports are too often cited with nothing to indicate that he was not a neutral observer, tended to rely on Royalist intelligence, and frequently expressed his conviction that England could never enjoy stability without monarchy.[48]

On the republican side, the negative case finds support in only a handful of less than reliable sources. These include the edited and *ex post facto* memoirs of Ludlow, the diary of the Scottish outsider Archibald Johnston, and the mutual recriminations of October.[49] But the main evidence remains the numerous conservative manuscripts.[50] The *a priori* decision to accept their interpretations, often without criticism has exercised a determining influence on all three modern narrative histories. Godfrey Davies, for example, commenced his account of this government by citing a contemporary report to the effect that the 'Parliament and council of state contained such a diversity of interests . . . that no harmony was likely to prevail'. This was a typical monarchist judgement, which is not surprising, since its source, described in the text only as a 'shrewd observer', was, in fact, the Scottish Presbyterian minister James Sharpe, who was hauled before the council on suspicion of Royalist plotting in the Commonwealth's first weeks. At an important moment in Parliament–Army relations, Davies relies on Ludlow, the foreign ambassadors and correspondence of the Royalist Secretary Nicholas to substantiate the crucial statement that the Indemnity Act 'instead of calming the troubled waters, intensified the storm and . . . nearly led to another ejection of Parliament'. As befits the reactionary paradigm, Davies reads

---

[48] CSPVen., 23, 29, 35.

[49] *The memoirs of Edmund Ludlow . . . 1625–1672*, ed. C. H. Firth, Oxford 1894. The problems arising from the multiple modifications of this text by its first editor are explained by Blair Worden in introducing his edition of part of the original manuscript, *A voyce from the watchtower: part five, 1660–62* (Camden 4th ser. xxi, 1978).

[50] Victory ensured the disproportionate survival of Royalist manuscripts, especially letters; nothing comparable to the collections of Clarendon or Nicholas exists for any major republican leader.

Johnston's account of momentary disputes between leaders such as Vane and Fleetwood as proof of ongoing 'feuds between individuals', and overlooks abundant evidence of their co-operation thereafter. Davies also follows the Republic's enemies, this time Nicholas's informants and the French ambassador, in representing the new militia as the result of the 'determination of Parliament to create a rival organization' to the Army, and hence the occasion of 'misgivings' amongst the officers, despite the complete absence of complaint on their part, even in the comprehensive grievances of October.[51]

The pessimistic interpretation presented by Davies is shared by Woolrych and Hutton. Woolrych uses the foreign ambassadors to support Harrington's assessment of Parliament's unpopularity in July, but ignores the partisan motives of all three; he then follows the Nicholas and Clarendon manuscripts in contending that the Parliament had received 'miserably few addresses of congratulation', and that even these were 'said to have been mostly concocted at Westminster'. Like Davies, Woolrych portrays the new militia as a major cause of 'suspicion' and 'discontent' in the Army, and, after citing a few more monarchist sources, asserts that Parliament–Army relations had deteriorated by July to such an extent that only 'the shadow of the common enemy kept [them] from quarreling openly'.[52] Hutton similarly affirms that 'observers agreed' that the 'mutual awareness of trouble brewing in the provinces' was the 'main force keeping officers and MPs together' in the summer, but almost all the observers to whom he refers were hostile. Though he recognises that certain pamphlets had a 'deliberate policy of rubbing salt' into Army wounds, he fails to relate these to the conservative campaign against the Commonwealth.[53]

Even more significant than direct reliance on negative evidence when documenting particular events is the omission, without comment, of all positive portrayal of republican policies, and the evidence for the containment of tensions between the Parliament and the Army. The result is the dominant historiographic portrait of the Republic as intrinsically self-contradictory, its constitutional debates as futile dreams, its financial difficulties and unpopularity as necessarily permanent, its difficulties with the Army as insoluble. So influential is this interpretation that an otherwise excellent recent study of Ireland confidently asserts, on the flimsiest grounds, that 'the restored members . . . antagonised their allies, alienated their friends, and conciliated no one'.[54] Zealous suppression of the memory of the defeated Common-

---

51 Davies, *Restoration*, 96, 114, 115.

52 Woolrych, 'Introduction', 97, 100. At this point Harrington was particularly anxious to promote his own constitution by disparaging Parliament as a narrow oligarchy.

53 Hutton, *Restoration*, 54.

54 Aidan Clarke, *Prelude to Restoration in Ireland: the end of the Commonwealth, 1659–60*, Cambridge 1999, 57. The judgement is based on a few selected 'facts' and exaggerations that amount to fictions. Though arrears were unpaid, and a constitution undecided, this was not, as Clarke alleges, for want of action on Parliament's part.

wealth's merits after the Restoration reflects intense fear as well as hatred on the part of those responsible. Historical acceptance of the victors' perspective makes teleological sense, since it provides a convenient and superficially plausible explanation for the Commonwealth's eventual collapse. It is, however, high time to re-examine Parliament's performance without the aid of such hindsight. It will then become clear that, though genuine problems existed, the case against the Republic so brilliantly propagated by its opponents had few foundations in reality.

2

Priorities and Policies

How much can be done (if they be pleased) even in one day against their faithful friends, and how little, in six months for the common and publick good: *THE ARMY'S PLEA For Their present Practice*, Oct. 1659.

Did they not get you a whole Years Tax to be paid in Three Months and a Three Months Tax more to be paid in Three Weeks . . .? Did they not prepare an Act for £100,000 per mensem to be immediately levyed for you; and Ordered to sell everything almost to pay you your Arrears? and thereby drew an odium upon themselves more than ever any other Parliament would do: *The Grand Concernments of ENGLAND ENSURED . . . With some smart Rebukes to the Army*, Oct. 1659, 58.

The effectiveness of past governments, operating by different, usually unwritten, standards, and lacking systematic surveys of enforcement, is always difficult for historians to measure. It has proved particularly difficult in the case of the English Republic. Both Gerald Aylmer, in his monumental history of Interregnum administration, *The state's servants*, and Blair Worden, in his detailed study of *The Rump Parliament's* first tenure of power, wrestle with the problems of interpreting the dry bones of institutional evidence and the abundance of intensely partisan contemporary comment, but reach significantly different judgements. Whereas Aylmer accorded a qualified assent to the charges of corruption and dilatoriness hurled by the radicals in 1653, Worden exonerates Parliament, as a body, from such imputations, using careful comparisons with 'other seventeenth-century governments' rather than saintly ideals to demonstrate that the members were no worse, if no better, than any other politicians.[1] As these were the men who returned to power in 1659, Worden's findings raise obvious questions of continuity: were MPs more, less, or equally effective? Aylmer asserted that they 'had learnt some lessons' from their critics, and were now more committed to administrative reform than the pursuit of private interests. Indeed, he went so far as to suggest that more rigorous ethical standards characterised republican government than its monarchical counterpart, concluding that, in general, 'the parliamentarians were trying to operate more honestly and efficiently a system which was definitely more open to talent'.[2] To estimate the relevance

1 G. E. Aylmer, *The state's servants: the civil service of the English Republic, 1649–1660*, London 1973, 332–3; Worden, *Rump Parliament*, 90, 93, 95, 101.
2 Aylmer, *State's servants*, 336, 290–1, 341–2.

of these insights for 1659, it is essential to examine the priorities and policies adopted by the reinstated republicans.

The restored Parliament of 1659 presents the same evidential problems as in 1649–53, with the added complication of brevity: it is much easier to evaluate policy initiatives or assess general trends over four years than over five months. Contemporary debate on the efficiency of this government raged more fiercely than ever after its second expulsion: the epigraphs that head this chapter reflect the irreconcilable positions advanced by each side. Seeking additional excuses for the disruption of civilian rule, the Army's propagandists revived the old accusations deployed most recently by conservative critics: far from pursuing the public good, this assembly had proved selfish and indolent, delaying not only settlement but essential financial legislation in order to perpetuate its own power. Parliament's supporters hotly defended its integrity, praising the members' diligence, and wisdom in addressing the many difficulties that had confronted them.[3] Dismissing the officers' censure as unsubstantiated, these pamphleteers referred readers who doubted that their representatives had 'laboured like horses night and day' to the 'Diurnals', insisting that 'every Book of our Weekly Intelligence [will] witness against [the Army] as very Lyers'.[4] Ample documentation of Parliament's activities does, indeed, exist: not only the biased and abbreviated accounts in the newsbooks, but detailed institutional sources such as the Commons' Journal and the minutes of the Council of State have survived. Despite their formal nature, these records reveal much about the day-to-day working of government, showing which business did and did not receive attention, and what action was taken. It is therefore possible to escape reliance on partisan testimony, and identify the republicans' actual priorities.

Contrary to the assertions of its detractors, self-aggrandisement was not a priority. Parliament, in fact, spent an even smaller proportion of its time debating private business in 1659 than during its first period of power. Five MPs, including such important figures as Sir Arthur Hesilrig and the earl of Pembroke, presented petitions which were committed, but only Robert Reynolds, the influential solicitor-general, obtained a favourable report.[5]

---

[3] THE ARMY'S PLEA For Their present Practice, 19–20; The Grand Concernments of ENGLAND ENSURED, 58.
[4] A TRUE RELATION OF THE STATE of the CASE Between the ever Honourable PARLIAMENT And the OFFICERS, That fell out on the 11th and 12th of October 1659, 6; The Northern QVERIES From The Lord General Monck His QVARTERS, Sounding an Allarum, to all Loyal Hearts and Free-born English men . . . Against the Tyrannical Power, & Domination of the Sword, 5.
[5] Reynolds's petition was read and committed on 7 July, and the committee reported in his favour on 20 July: Journal, 705, 725–6. The other MPs petitioning were Hesilrig, Michael Oldsworth, the earl of Pembroke and Lord Monson. The sixteen private individuals who petitioned Parliament fared even worse: satisfactory answers were granted only to Elizabeth Lilburne, widow of the famous Leveller, the displaced republican Colonel Alured and Henry Ogle.

Tangible rewards were, in practice, limited to occasional bucks from the Commonwealth's forests, and, for the more active, lodgings at Whitehall.[6] Although most leaders simply resumed their former suites, organising the remaining space consumed significant amounts of council time in July. Some petty rivalry occurred – possession clearly bred pride in certain individuals, such as the Scottish newcomer Johnston of Wariston. Yet there was little attempt to recreate the much-criticised material splendour of the early republican 'court'.[7] A Royalist satire published in June deplored the quartering of soldiers in the 'sad decaying Rooms', and declared that, in the rightful owner's absence, occupation by the council was a preferable fate for the palace. In the following month Giavarina remarked upon the sparseness of the furnishings, and the reluctance of those granted accommodation to take up residence. Republican probity in the face of Whitehall's dilapidation is further illustrated by the decision to forbid state funding for the repair of apartments assigned to MPs or councillors.[8] Instead of enriching or otherwise indulging themselves, the Commonwealth's new rulers consistently devoted the greatest attention to three pressing national problems: finance, domestic security and the resumption and effective functioning of a republican administration. To assess their achievement, it is thus necessary to consider what progress was made in these areas.

Dominating the agenda for the first month was the practical restoration of republican authority. As Parliament naturally did not recognise any previous regime established without its sanction, all commissions, decisions and legislation since the 'interruption' of April 1653 were technically invalid. The Republic's return thus threatened to bring government everywhere to a standstill. Judges in the courts at Westminster, collectors of essential taxes, JPs and sheriffs, all lost their official mandate to proceed. The removal of the Protector and his council left a vacuum at the centre of government: the republicans urgently needed to create a new and reliable executive to assume the responsibility for diplomacy, security and daily administration. Moreover, the forty-four MPs indisputably present in the House on the 7 May were scarcely adequate for the august role of 'Supreme Authority'.[9] To demonstrate

---

6 Council minutes record the allocation of deer to 52 individual members and two dining coteries; official lodgings went to 54, including the 18 resident councillor-MPs; in all, 69 MPs obtained at least one of these privileges.

7 The council gave substantial attention to the redistribution of lodgings on 8, 9, 12 and 14 July with occasional orders thereafter. Johnston was initially delighted to receive lodgings in a palace formerly occupied by the Stuarts and Cromwells, but later, upon losing two of his 'best rooms' to another councillor, reproached himself for 'vainglory and boasting': Johnston diary, 126–7. On the material culture of the early republican 'court' centred upon Whitehall, and the criticisms that it aroused see Kelsey, Inventing a republic, esp. ch. i.

8 WHITE-HALLS PETITION To The PARLIAMENT: That he may enjoy his former Priviledges (22 June); CSPVen., 45; council minutes, 8 July.

9 Though Presbyterians insisted that there was a bare quorum of 42, between them they list 44 MPs as present. See Prynne, Narrative, 35–6; [Annesley], England's confusion, 10–11.

the dignity of the legislature, and defeat the secluded Presbyterians' demand for entry, it was imperative to enforce the attendance of as many eligible members as possible.

The republicans took swift action to ensure that government continued without disruption and came increasingly under their own control. On the very first day, Parliament not only established a committee to consider the administration of justice and a temporary executive 'Committee of Safety', but also compiled a list of qualified absentees and despatched letters commanding their appearance. Within a week, a new great seal, modelled on 'the last great seale made by authority of the Parliament', had replaced that of the Protector. Pending its use to prepare new commissions, order was maintained by laws continuing the Easter term as if 'Judges authorised by Parliament sat', and confirming existing taxes and officials. The republicans were, however, careful to emphasise the short-term nature of these measures. They had no intention of using their power to legitimise the Cromwellian *status quo* once the immediate crisis was over. Quite the reverse: on 9 May they laid the foundation for a thorough purge by voting that all officers, civil and military, must be 'able, fearing God and such as have given testimony of their love for all the people of God and of their faithfulness to the cause of this Commonwealth'.[10] This qualification was a masterpiece of constructive ambiguity: though the biblical emphasis upon godliness and proven fidelity offered reassurance to purist militants fearing a sacrifice of principle, the absence of specific requirements extended hope of continuance to competent Cromwellians who were prepared to serve the new order.[11] In practice, Parliament's interpretation was broad enough to accept most persons who offered their services, excepting notorious trimmers: Marchamont Nedham, the much execrated editor of the official newsbooks, was sacked just six days after the Republic's revival.[12]

During the same period, the pretensions of the secluded MPs were firmly depressed by well-publicised votes, enforced by guards, to continue the exclusion of all those who had not sat since 1648 or taken the Engagement of 1650. Exemptions were contemplated only for the illustrious former lord general, Fairfax, who was not willing to sit, and Sir Anthony Ashley-Cooper, who was, and these cases were referred to a committee that never reported. Neither Prynne's personal and printed complaints, nor the private pleas of individuals such as Richard Tolson, who professed his 'Cordial and real

---

[10] These resolves were all reported in the official newsbook, *Politicus*, no. 566, 5–12 May, 432, 430. The qualification for office-holders clearly echoed that of ancient Israel's commonwealth, recorded in Exodus xviii.21.

[11] On the administrative changes see Aylmer, *State's servants*, esp. p. 57. Though he admits that the Republic did not lack competent officials, he suggests (pp. 328–38) that the failure to pursue more radical administrative reform contributed to its collapse. This seems unlikely: the need for able officials was more urgent than the demand for reform, while immediate causes afford a far more convincing explanation of the Republic's downfall.

[12] *Journal*, 652; *Politicus*, no. 567, 12–19 May, 437.

Activeness for the good-old-Cause . . . of this Commonwealth as a Free-state' in a letter urging the Speaker to support his readmission, produced any alter-ation in this policy.[13] Meanwhile, attendance of authorised MPs rose rapidly: seventy-eight were present at the council's election on 14 May. Less than a month after the initial summons, 115 MPs had arrived; as more drifted in, the total eventually reached 127, or 89 per cent of those pronounced eligible.[14] This remarkable proportion, though unimpressive in numerical terms, sufficed to staff the numerous committees, and was certainly not the pathetic handful depicted by hostile contemporaries and uncritical historians. Rather, the high percentage indicates an extensive willingness among MPs to make the onerous journey to London and resume arduous responsibilities. The ideal of self-sacrificial dedication to the 'public interest', whose importance for the earlier Republic Sean Kelsey has highlighted, had lost nothing of its rhetor-ical or motivational force during the interval.[15] Pledging all possible haste, Sir Michael Livesey assured the Speaker that there was 'no Joy under the sun more welcome . . . than to do service for this parliament'; though almost blind, John Gurdon stoically asserted his determination, providence permit-ting, 'to spend and be spent . . . in attending the service of the house'. That their professed zeal was sincere, not just assumed to escape censure for absence, is underlined by their subsequent appearance and cordial recep-tion.[16] But efforts to compel attendance from the recalcitrant minority, by calling the House and fining those absent without leave, were not wholly fruitless: at least one member accorded such treatment was thereby motivated to appear and secure remission.[17]

Despite increasing numbers, the members' enthusiasm for their duties was far from uniform. Though 40 per cent were at least moderately assiduous, since they were regularly appointed to committees, another 25 per cent made only occasional visits to Westminster, taking little interest, and playing little

---

[13] *Politicus*, no. 566, 5–12 May, 431; *Journal*, 646; Richard Tolson to the Speaker, 6/16 May, Bodl. Lib., MS Tanner 51, fo. 48.

[14] *Journal*, 653–4. The 115 MPs are listed in *A CATALOGUE of the NAMES of this Present Parliament*, collected by Thomason on 4 June. The presence of all but one can be corrobo-rated either from the journal or from the Presbyterian lists. This catalogue also listed 24 MPs who had not yet taken their seats; 9 of these subsequently appeared, as did 3 who were omitted. The total judged eligible to sit may thus be estimated at 142. Hence the inaccu-racy of Hutton's assertion that 'the total number declared eligible to sit was seventy-eight, of whom some never appeared': *Restoration*, 42.

[15] Kelsey, *Inventing a republic*, 209–10.

[16] Sir Michael Livesey to the Speaker, 12 May, MS Tanner 51, fo. 50; John Gurdon, 13 May, ibid. fo. 55. Both men excused their immediate absence by pleading ill health, but arrived in the House by 1 July; Livesey was assiduous enough to be allocated lodgings at Whitehall, while Gurdon was favoured with a buck: *Journal*, 700; council minutes, 12 July, 10 Aug.

[17] The House was called on 8 Aug. and 30 Sept. Edward Dunch, fined £100 on the first occasion, had arrived by 24 Aug., and, on 13 Sept., secured the remission of his fine: *Journal*, 751, 767, 777.

part in the government. At the opposite extreme, comprising about one-third of the total, were the dedicated MPs in constant attendance.[18] This hard-working group included not only such charismatic, multi-talented leaders as Sir Henry Vane and Sir Arthur Hesilrig, but the colourless professionals: lawyers William Say and Augustine Garland, who were frequently appointed to draft amendments and chair grand committees; the financial experts, John Downs and William White, who dominated the Committee for Inspection into the Treasuries; and the naval specialists George Thompson and Valentine Walton. These were the able men who had enjoyed the business of government during the early years of the Republic. In 1659 they devoted themselves anew to the work in which they had formerly excelled, serving on the principal standing committees, the important commissions for revenue, the admiralty, and the nomination of officers, and, especially, the Council of State, whose twenty-one MPs were, with four exceptions, elected from this elite of the most active and talented administrators.[19] Well might a Royalist caution that the present rulers were 'men of long experience, great expedition, and many of them singular parts'.[20]

Given the quality of those appointed, it is hardly surprising that the republican Council of State, which commenced work on 19 May, proved an effective solution to the problem of the executive. Recalling former precedents had expedited its establishment: the entire process occupied the House for just ten days. In addition to the MPs, the new council included three senior Army officers – Lambert, Disbrow and Berry – and seven civilians. Of these, Lord Fairfax and his Royalist kinsman, Sir Horatio Townsend, had co-operated with the republicans in Richard Cromwell's Parliament, but would not join them in government, while John Bradshaw, a former president, was

---

[18] These estimates were obtained by counting the days on which each member's presence was recorded in the journal; since a member's presence on a particular day was usually not recorded unless he were appointed to a committee, served as a teller or made some report, the figures tend to err on the side of underestimating occasional attendance. But, as committees were frequently appointed during the first four months, it is improbable that any member regularly present would have escaped inclusion. In all, 33 MPs appear on 7 or fewer occasions; 52 on 8–20 occasions, and 42 more than 21 times. The dedicated core group is plainly discernible: 23 MPs appear more than 30 times, and 7 over 50 times. If prizes had been awarded for diligence, the first would have gone to Richard Salway, who was not only a councillor and commissioner for both admiralty and revenue, but was appointed to no less than 56 committees. On the earlier achievements of these men see Worden, *Rump Parliament*, esp. ch. i.

[19] The exceptions were Oliver St John, whose prestige remained high despite his involvement in the Protectorate, but whose commitment to the restored Republic was at best lukewarm; Robert Wallop, who was never more than moderately active in Parliament, and vanished from Westminster altogether after securing a colonelcy in the Southamptonshire militia and the wardenship of the New Forest in August; John Dixwell, whose recorded appearances in Parliament were very infrequent, though he proved assiduous in his attendance at council; and Lieutenant-General Charles Fleetwood, whose military responsibilities necessarily limited his role in Parliament.

[20] Anonymous letter to Charles II, 17 June, *CSP* iii. 491.

for two months prevented by ill-health from fulfilling his ardent wish to serve the Commonwealth again.[21] The other four were: the plausible, but untrustworthy, Ashley-Cooper, another ally from Richard's Parliament, who retained secret links with monarchist conspirators; Josias Berners, a close friend of John Hobart, and ex-member of the Haberdashers' Hall committee; Vane's brother-in-law, Sir Robert Honywood; and a solitary Scottish Covenanter, Sir Archibald Johnston of Wariston, whose speeches in the Other House against Richard's recognition had attracted Vane's favourable notice.[22] The active service of these men on subcommittees eased the pressures on the members, enabling the council to continue work during their necessary absences in the House or at parliamentary committees.[23]

The council's workload was phenomenal. Besides executing specific orders and recommending necessary measures and appointments to Parliament, this body supervised all departments of government, managed Commonwealth property and overseas possessions, corresponded with local officials and garrison commanders, negotiated with the foreign ambassadors, and liaised with both the City and the Army.[24] The council also spared Parliament the majority of individual petitions: by June the quantity arriving was so great that preliminary screening by a subcommittee became necessary. When this failed to reduce the total to manageable levels, the council seized the opportunity to require all petitioners to subscribe to the Engagement.[25] The initial upsurge of petitions was due to the avid competition for favours from the new government: though radicals such as John Canne warned that the principles of 'good men' were incompatible with those of the 'servile mercenarie fellows' who came 'running . . . for places', prizes frequently went to the importunate, since the council had no leisure to solicit aid from those who remained aloof.[26] Later, however, the mass of petitions related to the rebellion, which

---

[21] Fairfax did not openly reject the Commonwealth, but resisted appeals to act, contacting his fellow councillors only when necessary to secure preferential treatment for his Royalist son-in-law, the duke of Buckingham: council minutes, 27, 30 July. Townsend consulted the exiled royal government on whether to take his seat, but withdrew instead after opposition from Fleetwood and the officers: CSP iii. 481; MS Clarendon 61, fo. 1; *Ludlow memoirs*, ii. 83–4. In a letter of 7 June Bradshaw explained that illness frustrated his desire to serve 'with all diligence and faithfulness': MS Tanner 51, fo. 89.

[22] *Johnston diary*, 113. Ashley-Cooper's Royalist connections are amply chronicled in Hyde's correspondence. For examples see CSP iii. 477, 487–8, 498–9, 555–8. Some of Berners's letters to Hobart survive in MS Tanner 51.

[23] The usefulness of the civilian councillors who were not also MPs is reflected in the exceptionally high attendance of all except Ashley-Cooper. They were present at 76% of all possible sessions, considerably more than the 54% overall average for active councillors; business was frequently referred to a committee of the non-MPs.

[24] Full details of attendance and all business are in the minute books: MS Rawlinson C79, 19 May–10 Aug.; PRO, SP 25/79, 11 Aug.–25 Oct.

[25] MS Rawlinson C79, fos 61, 213. In all, the council dealt with 180 petitions; Parliament received only 142, including many congratulatory addresses.

[26] John Canne, *A Seasonable Word to the Parliament-Men*, 3. A good illustration of the eventual, if sometimes long-delayed, rewards of petitioning is the case of the council

had substantially increased the council's burden: not only was it obliged to direct the military effort, but to find prisons and conduct the examinations of the multitude of suspects arrested and sent up to London. Notwithstanding these challenges, the council discharged its duties with an unrelenting diligence, sitting twice daily and, at moments of crisis, on Sundays as well. Its dedication and thoroughness won grudging admiration even from such hostile observers as the Venetian diplomat Giavarina.[27]

By early June the transfer of power was all but complete. Republican central government functioned smoothly, following a prescribed schedule: the House sat from 8.00 a.m. till noon, six days a week, leaving the early mornings and afternoons for committee and council meetings.[28] Commissioners loyal to Parliament had assumed custody of the new great seal, whose profits were sequestered to the Commonwealth. Despite the legal profession's rumoured dissatisfaction, a handful of properly authorised judges now presided over the Westminster courts.[29] Although Richard Cromwell still lingered at Whitehall, he did so rather to evade his creditors than to inconvenience the Republic, in which he had publicly declared his acquiescence.[30] One Royalist, disheartened by his party's failure to profit from the confusion accompanying the Protectorate's collapse, lamented that the new regime's overthrow was becoming 'every day more and more doubtful and difficult'; even the eternal optimist Mordaunt warned his sovereign that 'if before the end of the next Tearme we adventure not . . . these People may settle'.[31]

Secure at the centre, the republicans turned to asserting their authority in the provinces. As the summer assizes approached, it was important to demonstrate that the Republic, unlike Richard, who had postponed the Lent circuit, would dispense regular justice by reputable judges in a legal and orderly manner. On 7 June the council received instructions to 'consider with all

---

printer: in the first fortnight, petitions from two aspirants for this office were received and recorded. When, in September, the council at last discovered a need for its own printer, it duly appointed the first candidate: council minutes, 26, 31 May, 26 Sept.

[27] The council met on four Sundays, on 22 May, when a Royalist rebellion was feared, but did not materialise, and the three Sundays immediately before and during Booth's rising. For Giavarina's admiration of the council's 'sound precautions' and intense application to business during the emergency see *CSPVen.*, 30, 48, 53.

[28] This schedule was voted on 31 May, and worked well until July, when the complexities of the indemnity bill and the increasing urgency of settling the county militia necessitated increasingly frequent afternoon sessions.

[29] Patents for Newdigate, Archer, Atkins and Parker to continue until 30 June as judges in the courts of Upper Bench, Common Pleas and Exchequer were issued on 16 May, and on 11 June renewed until 30 Nov. Due to Bradshaw's illness, Chancery was slower to reconvene; on 6 June its officials were licensed to hear cases in the absence of the great seal commissioners: PRO, C231/6, fos 433, 434. The regime's enemies, predictably, spread rumours of the lawyers' discontent, and sneered at the small number of judges: for examples see *CSP* iii. 479, 485.

[30] Richard Cromwell's acquiescence was published in *Politicus*, no. 568, 19–26 May, 464.

[31] *CSP* iii. 491; Mordaunt to Charles II, 19 May, MS Clarendon 60, fo. 560.

speed how to provide [for] the Circuits this Summer, that the Circuits be not hindered'. When Parliament, nine days later, approved most of the council's nominees, the matter seemed virtually settled: *Mercurius Politicus* confidently published details of the judges, dates and places of the assizes, while local sheriffs also had orders to proclaim the arrangements.[32] Meanwhile, the House debated the appointment of new JPs, and prescribed a new Engagement of loyalty to 'the Commonwealth without single person, kingship or House of Lords'. Judges, county justices and all other officials were now required by law to swear allegiance in these words before commencing their duties.[33] This was a standard precaution, intended to ensure the reliability of those entrusted; the result was unexpected. Ten days before the first assizes were due to begin, the Speaker learned that a 'failure of Justice to the People' of 'evil consequence' was imminent, since very few of the eleven circuit judges had so far taken the oath, while three had refused point blank. Two of these, Archer and Atkins, were already serving in the Westminster courts, and had hitherto accorded Parliament the 'usual obeisance'; the third, Serjeant Earle, was an MP, as was a fourth, Baron Nicholas, who soon joined them in opposition.[34] Why these men, who had all consented to act when consulted prior to appointment, so suddenly developed scruples remains a mystery.[35] Parliament plainly interpreted their defiance as an intolerable affront, since it immediately reiterated the order imposing the Engagement, and subsequently refused to renew the patents of those who proved obdurate. Instead, the circuits were hastily reorganised.[36] Contrary to the expectation of Royalist commentators, Parliament declined to elevate 'unknowen or very ordinary gownemen' to the judiciary, but shared the six circuits among the

---

[32] *Journal*, 673, 682, 686, 687; *Politicus*, no. 572, 16–23 June, 521–2. Evidence of such orders to sheriffs, issued on 23 June, survives in PRO, ASSI 35/100/6, fo. 15.

[33] *Journal*, 672, 689, 693; the new law, passed on 16 June, merely formalised and broadened an order of 4 June for the great seal commissioners to administer this oath to the judges at Westminster, and so could hardly have surprised the latter.

[34] Great seal commissioners to the Speaker, 1 July, MS Tanner 51, fos 79–80; *Journal*, 672. Nicholas's opposition is evidenced by the council's recommendation of a replacement for him on 7 July, and his omission from the eventual list.

[35] The most detailed discussion of this incident occurs in S. F. Black, 'The judges at Westminster Hall during the Interregnum', unpubl. BLitt. diss. Oxford 1970, 231–3. Black's explanation in terms of the judges' latent Royalism or anticipation of the Restoration seems unconvincing, as Atkins, Nicholas and Earle had taken the earlier Engagement, while all were prepared to accept patents from Parliament. It is possible that they had hoped to evade the new oath, but were frustrated by the commissioners' energetic application of the law. Surviving contemporary comment on their motives comes only from a Royalist who likened the oath to the 'Popes Bull', and cryptically suggested that they refused because they were 'rich and would not be impoverisht' by the Republic: *Nicholas papers*, 165–6.

[36] The main changes – solitary circuits by Windham and Widdrington – were given minimum publicity in *Politicus*, no. 278, 7–14 July, 583; the whole revised list may be found in PRO, C181/6, fo. 369. From this, and a council order of 4 July for the commissioners to administer the oath to him, it is clear that Earle withdrew his objections.

eight previous appointees who eventually accepted the oath. Justice proceeded with no compromise of parliamentary authority; nevertheless, the absence of a full complement of judges did nothing to reinforce the intended image of the Republic's strength and stability.[37]

As the assizes coincided with the climax of the most ambitious conspiracy of the decade, it is hardly surprising that the projected demonstration of republican power did not proceed entirely smoothly.[38] The greatest disruption befell the Oxford circuit, whose judges appealed for instructions. On 5 August Parliament granted them permission to proceed or retreat as conditions dictated. In the event, they decided to withdraw from Gloucester to Hereford and Shrewsbury, where they remained until the rising was safely over; this delayed the Monmouth and Stafford assizes for almost a month.[39] By August, however, a hiatus in the distribution of justice was the least of Westminster's worries: security had long since succeeded administration as the overwhelming priority.

Emergencies always tended to bring out the best in the republicans, whose competence in such circumstances has commanded the admiration of most historians. Hutton observes that they 'responded with all the formidable energy of which they were capable in their own defence', while Davies deplores the folly of Royalists who failed to perceive that the Parliament was 'strongest on the battlefield and weakest in the council chamber'.[40] Yet such judgements ignore the fact that success in battle requires considerable prior skill in council. MPs were not content to await the onslaught of their enemies on 1 August; rather, they worked tirelessly throughout July to prevent disturbances if possible, and facilitate their suppression if necessary. The resultant measures ranged from proclamations for the surrender of suspects and the banishment of Royalists and Roman Catholic priests to laws requiring householders throughout England to report all horses, arms, ammunition and lodgers, on pain of imprisonment and fines of up to £50. To reduce the likelihood of false declarations, informers were promised the cash value of any concealed items discovered. But the most important initiative was the creation of the new militia in London and the counties. First proposed in response to rumours of invasion and insurrection in May, but shelved during

---

[37] *Journal*, 701; 'Miles' to Nicholas, 13 June, *Nicholas papers*, 154. The council, to whom the task of reorganisation was delegated, had recommended the elevation of the relatively obscure John Farewell; Parliament decided against this, opting instead to leave four circuits with only one judge: *Journal*, 708.

[38] The best general account of the rebellion remains Underdown, *Royalist conspiracy*.

[39] Parliament's vote was reproduced in *Politicus*, no. 582, 4–11 Aug., 646. Details of the proceedings of Wild and Hill, the judges on this circuit, survive in ASSI 1/2. Explicit evidence for the other circuits is meagre, except for the Home Counties, of which partial records are in ASSI 35/100. As the major problems encountered by Wild and Hill did secure Parliament's attention, it is probable that their colleagues elsewhere proceeded without serious incident.

[40] Hutton, *Restoration*, 57–8; Davies, *Restoration*, 126.

the greater tranquillity of June, the new militia emerged as a major under-taking while the storm gathered in July. The aim was, quite simply, to provide for local defence by raising new forces under the direct control of Parliament, which not only appointed commissioners to organise regiments and exact the necessary funds in each county, but retained the power to confirm all officers. Conscious that the effectiveness of this law would depend on the quality of the commissioners, the republicans took all possible precautions to ensure their reliability: Parliament not only inserted a clause requiring commis-sioners to take the Engagement, but encouraged county MPs to recommend candidates, and spent several days debating additions and deletions.[41] So great was Parliament's absorption, or confidence, in the militia, that it neglected certain other security measures urged by the council, including a proclamation against the horse races and other gatherings that so often afforded convenient cover to conspirators.[42]

Despite occasional inattention to its advice, Parliament usually supported the council's efforts, and authorised it to arrest suspects, conduct searches, seize arms and horses, and levy additional forces. The council rose to the emergency with predictable zeal, making full use of all available resources to uncover and counter the conspiracy. As the intelligence network, now again directed by Thomas Scot, proved as efficient as ever in infiltrating Royalist circles, the council could not only detain many conspirators before they were due to act, but even direct troops to forestall the intended rendezvous. Such timely action quashed most risings at their inception.[43] On 29 July the council created its own committee of safety to supervise the Army, the militia and various volunteer regiments in policing the London area; the strict precautions adopted effectively deterred hostile action in the capital. Mean-while, the council expanded its communication with the provinces, some-times sending as many as fifty or sixty letters a day to warn local authorities of the dangers, exhort them to greater vigilance, and enquire after their prog-ress. That only Sir George Booth, of all the rebel leaders, succeeded in gath-ering an army was due, in large measure, to the council's prudent exertions.

---

[41] The question of the militia was first raised on 9 May. The bills for London & Westmin-ster reached committee stage by the end of the month, but did not re-emerge until 27 June, when a committee was created to introduce a general militia bill: *Journal*, 647, 662, 663–4, 694–5. Militia acts for the capital and its environs had passed by 14 July; that for the coun-ties reached the statute book on 26 July, after a debate lasting eight days, spread over three weeks: *A&O* ii. 1293–8, 1316, 1320–41.

[42] On 13 July the council reported the need for a proclamation against races, cock fights and bull baitings, and urged the confinement of Royalists to a 5–mile radius of their homes. Parliament agreed to ban races, but failed to issue a proclamation to this effect. Undeterred, the council ordered local officers to prevent such meetings on its own authority: *Journal*, 715; MS Rawlinson C79, fo. 173.

[43] This was particularly true near London: on 31 July, troops ordered to Blackheath, Tunbridge, Redhill successfully prevented risings, and enabled the arrest of rebels as they arrived. See *Politicus*, no. 581, 28 July–4 Aug., 638; the troop movements in question are confirmed by the council's letter book, SP 25/98, fos 75, 99.

The easy suppression of his insurgents by Lambert's professionals also owed much to the council, which organised the essential supplies for the expeditionary force.[44]

Though the republican success against Booth and his fellow conspirators has justly been praised by historians, the financial achievements that undergirded that success have seldom, if ever, been acknowledged.[45] Indeed, first impressions of the Parliament's financial performance are distinctly unfavourable: despite the vast debts left by the Protectorate, the Republic sanctioned substantial increases in military expenditure, and failed to introduce an adequate revenue by the time of its interruption. Thus Hutton suggests, after surveying a few inadequate expedients, that the restored Parliament ignored the reports of its own committees, and was 'as reluctant to face fiscal realities as Richard's' parliament had been. Such criticisms do not, however, do justice to the complexity of the financial problem, and the determined, and by no means wholly ineffectual, efforts of the republicans. Far from neglecting the difficulties, Parliament consistently accorded finance a priority second only to security; during its five-month session, fiscal issues were debated on no less than eighty occasions, while almost a quarter of all legislation passed related to finance. Nor was this diligence unavailing: by October, the Parliament had begun to develop rational solutions to the financial predicament.[46]

No solutions could be devised without accurate information on the scale of the problem. Parliament's first move, on 9 May, was the creation of a standing Committee of Inspection of the Treasuries, instructed to sit daily to investigate the 'whole state' of the revenue and propose measures to improve it 'with least charge and most speed'. This committee, under the watchful care of John Downs, began work immediately: during the next two days it produced preliminary measures, which were readily adopted by the House. On 20 May Downs presented the first major report, in which, after calculations estimating the deficit at almost £1.5 million, the committee recommended better management of the customs and excise, and legislation to continue the assessment and recover debts to the state incurred during the

---

44 Instructions to committee of safety, MS Rawlinson C79, fo. 241. The sudden expansion of the council's communications is apparent in its letter book. From 20 July to 30 Aug. the council wrote 192 letters, excluding circulars. This was more than twice the total for the other four months of its existence. On five occasions the council sent out circulars to all the sheriffs and more than 50 militia captains. Orders concerning the supply of Lambert's forces frequently occur in its minutes: for examples see 12, 15, 19, 23 Aug.

45 This Parliament's former achievements in establishing the fiscal apparatus that made possible unprecedented military mobilisation have, however, received abundant coverage: see, in particular, James Scott Wheeler, *The making of a world power*, Sutton 1999.

46 Hutton, *Restoration*, 49. The index printed in *A&O* iii, pp. civ–cvii reveals that 11 of the 42 statutes recorded related to finance. The priority assigned that topic may be deduced from the fact that on four occasions in July and September Parliament listed money as one of only three subjects to be debated in the ensuing days: *Journal*, 706, 723, 776, 789. The frequency with which Parliament actually discussed it may be estimated from journal references.

interruption. As these debts were estimated at £205,000, Parliament within a week passed an act ordering payment; commissioners were appointed to enforce the new law and work with the committee to improve the administration of public revenue. Meanwhile, the committee continued the herculean task of untangling the web of Cromwellian accounts: on 8 June Downs presented a second report. This provided more detailed figures on the extent of the Commonwealth's obligations, but had no constructive suggestions, listing various fiscal expedients only to conclude that they could not produce an adequate or 'timely supply for accommodating the pressing Occasions of the Commonwealth'. Instead, the committee advised the House to seek alternative sources of income.[47]

Though the Committee of Inspection might be at a loss, there was no shortage of would-be advisors: few visions of a reformed Republic omitted the financial question, while several pamphlets were exclusively devoted to revenue. Parliament was quite prepared to consider advice from without, and, indeed, instructed its financial committees to receive any proposals offered.[48] Some suggestions had no hope of success: however emphatic their invocation of republican rhetoric, appeals to replace the excise with the old-fashioned and far less lucrative subsidies were unlikely to persuade the government of anything except the political correctness of an attack on those 'deformed Monsters . . . tyrannical oppressors and Monopolizers of our Freedom', the excise farmers.[49] More realistic were those, like the London merchant John Bland, who criticised abuses and recommended improved regulation of the existing system.[50] Mollified by praise for the equity of the excise itself, Parliament proved receptive to advice to replace corrupt farmers with public-spirited commissioners, who would use their position to encourage trade and hence increase revenue. Direct collection of the entire excise replaced partial farming in July. September saw the creation of new commissions headed by loyal London aldermen for both customs and excise, under the general oversight of the five revenue commissioners appointed in May to bring in arrears owed the Commonwealth.[51] In August the House had held a 'long Debate' on

[47] *Journal*, 647, 659–60, 675.
[48] Ibid. 669–70, 717. Some proposals considered by Parliament and the Committee of Inspection are described in S. E., *The Toutch-Stone of MONY and COMMERCE: Or an Expedient For increase of Trade, Mony, and Shiping*, published after Parliament's second restoration in December.
[49] *EXCISE ANOTOMIZD, AND TRADE EPITOMIZD: Declaring, that unequall Imposition of Excise, to be the only cause of the ruine of Trade, and universall impoverishment . . .*, 5–6. Other denunciations of the excise include *Trades Destruction is Englands Ruine, or Excise Decryed*, and the satire, *A Dialogue betwixt an EXCISE-MAN and DEATH*.
[50] John Bland, *Trade Revived, or, A way proposed to restore, increase, inrich and preserve the decayed and even dying trade of this our English nation, in its manufactories, coin, shiping and revenue, whereby taxes may be lessened if not totally taken away.*
[51] *Journal*, 702–3; A&O ii. 1349–51, 1276–7. The customs and excise commissions were led respectively by John Ireton, the reliable lord mayor, and Alderman Thomas Atkin, MP;

William Hawkins's proposal to replace taxes on English imports and exports with a new duty on the vice of alcohol and tobacco consumption. To this end JPs were ordered to report on the number of 'Taverns, Inns, Alehouses, and what was spent in them' during the previous year. Eager for ready money, Parliament also heeded calls to increase the supply of bullion, ordering the council to enforce the law against its transportation.[52] That suggestion had been echoed, less disinterestedly, by the goldsmith Thomas Violet, who presented his ideas in a lengthy pamphlet, complete with an elaborate frontispiece and poem celebrating his former services. Violet offered, if suitably rewarded, to gain the Commonwealth thousands of pounds by regulating the mint and exposing long-forgotten frauds. His schemes, supported by testimonials from some leading republicans, obtained serious attention from the council, but were never implemented – either the rebellion interrupted progress, or the councillors perceived the probability that Violet would profit rather more than the treasury.[53]

Notwithstanding the extravagant promises of individuals like Violet, there were in reality only four ways to improve the financial position: reducing expenditure; selling public assets; recovering outstanding revenue; and raising taxes. Republican policies exploited all these options to the full. Parliament constantly enjoined economy: much attention was devoted to devising alternative provision for the thousands of disabled soldiers enjoying state pensions, while significant savings were anticipated from reducing or abolishing the stipends of some officials.[54] MPs even considered recovering up to £100,000 disbursed in technically illegal salaries since 1653, but eventually decided against such divisive refunds; all positions granted during

the revenue commissioners included two MPs, Luke Robinson and William White. On the administrative history of these revenues see Wheeler, *World power*, chs vi, vii.

[52] *Journal*, 676, 761–2, 711; cf. Bland, *Trade revived*, 25–7, 48–9. Hawkins's scheme, described at length in *Toutch-stone*, 12–15, resembles and may well have been modelled on an idea of Bland's. In a postscript the latter professed his pleasure at some of his proposals, 'lately published by other hands', being 'at present under consideration': *Trade revived*, 57.

[53] Thomas Violet, *A TRUE NARRATIVE Of The PROCEEDINGS In the Court of Admiraltie . . . Together with several Humble Proposals, for the Profit and Honour of this Common-wealth, in saving them many score of thousand pounds.* The council appointed a committee for Violet's proposals on 20 June; on 27 July, when preparing its own report to Parliament on finance, it enlarged this committee and ordered it to report as soon as possible. No further action was taken: MS Rawlinson C79, fos 123, 223. Violet himself was, however, rewarded with office: by October the clerk of the irons was petitioning the council against him, alleging that he and other officers 'speak against Parliament, keep company with malignants, drink and are unfaithful': *CSPD 1659*, 230.

[54] Thus Parliament confiscated the profits of the commissioners for the great seal and second moyeties, and instructed committees to propose cuts in salaries and the number of officials: *Journal*, 648, 694, 731, 758. On 1 Sept. Parliament ordered careful investigation of the maimed soldiers and others receiving pensions, and imposed stringent requirements for eligibility; on 5 Oct. it ordered as many as possible to be transferred to garrison duty, and alternative maintenance for the rest: ibid. 771, 792. As the cost of pensions had been estimated at over £860,000 p.a., there was much to be gained from such economies.

the interruption did, however, revert to Parliament's gift.[55] Greater things were expected from the disposal of surviving assets – the forests, confiscated lands and, especially, the palaces of Whitehall, Hampton Court and Somerset House, which virtuous republicans loudly condemned as incongruous symbols of monarchical oppression.[56] Within a month of its return, Parliament had ordered the sale of virtually all Commonwealth property except Westminster.[57] Though Whitehall was soon reserved for the council's use, the non-appearance of the expected purchasers for the other palaces owed more to want of the 'ready cash' required, and the imprecations of George Fox, who deterred some Quakers from investing, than to any desire to live in unbecoming luxury on the part of the members, who ordered preparations to sell plate and furnishings even after resolving to retain the buildings. Under pressure that autumn, Parliament reiterated the orders to sell Somerset House and Hampton Court.[58] At the same time, efforts to recover all debts to the state redoubled: counterfeit receipts pleaded by the customs commissioners were cancelled, while the threat of sequestration and imprisonment was wielded with some success against the excise farmers. Preparations also commenced to repair the Commonwealth's depleted capital by confiscating the lands of the numerous prisoners of quality captured during the rising.[59]

At first MPs sought to avoid politically damaging tax increases, voting in June to continue all taxes at the existing rates, but collect the entire year's assessment by the end of the first quarter. Rising expenditure due to the rebellion necessitated an abrupt change of policy. In August Parliament resolved to impose a new assessment at the 1653 rate of £120,000 per month, subsequently reduced to £100,000, still nearly triple the current rate. The republicans were thus planning to redress the root cause of the deficit, the Protector's reduction of this crucial tax to a level incapable of sustaining the govern-

---

[55] Wariston, who stood to lose the position and proceeds of the clerk registership, anxiously noted the discussion of refunding schemes in June: *Johnston diary*, 119, 120, 121, 122. The eventual Indemnity Act of July guaranteed 'necessary Salaries' and affirmed the reversion of offices to Parliament's gift. On the divisiveness of this measure see ch. 2 below.

[56] A good example of such radical condemnation is *The Fifth Monarchy, or Kingdom of Christ, In opposition to the BEAST'S, Asserted*, 48, which excoriated Parliament for suspending the sale of Hampton Court in July.

[57] *Journal*, 655–6, 676, 689. An exception was also made for Somerset House chapel, used by French Protestants. The trustees duly advertised the sale of the palaces in *PI*, no. 182, 20–7 June, 524, and no. 183, 27 June–4 July, 557.

[58] *Journal*, 704, 708. One journalist reported that a Fleet Street goldsmith had bought Somerset House for £10,000: *WI*, no. 10, 5–12 July, 78. Confirmed only in *Ludlow memoirs*, ii. 102, this report is proved false by Parliament's October order: *Journal*, 791. Fox later boasted of preventing the sale: *The journal of George Fox*, ed. John L. Nickalls, Cambridge 1952, 355.

[59] *Journal*, 782–3, 788, 790, 793. Of 36 arrested on 21 Sept., 5 had made satisfactory arrangements to pay by 7 Oct. Sequestration commissioners were appointed as early as 2 Aug.; on 3 Sept. they were granted the additional power to examine witnesses: ibid. 745, 773.

ment's credit. During September the bill proceeded smoothly, if unhurriedly, through the usual stages.[60]

The truncation of most of these initiatives by the second interruption exacerbates the difficulty of assessing the Republic's financial accomplishments. Yet progress had clearly occurred. By August the council was no longer requesting the House to sanction short-term loans to supplement a 'weekly income bearing no proportion with the constant charge', as it had done repeatedly in June.[61] Late in July Vane, speaking for the council, had presented the third, and last, report on revenue: this stated that, even with the increases and extra pay voted to the soldiers, the deficit was only £700,000, and might be supplied from the recovery of debts. Such optimism might be dismissed as unrealistic, were it not for the testimony of modern experts on military finance. James Scott Wheeler has demonstrated the skill of earlier Interregnum governments in developing 'an effective way to finance a growing short-term debt without defaulting', and pointed out that even by 1660 the debt was 'equivalent to only one year's average revenue'. Henry Reece has suggested that, without the massive recruitment necessitated by the rebellion, ordinary revenue would have sufficed to pay the three armies, and that regular pay was much more important than the reimbursement of arrears, which became politically significant only at times of disbandment or transfer abroad.[62] Though the republicans naturally gave most attention to the provision of ordinary pay, they did not forget the problem of arrears: in October detailed arrangements were made to supply them from the sale of forests and delinquent lands. That these arrangements were not just concessions to Army pressure is indicated by the purposeful approach to fiscal problems from August onwards.

Parliament's newfound confidence was not lost on contemporary observers: to take one example, Giavarina, ever prone to exaggeration, stopped predicting imminent bankruptcy after the defeat of Booth, and instead lamented the likelihood that the Republic would recoup its fortunes at the expense of the imprisoned nobles.[63] Land sales had established the nascent Commonwealth's credit in 1649–50.[64] A similar, albeit smaller, capital injection could conceivably have restored confidence in 1659, and

---

[60] Ibid. 692, 762, 770, 771, 778. The new tax, described as a loan at its first reading, became a regular assessment when committed, and was ready to be engrossed by mid-September. For the disastrous impact of Cromwell's tax cuts on government creditworthiness by 1659 see J. S. Wheeler, 'Navy finance, 1649–1660', HJ xxxix (1996), 457–66.

[61] Journal, 689, 696.

[62] Ibid. 737–8; Wheeler, 'Navy finance', 461, 460; H. M. Reece, 'The military presence in England, 1649–60', unpubl. DPhil diss. Oxford 1981, 242. Reece estimates that 8,000 men were recruited, causing the monthly cost of the armies to rise by about £24,000.

[63] Journal, 791; CSPVen., 50, 69. Bordeaux made similar observations in early September: Guizot, Histoire, i. 426, 469–70.

[64] Wheeler, 'Navy finance', 460.

facilitated a return to successful deficit financing, supported by sufficiently high taxes.

The republicans' achievement in restoring parliamentary government, subduing opposition, and considering both immediate and more long-term financial needs, was therefore far from negligible. Their self-disciplined application to these national priorities in 1659 exposes the hollowness of hostile charges of irresponsible dilatoriness and corruption, and so confirms Worden's conclusions for 1649–53. The diligence and dedication of MPs also lends support to Aylmer's argument, suggesting that there was, indeed, a distinctive republican ethos marked by self-denial for the public good. Many years later, the former Royalist Roger Coke hailed the commonwealthsmen, in contrast to their monarchical successors, as 'a race of men indefatigably industrious in Business, always seeking men fit for it, and never preferring any for Favour nor by Importunity', and concluded that they 'excelled in their Management of Civil Affairs'.[65] This encomium, though extravagant, is by no means wholly unmerited. Despite the odium heaped upon them, both before and after the dissolution, the republicans proved abundantly capable of working together intelligently and efficiently. In so doing, they plainly demonstrated, to the joy of their supporters, and the dismay of monarchists, that the Republic was by no means an intrinsically impracticable form of government.

[65] Roger Coke, *A detection of the court and state of England*, London 1691, 363.

3

Containing Divisions

The joy in the three Nations is great and full for the Interunion of the Army with the Parliament, having espoused the interest of our Authority, and it is wished that no jealous disasters may disquiet or divorce them: *The Moderate Informer*, 12–18 May 1659.

The Chaos was a perfection in comparison of our order and government; the Parties are like so many floating islands, sometimes joining and appearing like Continents, when the next flood or ebb separates them that it can hardly be known where they will be next . . . [the Parliament] daily expects dissolution: Major Wood to Mr Simpson, 3 June 1659.

The Lord of heaven in great mercie lookinge upon this poore nation . . . to settle you and the rest of the worthy members of the ever honoured old Parliament . . . for the carryeing on of the good old cause . . . doth much rejoyce my heart . . . my prayers shall dayly be . . . for the uniting of the spirits of all his chosen to carrye on his cause, and that (tho in some things they may differ in judgment) yett that they maye not at all differ in affections: Richard Lobb to Robert Bennet, 29 June 1659.

Unanimity, however desirable in principle, is seldom, if ever, attained. In practice, the survival of governments owes much to their ability to accommodate internal disagreements and establish a *modus vivendi*. Republics, lacking the hypothetical unity supplied by the ultimate responsibility of a monarch, have been particularly vulnerable to charges of uncontrolled dissension and consequent inferiority. Collective decision-making does not, however, in itself entail greater ineffectiveness. Failure becomes obvious when differences escalate into breakdown, yet the extent of success is very difficult to measure. The mere presence of vociferously competing ideas or interests does not necessarily indicate irresolvable conflict – diversity may even, within limits, prove constructive. In the complex politics of the restored Commonwealth of 1659, practical co-operation long coexisted with the open communication of contrasting views. To appreciate the republican achievement in containing divisions and creating an effective government, it is necessary to examine first the extent of discord, then the ways in which it was handled in the House itself, and in the vital relationships among Parliament, the Army and civilian adherents.

That differences existed amongst the men reinstated in May 1659 is incontestable, since observed by contemporaries of all persuasions. Even before the breach of 1653, tensions had arisen between soldiers and civilians, godly and ungodly, proponents and antagonists of reform. Still more divisive was the legacy of the 'interruption': though almost two-fifths of the returning MPs had abstained from national politics since 1653, a similar proportion had been at least moderately active for or against the Protectorate.[1] These memories made for an uneasy atmosphere in the House, both at the start and sporadically thereafter, especially during the indemnity debate. Prominent Cromwellians could hardly hope to escape criticism from their late master's principled opponents, now enjoying the ascendancy.[2] Explosions occasionally occurred – within days of Parliament's reopening, Salway reportedly 'vilified St. John to his face' as 'an enemy to ye Republic and a builder of Protectordome . . . unfitt for public trust'. Yet such incidents, never frequent, soon ceased as old habits of co-operation regained strength.[3] More serious were the differences among convinced republicans, whose constitutional preferences had further diverged during the years of enforced retirement. Neville had become an ardent advocate of Harrington's elaborate model, while Vane developed his own vision of a godly commonwealth, and Hesilrig, no theoretician, but an immensely influential politician, took up an intermediate position, accepting some, but not all of Harrington's ideas. Conflicting views of what the eventual settlement might be were not, of course, confined to MPs; the flood of pamphlets arguing this question sought support from a much larger constituency of the 'well-affected', whose wishes were presented to Parliament in a stream of petitions advocating a wide range of reforms.[4] The most important constituency courted was the Army, whose most active and influential officers included few principled republicans, but many professedly repentant Cromwellians. Though there was no simple division between Army and Parliament, the survival of the restored Republic clearly depended on the successful partnership of these institutions.

If the differences themselves were undeniable, their implications for the Republic's future were, and are, highly debatable, as the preceding epigraphs show. Hostile commentators, like the Royalist Major Wood, saw the least

---

[1] 38% of MPs did not seek election to the Protectors' parliaments, and are not known to have been involved with the opposition. The other 62% were elected to at least one of these parliaments; of these 12% were active in opposition, while 10% held high office and/or accepted seats in the Other House.

[2] Bulstrode Whitelocke, who had favoured retaining Richard Cromwell, later recalled warnings that MPs were 'most of them discontented' by the memory of 1653, and would 'increase the divisions'; he went on to relate the failure of an early attempt to exclude both himself and Ashley-Cooper from the council, on suspicion of Royalist links reported by Scot: *Memorials of the English affairs*, Oxford 1853, iv. 344, 349.

[3] [?] Brodrick to Hyde, 23 May, MS Clarendon 61, fo. 15; 'Miles' to Nicholas, 13 May, *Nicholas papers*, 139. Though hostile, secondhand and possibly exaggerated, these accounts of Salway's behaviour probably have some foundation in fact: Royalist correspondents seldom substantiated their accounts of divisions with specific incidents, so are unlikely to have invented this. Salway soon fell under Vane's pacific influence, and subsequently collaborated with St John in committees and on the council without noticeable friction.

[4] The differing positions on the future constitution, inside and outside the House, are discussed in detail in chs 8 and 9 below.

signs of disunity as proof of irremediable instability, and gleefully predicted a second dissolution that would promote the king's cause. Loyal supporters of the Commonwealth, such as the Cornish official Richard Lobb, took a much more cheerful view of its prospects. Rejoicing in Parliament's seemingly miraculous restoration, these men were confident of continued divine intervention to overcome the remaining difficulties. Newsbooks and pamphlets resounded with the rhetoric of reunion and reconciliation; since Parliament and Army now recognised their common interest in the settlement of the Republic, there were reasonable grounds to expect the avoidance of 'jealous disasters'.[5] Historians, conscious that the Commonwealth eventually succumbed to just such a disaster, have tended to accept the negative evaluations, reading back the crisis of the autumn into the events of the spring and summer. Thus Godfrey Davies characterises Parliament–Army relations as 'inimicable' [sic], and insists that by August 'unsolved problems . . . had already provoked a crisis which the rising merely postponed'. Woolrych interprets the Parliament's approach as foolishly confrontational, rousing 'suspicion' and 'discontent' in the army by policies devised merely 'to show who was master in the new state'. Yet such dismissive judgements ignore the fact that contemporary optimism did not lack justification. Republicans everywhere shared their enemies' awareness that a Commonwealth divided against itself could not stand; far from pursuing a collision course, they endeavoured to establish a working alliance between Parliament, Army and 'well-affected' civilians. To evaluate their success, and the Republic's actual potential, it is essential to examine these endeavours in their original context, without the distorting shadow of October.[6]

That a substantial consensus among republicans existed in the spring is plain from the pamphlet literature. Military and civilian manifestos alike demanded a purge of Royalists and Presbyterians, the 'old and new malignants' who had 'crept into' civil and military office, and the reappointment of upright officers dismissed for their fidelity to the 'Good Old Cause'. The renewed Commonwealth was exhorted to reverse the conservative tendencies of the later Protectorate, and complete the 'work of Reformation', providing impartial justice by properly qualified officials.[7] The controversial immediate past was to be indemnified: John Canne, having warned against

---

5   [?] Wood to [?] Simpson, 3 June, CSP iii. 479; Richard Lobb to Robert Bennet, 29 June, FSL, MS X.d.483, fo. 124; The Moderate Informer, 12–18 May, 8.
6   Davies, Restoration, 102, 144; Woolrych, 'Introduction', 98–100.
7   Such counsels came from the broadsheets Twelve Plain PROPOSALS . . . to the Honest and Faithful OFFICERS and SOULDIERS, and Five PROPOSALS . . . To the General Council of the OFFICERS, from To the Right Honourable, the Supreme Court of Parliament The humble Petition of the Sentinels in the Regiment formerly belonging to Major General Goffe to Parliament, and from pamphlets such as that regiment's Humble remonstrance to Fleetwood, The Humble Representation of divers well-affected Persons of . . . Westminster, A LETTER of Addresse from the Officers . . . in SCOTLAND to Parliament, and The DECLARATION and PROCLAMATION of the ARMY of GOD.

confiding in those who 'lately Betrayed the *Privileges* of *Parliaments*, and the *Just Rights of the People*, into the hands of a *Single Person*', recommended a dec-laration on 'the *Good Old Cause*, so that it may be known far and neer, what a happy accord there is between the *Parliament, Army,* and the *Good people* . . . and how former divisions . . . are healed'. The Army had already declared its repentance and renewed devotion to that cause; Parliament swiftly followed suit, issuing, on 7 May, a declaration promising to 'endeavour the settlement of this Commonwealth upon such a foundation as may . . . secure the property and the liberties of the people' and to 'vigorously indeavour the carrying on of the reformation so much desired . . . to the end there may be a godly and faithful Magistracy and ministry'. These promises, with the published vote of 9 May to entrust office only to able candidates of proven godliness and fidelity to the cause, were universally applauded by the Republic's adherents, from the Leveller James Freeze, who praised Parliament's 'most Christian expressions' as harbingers of the revival of his 'Countries welfare', to the former Fifth Monarchist John Rogers, who longed for 'that Golden Vote' to be 'written upon a Pillar of Marble', to the Army itself, whose *Humble Petition* expressed 'great rejoycing' at a declaration that 'so fully answers what our hearts were drawn forth to desire'. By thus incorporating the republican consensus into official policy, Parliament consolidated its initial popularity with all well-affected groups and established a strong claim on their loyalty.[8]

Continued loyalty would, however, be closely linked to the interpretation and implementation of these promises. Here the consensus broke down, as two contrasting courses of action were urged upon the new government. On the one hand was the uncompromising, militant approach, much beloved of disguised Royalists fuelling the flames of contention, yet genuinely advo-cated, both by such unrighteous radical republicans as Henry Marten and by the many Quakers and Fifth Monarchists long critical of ungodliness in high places.[9] These individuals, not content to condemn the memory of 'the late Tyrant', Oliver Cromwell, and deny that his family deserved any public provi-sion, attacked his near relations and former servants, the Army grandees and prominent civilian officials, demanding their dismissal or, if truly penitent, their voluntary resignation in favour of the faithful saints. Thus the younger Isaac Pennington, now a Quaker, advised the Army officers not to rush into the 'work of reformation', but 'wait to be purged of this backsliding spirit (which sticks closer to you and makes you unfitter for this service then you

---

[8] Canne, *Seasonable word*, title, 4; *A DECLARATION Of The PARLIAMENT Assembled at Westminster*; James Freeze, *The OUT-CRY and Just Appeale of the Inslaved People of England, Made To . . . the PARLIAMENT*, 2; Rogers, *Diapoliteia*, 62, 113; officers' *Humble petition*, 3.

[9] For Marten's animus against those who had addressed Richard Cromwell as Protector, and motion that 'all addressers that were of . . . the house might be turned out as enemies to the Commonwealth . . . and betrayers of their trust to bring in government by a single person', see *Aubrey's brief lives*, ed. A. Powell, London 1949, 215. A certain social radi-calism was common to both sets of critics.

are aware)', and warned Parliament against the 'Apostasising Spirit, which would colour over the Apostacy, and make it seem as little as they could . . . though in persons never so great'. Others counselled stringent measures to ensure civil control of the sword in future: only by limiting the power of the senior officers, and asserting its own authority to grant commissions could Parliament check military ambitions and demonstrate its 'Self-denying Impartiality and Justice' to the satisfaction of former detractors. The most extreme tracts called for the compulsory restitution of all salaries and other profits made during the interruption, and even criticised the extension of indemnity to 'Apostate vassals' guilty of high treason.[10]

Opposing such harsh policies for their tendency to inflame divisions and narrow the basis of support for the Republic to impossibly low levels, were the advocates of a more moderate, eirenical and inclusive approach. Foremost among these was Sir Henry Vane, whose Healing question, first published in 1656, skilfully summoned all the 'good party', whether Cromwellians, Fifth Monarchists or godly republicans, to repent of past failings and reunite on the basis of 'fundamental' principles common to all.[11] Vane's professed moderation has often been dismissed as a transparent front for personal or partisan goals – hearing that he desired to restrict power to a qualified elite, Viscount Mordaunt, for example, cynically concluded that 'Vane's Religion is to make a Party, and solely interest leads him'. But to assume his insincerity is to accept a powerfully propagated inimical prejudice.[12] Reconciliation, within carefully defined limits, was, in fact, a central element of Vane's thought, in no way contradicted by his actions.[13] The Commonwealth's renaissance in 1659, through reconstruction of a coalition along the lines that he had envis-

---

10 Isaac Pennington, To the Parliament, the Army, and all the Wel-affected [unpagination]; Twenty Four QUERIES . . . Tending to Settlement, on the Basis of Justice & Honour, 2. Other tracts of this persuasion include The Army mastered; A Secret Word to the WISE: or Seventeen QUERIES; Margery Good-Cow . . . Or, a short DISCOURSE, Shewing That there is not a Farthing due from this Nation to old Oliver; DEMOCRITUS Turned STATES-MAN; and The First & Second Parts of Invisible JOHN made Visible: Or A Grand Pimp of Tyranny portrayed in BARKSTEADS ARRAIGNMENT. The most extreme pamphlets were Ambitious tyranny and Eight and Thirty QUERIES Propounded By One that is setting forth Sail. . . .

11 For a full discussion of the Healing question's appeal to the disparate elements of the 'good party' see R. E. Mayers, ' "Real and practicable, not imaginary and notional": Sir Henry Vane, A healing question, and the problems of the Protectorate', Albion xxviii (1996), 37–72.

12 Mordaunt to Hyde, 7 June, CSP iii. 483. The image of Vane the Machiavellian hypocrite was zealously propagated in print and manuscript, and became widely accepted – according to one not unsympathetic observer, Vane by 1660 suffered from 'the most catholique prejudice of any man': TSP i. 767. Historians have often been equally sceptical, if less scathing in their assessments. See, for example, the negative interpretation of Vane's appeal to Cromwellians by Blair Worden in 'Oliver Cromwell and the sin of Achan', in D. E. D. Beales and G. Best (eds), History, society and the Churches, Cambridge 1985, 125–45 at pp. 136, 138–9.

13 To fully substantiate this statement would require another book, which I hope someday to write. Within the limits of 1659, the centrality of reunion to Vane's brand of republi-

aged, owed much to his persuasive efforts.[14] Against Vane's detractors, John Rogers affirmed that the *Healing question* and its 'honourable Author' had been 'so great a *Means of Blessing* towards the *Recovering* and *Healing* of this *poor* ISLAND as . . . Children may live to . . . bless God for'. His confidence in this pamphlet's impact was shared by the publisher, Thomas Brewster, who reprinted it in response to rising demand for a work so 'very seasonable and of much use at this day'.[15]

But the urgent need to maintain republican unity also inspired a series of pamphlets expanding and applying the *Healing question*'s themes to specific contemporary issues. To deflate saintly pretensions to self-righteousness, eirenicists developed Vane's assertion that no members of the 'good party' were flawless enough to refuse the duty of humiliation before God and reconciliation with their fellows. Most of the individuals who now 'sharpened their tongues like a Serpent against the late Single Persons', *Twelve Healing Questions* reminded readers, had uttered equally 'bitter words against this very Parliament before their . . . interruption'.[16] If all the 'good party' were imperfect, none merited exclusion on that account. Several pamphlets defended the integrity and sincere affection to the cause of those who had acquiesced in the Protectorate.[17] Severe treatment of repentant Cromwellians would be contrary to 'natural reason and Justice': their services against the 'common Enemy' during Parliament's absence merited legitimate compensation, not punitive confiscations. For the Republic to thus discourage future obedience, and alienate 'those that formerly have been and may again with gentle usage become . . . cordial Friends' would be most imprudent. Instead of indulging in recriminations, 'old friends' were adjured to resist satanic schemes 'to chill [their] affection and harden [their] hearts one against another'.[18] Forgetting their 'particular animosities', the Commonwealth's adherents should seek to strengthen the 'whole bodie' by 'Souldring up the broken pieces of Antient friendship', and looking forward with 'meek and broken hearts' to the

---

canism is discussed in ch. 8 below; further evidence for his consistent political conduct is provided in chs 9 and 10.

[14] Vane had worked towards this goal with other commonwealthsmen since 1656; his efforts to overcome mistrust had most recently prospered in the talks, held at his house, between leading MPs and officers, which resulted in agreement to restore Parliament. Nehemiah Bourne acknowledged Vane and Hesilrig as 'our two eminent good Instruments for the accommodating things betwixt them': *Clarke papers*, iii. 214. See also *Ludlow memoirs*, ii. 74–5; *Johnston diary*, 108.

[15] Rogers, *Diapoliteia*, 41; *A healing question* (1659 edn.), publisher's note.

[16] *The Dispersed United: Or, Twelve Healing QUESTIONS*, 3.

[17] Such defences of Cromwellians include *Twenty seven QUERIES Relating to the General Good*; Thomas Le White, *AN ANSWER To A LETTER Sent To a Gentleman of the Middle-Temple*; and *Several REASONS why some Officers of the Army with Many other good People, did heretofore . . . subject to Oliver Cromwel as the Supreme Magistrate . . . Likewise, Why they have rejected the said Government, and earnestly desire the Long Parliament to sit*.

[18] *A Seasonable QUESTION Soberly Proposed*, 3, 7; *THE POOR MAN'S MITE, Unto the more large CONTRIBUTIONS of the LIBERAL*, 10.

glorious future – 'that blessed and saving work which God hath yet to work out'. Such blessing, anxious readers were assured, might reasonably be antici-pated from the reunion of ex-Protectorians and faithful republicans in the new government, since those MPs who had not already been 'refined in the furnace of sufferings' were now 'toucht . . . with a deep and godly sense of their fallings', while the greatest 'troublers of Israel' had been cut off by provi-dence.[19]

As Parliament clearly remained a mixed body, it is scarcely surprising that it debated both but opted decisively for neither the hardline nor the eirenical republican policy. Instead, it occupied a position between the two extremes, though usually closer to the second, veering one way or the other as induced by internal alignments and arguments, external pressures or the exigencies of the moment. The preference for intermediate courses is exemplified by the treatment meted out to the Protector's leading civil servants. To appease the militants' outcry against them, Parliament did deprive such controversial figures as Thurloe, Fiennes, Maynard and Glyn of their offices, but eventually dismissed motions to deny them indemnity or compel them to refund their profits.[20] Similarly, the kingling lawyers Whitelocke, Lisle and Widdrington, though active members, did not regain their former places as commissioners of the great seal, but suffered no further punishment.[21] Only those MPs who had merely continued to exercise offices conferred prior to the interruption were confirmed in their places: thus Prideaux remained attorney-general, and St John lord chief justice despite radical denunciations.[22] When another MP, Colonel Philip Jones, former councillor and controller of the Protector's household, was accused of 'Transcendent *Crimes*' and 'Oppressions', Parlia-ment demonstrated its concern for impartial justice by admitting the petition against him and appointing a committee to investigate the charges. Though this committee, despite periodic enlargements, never reported, Jones's volun-

---

19 *Seasonable question*, 8; *A Short DISCOURSE concerning The Work of God in this NATION, and The Duty of all good People, both Governors and Governed, in This their DAY*, 3, 4. Though the 'troublers' are deliberately not identified, Oliver Cromwell was almost certainly intended.

20 Under the Indemnity Act, all offices bestowed during the interruption reverted to Parliament's gift, unless granted by persons authorised by Parliament, an exception which relieved St John, but left others with the threat of resumption. Wariston thus lost his clerk registership; fearing financial ruin, he dissuaded his colleagues from including a refunding clause: *Johnston diary*, 122. Motions to except Thurloe and other notorious Cromwellians were debated in June and early July: *Ludlow memoirs*, ii. 97–8; *Nicholas papers*, 164; *CSP* iii. 532–3; *The Rawdon papers*, ed. E. Berwick, London 1819, 197. But only provisoes against Alderman Pack, the first mover of the kingship petition, Col. Barkstead, and Alderman Tichborne reached the record, and these were rejected: *Journal*, 707, 713, 714.

21 *Journal*, 671–2; Whitelocke, *Memorials*, iv. 348, 351.

22 Critiques of these prominent Cromwellians include *Democritus*; *Twelve QUERIES Humbly Proposed to . . . Parliament & Army*, and *A True Catalogue, Or An Account of the several Places and most Eminent Persons . . . where and by whom RICHARD CROMWELL was Proclaimed Lord Protector*.

tary retirement relieved the House of the embarrassment attending his presence.[23] Of the Cromwellians who remained at Westminster, most were obliged to accept diminished status and influence: Sydenham was the only member of Richard's council to be elected to the new Council of State, while St John and Whitelocke just scraped in at eighteenth and nineteenth in the ballot.[24] The inclusion of these men in the new council, did, however, indicate a willingness to forget former rifts and harness the ablest members to the service of the Republic.[25] Elevation by the Protector was, in itself, no barrier to MPs prepared to forget their former dignities and work for the new regime; thus the Stricklands, once Cromwellian councillors, were assiduous in attending the House, and sat on numerous committees, while the aged Major-General Skippon, late councillor and member of the Other House, was trusted with the important command of the new militia in London.[26] By accepting aid from almost all who would give it, while reducing the most infamous Cromwellians to obscurity, Parliament sought to ensure efficient government and maximise support from all groups within the republican alliance.

Inclusive policies did, however, threaten to impair efficiency by encouraging internal strife. The memory of past conflicts, interpreted as struggles between self-interested and self-denying MPs, was frequently invoked to substantiate fears of future instability. Thus the loyal Rogers, writing in July, urged Parliament to check such tendencies by clearly defining 'the true interest of the Commonwealth and Cause', and deplored the fact that it was 'too notorious and talk'd of already, as if such a faction were now in the House at the Old Game to the extraordinary Regret of your friends and rejoycing of your foes'.[27] The Republic's foes did, indeed, rejoice at every sign of discord, representing rare moments of conflict, such as Salway's outburst in May, the defeat of Vane's attempt to get the Quaker George Bishop into Bristol's militia commission in July, or the quarrel between Vane and Hesilrig over the proposed Engagement in September, as indications of the chaotic character of the regime and the crumbling credibility of leading politicians.[28] Some

---

[23] The charges were printed in *Articles of Impeachment of Transcendent Crimes, Injuries, Misdemeanours, Oppressions and high Breach of TRUST Committed by Col. Philip Jones . . . read in PARLIAMENT the 18th of May 1659. Together with . . . Jones' Answer*. The committee's appointment and enlargement are recorded in *Journal*, 663, 666, 684, 691.

[24] A list of the councillors of state, showing the votes received by each MP, survives in MS Tanner 51, fo. 29r.

[25] Even a Royalist remarked that St John was courted by his republican colleagues for his 'real or reputed abilities': MS Clarendon 61, fo. 15. Dismayed by the lack of reprisals, Hyde repeatedly sought elucidation of 'the mystery how St John comes to hold his credit': CSP iii. 482, 532–3.

[26] *Journal*, 707. Sir William and Walter Strickland sat on 17 and 29 committees respectively.

[27] Rogers, *Diapoliteia*, 94–5.

[28] For the response to the latter two incidents see the Royalist letters printed in CSP iii. 529–30, and *CSPD 1659*, 207.

went so far as to produce elaborate analyses of the divisions among the new rulers. The Royalist agent Mordaunt, for example, distinguished four competing 'Cabals' in early June: ex-Protectorians Fleetwood and John Jones, whom he supposed eager for the return of that government; oligarchical republicans led by Vane, Salway and Lambert; those who were 'perfectly Commonwealth's men', including Ludlow and Neville; and Fifth Monarchists. Hesilrig, in this view, oscillated between the second and third groups. More cautiously, the French ambassador Bordeaux, naming no individuals, identified three factions: degraded Cromwellians, 'true republicans' bitterly hostile to the Army, and a smaller clique of the most able MPs, who had conspired with the Army officers against Richard, but were more likely to restore him to nominal authority than to relinquish power.[29]

The perceptions of such hostile observers, whose understanding was necessarily circumscribed by their exclusion from the inner circles of power, are justly suspect. Had the Republic really been racked by constant conflict among coherent factions, traces of partisanship should appear in the lists of divisions, tellers, committees and even the council elections. Yet these institutional sources do not support this view. Though limited by the fact that controversial matters were not necessarily put to the question, the record of divisions does afford a rough guide to the incidence of conflict. If factional quarrels had predominated, many divisions on obviously partisan issues might be expected; in reality, there were few divisions relative to the total number of resolutions, and there was seldom any connection between the motions. Divisions rarely occurred in May and June. Though disputes over the Indemnity and Militia Acts produced more in July, their frequency decreased sharply thereafter until the gathering crisis of late September.[30] The lists of tellers suggest that in 1659, as in 1649–53, Parliament was characterised not by cohesive factions but by a kaleidoscope of shifting alignments, which coalesced and dispersed again as particular issues arose and receded. Individuals acting as tellers on the same side in one, or even two debates, served on opposite sides on other occasions.[31] There is, in 1659, no evidence of consistent partnerships amongst tellers, or even committee members: indeed, the only pairing to occur with even remotely unusual regularity in committee lists is that of Vane and Hesilrig, who have often been portrayed as the leaders of strongly antagonistic factions. The conclusion that consensus was far commoner than conflict finds further support in the election of councillors:

---

[29] Mordaunt to Hyde, 7 June, CSP iii. 483–4; Bordeaux to Mazarin, 6 June, Guizot, Histoire, i. 430–3.

[30] There were only 8 divisions in May and June; 9 in July; 6 between 1 Aug. and 22 Sept., and 9 between 23 Sept. and 10 Oct.

[31] Thus Vane and Neville served as tellers for the same side on 14 July and 5 Aug., but against each other on 23 Sept.; Luke Robinson and Henry Marten were tellers together on 4 July, but against each other on 27 Sept. On the uses of lists of tellers and committees for detecting groupings during the earlier period see Worden, Rump parliament, esp. pp. 400–1.

Hesilrig, Vane, Ludlow, Fleetwood, Morley, Salway and Scot each gained over 70 per cent of the available votes.[32]

To defend the importance of consensus in parliamentary decision-making is not to deny the political and religious differences among MPs, and the potential for disharmony. Spectacular clashes did at times occur, but these were personal rather than factional: three alarming quarrels between individuals are recorded in the diary of Archibald Johnston, who, as one of the most diligent councillors, was well placed to observe the daily interaction of the republican leaders.[33] Yet these moments of open strife were infrequent, and short-lived. Tensions in the House could be defused, at least temporarily, by the appointment of a committee, or simply by adjourning a contentious debate.[34] Heated altercations between MPs over one issue did not preclude their collaboration on a multitude of others. Vane and Neville argued vehemently over the question of settlement in late June, but worked hard in July and August to ensure that military responsibilities were entrusted to reliable individuals. Defeat in a specific division did not imply the declining influence of the politicians in question: though Vane and Neville failed to get George Bishop appointed a militia commissioner, they succeeded, three weeks later, in preventing the return to the Army of that loyal relative of Richard Cromwell, ex-Colonel Edward Whalley.[35] Some inkling of the breadth of the alliances between MPs of very different temperaments and beliefs may be gained from the letters of Robert Bennet. Himself godly enough to be stigmatised by Presbyterians as 'Sir Henry Vane's little second at Preaching', Bennet willingly worked not only with the equally godly Ludlow, but with his correspondent Richard Lobb's 'very good friends Mr Henry Nevil and Mr Thomas Scott', who were quite irreligious, to secure a reduction in the duties on Cornish tin and fish.[36] Practical co-operation generally prevailed over personal differences; the normal business of government proceeded with little or no interruption. Before September, the occasional disputes between MPs never escalated into public rifts, and did not become

---

[32] The names of Vane and Hesilrig appear together 11 times on committee lists; no other pairing occurs more than 3 or 4 times. As these men were appointed to the same committee on just 27 occasions, this frequency seems only mildly remarkable. The votes in the council elections show Hesilrig and Vane supported respectively by 71 and 68 of the 78 MPs present. On the pursuit of consensus by republicans and others in the last Protectorate parliament see D. Hirst, 'Concord and discord in Richard Cromwell's House of Commons', *English Historical Review* ciii (1988), 339–58.

[33] For these quarrels, between Vane and Neville in late June, Vane and Fleetwood in early July and Vane and Hesilrig in September, see *Johnston diary*, 120–1, 123, 134–5.

[34] These were the responses to the quarrel of Vane and Hesilrig on 6 Sept., and that between Vane and Neville on 17 June: *Journal*, 774, 688.

[35] Ibid. 717, 749.

[36] [Annesley], *England's confusion*, 11. Lobb first advised Bennet to co-operate with these MPs in a letter of 29 June; on 10 Oct. he praised the success of Bennet, Scot and Neville in accomplishing the desired relief: FSL, MS X.d.483, fos 124, 129.

common knowledge, even among those who listened most eagerly for such rumours.

If disputes within the House could be kept from outsiders, little secrecy attended the delicate relationship between Parliament and the Army. The breakdown of this partnership was, of course, the chief hope of all the Republic's enemies, who not only watched avidly for signs of tension, but often actively fomented distrust and discontent. Hostile sources therefore abound with rumours of the 'great jealousies' dividing MPs and officers, and the imminence of a second dissolution. Professions of unity were dismissed by Royalist commentators as transparent pretexts cloaking selfish ambitions: Parliament and Army were engaged in a struggle for power which could only end in another military triumph. Such perceptions, however, proceeded from wishful thinking more than actual observation. Even a few monarchists questioned the prevailing optimism, highlighting the soldiers' devotion to the Republic, and the improbability that so experienced a Parliament would deliberately alienate them. Similar scepticism was expressed by Bordeaux, who chronicled divisions in both Parliament and Army, but doubted the confident predictions of a 'notable dissolution' in July.[37]

Despite the provocative policies advocated by hardline republicans anxious to prevent a second tyranny, co-operation, not confrontation, dominated Parliament's dealings with the penitent officers. As in its treatment of civilian officials, the House steered a careful course between the extremes of leniency and severity. Far from proceeding 'recklessly to alienate the army that had restored it', as Woolrych suggests, Parliament carefully cultivated the grandees, approving the changes in command that they had already introduced.[38] Thus Fleetwood was confirmed as commander-in-chief, and given the care of St James's Park, while Disbrow and others who had deserted Richard in good time were also assured of their places. Officers cashiered by Cromwell for their fidelity to the Republic, including Major-General Robert Overton, Nathaniel Rich and the famous three colonels Okey, Saunders and Alured, regained their commands with Parliament's blessing. Only the most disreputable, and expendable, Cromwellians, such as John Barkstead, execrated for his conduct as lieutenant of the Tower, or the notoriously arbitrary ex-Major-General William Boteler, were sacrificed to the radical clamour for an anti-Cromwellian witch-hunt.[39] Such was Parliament's willingness to renounce mistrust that even Lambert, the principal architect of

---

[37] Antoine de Bordeaux-Neufville to Cardinal Mazarin, 7 July, Guizot, *Histoire*, i. 393. For Royalist scepticism see *CSP* iii. 491, *Nicholas papers*, 142, 154–5, and the intercepted letter printed in *CSPD 1659*, 88.

[38] Woolrych, *England without a king*, 44.

[39] For the rejection of Barkstead and Boteler see *Journal*, 679, 704. Barkstead was not only denounced in such tracts as *Invisible John*, but by Overton, who sought vengeance for his imprisonment. Barkstead's arrest at Overton's suit was reported in *Politicus*, no. 570, 2–9 June, 499.

the Protectorate in 1653, and the popular hero of many common soldiers, was entrusted with not one but two regiments, and the command of the vital expedition against Booth.[40]

Co-operation and mutual trust between Parliament and the officers were not negated by the natural determination of MPs, mindful of their humiliation in 1653, to maintain parliamentary authority over the Army in future. That objective was not in itself controversial: the officers accepted the principle that the sword should be subject to the civil power, and repeatedly promised to yield their 'utmost assistance' to the Parliament. They therefore had no reason to resent their official status as the 'subordinate partner' in the new government.[41] At first, Parliament merely formalised the existing alliance between republican leaders and the senior officers, who were appointed to the temporary committee of safety, then to the council. The preponderance of MPs on the latter was typical of such bodies, and certainly not intended to make 'the grandees . . . very conscious of their diminished role in national politics', as Woolrych supposes. Though Ludlow's *Memoirs* erroneously assert the soldier-councillors' infrequent attendance and 'unimaginable perverseness' when present, the contemporary council minutes provide ample evidence of their careful co-operation with civilians on important domestic and foreign business. Jointly entrusted with the responsibility for vital security measures, including the surveillance of London, the senior officers had little cause to think themselves marginalised.[42] Nor could the grandees complain that Parliament had deprived them of influence within the Army. On 13 May the ex-Cromwellians Fleetwood, Lambert, Disbrow and Berry, were appointed, together with the republican MPs Hesilrig, Vane and Ludlow, as commissioners to nominate officers. Responsibility for the ensuing purge was thus delegated to a commission dominated by the officers them-

---

40 Lambert's regimental commands, though 'smartly' opposed by 'some members' (*Nicholas papers*, 155), passed without question after two hours' debate: *Journal*, 668; *True relation . . . of the case between . . . Parliament and the officers*, 5.

41 For the Army's promises, implying recognition of this principle, see their *Declaration* of 6 May, the *Petition* of 12 May and, especially, the *Humble Representation* of October, reminding Parliament (pp. 3–4) of the constant obedience of its 'faithful servants'. On receiving commissions, individual officers explicitly affirmed their willingness to serve Parliament 'with all faithfulness and obedience': cf. *True relation*, 5; *A PARLIAMENTER'S PETITION TO THE ARMY*, 2; *Ludlow memoirs*, ii. 98. Retrospective suggestions that they resented their subordination occur in *Ludlow memoirs*, 84, Hutton, *Restoration*, 51, and Woolrych, 'Introduction', 98.

42 Woolrych, 'Introduction', 99; *Ludlow memoirs*, ii. 84; council minutes, passim, but especially the orders of 8, 29 July. Of possible council meetings (i.e. excluding those held during their absences on active service), Lambert and Disbrow appeared at 53% Fleetwood at 46%, Berry at 42% and Sydenham at 40%. Given their military responsibilities, the difference between this record and that of the most zealous councillors is understandable; besides, the figures compare favourably with those for several civilian MPs, for example Challoner (52%), Reynolds (48%), Downs (34%) an St John (17%).

selves; technically subject to parliamentary approval, their recommendations were seldom actually rejected.[43]

Although the *rapprochement* between Parliament and the grandees did not result in perfect harmony, it proved capable of withstanding the strain of disagreements over particular issues. Its first test occurred in May, when Fleetwood, Sydenham, Lambert, Disbrow and Berry announced conscientious objections to taking the oath prescribed for councillors. In this they were not alone. Archibald Johnston had considerable reservations, and consented only after assurances that the obligation should be understood as 'conditional' upon providence and 'the true good old Cause'.[44] Three civilian members, including the indisputably loyal Vane, who disapproved of oaths on principle, simply evaded the requirement, and were never challenged.[45] Unlike the judges' later recalcitrance, the officers' stance was essentially, as Ludlow observed, a 'difference about ceremonies', not a demonstration of disaffection, nor even a bar to full participation in practice. Perceiving no threat to their authority, MPs responded sympathetically. A mutually satisfactory compromise was swiftly devised, whereby Parliament authorised the council to dispense its members from the 'formality of the oath', in return for their 'declaration' promising 'to do and perform the things' contained therein.[46] The willingness to accommodate the officers' scruples in this matter suggests that Davies erred in depicting MPs as rigid anti-militarists, who 'would never stoop to conciliate' the Army. Rather, the Commwealth's leaders agreed that there was 'more real security to the State in the principles and interests of good men then all the . . . oaths of others', and abated official rigidity accordingly.[47]

That conciliation stemmed from a sensible concern to consolidate the

[43] *Journal*, 651, 674–5. The considerable influence of commanding officers on the selection of their juniors is plain from the surviving proceedings of the nominating commission, confusingly designated the Committee of Safety: SP 25/127. A comprehensive analysis of the commissioners' activities and the extent of the purge is provided in D. Massarella, 'The politics of the Army, 1647–60', unpubl. PhD diss. York 1977, 576–86. This demonstrates that Parliament rarely refused their recommendations.

[44] *Johnston diary*, 115; 'Reasons for not taking the oath as councillor of state', 30 May, *Clarke papers*, iv. 12–15. This document, although misdated, definitely corresponds to Johnston's summary of his speech on the subject. Its survival among these army manuscripts suggests that the officers were, at least, interested in his reasoning.

[45] The council minutes record that all active councillors, except for Vane, Dixwell and St John, took the oath or declared its tenor. St John, unlike Vane, may well have been actuated by dislike of the Commonwealth. No-one seems to have commented on this omission; certainly neither Parliament nor council sought to rectify it, or stop these men from serving.

[46] *Ludlow memoirs*, ii. 84; *Journal*, 664. The officers attended council meetings from 22 May, its third day, so were active on its business before Parliament resolved the question or they themselves made the requested declaration.

[47] Davies, *Restoration*, 102; *Clarke papers*, iv. 13. Johnston noted that the council president, Sir James Harrington, and the others present (including Hesilrig, Scot, Neville, Ludlow and Whitelock), assured him of their agreement.

reunion, and not, as Giavarina supposed, from a craven fear of displeasing the grandees, was revealed by Parliament's determined assertion of its authority over the Army in early June. Not content with their right to confirm appointments, MPs heeded calls to prevent the rise of a second Cromwell by publicly demonstrating the officers' dependence on Parliament rather than any senior figure. Over-ruling Salway, Vane and Ludlow, who warned against insisting on an insubstantial ritual, the House resolved that all commissions should be signed and delivered by the Speaker instead of, as originally proposed, the commander-in-chief, Lieutenant-General Fleetwood.[48] Given the officers' control over nominations, this vote required ceremonial submission rather than a real surrender of power. Nevertheless, as its opponents had feared, the unfamiliar procedure, together with the formal limitation of Fleetwood's authority, occasioned suspicion and resentment. That evening Johnston heard of 'great jealousyes' between Parliament and Army over this issue; next day, alarmed by reports that 'the officers resolved to taik no [new] commissions', he urged his colleagues to appoint 'som choyse men' to mediate. The malcontents were led by Disbrow. Army sources admitted that 'some . . . of our chief' had expressed 'dissatisfactions' in council at Disbrow's house, and that 'many feares and jealousies' had arisen through Fleetwood's failure to collect his commission at the earliest opportunity.[49] Yet within three days not only Hesilrig's satellite Colonel Hacker, but Fleetwood himself had submitted, an example soon followed by Berry, Lambert, Lilburne and the others in London. Even Disbrow at length 'declared fully his satisfaction to the parliament and . . . engaged for the fidelity of his officers'.[50] The defusing of this crisis owed much to the reassurance offered by Parliament, especially through those MPs, such as Ludlow and Hesilrig, who were officers themselves. Despite its anti-militaristic bias, the account in Ludlow's memoirs reveals that Lambert and Disbrow, far from harbouring deep designs against the Parliament, openly communicated their discontents and insecurities, including the fear of losing their commands, and listened to the members' explanations and exhortations not to entertain 'groundless suspicions of those whose interest was the same with theirs'. That some confidence was

---

48 CSPVen., 27; Journal, 673; Ludlow memoirs, ii. 88–9. One journalist interpreted 'the novelty' of this decision as a sign that the civil power really would control the military in the new Commonwealth (WI, no. 6, 7–14 June, 43); other newsbooks tactfully refrained from comment.

49 Johnston diary, 118; Clarke papers, iv. 17. Disbrow's leadership is emphasised in Ludlow memoirs, ii. 90, and in the contemporary Royalist sources, for example Nicholas papers, 156.

50 Worcester College, Oxford, MS Clarke 31, fo. 167. The Speaker delivered the first commissions on 8 June (Hacker), 9 June (Fleetwood and Ludlow), 10 June (Berry), 11 June (Lambert), 13 June (Lilburne), 14 June (Hewson and Biscoe), 15 June (Fitch and Salmon); a second group followed on 1 July (Okey), 2 July (Moss) and 7 July (Disbrow): Journal, 675–6, 677–8, 679–80, 680–1, 682, 684, 685, 700, 701–2, 706–7. The two-week interval was due not so much to greater obstinacy on the part of the later recipients, as some Royalists surmised (for example Edward Conway, Rawdon, 195) as to the fact that lists for their regiments had not yet been finalised.

restored by these representations is suggested by the Army newsletter of 9 June, which observed that the situation was 'generally satisfactory', if 'hardly so universalie', and that Parliament, though eager to 'keep the power in their own hands', had affirmed their 'love . . . of us, as the best instruments they can have to preserve them and the nations in peace'.[51] As a political move, the distribution of commissions by the Speaker succeeded, disgusting the Royalists and impressing the diplomats with a visible demonstration of the Republic's strength and unity.[52]

If Parliament worked hard to promote good relations with the senior officers, it did not neglect their inferiors. Provision for material needs had long been recognised as a vital element in securing the Army's allegiance; the republicans in Richard's parliament and printed propaganda had celebrated their past achievements in this regard, and promised renewed attention to the soldiers' welfare. Once restored, Parliament repeatedly demonstrated its care for the Army, showing much sensitivity to material grievances. On 16 May, following a report on the soldiers' sufferings, the House resolved to take 'speedy and effectual care' for their pay and arrears, and ordered the sale of the remaining palaces as an initial step towards this. Ten days later Parliament voted £3,000 to relieve the immediate needs of disabled soldiers, widows and orphans petitioning, and ordered a committee to consider long-term provision for them.[53] At the end of the month Parliament even increased the pay of the politically influential forces around London, which Cromwell had reduced. Given the chaotic state of the finances, and increasing recruitment, it is hardly surprising that these orders did not automatically resolve all problems: on the 28 June the council was authorised to raise short-term loans to satisfy the 'extreme wants of the Souldiery'. Complaints of exploitation, shortage of pay and lack of arrears were still voiced, but money was found to meet the most pressing needs.[54] Nor were the long-term prospects as bleak as some historians have suggested. Davies, for example, asserts that the Parliament was 'doomed to send [the soldiers] away

---

[51] *Ludlow memoirs*, ii. 89–90; *Clarke papers*, iv. 18–19. The same newsletter also suggested that Parliament could hardly be blamed for not granting desires regarding Fleetwood's power that had never been represented.

[52] See *Nicholas papers*, 154; *CSPVen.*, 31; Guizot, *Histoire*, i. 435, 431.

[53] *Journal*, 655, 667. This committee reported on 13 June, and was instructed to conduct a more thorough investigation and recommend legislation; meanwhile Parliament voted another £755 for immediate relief. Seven more MPs were added to the committee on 30 July, while the council was ordered to provide another 2 months' support. On 1 Sept. a second petition elicited further votes for provision, various resolves for economy and the transfer of the problem to the Worcester House trustees. Parliament made further provision on 5 Oct. Thus the expression of care for the maimed soldiers, widows etc. in May was not just a sop to the petitioners, but a recurrent concern throughout Parliament's tenure.

[54] Ibid. 669, 696–7. A good example of the complaints of loyal soldiers was the *Petition of the sentinels*, published in June. This not only described present sufferings, but recalled that Parliament had formerly been 'conscionably careful for their preservation by allowing them due Pays'.

empty', since any attempt to raise adequate supplies would have alienated their 'ardent civilian supporters'.[55] In fact, the obligation to provide for the common soldiers, if necessary by increasing taxes, was acknowledged even by those republicans who thought that officers with great estates should serve *gratis*.[56] Parliament's decision to raise the assessment to almost pre-interruption levels offered clear proof that the Republic, unlike the Protector, whose tax cuts had resulted in soaring arrears, was prepared to risk heightened unpopularity to satisfy the Army. Such signs of Parliament's concern, and the hope of eventual satisfaction, did much to sweeten the endurance of continued hardships. Despite assiduous attempts by Royalists and disaffected Cromwellians to exploit material grievances to breed distrust of Parliament's intentions, the soldiers remained remarkably loyal to the Commonwealth.

The soldiers' resistance to conservative blandishments is itself a sign that they had not yet become a 'mere mercenary army'. Enthusiasm for the principles of the 'Good Old Cause' had been much more prominent than material hopes in the agitation among junior officers and soldiers for Parliament's restoration. Within a week of this event, the officers presented a petition which combined warm congratulations with fifteen political proposals intended to secure the 'fundamentals' of 'that Righteous Cause, wherein the civil and religious Liberties of the People . . . were involved'. Several of these dealt with such immediate concerns as the ratification of Fleetwood's command, provision for Richard Cromwell, indemnity and the confirmation of laws and debts since the interruption. A high priority was, predictably, given to the promotion of godliness: four articles called for the encouragement of a 'painful Gospel-Preaching Ministry', reformation of the universities, 'equal protection' for peaceful believers in the Trinity and the authority of Scripture and the removal of ungodly, malignant or persecuting magistrates. Other familiar desires included the regulation of the law, and the protection of liberty and property by the 'Government of a Free State', without a single person or House of Lords. Though the petition respectfully requested government by successive legislatures including a 'select Senate' of the most eminent and godly, it was careful to avoid any appearance of dictation or invasion of Parliament's prerogative. The officers professed much admiration for the members' wisdom and past achievements, and concluded by invoking the divine blessing on their counsels for 'the bringing forth such a Settlement as may be for the honour of God, the union, joy and rejoycing of all the People of this Commonwealth'.[57]

Parliament soon proved its responsiveness to the Army's political desires. The petition was accorded an especially gracious reception: the Speaker returned 'very hearty thanks' for the expressions of 'love and affection', and admired the 'weighty matters' contained therein. As the House swiftly

55 Davies, *Restoration*, 116.
56 This argument was advanced in *Eight and thirty queries*, 6.
57 *Humble petition*, 1–2, 12–13, 14–15.

acceded to ten of the fifteen proposals, including the important qualification for religious protection, it is scarcely surprising that not only the newsbooks, but Army newsletters in May observed a 'very good understanding between these Parliament men and the army, they aiming both at the same things'.[58] More time was required for the other matters, but Parliament evidenced its readiness to address them. Committees were appointed to consider law reform, the debts and legislation inherited from the Protectorate, and Richard Cromwell, whose acquiescence was rewarded with the promise of a 'comfortable and honorable subsistence', and protection from his creditors.[59] Meanwhile, the House spent twelve days between the end of May and the beginning of July in a Grand Committee considering settlement and indemnity.

That these issues proved more controversial is hardly surprising. Debates on indemnity not only divided Parliament to such a degree that an exasperated member commented that there were 'not six of one mynd', but occasioned further tensions in its relationship with the Army. The long delay in enacting what had seemed a straightforward measure; the liberal reception of petitioners pressing complaints against individual Cromwellians; inaccurate journalism announcing the insertion of numerous exceptions, mainly of soldiers; the actual consideration of clauses for the refund of salaries, the restriction of protection to those purchasing pardons for forty shillings and the punishment of anyone 'guilty of Mal Administration' or illegal acts, all contributed to rising anxiety among the officers, who had requested a comprehensive and unqualified act. On 6 July Johnston witnessed 'hott words' between Vane and Fleetwood and, with habitual pessimism, feared that the 'jealousyes rooting both in the members . . . and the Airmye' would 'break out agayn into flammes'. Three days later, rumours that military discontents had already produced a second dissolution swept through London and Westminster, achieving such credence that sober denials were 'cryed down by the Multitude'. Once again, however, the wish of the regime's enemies was father to the thought: there is no evidence that the officers themselves ever contemplated such extreme action.[60]

The act eventually passed on 12 July was not ungenerous: all those who had acted since April 1653 were 'fully acquitted and pardoned', and their 'necessary Salaries' guaranteed. Only customs and excise farmers who failed to pay their arrears were excepted; everyone else could claim protection

---

[58] *Journal*, 651, 661, 662, 665, 674; *Clarke papers*, iv. 8. Newsbooks reported that Parliament's response to the petition tended to the Army's 'great satisfaction', and emphasised the mutual interest of both in 'Interunion': *WI*, no. 3, 17–24 May, 24, 17.

[59] *Journal*, 665, 704, 720. Parliament assumed responsibility for Richard's debts; in mid-July the committee recommended settling lands worth £5,000 *p.a.* on him, but was ordered to further investigate his assets.

[60] *TSP* vii. 686; *CSP* iii. 505; *WI*, no. 9, 28 June–5 July, 72; *Journal*, 707, 713–14; *Johnston diary*, 123; *WI*, no. 10, 5–12 July, 80.

simply by taking the standard engagement of loyalty to the Commonwealth as established without a single person or House of Lords.[61] Some imperfections inevitably remained. An Army newswriter reported that the salaries' clause, challenged unsuccessfully at the last moment, was situated 'so as to the worst advantage', since Parliament was sole judge of necessity.[62] In private conversation the next day Lambert protested that this left all soldiers 'liable to be questioned for whatsoever they had received', and still appeared dissatisfied despite Ludlow's confident guarantee that soldiers were safe, and Hesilrig's assurance that Parliament was their 'good friends'. Though this account of Lambert's 'very harsh' words, amounting to veiled threats, is distorted by hindsight, the admission of insecurity seems genuine, and may well have left doubts concerning his allegiance in Hesilrig's mind; how far others may have shared this unease is less clear.[63] Lambert did not advertise his discontent, but remained a trusted participant in government, to which normality quickly returned. That the act succeeded, by and large, in allaying suspicions and restoring good relations is indicated by the fact that even Bordeaux observed, five days after its publication, that 'the storm [was] dissipated' and 'the Parliament [seemed] without distrust of the Army'. Davies therefore seems mistaken in his assertion that the Indemnity Act served rather to 'intensify the storm' than to calm it. Moderate counsels had narrowly prevailed with MPs, who rejected the most divisive clauses, and reaffirmed their determination to protect the Army.[64]

In light of the abundant evidence for Parliament's responsiveness to Army concerns, the fruitful co-operation between MPs and senior officers in the administration of government, and the resolution of such problems as arose, grave doubt may be cast on the contention of Woolrych, Davies and Hutton that only 'the shadow of the common enemy kept the army and the Rump from quarreling openly' in the summer.[65] Recent research on the Army has shown that the new militia, fondly perceived by the regime's enemies, and hence historians, as an attempt to supplant the regulars, was not, in fact, a grievance at all, since the officers superintended the reorganisation,

---

61 The provisions of the Indemnity Act were summarised in *PI*, no. 185, 11–18 July, 587; it appears in full in *A&O* ii. 1299–304.

62 Army newsletter, 12 July, MS Clarke 31, fos 168–9. A motion to delete the word 'necessary' was defeated by 8 votes; Col. Sydenham was a teller in favour, opposed by Hesilrig and the republican Col. Rich: *Journal*, 712. The majority of MPs are unlikely to have intended to expropriate the Army – qualifying the salaries' clause left open the option of prosecuting the much execrated enemies of the Commonwealth who had enriched themselves at its expense.

63 *Ludlow memoirs*, ii. 100–1. That Lambert's protest indicated a military 'design' against Parliament, as this narrative suggests, is most improbable; it is much more likely that Hesilrig's abrasive personality undermined the calming effect that his words might otherwise have had.

64 Bordeaux to Mazarin, 14 July, Guizot, *Histoire*, i. 411; Davies, *Restoration*, 114.

65 Woolrych, 'Introduction', 100. See also Davies, *Restoration*, 144, and Hutton, *Restoration*, 54.

commanded the new forces and expressed eagerness for the completion of the necessary legislation.[66] Parliament's faith in the grandees was demonstrated again in late July, when Major Harlow, a Presbyterian who had, in the spring, engaged in secret intrigues with both Royalists and republicans, but eventually thrown in his lot with the latter, was arrested for accusing Fleetwood, Lambert and others of conspiring to restore Richard Cromwell.[67] Had the members been eager for an excuse to remove distrusted individuals, they could easily have used Harlow's revelations against them. Instead, they readily accepted the Army's assurances 'that there [was] noe danger at all', and publicly proclaimed their confidence in the accused officers, voting the allegations 'false and scandalous', and depriving Harlow of his positions as JP and militia commissioner. After hearing Harlow's examination before the council, Johnston, ever inclined to credit reports of 'great jealousyes', concluded with relief that 'artificial rumours [had been] spread to devyde Parliment and Airmy'. The partnership between officers and MPs had, if anything, been strengthened by the evidence of their mutual commitment to each other, and was certainly not characterised by ever-increasing suspicion and acrimony.[68]

Though Parliament naturally accorded a high priority to its relationship with the soldiers, it did not forget to cultivate 'well-affected' civilian supporters. The House encouraged the respectful petitioners who flocked to its doors with grateful answers, assuring them that their views had been noted and their 'good affections' appreciated. Especially gracious, if non-specific, responses were often accorded to the most radical petitions. Thus the 'Assertors of the Good Old Cause' in Buckinghamshire, who pleaded for the speedy removal of all 'oppressions and tyrannie', including tithes, were not only thanked for their 'Constancy in that . . . Cause', but promised that the Parliament would, indeed, proceed to settle a 'Commonwealth in nature as in name'. Similarly, the 'well-affected' inhabitants of Bedfordshire, who combined an attack on tithes with demands for the decentralisation of justice and extensive religious toleration, received thanks and assurances that the House would consider 'such of the [particulars] as they shall find good for the Nation . . . in due time'. But Parliament was careful to avoid the semblance of commitment to any one faction, granting some equally favourable replies to those who solicited the preservation of tithes and a more modest regulation of the law.[69] As these answers, and sometimes the petitions themselves, were

---

66 Reece, 'Military presence', 238–9.

67 On Harlow's earlier intrigues, and the Royalists' disappointment when he and John Wildman defected to the Commonwealth's adherents, where they associated with Neville, see the letters in MS Clarendon 60, fos 466, 475, 534, and CSP iii. 511.

68 Major Barton to Col. Saunders, 21 July, DRO, MS 1232, fo. 80; MS Journal, 20 July. This vote, deleted in 1660, does not appear in the printed version, but was published in *Politicus*, no. 580, 21–8 July, 613; *Johnston diary*, 125.

69 *Politicus*, no. 569, 26 May–2 June, 471–2; *The Humble Representation and desires of divers Freeholders and others well affected to the Commonwealth . . . ., inhabiting within the County of*

reproduced in the newsbooks, or published at large, Parliament's readiness to receive grievances was rapidly communicated to a wide audience. By the same medium, the initial steps towards redress were presented as proofs that the House was sincerely concerned for the people's welfare, and would ultimately provide the desired relief. The *Faithful Scout* in June, for example, enthusiastically proclaimed the '*long lookt for, & gallant Resolves, for the taking off unreasonable Fees . . . and poor prisoners to be preserved from being buried alive in* Gaols'; a month later, the same newsbook proudly announced '*The Parliaments Decree and Proceedings touching Prisoners of Debt & the releasing of such as are not able to satisfie their Creditors*'. Such glowing accounts of Parliament's intentions and progress in the midst of other pressing affairs encouraged its adherents to hope that substantial reforms might well be achieved once the immediate crisis had passed. Milton, for example, was emboldened to offer his own anti-clerical counsel by 'seeing daily the acceptance which they finde who in thir petitions venture to bring advice'.[70]

It was, of course, impossible for Parliament to satisfy the conflicting desires of all the 'well-affected'. Disillusionment did occur, especially among those who saw in the frustration of their own hopes for financial and political advancement the Commonwealth's betrayal by corrupt and apostate MPs. Such an individual was ex-Protectoral poet George Wither, who accentuated his personal quest for reparation and reemployment with emotive evocation of the 'poor distressed Men, Women and Orphans . . . attending early and late . . . solliciting for the relief of their urgent necessities' but receiving only 'such a dissembled regard as increased their necessities by giving false hopes of that performance which they never made'. In his view, the familiar excuses of state poverty or more urgent business thinly disguised 'Malice, Covetousness, Selfness, Vanity, or Negligence' at the centre; unless the government reformed itself and redressed just grievances, he prophesied that no settlement securing freedom could prosper in its hands. Yet Wither did not despair of Parliament, but acknowledged it to be 'Englands Representative' and a 'true and lawful power'. Depicting himself throughout as a 'faithful servant to this *Republick*', he pledged his help to strengthen MPs, whatever their decision in his case, and, indeed, exhorted dissatisfied people to 'aide them with a liberal hand And loyal heart'.[71] This strategy produced at least partial results: within weeks of publishing his complaint, Wither was reappointed to the

---

Bedford. For an answer encouraging less radical groups see the response to the petition of the Sussex ministers and JPs printed in *PI*, no. 183, 27 June–4 July, 552–3.

[70] *Scout*, no. 9, 17–24 June, and no. 15, 15–22 July, headlines; Milton, *Considerations*, preface: *CPW*, 275.

[71] George Wither, *Epistolium-Vagum-Prosa-Metricum: or, An Epistle at Random, in Prose and Metre . . . first intended only, for . . . the Authors Friends in Authority . . . to meditate in Parliament, the Redress of his destructive Grievances*, 9, 25, 30, 1, 19, 20. Norbrook has done much to illuminate the tergiversations of Wither's literary/political career, and analyses this pamphlet's fumbling attempt to demonstrate its author's constancy in the Commonwealth's cause in *Writing*, 402.

commission of the peace in his native Hampshire.[72] Strong resentment of the regime's shortcomings was therefore compatible with commitment to, and even reinforcement of, its authority.

Potentially more dangerous than the discontent of isolated suppliants like Wither was the displeasure of the Fifth Monarchy-men, who had never had much enthusiasm for restoring this assembly, and increasingly resented its failure to concede a monopoly of office to the saints. Late in the summer extremists published vehement allegations that Parliament, by not purging itself of the 'many scandalous persons', 'unworthy Mercenary Lawyers' and persecuting members of 'the late Tyrants Council', had reneged on its commitment to a 'thorough and vigorous Reformation'. Specially reprehensible was the 'Act of Indempnity sufficiently justifying the wicked, and consequently condemning the righteous'. As ultimate proof that the government was dominated by a 'corrupt party' heedless of Christ's interests, these writers cited the reinstatement of Marchamont Nedham, that 'Rabshakeh against the people of God', as editor of *Politicus* in place of their own polemicist, John Canne. Such ferocious denunciations were not, however, politically very adept. Questioning the Army's repentance while condemning most religious groups as apostates was unlikely to commend the theocratic alternative to, or destroy the regime's credibility with, the wider constituency of the well-affected.[73] More compelling was the comparatively moderate approach of Overton and the other signatories of *An Essay towards Settlement*, which attracted widespread support from the Baptist churches, and provoked two refutations.[74] Although this text, too, criticised the continued employment of Cromwellians without 'good proof of repentance in truth', it affirmed the preservation of a 'faithful Seed' in Parliament, and presented the godly with positive proposals to inaugurate Christ's reign through biblically qualified representatives and righteous, accessible laws.[75] Thus the dissatisfied Fifth

---

[72] Thomason collected the pamphlet on 19 Sept.; Wither's appointment was recorded on 5 Oct. in the chancery clerks' docket book: PRO, C231/6, fo. 443. Besides his financial losses, which remained uncompensated, Wither had emphasised the indignity of exclusion from the commissions of the peace and the militia: *Epistolium*, 11. Under the Cromwells he had also been a JP in Surrey and Essex: C193/13/5.

[73] *Fifth Monarchy . . . asserted*, 47, 51–2; *True catalogue*, 53, 76. Shorn of the negative rhetoric, the Fifth Monarchist vision looked much more attractive. One editor presented brief excerpts from *Fifth monarchy* as 'tending much to' godly unity and 'settlement upon a Righteous Foundation': *Scout* [no. 16], 12–19 Aug., 132.

[74] *A WARNING-PIECE To The General Council of the ARMY, Being sundrey Concurrent ESSAIES, Towards a Righteous Settlement*, published in November, reprinted the *Essay* with endorsements, mostly written before the coup, from Baptist churches in Berkshire, Oxfordshire, Devon, Cornwall, Leicestershire, Nottinghamshire, Rutland, Derbyshire, Salop and Warwickshire; the Berkshire churches had previously published their response separately as *A Testimony to truth, agreeing with an ESSAY for Settlement*. The refutations were *A Word To the Twenty Essayes towards a Settlement*, and Edward Johnson, *AN EXAMINATION OF THE ESSAY: OR, AN ANSWER TO THE Fifth Monarchy*.

[75] *An Essay towards Settlement upon a sure Foundation being an humble Testimony for God in*

Monarchists were divided. Overton and his military associates had accepted Parliament's commissions, and proved remarkably loyal to its authority.[76] Former leaders and MPs, Thomas Harrison and John Carew, whom some reactionaries suspected of meditating violent intervention, remained ostentatiously aloof from politics, while the rest contented themselves with verbal attacks, which did the Commonwealth little actual damage.[77]

Verbal denunciation was also a speciality of the Quakers, who shared the Fifth Monarchists' antipathy to tithes, the national ministry, persecution and the exclusion of the godly from office. Unlike hardline Fifth Monarchy-men, however, many Friends welcomed Parliament, and hoped for a reversal of the repressive tendencies of the later Protectorate. Apprehension that 'the old nature' persisted in the new government despite the 'change of name' qualified expectations, and inclined some leaders, notably George Fox, to detachment, but did not discourage others from engaging in a vigorous, well-concerted campaign for the removal of persecuting magistrates and introduction of far-reaching reform.[78] Thus Edward Burrough could privately inform Vane that his coreligionists anticipated from Parliament no 'more than what one of the ten horns that sprang out of the head of the beast can bring forth', yet he publicly hailed MPs as the 'first Assertors of and contenders for

this perilous time by a few, who have been bewailing their own and others Abominations, and would not be comforted, until their Redeemer . . . be exalted in Righteousness.(broadsheet), signed by Overton and 19 others, including the eirenical Baptist leader Henry Jessey. Although Barbara Taft has questioned whether this text should be termed 'Fifth-Monarchist', because it reflects the 'aspirations of moderate theocrats', and lacks 'millenarian prophecy', its language and programme, envisaging the millennial kingdom, do resemble those of the longer, more extreme texts, while contemporaries denominated it thus: Barbara Taft, ' "They that pursew perfection on earth": the political progress of Robert Overton', in I. Gentles, J. S. Morrill and A. B. Worden (eds), Soldiers, writers and statesmen of the English revolution, Cambridge 1998, 286–303 at p. 293.

[76] Overton refused to endorse the Derby petition in September. Instead, he and his officers in the Hull garrison professed 'stedfastnesse to the Parliament . . . in all their just and Warrantable proceedings': A LETTER From Ma. Gen. OVERTON. After the breach Overton attempted to mediate, publishing Humble and Healing Advice to both sides; had the military situation permitted, he might well have joined Monck in opposition.

[77] Harrison and Carew, in retirement since the failure of the Nominated Parliament in 1653, were listed as eligible members not yet sitting in the Catalogue . . . of this present Parliament, printed in June; neither ever appeared. For conservative suspicions of Harrison and his co-religionists see CSP iii. 479, 481, 484. Not all Royalists shared these fears. Brodrick, for example, thought scarcely 100 Fifth Monarchists were desperate enough to act, and compared the majority to 'women, whose tongue is their best weapon, therefore unlike to prevail': CSP iii. 505–6.

[78] Letters of early Friends, ed. J. Barclay, London 1811, 68, 69–70. Fox was a leading, if ambiguous pessimist: though he did not absolutely forbid political participation, he warned Friends against 'running into places', counselling would-be militia commissioners that there was 'little but filth and muck and dirt and drosse to be expected among them': FHL, MS vol. 359, fo. 157. The co-ordination of the campaign to reform the commissions of the peace is apparent from the various lists sent in by local Quakers. These are summarised in CSPD 1658–9, 358–60.

Englands Liberty', and sought repeatedly to influence their counsels.[79] A spate of petitions and tracts not only highlighted particular grievances, but sternly admonished the reinstated rulers to fulfil their 'fair promises' to end oppression in the only possible way – completely renouncing civil authority in religious matters.[80] Such a radical course might command support from a few MPs – Vane, for example, was an innovative thinker who stood on cordial terms with some Quakers, and had independently reached the same conclusion.[81] But a Parliament that also comprised men as strongly conservative as Herbert Morley and John Fagg, who reputedly preferred loose-living episcopalians to godly witnesses, was, predictably, unwilling to take any extreme step.[82] A massive Quaker petition – estimated at twenty-five yards long, with 'twenty thousand hands' – only elicited a vote to continue tithes unless a better alternative was found. MPs also created a committee to devise legislation to 'punish disturbances in the Worship of God', so frequently caused by Quakers.[83] Those guilty of such offences, or of denying the doctrines of the Trinity or the Bible's authority, were not to expect 'equal protection' in the future Commonwealth.[84]

These disappointing decisions did not, however, entail a wholesale rejection of the Quaker agenda. Despite the official limits on toleration,

---

[79] Edward Burrough to Vane, FHL, MS vol. 316, fos 27–9; idem, *To the PARLIAMENT of the Common-wealth of ENGLAND who are in place of Authority to do Justice, and in present power to ease the oppressed Nation from its Bonds. Councel and Advice*, 6 (this was one of at least five addresses to Parliament; three were published, while two survive in manuscript).

[80] Idem, *To the PARLIAMENT . . . A Presentation, by a faithful Friend to the Nations . . . That you may take off oppression . . . that Truth, justice and Righteousness may come nigh unto us* (broadsheet). Other examples include J. Hodgson, *Love, Kindness and due Respect, By way of Warning to the PARLIAMENT; That they may not neglect the great opportunity . . . for the redemption and freedom of these Oppressed Nations*; Humphrey Bache, *A Few Words in true love written to the old long sitting PARLIAMENT who Are yet left alive, and do sit there now*; Richard Hubberthorn, *The REAL CAUSE Of The NATIONS Bondage . . . Demonstrated And the Way of their Freedome . . . Asserted. Presented unto the PARLIAMENT . . . Who have a Power and Opportunity to do good, and to fulfil the expected ends of many*; William Morris, *To the Supream Authoritie (Under God) of the COMMON-WEALTH, The Commons in Parliament Assembled*; and R. H., *The Good Old Cause Briefly demonstrated With ADVERTISE-MENTS To AUTHORITY . . . to the end, All persons may see the Cause of their Bondage, and way of deliverance.*

[81] Though socially conservative, Vane engaged in dialogue with various Quakers, including Burrough. He first expounded his vision of the state's separation from the ecclesiastical sphere in *Zeal Examined: Or, A Discourse for Liberty of Conscience*, published in 1652; since then it had featured both in his *magnum opus*, *The Retired Mans Meditations* (1655), and, more briefly, in the *Healing question*.

[82] Ambrose Rigg denounced the anti-Quaker proclivities of Morley and Fagg in *OH YE HEADS Of The NATION Who are set in the SUPREAM AUTHORITY Thereof, and at this time Assembled in PARLIAMENT*, 7.

[83] *Journal*, 694, 700. The estimate is from Thomas Hall's commentary on Hosea xiii, *Samaria's Downfall* (published in 1660, but completed by Nov. 1659), 91. Even allowing for the exaggeration born of prejudice, this petition was clearly an enormous document.

[84] *Politicus*, no. 590, 6–13 Oct., 792.

persecution declined or virtually ceased in many areas.[85] Prompted by petitions, Parliament had established a committee, chaired by Vane, to investigate cases of imprisonment for conscience sake. Initial disputes over hat honour ended in accommodation of Friends' scruples, to the disgust of some observers.[86] But this conciliatory approach earned committee members the Quaker community's respect, even before their sympathetic exertions began to release numerous sufferers, not excepting even the 'notorious blasphemer' James Naylor. In the liberal climate that accompanied the revival of the the Commonwealth, Friends rejoiced to find an unprecedented 'great advantage' and 'open door' for their message 'in most places'.[87] Several obtained positions as magistrates, militia commissioners or members of volunteer regiments; though some hesitated to act, the presence of others among the Republic's most responsible servants stoked the fears of its enemies.[88] Discounting rumours of Quaker conspiracies, the House remained open to their political representations – on the 5 September MPs resolved to read a paper then presented by Burrough before the next debate on the government.[89] Such conciliatory gestures exploited the movement's internal divisions.[90] Purists prophesied the downfall of a Commonwealth conserving the 'Antichristian yoke of bondage' and advised the faithful to eschew any polit-

---

[85] Though the months of Parliament's rule saw a few riotous assaults on Quakers, for example in Liskeard, Derbyshire, Hertfordshire and London, many counties reported no sufferings whatsoever, or substantially fewer than in previous or subsequent years; of those incidents dated, most occurred before May or after October: FHL, MS Great Book of Sufferings.

[86] *Journal*, 648; Fox, *Journal*, 353. Among those appalled by such leniency towards recalcitrant Quakers was Thomas Underhill, who judged it the 'greatest dishonour of the Authority of England, as ever was admitted': *Hell broke loose: Or An HISTORY of the QUAKERS*, 31.

[87] *Letters of early Friends*, 69–70. The Great Book of Sufferings records the committee's intervention in nine cases; Naylor's release required a warrant from the Speaker: *Journal*, 775. His description is that of the Scottish Presbyterian minister Robert Baillie, who was alarmed by this apparent sign of the 'prevalencie of the Quakers and Fifth-monarchy men': *Letters and journals of Robert Baillie*, ed. D. Laing, Edinburgh 1842, iii. 429. To refute reports that he had recanted, Naylor published his own account of this episode, *Having heard that some have wronged my words which I spoke before the committee of Parliament . . . I shall speak a few words which may satisfie such as loves the truth.*

[88] On the Quakers' involvement in the militia etc. see B. Reay, *The Quakers and the English Revolution*, London 1985, ch. v. For his account of the Quaker fear see especially 'The Quakers, 1659 and the restoration of the monarchy', *History* lxiii (1978), 193–213.

[89] *Journal*, 774. The paper in question was probably Burrough's address 'To the Parliament of the Commonwealth . . . Sitting in Westminster', MS Rawlinson D397, fo. 17. This advised the creation of a committee comprising the 'ablest and soberest men' of 'all sortes', religious and others, to consider the future constitution. Instead Parliament appointed a committee of MPs.

[90] On Quaker divisions in the preceding years, and the split over Naylor see Leo Damrosch, *The sorrows of the Quaker Jesus: James Naylor and the Puritan crackdown on the free spirit*, Cambridge, Mass. 1996.

ical participation which might avert the divine judgement the regime so richly deserved.[91] Pragmatists, though deploring certain policies, refused to disown Parliament altogether or despair of persuading it to deliver.[92] The dilemma that these tensions could cause individuals is exemplified by Burrough. Torn between dissatisfaction with Parliament's failures and the desire to influence the good he saw in its members, he penned an impassioned remonstrance which alternatively threatened withdrawal in time of danger and promised assistance 'in all righteous Things'. Yet he refrained from publishing these reproaches, issuing instead a firm, but positive exposition of the proper programme. Though others were less restrained, the passivity of discontented Quakers, who would not 'exalt Christ's kingdom by an outward sword', posed little practical threat to the Republic.[93]

Denying the Quakers substantial concessions was expected to please rival Puritan groups, especially Presbyterians, Independents and Baptists. These, too, were divided. Even the Presbyterian clerics, who most consistently opposed the Commonwealth in principle, differed significantly in practice. Some advocated active or passive resistance, regardless of the regime's placatory policies; others affected neutrality, at least in public, exhorting all parties to 'love one another as Christians'.[94] A few approached Parliament

---

[91] *Good Old Cause briefly demonstrated*, 9. That summer, Fox obliquely warned against any action that might 'save them [unrighteous authorities] from the wrath & the rod'; by January he was flatly forbidding active participation in the militia: FHL, MS vol. 359, fo. 157; vol. 356, fo. 219. Quaker tracts denouncing Parliament's policies and predicting doom unless it repented include Samuel Fisher, *To the Parliament of England*; Francis Howgill, *The MOUTH Of the Pit Stopped*; and *These several PAPERS Was sent to the PARLIAMENT The twentieth day of the fifth Moneth, 1659 Being above seven thousand of the Names of the HAND-MAIDS And DAUGHTERS Of the LORD, And such as feels the oppression of Tithes*.

[92] Among the tracts by Quakers who still hoped to persuade Parliament, or at least profit from its government were Burrough, *To the Parliament . . . councel*, published in October; *To the PARLIAMENT . . . A Representation of the Outrages and Cruelties acted upon the servants of Christ, at two Meetings at Sabridgworth in Hartfordshire*; and its sequel, *A FURTHER EVIDENCE Of . . . THOMAS HEWET His DISAFFECTION To the PRESENT AUTHORITY*. The latter cleverly attempted to connect persecution with political disloyalty, using the Hertfordshire riot to argue that Parliament should replace ungodly JPs with the upright and faithful, i.e. the Quakers.

[93] Edward Burrough, 'To the Parliament and Army (in generall) of the Commonwealth of England' (Aug.), MS Rawlinson D397, fo. 13, and *To the Parliament . . . a presentation* (Sept.). Burrough stressed Quaker pacifism, denying rumoured plots, in his advice to Vane: FHL, MS vol. 316, fos 27–9.

[94] The first type is well exemplified by Henry Newcome, whose conviction that 'the Rump Parliament' consisted of 'such as hate us' was unshaken by the vote to maintain tithes etc, and led him to promote Booth's rising: Newcome, *Autobiography*, 104, 107. His fellow Cheshire minister Adam Martindale privately sympathised with the rebels, but adopted the prudent public course and joined other cautious colleagues in protesting his innocence to Parliament: *The life of Adam Martindale, written by himself*, ed. R. Parkinson (Chetham Society, 1845), 134–5, 141.

directly, dissociating themselves from the defeated rebellion and applauding the votes to encourage preaching and vindicate 'just rights as Men and Christians'.[95] Support for a national ministry, tithes and restricted toleration also suited the aspirations of the 'sober godly' interest led by John Owen and other Independent pastors, who exercised considerable influence, both openly, through sermons, and obliquely, by counselling individual hearers in high places.[96] Though generally well-disposed towards the Commonwealth, the gathered churches' enthusiasm for political action varied. The Yarmouth meeting rejoiced in the 'delivering mercy' of Parliament's restoration, and devoted a day to prayer for divine direction, yet declined an invitation from Wallingford House to opine on 'civil business'. London's congregational churches not only prayed, but offered to raise two volunteer regiments, no mean contribution to the campaign against rebellion.[97] Also zealous in the Republic's service were numerous Baptists.[98] While some did denounce the retention of tithes sustaining an 'Antichristian ministry', and would endorse the *Essay*'s desire for 'effectuall reformation' detached from Parliament, not all so-called 'Anabaptists' deserved their frequent classification with Quakers and Fifth Monarchists on a feared fanatic fringe.[99] Moderates, who had sought reconciliation with godly Presbyterians and Independents until, or, in a few cases, even after, the Commonwealth's return, professed greater confidence in parliamentary authority.[100] Parliament, for its part, took care to encourage all influential sects. Invitations to preach at Westminster and Whitehall went to distinguished Independents. The 'Baptised Congregations' of southern England were thanked for the 'sobriety and many temperate expressions' of their petition; Leicestershire ministers received

[95] 'The Humble Representation of divers well affected Ministers of the Gospel in the County of Leicester' to Parliament, summarised in *Politicus*, no. 586, 8–15 Sept., 721–2.

[96] Owen's church at Wallingford House included Fleetwood, Disbrow and other influential officers. Parliament's ecclesiastical resolves closely resemble his counsel in *Two Questions concerning the Power of the Supream magistrate about Religion, and the Worship of God with one about Tythes*, composed in answer to an influential enquirer.

[97] Dr Williams' Library, 'Copy of Yarmouth Congregational Church Record 1642–1855', 61; council minutes, 9 Aug.

[98] So prominent were the Baptists in public life under the Commonwealth that the Quaker Richard Hubberthorn, looking back in December, could plausibly contrast their eagerness for 'Offices and Places and Commands' with his co-religionists' comparative reticence: *An ANSWER To a DECLARATION Put forth by . . . the People called ANABAPTISTS In and about the City of LONDON*, 16.

[99] *Warning-piece*, 19. Differences among Baptists are detailed in B. R. White, *The English Baptists of the seventeenth century*, London 1983.

[100] Among the main Baptist believers in godly reconciliation were Richard Baxter's correspondents William Allen, John Tombes and Thomas Lambe; though these continued their efforts, Baxter complained in September that London's Baptists grew 'too high for our accommodation' once 'the turne [to a Commonwealth] set them up': *Calendar of the correspondence of Richard Baxter*, ed. N. H. Keeble and G. Nuttall, Oxford 1991, i. 407–8. The *Essay*'s critics commonly enjoined prayerful submission to Parliament's wisdom.

praise for the 'Gospel-spirit of Meekness, Sincerity and Holiness' pervading their representation. Meanwhile, the London churches' offer had been gratefully accepted and celebrated by *Politicus* as a 'good example' to the rest of the nation.[101]

The divisions among the well-affected thus tended to work for, not against, the restored Republic. It was unnecessary to satisfy all parties, since none was united, and undesirable to identify entirely with any one faction, lest the rest be alienated. By displaying a willingness to entertain contentious proposals, and conciliate their advocates when possible, support could be maximised. Some disappointment and censure was inevitable, but did not represent a serious threat: Parliament in 1659 encountered only a feeble reflection of the radical agitation against it in 1651–3. Given the state of emergency, the scarcity of concrete reforms was excusable, in the opinion of many, and had not 'diminished much of the enthusiasm' for the regime 'among reformers, particularly Quakers', as Hutton contends. After a lull during the rising, the late summer and autumn witnessed yet more schemes for reform. As late as October, Edward Burrough was still advising Parliament to repeal all 'unrighteous Lawes' dating from the 'dark night of Apostacy'. John Rogers, in September, published a monumental work which praised the progress already made towards the 'holy Commonwealth', but sought to warn its rulers against the admission of 'some of the most dangerous remains of the late Apostacy' to their 'former Places', and the neglect of some faithful and deserving persons. Criticism of particular policies could therefore coexist with optimism and confidence in the Parliament's overall integrity. Rogers devoted much space to defending Hesilrig, Vane, Ludlow, Fleetwood, Lambert and other leaders, whom he pronounced 'the most Active and eminent Dignitaries in our Orb; Whose sparkling virtues and Twinkling lustres . . . outshine all . . . Reproaches of the lower Region'.[102]

Such tributes, though overstated, were not undeserved. Amidst a galaxy of differences, the republicans had succeeded in constructing and maintaining a working alliance. By exploiting consensus when possible, and preferring latitudinarian counsels to the most divisive proposals, Parliament expanded the narrow basis of its support to the widest possible extent. Contrary to the assertions of its enemies, the House was neither paralysed by factional strife, nor united by hostility to the soldiers. Rather, it showed a consistent concern to consolidate the official reconciliation with the Army, accepting the senior officers as trusted members of the government, providing for the soldiers' needs, and responding favourably to most of their political desires. Far from teetering on the brink of a fatal rupture, the partnership between Parliament

---

101 *Politicus*, no. 569, 26 May–2 June, 469; no. 586, 8–15 Sept., 722; no. 582, 4–11 Aug., 656.
102 Hutton, *Restoration*, 53; Burrough, *To the Parliament . . . councel*, 6, 8; Rogers, *Diapoliteia*, 62, 100, 16.

and Army proved capable of resolving successive problems without sowing the seeds of irreparable distrust. Considered in the light of the vast potential for discord, the occasional complaints and conflicts pale in comparison to the republican achievement in containing divisions.

4

The City of London and the Republic

The City Magistrates congratulat[ed] the Members with Cordial affections and elegant Speeches, desiring that God would crown them with the honours of making these Nations happy by such a Government that the Liberties and Rights of the good people of these Nations may be preserved to them and their Posterities: *Loyal Scout*, 30 Sept.–7 Oct. 1659.

> From a senseless Mayor not fit to rule Hoggs,
> From such as obey him like Spaniel Doggs . . .,
> From a City that lyes on his back to be gelt,
> From such as won't stir till famine be felt . . .
> From the City Militia that stares like Hectors
> From Taxes, Red-coats and Collectors . . .
> From the luke-warmness of a perjured City . . .
> *Libera nos Domine*: THE NEW LETANY, Sept. 1659.

The greatest number, as well of the richer sort, as of poor Artificers, Tradesmen, Apprentices, Clerks and other debauched, despicable and giddy-headed persons . . . are filled with malice, and their mouths . . . with hellish Curses . . . against their Superiors and those things which they understand not, manifesting in them, a proneness to desperate Mutinies and Insurrections . . . [it is only by God's mercy] that this great City hath not been in a flame long since: George Wither, *A Cordial Confection*, Oct. 1659.

To survive at all, the Republic had to succeed in governing London. Contemporaries of all persuasions, including those most critical of its judicial, economic and demographic dominance, acknowledged the supreme importance of the capital. Complaining that 'the whole riches of the Country is here rifled away in riot', an ardent republican theorist denounced the City as an improvident 'Mother' neglecting the welfare of her 'daughters', the provinces, and demanded radical decentralisation. More flatteringly, Marchamont Nedham, worming his way back into Parliament's good graces, saluted London as the 'Metropolis and Imperial Chamber of England', and sought to persuade the inhabitants that the prosperity of their 'Renowned City' was inextricably linked with that of the Republic. From the other end of the political spectrum, the Royalist plotter Viscount Mordaunt regarded London as the 'Master wheel, by whose motions the successive rotations of all the lesser must follow'.[1] The provinces had, indeed, followed London's lead in all the

---

1   CHAOS: Or, A DISCOURSE, Wherein Is presented . . . a Frame of Government by way of a Republique, preface; [Marchamont Nedham], Interest will not Lie. Or, a view of England's

political changes of the past decade, including the coup that destroyed Richard Cromwell's Protectorate. Though distinguished by its proximity to the seat of government, London exhibited, with peculiar intensity, almost all the problems encountered by the regime elsewhere. Its relations with the restored Parliament therefore merit examination, not only because of the capital's intrinsic importance, but as a case study in republican government.

Contemporaries often thought in terms of a simple dichotomy between 'City' and 'Country'. Reality was, however, much more complex. London was not one city but a vast conurbation containing a multitude of jurisdictions, of which the ancient corporation was only the most prestigious and influential. Like the provinces, London had no single identity, but was a compound of competing interests, economic, religious and political. Stronghold of the sects, London was also the capital of Presbyterianism; hotbed of radical political ideas, London remained the centre for reactionary thought. These tensions resulted in divergent responses to the new government: the epigraphs that head this chapter reveal some contrasting perceptions of the relationship between Londoners and the Republic. The *Loyal Scout*, reporting the banquet given in Parliament's honour by the City authorities, emphasised harmonious co-operation founded on the common commitment to the cause of righteous settlement. Such lofty principles and motives were contemptuously dismissed by the Cavalier ballad, *The New Letany*, which condemned the City's submission to republican tyranny as the consequence of pure stupidity and wilful indifference to its former allegiance to the Stuart kings. Equally critical, for opposite reasons, was the aggrieved republican poet George Wither, who saw in Londoners an antipathy to the regime that transcended differences in wealth and occupation, and awaited only an opportunity to manifest itself in open rebellion.[2] Inadequate though they were as generalisations, all these perceptions nevertheless contained elements of truth. To appreciate the republican achievement in governing London, it is necessary to examine the complex interaction between Parliament and the diverse constituencies of which the capital consisted.

Most vociferous of all London constituencies was the broad alliance of the 'well-affected', who were concentrated there in particular strength.[3] Proximity to the powerful gave such Londoners advantages that they did not hesitate to exploit: the Army's decision to restore Parliament owed much to the determined agitation of '*several Thousands of faithful Friends to the Good*

True Interest: In reference to the Papist, Royalist, Presbyterian, Baptised, Neuter, Army, Parliament, City of London: In refutation of a treasonable Pamphlet, entituled, The interest of England stated, 42, 46; Mordaunt to Charles II, 26 Jan. 1660, in *The letter book of John, Viscount Mordaunt, 1658–1660,* ed. M. Coate (Camden Society, 3rd ser. lxix, 1945), p. xviii.

[2] *Scout* (no. 23), 30 Sept.–7 Oct., 190; *The NEW LETANY* (broadsheet); George Wither, *A Cordial Confection,* 22.

[3] Of 99 private informers included in a post-Restoration list, 23 were London artisans or tradesmen: BL, MS Stowe 185, fos 165–7.

old Cause *in and about the City*.[4] Liberated from all restraint by Richard Cromwell's fall, these Londoners shared the limitless expectations and eager enthusiasm for the Republic of their provincial counterparts, and set them an example of appropriate action. Within a week of Parliament's return, three congratulatory petitions had been presented by the 'well-affected' citizens of London and the adjacent suburb of Southwark. These not only expressed thanksgiving and wonder at the miraculous providence that had restored the Republic, but exhorted MPs to improve their new-found opportunity to introduce a righteous settlement. Thus Samuel Moyer, spokesman for the 'Humble Petition of many inhabitants in and about the City of London', represented Parliament's reappearance as 'the very joy of our hearts', and urged members to 'make it your great work . . . to do that wherein you may have glory by the establishment . . . of these poor Nations upon a righteous and just foundation of Judgment and Justice'.[5] Loyal citizens were not slow to offer detailed prescriptions for the future settlement, producing a flood of reforming pamphlets in the months following Parliament's return. Indeed, London's dominance of the book trade fostered republican creativity there, affording the 'well-affected' unique opportunities to shape opinions, and hence the outcome of events.

But the new-found liberty of 'well-affected' Londoners to publish and debate also exposed their differences, and alarmed conservatives. Certain Quakers, emboldened by the appearance of a regime that seemed more sympathetic to their sufferers, dismayed the authorities and outraged sober opinion by a series of spectacular gestures, ranging from by now familiar practices such as going naked through the streets and disturbing ministers to administering public rebukes to the lord mayor himself.[6] And Quakers were not the only ones to inspire apprehension for the established order. Fifth Monarchists fuelled fears of a radical coup by holding mass meetings near London, and printing demands for massive reforms of the corporation, including the abolition of the lord mayor's office and 'all remaining badges . . . of the Monarchical Foundation'.[7] Nor was anxiety over the implications of

---

4   This phrase described the signatories of an address *To his Excellencie the Lord Charls Fleetwood, and the rest of the Officers* . . . for Parliament's return; similar assertions were made in tracts such as *Five proposals*; *A DECLARATION Of the Well-affected to THE GOOD OLD CAUSE In the Cities of London, Westminster, and Borough of Southwark*;; and the *Humble Representation of divers well-affected persons of the City of Westminster*. 'Well affected' members of the City militia contributed to Richard's downfall by affirming solidarity with the Army in pursuit of the 'Good Old Cause': *The Humble Representation and Petition of the Field Officers & Captains of the . . . Trained-bands, of the City.*

5   *Journal*, 649–50, 647, 648.

6   Most of these incidents were catalogued in September by Underhill in *Hell broke loose*, 32–3. Further confirmation, and the affront to the lord mayor, may be found in the indictments in CLRO, sessions files for 27 June, 14 Aug. and 10 Oct.; a fascinating narrative of one London Quaker's disruptive impulses is Solomon Eccles, *In the year 59, in the fourth month*. On the fears roused by such assertiveness see Reay, 'Quakers, 1659'.

7   *True catalogue*, 66. For the fears occasioned by Fifth Monarchist meetings see CSP iii.

the Republic's return diminished by attempts to rekindle enthusiasm for Leveller ideas, reviving the tactics that had made London the principal stronghold of the Leveller movement during the previous decade.[8] John Lilburne's widow and some of his associates now returned to the political forefront, producing new pamphlets and petitions to Parliament which not only resurrected the former programme but represented it as the only means to unite all the godly in the cause of 'Justice and Righteousness'. In a curious blend of Leveller, Fifth Monarchist and chivalric rhetoric, one writer summoned all 'noble spirits' recognising Christ as 'King, Priest and Prophet' to meet regularly at the tomb of 'that famous and worthy Sufferer for his Countrys Freedom', John Lilburne, in order to 'compassionate one anothers burthens' and promote the 'Work of the Lord' as 'true English-men'.[9] A short distance, but a vast gulf, separated the passionate godliness of these neo-Leveller meetings from the rarefied intellectual atmosphere prevailing at the Nonsuch tavern in Bow Street where James Harrington and the virtuosi, including such other former Levellers as John Wildman, discussed constitutional theory.[10] Only in London were the contrasting tendencies among the 'well-affected' so closely juxtaposed, and so clearly manifested.

Quick to exploit the differences between the regime's adherents were, of course, its enemies, who also congregated in the capital in unusual numbers. Royalists not only resumed secret, and unsuccessful, intrigues with Wildman and other sober commonwealthsmen,[11] but used the Hobbesian argument that the extravagance of newly-tolerated Quakers, Fifth Monarchists and other radicals 'proved' that the Republic would not provide adequate protection, and hence had no claim on the citizens' allegiance. Among the more notorious results of their labours was the broadsheet entitled *An Alarum to the City and Soldiery*, disseminated early in June, which purported to reveal that Fifth Monarchists, encouraged by Parliament, intended 'to Fire the City, and

479, 485. The activities of Fifth Monarchists in 1659 are briefly recounted in B. S. Capp, *The Fifth Monarchy men: a study in seventeenth-century English millenarianism*, London 1972, 123–30.

8 For such attempts see Freeze, *Out-cry*, H. N., *An OBSERVATION and COMPARISON Between the Idolatrous Israelites and Judges of England*, and the reproduction of the petition and invitation to regular meetings in the *Scout*, no. 4, 13–20 May, 31. To Royalists a Leveller resurgence was as bad as the Quaker menace: *Nicholas papers*, 152–3; *CSP* iii. 505; MS Clarendon 61, fo. 104. The fullest history of the Leveller movement in the 1640s remains H. N. Brailsford, *The Levellers and the English Revolution*, London 1961.

9 H. N., *Observation*, 9, 4.

10 Though evidence concerning this club is disappointingly meagre, it seems reasonable to suppose that its discussions resembled those of its successor, the famous Rota of the autumn. On the activities in Bow Street see Brasy to Hyde, 8 July, MS Clarendon 62, fo. 25, and the additional references cited in M. Ashley, *John Wildman, plotter and postmaster: a study of the English republican movement in the seventeenth century*, London 1947, 142, 307.

11 For these intrigues, and their failure to win support from Wildman and those who hoped for a permanent republic, see the letters in *CSP* iii. 511, 525–6, and MS Clarendon 60, fos 475, 563.

to Massacre all considerable People' on 'Tuesday next', and exhorted the inhabitants to avert 'Ruin and Destruction' by a preemptive revolt. In the unstable climate of the summer of 1659, the inflammatory potential of such disinformation was considerable, as the lord mayor, and the 'much amazed and alarmed' citizens who presented the paper to him, immediately realised.[12] Nor did the danger disappear when events disproved the *Alarum*, for similar themes were sounded, in slightly more sophisticated form, by a stream of subversive pamphlets, culminating in *The Londoners Last Warning*, an eloquent appeal to support Booth's rising. The sectarian menace was not, of course, the only theme of such propaganda, which also courted Londoners by extensive appeals to civic pride and economic grievances. Republican rapaciousness received the blame for the 'present deadness of trade'; the massive 'Contribution and Militia' extorted with unprecedented 'excesse and rigour' was attributed to deep designs to destroy the City's ancient privileges and property. Monarchists repeatedly urged citizens not to be 'tamely . . . led, or cowardly . . . frightened into a perpetual Slavery to the worst of [their] fellow Subjects': resistance would be not just 'glorious and honourable' but eminently feasible, since London possessed 'a power so great' that only 'resolution' was required to sweep away the republican tyrants.[13]

Efforts to capture London featured so prominently in counter-revolutionary propaganda because of the capital's centrality to the conspiracy against the Commonwealth. Despite the proclamation for their departure in the last days of Richard's Protectorate, many delinquents remained throughout the spring and early summer.[14] It was therefore in London that the crucial meetings between Presbyterian and Royalist leaders were held, and around London that their plans revolved: once provincial uprisings had diverted the regular forces usually concentrated there, rebellion in the City would overthrow the central government. To this end, considerable confidence was reposed in the interest of former merchant and major-general Richard Browne, who was to raise an army of citizens and apprentices; appropriate inspiration was also anticipated from the influential Presbyterian clergy.[15] As the plot ripened, signs that Londoners were dissatisfied with the Republic fed

12 Ireton to Charles Fleetwood, 6 June, MS Tanner 51, fo. 74.
13 *Interest of England*, 11; *Londoners*, 4, 6–7. Other examples of propaganda addressed to the City include *Several new cheats*, which concluded with a poem alerting London to its enslavement; *Mercurius Pragmaticus*; *An EXPRESS from the KNIGHTS and GENTLEMEN now engaged with Sir GEORGE BOOTH; To the City and Citizens of London, And all other Free-men*; and *Englands remembrances*, which stressed the king's concern for the prosperity of 'the great Metropolis', and urged citizens to 'Repent . . . and Redeem the innocent blood' of his father (pp. 11, 10).
14 The April proclamation occasioned little complaint, and no interruption of Royalist correspondence, and does not seem to have been vigorously enforced by the Army, which had assumed practical power. The proclamation naturally lapsed once Parliament was restored, since it did not recognise its predecessor's decrees.
15 For these expectations, and London's place in the plot, see especially *Nicholas papers*, 99; MS Clarendon 61, fos 496, 541, 553.

optimism regarding the outcome. Letters to the exiled court in July and early August reported that the new militia had occasioned 'much discontent', and that the 'meaner sort' were openly, the 'better sort' secretly disaffected. Conspirators also found encouragement in the general reluctance to contribute financial aid.[16] The Venetian Giavarina remarked that those charged with the new militia 'rail[ed] at the injustice, freely expressing improper sentiments without the slightest fear', and so was easily convinced that the 'citizens and guilds [were] . . . mostly royalists'. More cautious, Bordeaux simply noted the importance and discontent of the Presbyterians. Foreigners were also impressed by the availability of anti-republican propaganda and its appeal to the citizens. Giavarina, who witnessed only events in London, claimed to have heard the 'common people crying for the coming of King Charles', and leapt to the conclusion that the English were 'altogether disgusted and thoroughly tired' of the Republic.[17]

By their extraordinary vigilance, the republicans frustrated expectations that discontent would produce rebellion in the City. Acutely aware that London, as political centre and principal source of revenue, must be retained at all costs, Parliament and council responded vigorously to the least signs of danger. On its very first day, the House ordered the lord mayor to take 'special care of the preservation of the peace and safety' of the City; a false alarm the following night resulted in a violent search for weapons and suspects, from which even the foreign ambassadors were not entirely excepted.[18] While the council instituted surveillance of the arms trade, Parliament prepared special legislation to settle the militia in London, Westminster, Southwark and the Tower Hamlets.[19] Though these bills languished in committee during the greater calm of June, they became law in early July as part of a series of moves against the gathering conspiracy. The other major initiatives were the Act against Delinquents, banishing known Royalists from the capital, and the Act for Householders, requiring registration of all lodgers, arms and horses in the London area.[20] Superintending enforcement was the council, which not only issued commands to the City authorities and militia commissioners, but also established its own committees for London security to carry out searches and seize and examine suspects. The council's proceedings in late July and August abound with preventive measures: constant patrols by the militia and regular forces, the stationing of more and more barges manned with musketeers to scrutinise travellers crossing the river, the issue of passes to all those

[16] MS Clarendon 62, fo. 16; 63 fo. 193; *Nicholas papers*, 174.

[17] *CSPVen.*, 48, 54, 59–60; Bordeaux to Mazarin, 8 Aug., Guizot, *Histoire*, i. 395; *CSPVen.*, 42, 50. Giavarina admitted that his correspondence with the 'most notable places' in the provinces had been cut off since the recent 'revolutions': *CSPVen.*, 55–6.

[18] *Journal*, 646. On the impact of the search see the accounts in *WI*, no. 1, 3–10 May, 8; MS Clarendon 60, fo. 540; *CSPVen.*, 20.

[19] Council minutes, 22 May; *Journal*, 647, 662, 663–4.

[20] The various London militia acts were passed between 28 June and 14 July; the Act against Delinquents on 13 July, and the Act for Householders on 22 July.

with 'lawful occasions' to enter or leave London.[21] The effectiveness of these precautions was acknowledged on all sides, from newsbooks admiring the divine blessing on the council's efforts to keep 'all quiet in and about London', to monarchists moaning that the 'inquisition' there had made life impossibly dangerous.[22] Their complaints substantiate a Middlesex militia commissioner's observation that the 'sudden seizing' of horses and 'extraordinary Strict Guards' in London had left many Royalist leaders stranded and vulnerable to arrest. Pre-emptive action at the centre had thus not only thwarted counter-revolutionary ambitions there, but played a significant part in the failure of the provincial risings.[23]

Credit for the preservation of 'perfect Tranquillity' in London[24] was, however, due in large measure to the intelligent co-operation of the City magistrates with republican initiatives. Tribute to their contribution was paid by all parties: newsbooks applauded, the council thanked, the lord mayor and aldermen for their 'great Care of the publique peace'.[25] Less complimentary were the foreign ambassadors: Bordeaux attributed elite support for the Republic to fear of the populace and a vested interest in confiscated property, while Giavarina's hostility to the regime moved him to conclude that the 'mayor and aldermen' were 'almost all creatures of the government [who] mortally hate his Majesty'.[26] Royalists invariably ascribed the worst motives to a collaboration so fatal to their aspirations; their propaganda vainly attempted to destroy respect for the magistrates by vilifying the lord mayor as a 'false villain' and traitor to the City's true interest, and accusing the aldermen of 'Compliance for gain without conscience'.[27]

Accurate only in the assertion that there was much to be gained from compliance, such censure did the City magistrates an injustice. As little as any provincial office-holders did London's mayor and aldermen desire disturbances that would jeopardise their own standing, together with the social, economic and religious order. Their priority was the smooth running of the

---

21 Council minutes, 8, 29 July (committees), 29, 30, 31 July (barges), 5, 12 Aug. (passes), 29, 30 July, 9 Aug. (guards and patrols).

22 *Politicus*, no. 581, 28 July–4 Aug., 639; *Nicholas papers*, 176, 174. It is surely no coincidence that the letters from the mysterious 'Miles' to Nicholas cease after that of 8 Aug. reporting the acute danger from republican security measures. For other Royalist complaints of the tranquillity enforced by these measures see the letters in MS Clarendon 63, fos 14, 203; *CSPD 1659*, 74, 88.

23 Barkstead to Scot, MS Clarendon 63, fo. 95.

24 This phrase was used by both *Politicus*, no. 581, 28 July–4 Aug., 639, and *Scout*, no. 14, 29 July–5 Aug., 117. Similar comments were made by various writers in early August: see the letters in *CSPD 1659*, 74, 88, 114.

25 Council order to the lord mayor, 9 Aug.; *Post*, no. 13, 26 July–2 Aug., 108. For other expressions of the council's gratitude see the letters to Ireton of 8 July and 2 Aug., and Whitelocke's speech to the mayor and aldermen on 9 Aug., reported in *Politicus*, no. 582, 4–11 Aug., 658.

26 Guizot, *Histoire*, i. 430, 423; *CSPVen.*, 54.

27 *Londoners*, 5; *Bibliotheca*, 1.

ordinary machinery of government: managing City property, receiving citizens' petitions and regulating companies. Justice proceeded as usual in the mayor's court, where Londoners continued to sue each other for debt, and at sessions, where JPs prosecuted the most flagrant misdemeanours of the Quakers, together with the multitude of more mundane offences, chiefly theft and assault. Law and order thus functioned normally, disproving reactionaries' allegations of republican anarchy. In London, as elsewhere, the Commonwealth's return brought no sudden change in the composition of the corporation; most magistrates continued to discharge their duties rather than hazard their places by open disloyalty to the new regime.[28]

But the City elite, exposed to the danger of Parliament's immediate displeasure, and sitting on a powder keg, could not afford to emulate those provincial magistrates who conceded only a tacit submission to the central government. Though Woolrych, crediting Royalist assertions that the lord mayor's influence was exerted in vain, contends that 'the City of London could not be stirred to produce' an address of loyalty, the Common Council in fact appointed a committee to consider the City's response within days of the Republic's return. Less than three weeks later, Parliament received *The Humble Petition of the Lord Mayor, Aldermen and Commons of the City of London*. This address was certainly less ecstatic than the effusions of the 'well-affected', but Woolrych errs in supposing that its purpose was 'not so much to pledge allegiance as to press for a guarantee of the city's liberties and for relief from over-taxation'. London's governors not only acquiesced in the 'almighty power and providence of God' that had restored the members to their places, but praised Parliament's initial *Declaration* and affirmed their shared commitment to 'the maintenance of Religion in its power and purity and our Civil Rights and Liberties inviolably'. These were, of course, the objectives of the 'Good Old Cause' so much celebrated by the 'well-affected'. Recalling their 'many and free Ingagements . . . against the old Common . . . Enemy', the City magistrates insisted that their 'affections still remain[ed] upon the same principalls and to the same ends'. The specific requests of the petition made few allusions to London's liberties, and none to taxes, but were formulated in national terms: the protection of property and corporation privileges everywhere, the reconciliation of the godly, the prevention of all oppression of conscience. Moderate clauses asking Parliament to preserve the universities 'in piety and learning', maintain a 'Godly Learned painfull Gospel preaching Ministry' and regulate the laws and courts for the benefit of the poor echoed the Army petition presented on the 12 May. In desiring the

---

[28] Continued attention to the normal functioning of government is plain from the records of Common Council, the repertory court of the aldermen, the mayor's court and sessions. Conformity to successive regimes, including the Republic, is evident from the fact that 50% of the aldermen active in 1658 would still be in office in 1661. On the gradual nature of change see G. V. Chivers, 'The City of London and the state, 1658–64: a study in political and financial relations', unpubl. PhD diss. Manchester 1961, esp. p. 66.

revival and regulation of trade and the settlement of the militia and the government in godly and faithful hands, the City's rulers reiterated earlier requests of their 'well-affected' subordinates. The petition was respectful, though not excessively subservient in tone, and concluded with a submission to the 'great wisdoms' of the members. A recognition more befitting the dignity of the first city of the realm could hardly have been imagined. Parliament certainly professed satisfaction, admiring the 'great Wisdom and Judgment' of the contents, and returning thanks for the 'good expressions and affections'.[29]

On this promising note of mutual congratulation began a real partnership between Parliament and the City authorities. The latter were far from blind to the advantages of good relations with a central government capable of redressing grievances and protecting City interests. In June the court of aldermen and Common Council contemplated recourse to Parliament on issues ranging from the suppression of 'low watermen' to compulsory work for prisoners, to prevention of the naturalisation of strangers.[30] The republicans, for their part, were anxious to demonstrate their concern for the City's welfare whenever more pressing business permitted. The City had able spokesmen within the House: not only Aldermen Pennington and Atkins but various merchants, including John Trenchard and the diligent councillors Richard Salway and George Thompson. These MPs had a long history of co-operation on commercial matters, and regularly served on committees concerning City affairs.[31] Thus a petition from the aldermen against the monopoly on the dredging of ballast, presented on 10 June, was referred to a committee chaired by Trenchard, whose report, when admitted on 30 July, firmly supported the City.[32] A petition from the merchants trading with Spain received a sympathetic hearing from those republicans who considered Cromwell's war a self-serving enterprise that had caused the decay of trade. The council, to which the petition was committed, showed no interest in prosecuting the war, but began tentative, albeit inconclusive, moves towards peace on 'reasonable terms'.[33] Parliament did make considerable, if sporadic, advances with a bill to satisfy the citizens who appealed for the settlement of Irish lands long promised to the adventurers, while the council responded positively to petitions from interested Londoners to regulate trade so as to ameliorate the 'deadness of the market here'.[34] During August's emergency

---

[29] Woolrych, 'Introduction', 97. On 13 May Common Council created the committee, which reported on the 31st (CLRO, CCJ, fos 204–5). The petition was printed with Parliament's answer both in Politicus, no. 570, 2–9 June, 486, and separately.

[30] CLRO, Rep. 66, fos 254, 262; CCJ, fo. 205.

[31] On the earlier cooperation of such members on City and commercial business see Worden, Rump Parliament, 31–2, 256–7.

[32] Journal, 679, 705, 735, 740.

[33] The merchants' petition was presented to Parliament on 26 May, and debated by the council on 13 June. Policy towards Spain is analysed in ch. 6 below.

[34] Journal, 706, 752, 761, 763–4, 767, 774–5, 778–9. On 14 June the council forbade the

Whitelocke could remind the lord mayor and aldermen, with some plausibility, that Parliament had 'testified their intention of advancing the Trade of this Nation', and already made 'good progress'. More realistically, Nedham warned Londoners not to allow 'the want of [trade] at present . . . [to] irritate you to fall out with the publick Interest of your Country', and predicted that close adherence to Parliament would soon produce a settlement enabling 'Trade and all other Concernments [to] flourish again'.[35]

As Nedham covertly admitted, London had, by August, received few tangible blessings from its association with the Republic. Parliament, on the other hand, derived substantial immediate benefits from the compliance of the City elite. As the London area supplied nearly 10 per cent of the assessment, and the greater part of the customs, the obedience of its taxpayers was of the first importance to a government in grave financial difficulties. By maintaining order among their inferiors, London's magistrates facilitated the continued inflow of ordinary revenue. The last six months of the Cromwellian assessment had been paid, according to schedule, and with a shortfall of only 0.0006%, by the end of June.[36] On 5 July Parliament, anxious for ready cash, ordered the London assessment commissioners to levy the first payment on the next instalment within six days, instead of the six weeks prescribed by the act. Though Giavarina mistook widespread resentment and reluctance for a popular refusal to pay, even Royalists remarked, with disgust, the City's submissiveness beneath the increased tax burden.[37] Supervised by the council, the commissioners effectively doubled the pace of collection: by 4 August receipts on this account amounted to nearly £8,000 – more than half the entire sum raised in the preceding six months. By 12 October the total stood at over £15,000 – an impressive achievement by any standard but Parliament's desperately ambitious timetable.[38] Less successful, however, were the republicans' attempts to raise loans. Though the East India Company did provide £15,000, secured on their own customs, this represented only half the

export of 'frames or engines for knitworkers of silke stockings' in response to a petition from the London framework knitters; exactly three months later it granted the London merchant John Hill and his company a licence to import 300 tonnes of oil and 100 tonnes of whalebone in order to provide employment for the Commonwealth poor.

[35] *The Humble ADDRESSE of the Lord Maior, Aldermen and Common-Council of the City . . ., on the 9th of this instant August to the Council of State . . . with the Lord Whitlock's SPEECH In Answer*, 7, 4; [Nedham], *Interest*, 46.

[36] The account book of Robert Barrett, City receiver-general, reveals that the £56,000 assessment required for the period from 24 June 1657 to 24 June 1659 was paid with a shortfall of only £36: SP 28/334.

[37] *Journal*, 705; CSPVen., 50; *Pragmaticus*, 2–3; *Nicholas papers*, 140, 168.

[38] These figures are derived from the receipts and dates listed in Robert Barrett, 'A particular account of money received on the 12 months assessment at £35,000 from 24 June 1659': SP 28/334. Parliament had ordered payment of the whole year's tax by the end of the first quarter – an impossible goal. By 12 Oct. 56% had come in; by 24 Dec. 92%. Had the assessment commissioners seemed negligent, it is inconceivable that the council would not have obeyed Parliament's instruction to report 'any remissness'.

sum the council had requested.[39] The fiat for the immediate collection of the assessment went forth only after the further failure to persuade the lord mayor and aldermen to lend the shortfall on that security. One Royalist asserted that the aldermen had absolutely rejected both pleas of necessity and threats of force, but his account of their defiance is so inconsistent with their usual conduct, and so confused and inaccurate as to details that it may surely be discounted.[40] Some money may have been supplied by wealthy individuals, at the instigation of the lord mayor,[41] yet the refusal to provide an official loan exposed the limits of co-operation. Anxious as they might themselves be to oblige MPs, the City magistrates nevertheless recognised their inability to persuade the majority of citizens to lend to a regime so exacting and unpopular as the Commonwealth.[42]

The responses to the new militia showed even more clearly that the City fathers were not simply creatures of the central government, but determined to communicate the citizens' concerns. Eager to secure magisterial support for this, the cornerstone of the campaign to secure London from the Royalist menace, Parliament included the lord mayor, sheriffs, twelve aldermen, and at least twenty common councillors among the commissioners to put the militia into execution. Although the House had already made the ageing, but highly respected major-general and MP Philip Skippon supreme commander of all forces raised, the appointment of these City dignitaries to the commission went some way to meet their request, in the recognition address, for the privilege of proposing militia officers. Tensions arose, however, because Parliament was not prepared to entrust the entire responsibility for the militia to the City officials, who were outnumbered on the commission by a host of

---

[39] Council minutes, 21, 22, 30 June; *Journal*, 699.

[40] On 30 June the council sent a committee to meet the City magistrates and assessment commissioners concerning this loan; failure is evident from the absence of any report, and the silence of City records. The colourful account of the conversation is in a letter of 27 June, which erroneously claims that the committee was sent by Parliament on 22 June (*Nicholas papers*, 163). The writer, or his informants, may have confused the council's request for a loan with Parliament's earlier committee to negotiate the exchange of Greenwich for New Park, an equally unsuccessful mission. On 28 June Bordeaux composed a similar report: Guizot, *Histoire*, i. 409.

[41] The evidence at this point is inconclusive: the same Royalist went on to report that the lord mayor had managed, after a 'great debate', to persuade Common Council to 'supply the present necessities of the State'. On 18 July another Royalist reported that London had lent a substantial sum: MS Clarendon 63, fo. 34a. It is improbable that an official loan could lack documentation in City or council records; individual contributions, however, could easily have been unrecorded. It is also possible that the Royalists simply interpreted tax payments as loans.

[42] There is a marked contrast between the reluctance to lend money in the summer and the alacrity with which the City elite responded to Parliament's appeal for a loan as citizens celebrated the restoration of the secluded MPs in February 1660: CCJ, fo. 220. That the aldermen were perfectly willing to oblige individual MPs earlier is plain from their positive responses to minor requests from influential figures such as Vane and Fleetwood: Rep. 66, fos 218, 271, 310.

the Republic's most loyal, if more radical, servants, including Samuel Moyer, Praise-God Barebone, Slingsby Bethel and the Baptists William Kiffin and William Allen.[43] The contrasting priorities of the committed republicans and the conformists among the City elite became apparent when the latter, outvoted at the commissioners' meetings, induced Common Council to appeal directly to Parliament, in an address pleading the 'Inability and unfitness' of the City to furnish more than two horse troops, and requesting an additional act to confirm the provisions of charters and 'all former ordinances and Acts' against compulsory service outside London. Although its principal aim was to protect the privileges and reduce the burdens of the citizens, the petition avowed no conflict between their particular interest and their allegiance to the national government. Asserting the reciprocity at the heart of all government, the City, with great respect for 'this Honourable Parliament', reminded MPs that Londoners had been 'cheerful in all your Streights' to come to 'your and the nations help', and confidently expected them to rule, as formerly, in a manner 'very much to the satisfaction of the City, and encouragement of persons of worth and Interest'.[44]

There was danger even in an implicit challenge to the new militia, and Parliament's control thereof, coming as it did from the capital whose support was so essential, and whose example might prove so influential. The government's answer, published with the petition in *Mercurius Politicus* as a lesson to the entire nation, was a judicious blend of firmness and tact. Refusing to compromise its authority and endanger London's security by rescinding its authorisation of the six horse troops recommended by the commissioners, Parliament nevertheless offered a reassuring explanation, promising to be 'very tender of the Priviledges of all the good people', especially in London, yet only 'so far as consists with the necessary welfare and safety of the whole'. To remain true to their own assertion of the harmony between local and national interests, the City magistrates could hardly reject this appeal to the over-riding and unimpeachable imperatives of necessity and general security. Insisting that the present was a 'time of eminent danger', Parliament exhorted 'Magistrates and other good people' to give 'all encouragement . . . to what may conduce to the safety and good of this Commonwealth'. Thus the republicans attempted to inspire recalcitrant subjects in London and elsewhere with a vision of the general good that might transcend their preoccupation with local or individual grievances.[45]

---

[43] The London Militia Act appointed 100 commissioners: aldermen and common councillors therefore comprised approximately one third of the total.

[44] The petition, with Parliament's answer, is printed in *Politicus*, no. 579, 14–21 July, 599–600. Parliament had ordered the first meeting of the commissioners on 9 July, two days after the passage of the act. On 15 July Common Council appointed a committee dominated by commissioners to draft the petition that was presented to Parliament the next day: CCJ, fo. 206.

[45] *Politicus*, no. 579, 14–21 July, 600.

In practice, Westminster and Whitehall kept the promise to protect local privileges as much as possible, displaying considerable sensitivity towards London sensibilities. Though they refused to guarantee that the militia would not be called to involuntary service beyond the walls, the council never sent it further than Blackheath: its principal duties were to guard the gates and patrol the streets of London.[46] As the City had requested, command of the new forces was entrusted to 'persons of quality, Freemen and Inhabitants': the senior officers in every regiment were selected from the most respectable militia commissioners, with the lord mayor, John Ireton, himself at the head of the controversial horse regiment.[47] Conciliated by this attention to their wishes, the City elite continued to co-operate with the Republic. Though some hostile observers had interpreted the petition as a refusal of the new militia, the citizens, in fact, remained acquiescent, even when Parliament authorised the commissioners to raise an extra three months' assessment to pay for the drums, provisions and other 'incident charges'.[48] On 3 August Politicus announced that one cavalry and six infantry regiments had commenced their duties, and represented London's militia as a 'remarkable' success that the rest of the nation would do well to imitate. Not just official sources, but Royalists and diplomats acknowledged the militia's important part in deterring rebellion in London after the removal of most of the regular forces to oppose Booth.[49] The triumph was Parliament's, since it had preserved the vital partnership with the City magistrates without hazarding either its authority or its initial objective, the capital's security.

No individual did more to foster the partnership between the Republic and the City than the lord mayor, whose energetic obedience cannot be ascribed to a purely conformist concern for order and stability. As mayor, Ireton was necessarily an important mediator, transmitting commands from Parliament and council to his colleagues in the City government; the precepts issued to the aldermen in Common Hall testify to his promptitude in discharging these duties.[50] But Ireton was not just the passive recipient of

---

[46] On 30 July, with the rising imminent, the council ordered the London militia commissioners to send two troops to join the regulars at Blackheath. There is no evidence that the militia went unwillingly: when the danger was over, the council not only thanked the lord mayor, but asked the army colonels to convey its appreciation of 'soe good an affection in those of the Country which appeared with you': SP 25/98, fo. 99.

[47] The list of officers is printed in Politicus, no. 580, 21–8 July, 620, 622.

[48] For such misinterpretations see Broderick to Hyde, 19 July, CSP iii. 529–30; CSPVen., 48. The act for the additional three months' assessment passed on 2 Aug., justifying itself on the grounds that a tax on real property was the most 'easie and indifferent' method of raising the necessary supplies: A&O ii. 1343.

[49] Politicus, no. 581, 28 July–4 Aug., 639. For other acknowledgements see the letters in CSPD 1659, 88; MS Clarendon 63, fos 193, 203, 243, 263; Nicholas papers, 176; CSPVen., 57; and Guizot, Histoire, i. 466–7.

[50] The promptitude becomes evident when the dates of the precepts are compared with those of the orders of Parliament and council. The precepts are recorded in CLRO, Common Hall minutes, 1659, fos 358, 379–80, 408, 416.

orders from above; rather, he actively investigated and informed the council of potential problems. Royalists combing the state papers after the Restoration found 'proof' of Ireton's 'implacable malice' in no less than seven letters that he had written to various councillors.[51] Their resentment is understandable, since his zeal had so often impeded their agents and foiled their plans. It was, for example, Ireton who interrogated and imprisoned Royalists caught recruiting for Browne in the neighbourhood of Thames Street, and thereby discovered vital details of a 'Design . . . in favour . . . of the late Insurrection in Cheshire' only the day before it was due to happen. His electrifying revelations not only inspired Parliament to issue a declaration warning the 'good people of these Nations and in the City' against Booth's treasonable schemes, but enabled timely practical precautions to be taken. A mayoral precept commanded householders, at their 'utmost perills', to 'strictly look after and keep in their servants and apprentices', unless employed in the City's forces. Besides summoning the extra foot soldiers that Ireton had requested, the council brought in four great guns, doubled all the guards, and enjoined especial vigilance upon the militia commissioners, who conducted a massive search for horses.[52] Meanwhile, Ireton used all the prestige of his office to resist tremendous pressure to summon Common Hall or Common Council, at which assemblies the Presbyterians intended 'to petition for a free Parliament to cause a general insurrection'.[53] Instead, the lord mayor, to the disgust of the Royalists, succeeded in leading the aldermen and common councillors to the Council of State, as Parliament had ordered, and once there set an example of respectful, if silent, attention to the proclamation against the rebels and a 'long harangue', delivered by Whitelocke, requiring the City to aid in the 'preservation of the Commonwealth'.[54] To Ireton therefore belonged a considerable share of the credit for the prevention of the intended rising on this, and other occasions. Ireton's military command was no sinecure: as colonel of

---

51 MS Stowe 185, fo. 157. The list records the recipients – Fleetwood, Scot, Whitelock and Bradshaw – but not the subjects of the letters. One to Fleetwood was almost certainly the letter reporting the *Alarum* cited above; another to Fleetwood, and two to Bradshaw are in MS Clarendon 64, fos 116, 41, 93; council minutes for 7 July, 3 and 9 Aug. indicate the contents of three more.

52 Mayoral precept, 31 July, Common Hall minutes fo. 380; council report to Parliament, *Journal*, 753. Some of Ireton's examinations survive in MS Clarendon 63, fos 167–9. Sessions files for 17 Aug. show three conspirators remanded in custody without bail, while another man, committed by the lord mayor 'for speaking words against the State', was released on providing security for his appearance at the next sessions. The precautions are listed in a report to the council of 9 Aug.

53 Newsletter, 9 Aug., *Clarke papers*, iv. 40. For other references to the anxiety occasioned by the Presbyterian agitation, and its disappointment through Ireton's influence see SP 25/98, fo. 94; *Johnston diary*, 129; Guizot, *Histoire*, i. 395; and *CSPVen.*, 57.

54 The fullest account of the speech, and the lord mayor's reaction, was published in the misnamed *Humble address of the Lord Maior*, 6. The description is that of the displaced council president Wariston: *Johnston diary*, 129. For the Royalist reaction see *Londoners*, 5–6.

the horse, he not only led the City militia to Blackheath at the outset of the rebellion, but thereafter directed nocturnal patrols whenever trouble threatened.[55] As militia commissioner, Ireton's responsibilities did not cease with the raising of the new forces; rather, he was assigned oversight of the important committees for the issue of passes and the collection of the lists of arms required by the Householders' Act, answering to the council for any negligence on the part of his fellow commissioners.[56] The defence of the Republic's interest in the City was clearly an onerous, but not an ungrateful task: though his performance was not invariably satisfactory, the lord mayor received the council's thanks for his 'great Care of the publique peace' on at least three occasions.[57]

The incontestable importance of Ireton's contribution has generally been viewed as an adequate explanation of Parliament's controversial resolution, on the 2 September, to recommend him for a second term, instead of allowing a free election. Woolrych views this as an indication that relations with the City, bad ever since the Militia Act, were now 'deteriorating', and asserts that, despite the defeat of the rebellion, 'the Rump' still felt 'so dependent . . . on Ireton's loyalty' that it could not bear to dispense with his services. Hutton, too, considers that Ireton had rendered himself 'invaluable', but goes further, situating the intervention on his behalf in the context of the annulment of Chester's charter two weeks later, and suggesting that MPs were attempting a 'similar coup' in the corporation of London.[58] Parliament certainly did justify its decree with a vague appeal to the 'safety of the Commonwealth as of the City', but these interpretations seem mistaken, since they ignore the immediate context. At the height of the rising, a decision that the danger required Ireton's continuance in office would have been understandable, though even then London's security had rested on much more than the loyalty of one man, however great his influence. Describing the dramatic events of the 9 August, the council singled out the lord mayor for special praise, but accorded equal recognition to the efforts of the Army and 'other good men well affected', who had furnished intelligence and served in the volunteer regiments raised to supplement the militia.[59] Since

---

[55] Ireton's role in the Blackheath expedition is plain from the council's letter of thanks: SP 25/98, fo. 99; for his subsequent activities see the army newsletter of 20 Aug. in *Clarke papers*, iv. 47.

[56] MS Rawlinson C79, fo. 290. On 11 Aug. the council ordered the mayor to investigate allegations that those granting passes were 'too liberall of their trust & that any one may have A pass for 6d', and to ensure that he maintained a 'strict observance' of the proceedings: SP 25/98, fo. 151.

[57] MS Rawlinson C79, fo. 402. The council also expressed its thanks to Ireton on 8 July and 1 Aug. The incident of the passes reveals its occasional dissatisfaction with Ireton's performance. In October, as Ireton neared the end of his mayoral term, the council twice had to remind him to enforce publication of the declaration for thanksgiving for the rebellion's defeat: SP 25/98, fo. 212.

[58] Woolrych, 'Introduction', 110–11; Hutton, *Restoration*, 60.

[59] *Journal*, 773; council to the Irish commissioners, 9 Aug., SP 25/98, fo. 94.

the collapse of the conspiracy, the republican hold on the capital seemed stronger than ever. Reports in late August of a 'general Ingagement of Apprentices to make some disturbance' had little foundation, and failed to alarm the council.[60] Even the eternal optimist Mordaunt lamented that those London Royalists still at liberty were plunged into 'general despair' – a 'sad change' from their former hopefulness; Hyde counselled him not to risk himself by further endeavours to rouse them, since it was now 'plain that they have not the courage to do any thing'. By early September the council felt secure enough to accede to the militia commissioners' request to reduce the 'great expense' of constant duty by returning the horses to their owners.[61] Renewed confidence was thus replacing the acute anxiety of the summer. With the Royalists so thoroughly subdued, and the situation apparently stable, Ireton was, if anything, less necessary than before. Contrary to Woolrych's supposition, MPs were not usually given to irrational fears, and disliked dependence on overmighty individuals. Nor had they as yet shown much inclination for radical schemes to reform even such obviously delin-quent corporations as Chester, much less the ostensibly loyal City of London. The fragile calm after the summer storms was surely the last moment at which men as politically astute as the Commonwealth's leaders might have been expected to hazard the delicate partnership with the City elite by engaging in gratuitous experiments.

That Parliament suddenly assaulted ancient privileges at this moment was, in fact, due to unexpected provocation offered by the City. It is no coinci-dence that the resolve regarding the lord mayor immediately followed the presentation of a City petition against the 'Creation of new markets in places adjacent'. This address, unlike the two previously offered in the name of the lord mayor, aldermen and Common Council was not published in *Mercurius Politicus*, and appears to have been entirely overlooked by historians. Despite the unpromising subject matter, the text is most illuminating. The City had a long tradition of hostility to new markets outside its control: the new petition boasted that since the fourteenth century all attempts to establish them had been 'rendered fruitless, the City insisting upon their rights by Quowarrants and otherwise'. In particular, it attacked 'the now Earl of Clare', for whose benefit the notorious republican Henry Marten had recently steered a bill for the creation of a free market in Lincoln's Inn fields through its first two read-ings.[62]

---

[60] Ireton to Bradshaw, 27 Aug., enclosing information on an apprentice plot to seize the Tower: MS Clarendon 64, fos 93, 91. The story rested on the unsupported, secondhand testimony of one junior apprentice against his senior, who was arrested. As no disturbance had occurred on the evening in question, the council took little notice, and on 6 Sept. it ordered its committee for examinations to release the suspect on security.

[61] Mordaunt to Charles II, Sept., and Hyde to Mordaunt, 19/9 Sept., CSP iii. 558–61; council minutes, 2 Sept.

[62] The text of the petition survives in CCJ, fo. 207. The bill for a free market was first read

Had the City been content to appeal to the 'Justice of Parliament' to protect the 'Libertyes and priviledges . . . so Legally Established and long enjoyed', it is improbable that MPs would have been alarmed. But the petition went far beyond such modest objectives. Foretelling that Clare's activities, and by implication Parliament's bill, would 'destroy the very being and subsistence of this great and populous City by drawing away the Trade thereof', it threatened that the citizens would become 'unable to bear any Considerable part of that great Tax which they have readily paid'. The City even offered tactless, if accurate, criticism of the 'great disproportion' between its tax burden and that of 'the rest of the Nation and specially . . . their neighbours in Middlesex'. By claiming that London's very survival was at stake, the petitioners sought to deny Parliament any freedom of manoeuvre, insisting that only compliance with their demands would produce a 'higher Engagement of . . . the whole City upon all Occasions to adhere to . . . the Government of the Commonwealth'. There was, of course, another side to this story: the vilified Clare, in a letter to Marten, expressed astonishment that the City had even demanded another hearing, and vividly recalled the unanimous vote against them at a committee meeting in 1652, after a lengthy debate attended by the City's lawyers, 'sheriffs and all their officers'. Not just the petition's extravagant expressions and substantial criticisms, but the attempt to reverse this previous vote gave Parliament good cause to resent an affront to its authority. Though the petition itself could be dismissed to the appropriate committee, it is hardly surprising that the anxious members, remembering that the mayoral election was due to take place at the end of the month, hastily resolved upon Ireton's continuance, in the hope that he could prevent further challenges from his colleagues.[63]

Such hopes were destined to disappointment. As the election drew near, it became apparent that the decision to dictate the result had been a miscalculation of potentially disastrous proportions. Ireton himself had not been consulted, and proved unwilling to comply with an invasion of privilege denounced by the increasingly discontented citizenry as worse than anything that monarchs or previous Parliaments had ever attempted. Rather than recommend Parliament's resolve to the aldermen, he readily acceded to their request to summon Common Council, ostentatiously absented himself from the meeting and presented his own petition of protest.[64] Yet even at this critical juncture, Common Council, chastened by the demonstration of Parliament's displeasure, produced a conciliatory petition which resembled the previous one only in requesting continued protection for the City's 'rights

on 8 Aug. and reached committee stage four days later; on 20 Aug. the committee was enlarged: *Journal*, 751, 757, 763.

[63] John, earl of Clare to Henry Marten, 2 Sept., Bodl. Lib., MS Dep. C. 159, fo. 165.

[64] Rep. 66, fo. 311; Ireton's own petition was presented with that of the City on 28 Sept. On the discontent caused by Parliament's invasion of privilege see the letters in Bodl. Lib., MS Carte 213, fo. 301; CSP iii. 568–9; Guizot, *Histoire*, i. 478; CSPVen., 70–2.

and privileges'. Instead of dwelling on the dangers of innovation, the City fathers stressed the order and stability founded upon the 'strong supports' of 'Laudable Customs' and 'Ancient Charters'. Far from complaining, this petition respectfully recalled Parliament's many promises to 'be mindful of the merit of the City', and extolled 'the love, peace and happiness this great and populous City hath enjoyed under this Government'. More important, the petition attempted to reconcile the City's freedom and Parliament's authority: confident that there were those, 'among the several very worthy persons whom God . . . hath given us in succession', who would be both 'Serviceable to the Peace and Safety of the City' and 'acceptable to your honors', London's magistrates promised to 'cheerfully submit' their choice to the authority of the 'Supreme Power'. As willing alternatives were available, Ireton was clearly not so central to the safety of City and Commonwealth as MPs had momentarily supposed.[65]

This compromise, offered with due deference and assurances of the City's hostility to the 'Common Enemy', proved acceptable to Parliament. Despite opposition from an obdurate minority, including Vane's satellite Richard Salway and Colonel Nathaniel Rich, a Fifth Monarchist who may well have shared his co-religionists' impatience with the 'pomp and fooleries' of ancient forms of government, the ungodly Marten led a substantial majority of MPs in voting, on 28 September, to concede the City its cherished 'liberty to make choice of their Mayor according to their Charter'.[66] Parliament was therefore wise enough to perceive and correct misguided policies, recognising that Ireton was not, in fact, the only candidate who could be trusted with the reins of the City. The reversal of the former vote had two immediate results: the election of the unexceptionable Thomas Allen, whom Giavarina, with typical exaggeration, characterised as 'entirely devoted to parliament and utterly opposed to monarchy', and the restoration of good relations between City and Parliament. On the very next day Common Council resolved to invite MPs, councillors, Army officers and other Commonwealth dignitaries to a banquet after the public thanksgiving for the defeat of the rebellion. Explaining the invitation as an expression of 'our real affections and the surety of our hearts to this Parliament and our desire to strengthen your hands', the aldermen and deputies sent to Westminster returned with Parliament's grateful acceptance of their 'message of great Civility'.[67] Not only the sermon, which proclaimed the 'Union, Union Union . . . of hearts, of Parliament, City, and Armie', but the expensive entertainment that followed affirmed the harmony between London's rulers and the Commonwealth. Free markets seemed to have been forgotten by all parties; the only discordant

---

65 The text of this petition is in CCJ, fo. 208 (23 Sept.).

66 *True catalogue*, 66; *Journal*, 788. Salway and Rich were the tellers for the Noes, who gained only 13 votes; Marten and John Lenthal were tellers for the majority, who numbered 38.

67 CSPVen., 75; CCJ, fo. 209; *Journal*, 791.

note was struck by a Quaker who attempted to prophesy imminent judgement, and he was swiftly silenced. Even the diplomats were impressed by the 'great splendour' of the occasion; loyal newsbooks printed glowing reports of the City's 'new testimonies of their old fidelity, honour and good affection towards the Parliament', and the 'mutual congratulations' of the distinguished persons present.[68]

With due allowance for editorial overstatement, there seems to be little reason to doubt the sincerity of these professions of solidarity between MPs and City magistrates. The evidence simply does not support Woolrych's contention that relations declined from bad to worse, with the City resentful and sullenly 'on its guard' even after Parliament responded favourably to its protests.[69] If anything, relations had improved: the willingness of both sides to compromise had resolved the impasse over the election of the new lord mayor, and established their partnership on a firmer foundation than ever. Disaffection was certainly a major problem, especially among the apprentices, but it was counterbalanced in London, as elsewhere, by the enthusiasm of the 'well-affected', and the acquiescence of the majority, who preferred the stability offered by the Republic to the perils of rebellion. London's peculiar importance, however, necessitated extraordinary security measures, and unusually heavy fiscal demands. Thanks to the compliance of the elite, which did much to maintain order, and the zeal of the most loyal citizens, these policies – however unpopular – proved effective. Aided by the lord mayor, Parliament actively pursued a good understanding with the City rulers, responding to grievances and attaining the majority of its goals by a judicious mixture of firmness and flexibility. That the republicans succeeded, despite the glare of publicity and the outpouring of inimical propaganda, in governing London, 'the chief Theater of publick Affairs', was surely one of their most significant achievements.[70]

---

[68] Nathaniel Holmes, A SERMON Preached before the Parliament, the Councill of State, the Lord Major, Aldermen & Common Councill of the City of London, and the Officers . . . Oct. the 6th, 37; CSPVen., 77; Guizot, Histoire, i. 492; PI, no. 197, 3–10 Oct., 777; Scout 30 Sept.– 7 Oct., 190. Bordeaux, however, was most impressed by the disturbance caused by the Quaker, Daniel Baker, who published his own condemnation of the festivities: The PROPHET APPROVED By the WORDS Of his Prophesie coming to passe.

[69] Woolrych, 'Introduction', 111.

[70] This description of the capital was employed by William Sprigge in his Modest Plea For An Equal Common-wealth Against Monarchy, 52.

5

Ruling the Provinces

There is a general disaffection, nay hatred throwout the Counties, unto the Government; and that more now then in the time of the late Usurper: James Harrington, A *DISCOURSE Shewing That the Spirit of Parliaments . . . Is not to be trusted for a Settlement*, July 1659.

All men in Citty, Towne and Country [are] soe Inclyned to his majesties service as Cannot be believed, and people Engaged soe impatient for the tyme to begine: Sparke to Hyde, 28 July 1659.

William Parsons said about midsummer that the Parliament . . . were not men sufficient but were fools and turncoats and lived on other mens means . . . that it would not be peace until there was a King . . . that we should see the Parliament turn for that the King would be here the next week: information against William Parsons of Kingsbury, 22 Sept. 1659.

We are ready to our utmost to promote that great and pretious cause for the welfare of this Commonwealth which you have soe highly asserted . . . and doe blesse the Lord that through this capacity . . . we can freely declare ourselves . . . owners of that interest which shall be dearer unto us than our lives & estates: Somerset militia commissioners to the council, 11 July 1659.

No analysis of the restored Commonwealth could be complete without exploring the relationship between the centre and the provinces. In recent decades, numerous local studies have rightly challenged the primacy accorded the view from Westminster by the older narrative histories. Central initiatives without implementation are clearly as unavailing as central perceptions alone would be misleading. Important as the capital was, the vast majority of subjects never visited it, experiencing national changes only as they affected their local communities. Evidence of provincial reactions thus not only corrects the distortion inherent in central sources, but affords a significant test of the regime: the republicans were keenly aware that failure to establish their authority in the localities would be no less fatal than the loss of London. Appraising their success requires careful exploration of the complex interaction between the members at Westminster and the various interests of their constituents.

In local government, as so much else, the Republic's achievement has been obscured by conflicting contemporary perceptions. Hostile propagandists, eager to maximise discontent, portrayed the new regime as arbitrary, anarchical and indifferent to local needs; Parliament's defenders, predictably, affirmed the contrary. The epigraphs that head this chapter exemplify the partisan positions. Reactionary optimists were quick to detect a ubiquitous readiness to rebel. Dissatisfied republican theorist James Harrington commended his ideal constitution by contrasting its potential popularity with the 'general disaffection' from the imperfect existing Commonwealth. That discontent existed is indisputable: William Parsons was one of many ordinary Somerset residents who audibly disparaged Parliament, and anticipated the king's return. Such murmuring, however, suggests resentment of the prevailing taxes and instability rather than sufficient affection for Charles Stuart's person to risk anything in his cause. Nor was disrespect for the Republic universal: the 'several persons' who reported Parsons's seditious comments to a magistrate plainly did not share his attitude. Far from resisting or refusing to co-operate, Somerset's serving militia commissioners were eager to impress the council with their zeal and dedication to Parliament's service.[1]

Historians have inclined towards the negative view, portraying the Republic's unpopularity in the provinces as a major factor in its failure. Thus Woolrych substantiates his assertion that 'the return of the Rump was most unwelcome' by quoting Harrington without acknowledging his bias, and suggests that the Commonwealth could only have survived by conceding 'reasonably representative Parliaments' to the 'uncommitted country gentry' and corporations. Davies contended that the Republic faced the 'indifference or passive resistance of a large class . . . alienated by . . . the work of reformation', and progressing inexorably towards 'open revolt'. These judgements not only overlook the evidence of enthusiasm and commitment, but assume that a successful government must be generally popular, or at least representative. According to Woolrych, Richard Cromwell's Protectorate, its popularity attested by a 'great sheaf' of loyal addresses, could have provided a lasting settlement; Parliament, necessarily unpopular, since restored by the 'hated swordsmen', could not. Yet popularity, however desirable, is notoriously difficult to measure, and by no means indispensable: effective government owes far more to efficient administration and the monopoly of force than to the nebulous asset of popular support. Moreover, the simple dichotomy between 'popular' and 'unpopular' is inadequate, since it conceals the whole spectrum of responses between the extremes of outright opposition and enthusiastic support. Without considering such diversity, and the policies adopted by Whitehall, it is impossible to rightly appreciate the Commonwealth's impact on the provinces.[2]

Rebellion, and its precursor, conspiracy, were, of course, the local reactions that Parliament most feared. At considerable risk of capture, Royalist agents,

---

[1] [?] Sparke to Hyde, 20 July, MS Clarendon 62, fo. 158; James Harrington, *A DISCOURSE Shewing That the Spirit of Parliaments, With a Council in the Intervals, Is not to be trusted for a Settlement: Lest it introduce MONARCHY, and Persecution*, 5; *Somerset quarter sessions records*, ed. E. H. Bates (Somerset Record Society, 1907), iii. 368; Somerset militia commissioners to the council, 11 Aug., MS Clarendon 63, fo. 185.

[2] Woolrych, 'Introduction', 97–8; Davies, *Restoration*, 96.

such as Mordaunt in the south-east and Massey in the west, toured the provinces, trying to transform antipathy to the Republic into practical assistance, financial and military, for the Stuart cause. Urging the advantages of an immediate insurrection, they insisted that Charles II had 'never had a fairer game than now', since the Protectorate's demise had left his enemies divided and 'discontents general every where'.[3] Nor did their arguments fall entirely on deaf ears: correspondence with the exiled court abounds with allusions to the contacts established and promises obtained from influential local figures. Great things were expected both from Presbyterians, including Sir George Booth in Cheshire and Alexander Popham in Bristol, and Royalists, especially Sir Marmaduke Langdale in Yorkshire and Sir Horatio Townsend in Norfolk. From such individual interests the activists wove an elaborate design for a universal uprising on 1 August. By the eve of its outbreak, Mordaunt considered 'the confusion . . . now so great' that 'dayly and hourely considerable people turn to the King'.[4] Yet the rising itself belied his optimism. In most areas, the conspirators either failed to assemble at all, or else were easily dispersed and arrested. Even in the north-west, where Sir George Booth scored a remarkable immediate success, gathering 4,000 men and seizing control of Cheshire and adjacent parts of Lancashire, many gentry, including such former Cavaliers as Somerford Oldfield, avoided involvement.[5] So, too, did large numbers of their social inferiors. Notwithstanding desperate efforts to rally support by suitable propaganda, the Cheshire revolt failed to inspire similar movements in other provinces, and so was easily suppressed. For all the hopes and endeavours of Mordaunt and his fellow plotters, rebellion itself was clearly the preferred activity of only a small, if vocal, minority of the regime's enemies.

That there was no automatic progression from resentment to actual resistance was due not only to the effectiveness of government precautions, but to the superior attractions of alternative responses. Many of Charles's most loyal adherents rejected, or gave only a lukewarm or conditional assent, to the calls for rebellion. Instead, they chose inaction or even a humiliating submission to the Republic. Very soon after July's Act against Delinquents, the council was inundated with petitions from former enemies promising peaceful

---

3   Brasy to Hyde, 13 May, MS Clarendon 60, fo. 541. For similar assertions see ibid. fos 466, 500, and *Nicholas papers*, 130.

4   Mordaunt to Hartgill Baron, 26 July, printed in *Mordaunt letter book*, 32. For the hopes of Booth etc. see *CSP* iii. 477, 498; *Nicholas papers*, 97–8, 157, 175; and MS Clarendon 63, fo. 49.

5   On Booth's revolt see J. S. Morrill, *Cheshire, 1630–1660: county government and society during the English Revolution*, Oxford 1974, 300–23. Morrill asserts that only 28 leading gentlemen are known to have identified with Booth. If Somerford Oldfield's diary is accurate, the rising had little impact on his ordinary routine of visiting, hunting, churchgoing and supervising agricultural activities. The diary survives in Cheshire Record Office, Chester, DSS/Drawer 5.

demeanour in return for exception from banishment.[6] The conflicting counsels of the Royalists in 1659 were rooted in the longstanding rivalry between
the Sealed Knot and the 'Action Party'. Mordaunt and other activists bitterly
attacked the excessive caution and delays advocated by the Knot, and attributed the eventual failure of the rebellion to the combination of 'unhappy
accidents, ill management in some particulars', and, supremely, 'cowardice,
which this degenerate age calls prudence'.[7] Self-preservation was, indeed, a
powerful disincentive to revolt among those who still had much to lose:
Bordeaux shrewdly observed that 'many talk or spread rumours without
intending to risk themselves'. As the risks to life and estate remained considerable, there was an understandable reluctance to support another rising
before its success seemed probable. In Gloucestershire, Massey complained
that the most generous contributions came from the least prosperous 'friends',
and that the 'great ones' gave nothing at all.[8] Though it was easy for the exiles
to condemn the wariness of such individuals as simple self-interest, the case
for inaction did possess considerable merits. On the one hand, it could claim
superior realism: the memory of past failures amply justified the depressing
conclusion that monarchists could not prevail without external assistance.
As late as July, pessimists implored Hyde to prevent a rising until the king
could 'appear with a force which may be a sanctuary for some and an encouragement for others', and warned that premature action would be a useless
sacrifice, enabling the republicans to establish themselves by making a
'plaister of the Cavaliers' blood to cure their own wounds'. Such emotive
appeals made ideological as well as practical sense: since the Commonwealth
was an intrinsically anarchical form of government, its enemies had only to
wait for its chaotic tendencies to produce renewed divisions among Army and
Parliament. As rebellion threatened to check those tendencies and reunite
republicans, it was not just impolitic but potentially ruinous – 'the most
destructive thing in the world' for the royal cause.[9]

If passive obedience to the Republic pending the cataclysm appealed so
strongly to convinced monarchists, it was equally attractive to the many
neutrals who had never sought entanglement in national quarrels. Passivity

---

[6] The Act against Delinquents passed on 13 July: two days later the council was obliged to
establish a subcommittee to receive the petitions and make recommendations; on the
30 July the council accorded 58 Royalist petitioners an additional fortnight in which to
gather sufficient security.
[7] [?] Cooper to Hyde, 12 Sept., CSP iii. 555. For earlier attacks on the Sealed Knot see
Mordaunt's letters ibid. 517–18, 518–19, 524–5, and Mordaunt letter book, 32.
[8] Bordeaux to Mazarin, 24 May, Guizot, Histoire, i. 403; Massey to Nicholas, 23 June,
Nicholas papers, 138–9.
[9] [?] Ashton to Hyde, 15 July, CSP iii. 525–6. Activists, of course, condemned such
passivity as an abdication of responsibility: see, for example, the critique of Gervase Holles,
who deplored the fact that 'we sleep and appear not, expecting . . . that God . . . shall
perform our partes for us', and insisted that 'if we keep our swords in ye sheath, you will
hardly heare that they cut their own throates': Nicholas papers, 139.

could, however, take various forms. At one extreme were those, especially evident among the greater gentry and nobility, who withdrew completely from public affairs, declining either to serve or oppose the central government. The felicity of such seclusion may occasionally be glimpsed in private correspondence: in Somerset one former Royalist, though beset by the attentions of the regime's spies, contrasted the 'Jangling' of the 'publick Governments' with the calm of his 'private . . . lytell Commonwealth . . . which shall have no relation . . . in the old trubelsome Cause of this place'. Retirement to the private sphere of 'good Company good firs good cheer and good fidlers' was, of course, neither a new nor an exclusively Cavalier reaction.[10] Several important ex-Parliamentarians, including Fairfax and Booth himself, had remained aloof for most of the decade, resisting all attempts to secure their participation. Others, encouraged by the conservative trends of the later Protectorate, had proved more susceptible to Cromwellian blandishments, and begun to drift back into their traditional role as JPs. The retreat of these men upon the Republic's revival resulted in a sharp decrease in the number of active justices in some areas, such as the North Riding of Yorkshire, where the magistrates had shown particular enthusiasm for the Protector.[11]

Complete withdrawal from public service was not, however, the commonest elite reaction to the restored Republic. More frequently, local office-holders acquiesced in the changes, and continued to transact business as usual. In many counties, including Devon, Warwickshire, Kent and Wiltshire, pre-existing trends at quarter sessions persisted, since a majority of the same justices remained active.[12] There was therefore no 'inexorable withdrawal of cooperation by the gentry as JPs' from May 1659, as John Morrill and John Walter have suggested.[13] Corporations, whose magistrates could

---

10 A. Poulett to Hugh Smyth at Long Ashton, Somerset, St Stephens Day (26 Dec.) and 4 Dec. (years unspecified), Bristol Record Office, Ashton Court MS C/C64, fos 9, 15. On the general phenomenon of retirement, and its variations, see Maren-Sofie Rostvig, *The happy man: studies in the metamorphoses of a classical ideal*, I: 1600–1700, Oslo 1962.

11 Of 14 JPs present at the North Riding sessions in 1658–9, only 5 continued to attend after the fall of Richard Cromwell. Though 2 of the absentees, Luke Robinson and Sir John Bourchier, were active in the restored Parliament, a 50% decrease in attendance had taken place. The JPs in this area had been unusually zealous in prosecuting those accused of 'seditious and scandalous words' against the Lord Protector: *North Riding quarter session minutes & orders*, ed. J. C. Atkinson (North Riding Record Society vi, 1888), 14, 17, 18.

12 On Devon see S. K. Roberts, *Recovery and Restoration in an English county: Devon local administration, 1646–70*, Exeter 1985; on the Warwickshire JPs see the tables in Ann Hughes, *Politics, society and civil war in Warwickshire, 1620–1660*, Cambridge 1987, 353–7. In Wiltshire, comparison of the JPs recorded in the order book as present at the various sessions reveals that 63% of those active in 1658 continued as usual; the withdrawal of the rest was partly compensated for by the reappearance of four nominated but inactive in that year: WRO, A1/160/2, 1654–68. A similar comparison for the Kent JPs whose presence is recorded in the quarter sessions order books (KRO, E. Kent 1, W. Kent 2) and at the assizes (ASSI 35/100/4) reveals a 61% continuity rate.

13 J. Walter and J. S Morrill, 'Order and disorder in the English Revolution', repr. in J. S. Morrill, *The nature of the English Revolution*, London 1993, 359–91 at p. 389. This

seldom afford the luxury of retirement, manifested equal continuity: surviving borough records chronicle mundane administrative matters, and seldom or never allude to national events. But the general silence did not denote ignorance or indifference to possible local implications of the return of the Commonwealth. Parliament's refusal to concede retrospective validity to the Protectorate's legislation invited scrupling. The city of York was unusual only in its formal suspension of one law made since the interruption until confirmed by Parliament. In Leicester a humble hospital trustee, alarmed by the news that 'what hath byne done since the parliaments late disturbance is null', expressed unwillingness to act without the endorsement of the mayor and a majority of his fellows.[14] Though only nine corporations formally recognised Parliament by preparing petitions, others approached the new government by indirect means, sending delegations or addressing letters to individual MPs or Army officers.[15]

Mere activity at the local level was, of course, compatible with a distinct lack of enthusiasm for the Republic. The clerk recording the July sessions in Lancashire abandoned the Lord Protector's name, but failed to substitute the new official style, the 'Keepers of the Liberty of England by Authority of Parliament' – that appeared only in October, after the suppression of the rebellion. Whether his conduct was due to actual disaffection or mere inertia, it still betrays a distinct absence of zeal for the new government. At Sawbridgeworth, Hertfordshire, Sir Thomas Hewet, a long serving JP related to Fleetwood, expressly refused to swear allegiance to the Commonwealth, yet still called himself a 'civil Magistrate', and was 'active beyond measure and beside his Authority'. Or so the local Quakers who suffered from his exertions reported.[16] Such recalcitrance was not unique. In September Major Waring, commander of the Shrewsbury garrison, complained that only three Shropshire justices had taken the new engagement of loyalty: as eight had

---

article links decreasing co-operation to the erosion of army unity, but as the latter process did not begin until October, that judgement seems premature. In May Parliament established its *de facto* authority as successfully as any previous regime.

[14] York City Archives, York Corporation Assembly minute book, fo. 127; *Records of the borough of Leicester*, ed. H. Stocks, Cambridge 1923, iv. 460.

[15] The nine were Colchester, Newcastle, Berwick, Worcester, Norwich, York, Stamford (*Journal*, 666, 673, 693, 706, 723, 734, 755), Salisbury (whose petition was never actually presented, but is in its minutes: WRO, G23/1/4, Ledger D, fo. 117) and Ipswich (whose petition also failed to secure a reading, but the existence of which is attested in a letter to the Speaker of 23 Aug.: MS Tanner 51, fo. 121). Corporations preferring indirect approaches include Leicester, which turned to Hesilrig and Fleetwood (*Leicester records*, iv. 457), and Beverley, which sent a delegation, and later a letter, to James Nelthorp: Humberside Record Office, Hull, Beverley Corporation minutes, BC II/7/4/1, fos 100, 101.

[16] Lancashire Record Office, Preston, quarter sessions order book, QSO/2/32 1659; *Further evidence of . . . Thomas Hewet*, 2, 4. For another side to this story, defending Hewet's respectability without denying his disaffection, see *QUESTIONS Propounded to George Whitehead and George Fox, who disputed by turns against one University-Man in Cambr. Aug. 29 1659*, 1660, 24.

appeared at the midsummer sessions, it was clearly possible to be diligent in provincial administration yet avoid direct commitment to a distasteful central authority.[17]

The division among the Shropshire JPs reflected a fundamental tension in the relationship between the provinces and the centre. Though the readiness of so many office-holders to discharge their ordinary duties was welcomed at Westminster, since it ensured that local government continued to function normally, their loyalty to the Republic was justly suspect, since they were often unwilling to implement its extraordinary directives. The limits of acquiescence were thoroughly exposed by the reaction to the Militia Act, an ambitious attempt to mobilise all the provinces against the anticipated rising by creating a new militia. Enforcement was entrusted to approximately 1,600 commissioners, of whom over half were JPs or corporation officials not known to be disaffected.[18] Hopes that the involvement of such worthies would unite the localities against the common enemy were soon dashed. The vast majority were not prepared to engage in the unpopular task of assessing their neighbours and raising yet more forces: surviving correspondence from the county commissioners suggests that never more than 40 per cent, and sometimes as few as 13 per cent, of those nominated actually served.[19] A significant stumbling block, or, in some cases, a convenient excuse, was the required engagement of loyalty. In Northamptonshire, one-third of the available commissioners never even answered the summons to meet; less than half of those who did assemble consented to the oath, and these proceeded to decide the necessary forces only after spending most of the day in fruitless endeavours to persuade the rest to a 'union in the Commonwealth'. Major Rainsborough, reporting this debacle to his fellow commissioner Adam Baynes in London, nevertheless emphasised the essential unity and loyalty to the Republic of those appointed. The non-jurors would, he insisted, explain 'their constant affections to the Parliament and the scruples that hindered

---

17 Waring to Lenthall, Shrewsbury, 3 Sept., MS. Dep. C. 159, fo. 187. The eight present at midsummer are recorded in *Orders made by the court of quarter sessions for Shropshire*, i, ed. R. L. Kenyon, Shrewsbury 1901.

18 Comparing the militia commissions with the 1658 commissions of the peace gives a national minimum average of 57%; this rises to 66% for counties where the 1659 commissions are available. This proportion represented around 45% of the JPs nominally available; it included both the activists and some others whose involvement at sessions was minimal or non-existent.

19 These estimates were derived by counting signatories of commissioners' letters to Parliament or the council, and comparing them with the total number of commissioners for that county listed in the Militia Act and not engaged in the Republic's service elsewhere. As many of these letters do not survive, this method offers only a rough and partial guide to activity. The highest percentage is that for Somerset, where 22 of 56 possible commissioners signed; the lowest that for Warwickshire, where only 4 of 30 commissioners signed. Corporations generally had higher percentages, since fewer commissioners were appointed: thus in Canterbury 83%, or 10 of a possible 12, were active, while for Bristol and Newcastle the figures were 54% and 53% respectively.

them from acting'; many of them had agreed that the recommended forces represented a 'fitt proportion'. To Rainsborough, the readiness of the larger number to serve and obey the new government clearly outweighed their reluctance to swear allegiance – a judgement substantiated by his earlier success in securing an official address, which advised placing the militia in 'safe hands', from the sheriff, justices and grand jury assembled for the county assizes.[20] But other activists showed far less sympathy for the objections of their proposed colleagues. In Shrewsbury Waring, eager to arrange an early meeting, was frustrated by the refusal of half the nominees in town to appear at all, and the reluctance of the remainder to act until all those resident in the county had been summoned; he ascribed these setbacks to the deplorable influence of the 'sordid spirits of formerly profest friends in this town, and now secret inimyes', and gloomily predicted that very few commissioners would serve.[21]

Not Rainsborough's tolerance but Waring's impatient distrust was the more typical reaction of zealous republicans to obstructive local elites. The 'well-affected' minority quickly perceived the discrepancy between Parliament's promise to entrust office only to faithful godly commonwealthsmen and the actual survival of so many unrighteous and reactionary magistrates. As militia commissioners, some Quakers 'madded the rest' of their more pragmatic colleagues by cross-examining officer-candidates on their conformity to the virtuous standard prescribed. Disillusioned Fifth Monarchists protested at the failure to appoint JPs with a 'through principle of godliness', and attacked the plans for 'Raising such a Militia in the Nation as hardly ever was the like, & that it should be put into the hands of such retches as some of them are'.[22] The summer's experiences did nothing to disprove such denunciations. Reports to Westminster from military commanders and loyal officials from Lambert downwards resound with the frustrations and dangers that resulted from trusting authority to unco-operative and disaffected local elites. In Staffordshire, Captain Backhouse treated the emergency as an excuse to arrest not only known Royalists and Roman Catholics, but several important officials, including Thomas Whitby, a JP and receiver-general of the county revenues, and the mayor of Stafford himself. Backhouse justified his actions on the grounds that these men had been 'slow in this Juncture of time to give incouragement though much desired to assist . . . in the putting the towne in a posture of defence'. At Harwich, Major Nehemiah Bourne accused the local governor of having 'too lightly passed over' an attempt to declare for the king, and complained that the 'spirit and temper of this country . . . [like] the rest of

[20] Rainsborough to Adam Baynes, Northampton, 6 Aug., MS Add. 21425, fo. 104. The Northamptonshire address, presented to Parliament by Rainsborough on 19 July, was printed in *PI*, no. 186, 18–25 July, 594–5.
[21] Waring to the council, Shrewsbury, 3 Aug., MS Clarendon 63, fo. 111.
[22] George Fox to Bristol Friends, recommending this example if they agreed to act: FHL, MS vol. 359, fo. 157; Jo. Christal to Fleetwood, 26 July, BL, MS Sloane 4165, fo. 28.

the nation . . . are embittered and malignant, and want nothing but opportunity and power to give trouble to the Army'; the brunt of the blame for this state of affairs he assigned to the inflammatory preaching of the local clergy. At Exeter, one of Bennet's correspondents believed the influence of the Presbyterian ministers so great that 'to Arme this Cittie & Countie by way of militia [was] to Arme . . . enemies', and prophesied an immediate rebellion in both 'City & County' if news ever came that 'our forces [had been] worsted or foiled'. After the rebellion, sequestration commissioners delighted in humiliating Chester's disloyal magistrates, scandalising conservatives by making the mayor stand 'hat in hand while they [sat] in his place', and imprisoning the minister and several recalcitrant aldermen.[23]

Conscious of their own isolation, and the vociferous discontent of the Presbyterians, 'well-affected' individuals tended to live in a state of siege, viewing the localities as so much dynamite apt to explode at the least spark of rebellion. That Booth's rising did not, in the event, produce the general conflagration expected did nothing to diminish this anxiety. Behind the least opposition, even the absence of enthusiasm for the Republic, its dedicated supporters discerned a deep-seated disaffection that demanded radical remedies. Existing office-holders consequently occasioned a desperate critique, culminating in Lambert's officers' attempt, in the Derby petition, to expose the 'grand Apostasizing and Newteral Spirit . . . through the Nations . . . amongst many of those who were intrusted for the safety thereof, very few acting or appearing in several Counties'. This bleak portrait of near-universal local untrustworthiness was, of course, influenced by the need to convince Parliament that it must appoint only reliable and godly officials. Struggles with their opposites simply strengthened the longstanding desire of the 'well-affected' to secure the Commonwealth by achieving a monopoly of power for themselves.[24]

Even without the monopoly that they craved, the 'well-affected' remained an exceptionally influential constituency, whose contribution is hard to underestimate. It was not, of course, homogeneous: scattered in varying numbers throughout the provinces, the faithful included men and women from a wide range of socioeconomic conditions, holding diverse political and religious opinions.[25] What identified these individuals as a meaningful cate-

---

[23] List of persons secured in Stafford by Capt. Backhouse, MS Clarendon 62, fo. 222; Nehemiah Bourne to navy commissioners, Harwich, 18 Aug., *CSPD 1659*, 125–6; Banchild to Bennet, Exeter, 29 Aug., FSL, MS X.d. 483, fo. 126; Randal Holme's Cheshire compilaton, BL, MS Harley 1929, fo. 21.

[24] *The Armies Proposalls to the PARLIAMENT*, 3. Of the same ilk was the *Essay towards settlement*'s attack on the 'abominable treachery, malignity and enmity in many in eminent power and in Armes under them'.

[25] Some indication of the geographic and socioeconomic diversity of the well-affected may be gleaned from post-Restoration use of the surviving papers to identify 230 individuals 'eminently active in informing against and apprehending the Kings Loyall subjects upon the returne of the Rump'. These include not only active militia commissioners and

gory, distinct from their neutral or disaffected neighbours, was their enthusiasm for the Republic. That enthusiasm was first manifested in the
extravagant rhetoric of the congratulatory petitions presented to Parliament:
celebrating its past achievements, together with the 'wonderfull Providences
of God' in its restoration, these announced high hopes for the future settlement of a 'Happy Free-state'.[26] Though Woolrych dismisses such addresses as
'miserably few', they in fact amounted to a considerable achievement. In its
first three months, Parliament received thirty-four petitions of this kind,
representing twenty counties and thirteen towns, mainly in the South and
Midlands. This was just over one-third of the total presented to Richard
Cromwell in twice that time, a total that Woolrych judges remarkable. Even
Giavarina, no friend to the Republic, was temporarily impressed, reporting in
mid-June that Parliament was 'receiving daily the congratulations of the
people and assurances of absolute concurrence'.[27] Unlike those to Richard,
which were primarily official responses from local authorities, the majority of
addresses to Parliament were independent initiatives by its eager adherents in
a particular area – for example, 800 'Assertors of the Good Old Cause, Inhabitants of . . . Buckinghamshire' signed a radical petition applauding the
members' 'honourable resolves' and pressing for a 'just and equal Commonwealth'.[28] Since all the formal professions of loyalty to Richard had produced
no protest at his downfall, the spontaneity of those directed to his successor
need not be taken as a sign of weakness. It is quite unnecessary to follow
Woolrych in crediting unsubstantiated Royalist assertions that these petitions had been 'mostly concocted at Westminster'.[29] Such evidence of their
genesis as exists points to the contrary: Richard Lobb was confident that an
'affectionate petition to the Parliament' subscribed by 'many thousands' of
Cornish tinners would 'speedily' be forthcoming once suitable concessions
were granted, and consulted Robert Bennet only as to the proper style and
timing. The Leveller author of *Panarmonia, or the Agreement of the People
Revived* plausibly maintained that his tract began life as an expression of the
'cordial salutations and well wishes' to Parliament of some 'sober and
well-minded people' in Gloucestershire; its development into a petition was
only prevented by the 'too early rise of another Address, pre-ingaging' many

army officers, but a wide variety of others, ranging from private soldiers, apprentices and
servants through substantial artisans to gentlemen, ministers and one gentlewoman: MS
Stowe 185, fos 157–67.

26 *To the PARLIAMENT . . . The Humble Petition . . . of divers well-affected of the County of
South-hampton.* The similar optimistic themes pervading the petitions reflected common
sentiments, not central manipulation, as cynics supposed – the specific prescriptions
varied, as did the degree of warmth with which Parliament responded.

27 Woolrych, 'Introduction', 97; CSPVen., 33.

28 The Buckinghamshire petition was printed in *Politicus*, no. 569, 26 May–2 June, 471–2.
A manuscript copy, with five additional pages listing 800 signatories (748 if all repeated
names are accidental), survives in BL, MS Egerton 1048, fos 163–9.

29 Woolrych, 'Introduction', 97; cf. *Nicholas papers*, 153.

potential subscribers.[30] Elite involvement in the Buckinghamshire petition seems to have been minimal – just 1 per cent of the signatories were prominent local administrators, a statistic suggesting that a genuinely popular republicanism had revived there, as elsewhere.[31]

Orchestrating loyal addresses that enhanced Parliament's prestige was, however, the least of the services performed by the 'well-affected'. Their enthusiasm also afforded the Republic invaluable assistance in local government, since they were most active in implementing Parliament's policies, and so compensated for the non-performance of the elite. As assessment commissioners, many responded rapidly to the unwelcome command to collect the entire year's tax in three months – at Somerton, the commissioners not only made the necessary apportionments within a week of receiving these orders, but sent a letter to the Speaker promising 'with all possible speede do our utmost that it may be payd in according to your desire'.[32] These were not empty words: though Parliament's targets proved unmeetable, extant accounts reveal a substantial acceleration in collection. Cornwall's receivers delivered a quarter of their annual charge in less than six weeks, and over half by 11 October. Middlesex achieved similarly high proportions, while Shropshire, which suffered greater disruption due to the rebellion, started more slowly, but had paid in a third of the required sum by 5 October.[33] Such energy was rooted in appreciation of the financial problems: despite strong sympathy for the human suffering occasioned by high taxes, Richard Lobb, a Cornish assessment commissioner, understood that 'Parliament [was] much necessitated considering the great debts they found due when they were restored to their iust power to sett againe'. This, the constant explanation offered by the House itself, was naturally more acceptable to loyal citizens than to ordinary taxpayers.[34]

Living among less loyal neighbours, it is hardly surprising that the 'well-affected' were equally convinced by Parliament's call for drastic security measures. Undaunted by their minority status, they proceeded to raise funds

---

[30] Lobb to Bennet, 19 June, Oct., FSL, MS X.d. 483, fos 124, 129; *Panarmonia, Or, The AGREEMENT Of The PEOPLE Revived*, 2.

[31] Nine signatories were JPs or militia commissioners. Buckinghamshire had earlier been a stronghold of Leveller/Digger ideas; the requests in this petition for the supremacy and 'continual succession' of the representative, abolition of tithes etc reflect the 'neo-Leveller' ideas that resurfaced in 1659, and are discussed in ch. 8 below. On the broader phenomenon see Smith, 'Popular republicanism'.

[32] Assessment commissioners to Lenthall, Somerton, 1 July, MS Tanner 51, fo. 90.

[33] Parliament's demand, on 23 June, for half the year's tax to be paid in by 1 Aug., the rest by 10 Oct., was hopelessly unrealistic. Cornwall came closest to meeting the first deadline, delivering 25% by 2 Aug., but only 55% by 11 Oct.; the remainder was paid by 1 Dec.; the sum collected in these six months exceeded the totals for the previous 2 years. For Middlesex the corresponding proportions were 23% by 9 Aug., 56% by 12 Oct. and 98% by 6 Dec., while Shropshire produced 3% by 2 Aug., 33% by 5 Oct. and 92% by 25 Nov. Detailed accounts for these counties may be found in SP/28/334.

[34] Lobb to Bennet, Sept., FSL, MS X.d. 483, fo. 128.

and forces for the new militia, following the instructions in the act almost to the letter. Some experienced much greater difficulty than others. Staffordshire's commissioners rapidly recruited one foot regiment and two horse troops, but pleaded inability to raise the 'very great charge . . . at a very bad tyme', and were briefly detained, in September, by militiamen determined not to be disbanded without pay.[35] The Leicestershire commissioners suffered no such humiliation, but, due to obstinate defaulters, still owed their forces 'considerable sums' in October. Supremely successful, however, were the six activists serving in Sussex, who had collected the charges so efficiently that a £300 surplus remained in December.[36] During the summer emergency, the 'well-affected' also agreed to raise over sixty volunteer companies, usually at the council's invitation, but sometimes on their own initiative: in August one Edward Downs persuaded the council to allow him to form a volunteer horse troop in Staffordshire on the strength of his speed in so doing during the Scottish invasion of 1651.[37] Such forces did play a significant role in local policing – they set watches, conducted searches, made arrests and deterred or dispersed Royalist gatherings in some areas.[38] Stafford's governor, Colonel Crompton, asseverated that the militia had 'under God . . . preserved the Town . . . and Countrie from ruin' during the rising. So strongly did Lobb believe in the efficacy of Cornwall's new militia that he protested hotly against Parliament's decision, in September, to disband it, insisting that 'many honest people [had been] very forward [in it], hoeping future troubles might thereby be prevented'.[39] Less visible than their military activities, but just as valuable, was the role of the 'well-affected' in intelligence – by reporting their neighbours' suspicious behaviour, and giving advance warning of dangerous meetings, they enabled the government to suppress much trouble before it could begin.[40]

[35] Staffordshire militia commissioners to Bradshaw, 22 Sept., MS Dep. C. 159, fo. 183. Suffolk's commissioners suffered similar treatment: ibid. fo. 181. Parliament responded by ordering the fining of defaulters, the proceeds to go to pay off the forces: *Journal*, 779–80.
[36] The proceedings, and accounts, of the Sussex commissioners survive in SP 28/335, fos 50–80; the orders of Leicestershire's militia commissioners are in Bodl. Lib., MS J. Walker C11. Whereas the former charged nearly 200 individuals, and raised over £1,000, the latter assessed only 68 persons, of whom 12 are listed as at least partial defaulters.
[37] These commissions are all recorded in the council minutes; that to Downs was issued on 15 Aug.
[38] See, for example, the glowing account of Thomas Hesilrig's activities as colonel of the Leicestershire new militia in *Politicus*, no. 584, 18–25 Aug., 680. It is not, of course, coincidence that Thomas was the son of leading republican politician, Sir Arthur Hesilrig.
[39] Crompton to the council, 14 Sept., MS Dep. C. 159, fos 185–6; Lobb to Bennet, Sept., FSL, MS X.d. 483, fo. 128.
[40] For example, John Dalron informed Fleetwood on 26 July that he had summoned additional troops as a precautionary measure at the 'Intreaty of most of the honest men' following 'many Alarrarms and strainge Reports dayly that Brisstoll faire would prove annother Salsbury business': MS Clarendon 63, fo. 20. The expected trouble did not materialise. Some indication of the scale and resentment provoked by the spying of the well-affected may be gained from the post-Restoration list identifying 99 private informers,

But active loyalists were not automatons obeying orders from Westminster regardless of their communities. Rather, they sought to communicate local problems to the centre, and offer constructive advice, and even criticisms. Richard Lobb, for example, seems to have seen himself as a mediator between Bennet and his constituents. By representing the latter's needs, Lobb not only hoped to secure redress for specific grievances, such as the high duties on fish and tin, but to recommend local solutions for the national problems of security and finance. In his view, the new militia, once perfectly organised in 'faythful hands', would guarantee Cornish security with troops to spare to quell disturbances beyond the county; he therefore challenged its abandonment as a short-sighted policy that would prove more costly in the long term. Sympathy for the sufferings of impoverished taxpayers induced Lobb to condemn the proposed new assessment of £100,000 as equally misguided: he volunteered to pay an extra £100 himself under a fairer system rather than 'put pen to paper to charge the poore to paye money that have not enough to fynde themselves bread'. More profitable alternatives were available – new rates for the customs and excise, a tax on alehouses and delinquents, and, especially, the extraction of subsidies from 'the worser sort'.[41] Nor was Lobb's advocacy of Cornish interests unique. In the north of England, the Leeds clothiers looked to Adam Baynes and Lambert, his patron, to relieve them of 'the tyranny and oppression of this corporation', warning that the latter's emissaries to London were secret enemies of the Commonwealth. At Hull, Robert Stockdale apprised Baynes of the abuses resulting from the customs officials' drunken and disorderly conduct, and outlined a comprehensive scheme to reform administration of the customs and excise in Yorkshire. His proposals would, he maintained, not only increase revenue but rescue the new government's reputation from the 'rash and irregular actions' of its predecessor's servants: it was especially necessary to conciliate merchants and seamen by just administration 'at such a time as this, when the Commonwealth is but newly restored after a relapse'.[42] For Stockdale, Lobb, and perhaps the majority of loyal individuals who left no record of their views, the Republic's welfare was plainly inseparable from that of the particular local interests that they espoused. And in this they echoed the calculus of local friends of every other regime.

Parliament could not and did not disregard its most faithful and zealous local servants. Instead, the republicans at Westminster devoted much atten-

---

said to have been motivated mainly by 'malice', though sometimes by 'hope or fear'. Though most informers came from closely governed London and the home counties, some resided in regions as distant as Lancashire and Shropshire: MS Stowe 185, fos 165–7.

[41] Lobb to Bennet, Aug., Sept., FSL, MS X.d. 483, fos 127, 128.

[42] Robert Hurst to Baynes, 10 June; Robert Stockdale to Baynes, 16 July, MS Add. 21425, fos 68, 93. On the complex interconnection of central and local interests at Leeds in the 1650s see D. Hirst, 'The fracturing of the Cromwellian alliance: Leeds and Adam Baynes', EHR cviii (1993), 868–94.

tion to the task of retaining their loyalty and encouraging them to persist in their labours. The House returned grateful answers to congratulatory petitions, and graciously signified its acceptance of outstanding services: thus Gloucester received especial thanks and promises of pay for 300 foot raised on the eve of the rebellion. In correspondence with provincial officials, the council customarily preceded exhortations to continued diligence with expressions of gratitude for past efforts: Oxfordshire's militia commissioners, for example, were praised for their 'good affections, unanimous Care and the progress' that they had already made, and rewarded with a buck from Whittlewood forest.[43]

Members themselves showed signs of taking their role as representatives seriously, liasing between the centre and the provinces. To some extent, this was official policy. MPs were appointed to the commissions of the peace and the militia; in late July the House debated sending 'all considerable' members to enforce the Militia Act in their constituencies.[44] Although it then resolved in the negative, such influential individuals as Thomas Purys in Gloucester,[45] William Purefoy in Coventry,[46] Robert Wallop in southern Hampshire and John Fagg in Sussex, did return to serve as militia commissioners with Parliament's approval.[47] Their energetic leadership not only stimulated the 'well-affected' to adopt essential security measures, but secured the central government's swift attention to local needs.[48] Yet less formal contacts were also important. Though he remained at Westminster, Sir Henry Vane had promptly informed his constituents in Hull of Parliament's return, assured them of his constant desire to see the 'Prosperity of [their] town included in the weal of the publike' and invited them to tell him how he could be 'usefull and serviceable'. When radical residents arrived with a

---

43 *Journal*, 743; council to Oxon. militia commissioners, 11 Aug., SP 25/98, fo. 105.

44 Brodrick's report on 22 July of a 'very hot debate' on the question whether to send out MPs or retain them to discuss settlement (MS Clarendon 63, fo. 4) is partly substantiated by that day's resolution requiring constant attendance for two weeks: *Journal*, 728.

45 On 27 July Thomas Purys reported success in raising forces and the need for speedy pay: MS Tanner 51, fo. 97. The council praised their 'great affections Care and Circumspection', promised provision and requested intelligence: SP 25/98, fo. 56.

46 Purefoy declined a military command, pleading age and infirmity, but insisted that his 'vigorous affections' to Parliament's service and 'the welfare of the good people' would not let him be idle, and reported 'good progress': MS Clarendon 63, fos 179, 189.

47 Parliament gave Wallop command of Southamptonshire's horse and foot regiments and sent him to settle the militia there on 15 Aug., after an urgent appeal from the well-affected: ibid. fo. 140; *Journal*, 759. Fagg received command of the Sussex militia, and spent much of the summer riding around the country, conducting searches, arresting suspects and earning the council's commendation for his 'Circumspection and care': SP 25/98, fos 121, 98.

48 MPs' activity in the militia was not always an unmixed blessing, however. In Pembrokeshire a disgruntled officer accused the 'chief Commissioner', Thomas Wogan, who rarely graced Westminster, of using his position to protect, even empower, Royalists and Roman Catholics: MS Clarendon 63, fo. 66.

petition deploring the 'late Apostacy from the Good old Cause', Vane duly introduced them in the House, and obtained its thanks for their 'good affections' after a close division.[49] Herbert Morley used his considerable influence over Sussex affairs to more tangible effect, relieving his 'honoured friends' at Rye of an impecunious, and therefore burdensome, company of regular foot. Robert Bennet carried on an extensive correspondence, explaining central policies to his fellow Cornishmen and representing their views to the House. Through his means, Parliament accepted some advice from its local adherents, and so encouraged them to anticipate further favours. Thus Lobb responded with ecstatic gratitude to the desired reductions in the excise on Cornwall's tin and fish, and hoped that Parliament might now proceed to confirm the tinners' charter.[50]

Such concessions did not, however, imply a willingness to grant all the desires of the 'well-affected'. Until the autumn, Parliament doggedly resisted demands for structural change in local government, and declined to undertake a sweeping purge of provincial elites. In county after county, commissions of the peace were simply renewed according to general lists retaining on average 60 per cent of the Protector's appointees. Cromwellians who had owed their previous inclusion to now redundant official positions rather than local standing were the one group consistently omitted. Despite the numerous recommendations, less than a quarter of the Commonwealth's JPs were new to the bench.[51] Substantial continuity, at least on paper, held good even in those areas where power had reverted to a faction headed by particular MPs, such as John Pyne in Somerset, or Herbert Morley and his kinsmen John Fagg and William Hay in Sussex.[52] Only serious charges of disaffection could provoke central intervention against a particular magistrate, and even then his removal rarely followed. Thus the House summoned Samuel Northcote, the mayor of the strategically sensitive town of Plymouth to answer allegations that he had refused his 'contenance and assistance in the Publication'

---

49 Vane to the mayor and aldermen of Hull, 10 May, Hull Record Office, L.635; *Journal*, 689, 690. Though unpublished, this controversial petition evidently circulated since eclectic republican William Sprigge cited its request for government by the 'holy just righteous Laws' of God: *Modest plea*, 74.

50 Herbert Morley to 'the Mayor, Jurats . . . of Rye', 6 Sept., answering theirs of 30 Aug., ESRO, Rye MS 47/161/2; Lobb to Bennet, 10 Oct., FSL, MS X.d. 483, fo. 129.

51 Such renewals for almost all counties are recorded in the chancery clerks' docket book: PRO, C231/6. The estimated average was obtained by comparing the lists for 1658 and 1659 in six counties: Surrey, Sussex, Kent, Essex, Hertfordshire and Devon. The discrepancy between the proportions of new nominees and survivors from the 1658 list is due to the reduced length of the 1659 list. No other political motive for the omissions is discernible, even where the difference was greatest: in Essex, for example, the 49% reappointed included all those whom the Quakers had denounced as persecutors.

52 On their activities see, respectively, D. Underdown, *Somerset in the civil war and interregnum*, Newton Abbot 1973, and A. Fletcher, *A county community in peace and war: Sussex, 1600–1660*, London 1975. In Sussex continuity was especially pronounced, with 74% of the JPs from 1658 reappointed in 1659.

of the proclamation against Booth, and encouraged ministers and officials to do likewise, so delighting the populace and infuriating the 'well-affected'. The council eventually released him upon mitigating evidence that the proclamation had arrived irregularly, without the sheriff's warrant.[53] This case was, however, extraordinary in that Westminster immediately took control; responsibility for investigating charges was more commonly delegated to authorities on the spot. Thus the council referred a petition complaining that the magistrates of Leeds, in Kent, were 'such as have manifested themselves ill affected to the Parliament' and 'by the law ought not to bear office' to a committee of local officials. Similarly, when a Chichester serjeant was accused of 'scandalous words . . . against the Parliament', the council contented itself with a letter approving the action taken by the town's magistrates and prohibiting his future employment.[54]

Parliament took drastic direct action solely in the case of Chester, rejecting the excuses of its mayor and aldermen, and voting on the 17 September to punish its part in the rebellion by abolishing its charter and status as a separate corporation. As effective power in the city passed to the sequestration commissioners, who duly confiscated the charter and arrested several aldermen, the hopes of 'well-affected Citizens and Inhabitants' for a new government by a smaller number of 'men of approved faithfullness to the Commonwealth' seemed to be on the verge of fulfilment.[55] By this time the House was beginning to contemplate more general reforms, progressing from a bill for the better government of Newcastle to appoint a committee to propose 'fit qualifications of persons to govern the several Corporations within this Commonwealth for the year ensuing'. Meanwhile, the council requested militia commissioners to identify and recommend reliable replacements for all JPs who 'did not actually appear for and own the Parliament in the late tyme of trouble'.[56] But this shift in policy owed less to the arguments of the 'well-affected' than to Army pressure and the experience of recalcitrance among local office-holders during the summer emergency. Contingency rather than planning was always crucial.

---

[53] Sampson Larke to the council, Plymouth, 23 Aug., MS Tanner 51, fo. 125. On 26 Aug. Parliament ordered the mayor to be 'sent for in custody as a Delinquent', and rewarded the constable who had made the proclamation; the council finally released him on 10 Oct. Excuses for the mayor were presented by Edmund Fowell in a letter to the Speaker of 9 Sept.: MS Dep. C, fo. 172.

[54] Council minutes 19 July, MS Rawlinson C79, fo. 175; council to Chichester, 25 Aug., SP 25/98, fo. 174.

[55] Humble proposals of the 'well affected Citizens and Inhabitants' of Chester, MS Harley 1929, fo. 11. For the assumption of power by the sequestration commissioners see ibid. fo. 21. Chester's magistrates denied voluntary involvement in the rising in an indignant letter to the council of 26 Aug.: MS Tanner 51, fo. 123. Given the weight of contrary evidence, it is hardly surprising that this failed to convince Parliament.

[56] *Journal*, 778, 780; SP 25/78, fo. 199.

In general, Parliament did not seek confrontation with existing magistrates unless they were known delinquents or active opponents, preferring stable, if unenthusiastic, local government to the disruption that might attend the exclusive elevation of its most loyal adherents. Anxious to demonstrate their concern for the whole nation, not just the 'well-affected', MPs received and committed petitions from various local interest groups, and granted some favours solicited by corporations that had not hastened to welcome their return.[57] Charitable contributions to relieve fire victims, whose sufferings were represented in petitions from their JPs, constituted a particularly impressive, and inexpensive, method of advertising Parliament's sensitivity to local needs.[58] To extend the basis of support for their rule as far as possible, the republicans tried to conciliate powerful local figures by including them in government, as justices and militia commissioners, and acceding to their requests. Fairfax, for example, was courted by the compliment of appointment to the council; his name headed the Yorkshire militia commission, and his intercession for the duke of Buckingham's exception from the Act against Delinquents was accepted with flattering speed. Such efforts had little success in transforming passive acquiescence into active obedience, but were not wholly ineffective: though Fairfax remained aloof from the Republic, he was equally deaf to Royalist overtures.[59]

As long as provincial rulers appeared compliant and competent, the republicans, preoccupied with urgent national problems, spared no time to supervise their activities. Direct interference in ordinary local government occurred only to reverse changes made during the Protectorate, or quell disorders threatening the Commonwealth's prestige or property. Thus the council in June revoked restraints imposed by its predecessor on the town of Sandwich, whose burgesses were authorised to 'exercise [their] fredomes according to [their] Charter'.[60] In a similar reaction against the illegality of the interruption, Parliament later cancelled charters that Oliver Cromwell had granted to Colchester and Salisbury. Though this resolve was a decisive victory for

---

[57] On 28 May Parliament committed a petition from the 'Pilotes Seamen Fishermen' etc of Lower Deal, Kent, and halted the sale of contested land in that parish pending the investigation: *Journal*, 668. For other examples of responsiveness to petitions from local interests see ibid. 670, 697, 744, 755.

[58] Parliament acceded to four petitions for such contributions, and was celebrated for so doing in *Politicus*, no. 568, 19–26 May, 453; no. 571, 9–16 June, 503; no. 572, 16–23 June, 526; no. 574, 30 June–7 July, 574.

[59] *Journal*, 738. The council had received Fairfax's letter on 26 July; three days later Parliament voted Buckingham's exception, pending the receipt of suitable security; the council then informed Fairfax and requested his attendance with Buckingham. According to one Royalist, they arrived in London by 8 Aug. with 'all maladies and gouts unleft behynde'. By this juncture there was therefore little likelihood that they would act for Charles Stuart: *Nicholas papers*, 179.

[60] Council to Sandwich, 29 June. This letter was not copied into the council's letter book, but the original survives in KRO, 'Miscellaneous letters to Sandwich', fo. 173. Its authenticity is plain from the council minute for 21 June.

the old charter's adherents at Colchester, who had eagerly solicited intervention on behalf of the mayor of their choice, it had little effect on the internal politics of Salisbury, whose aldermen dutifully surrendered their new charter but elected to continue the same mayor and recorder until the end of the year.[61] To repress disorders, the central government normally relied on local justices and sheriffs, to whom it addressed reproving letters enjoining greater diligence. Thus the council, hearing that Sir Charles Howard's tenants at Riddlesdale had been expelled by an 'unlawful assembly' of persons 'taking opportunity of the unsetledness of Government' just before Parliament's return, ordered the JPs and high sheriff of Northumberland to proceed 'according to Law and Justice'. The council's somewhat belated intervention in this instance was clearly motivated by the need to demonstrate the Republic's authority and determination to uphold the law in the remotest regions. Concern to defend the Commonwealth's reputation – in these cases, from aspersions of religious radicalism – also produced council commands that magistrates investigate tumults reportedly caused by Quakers at Brentford and Canterbury.[62]

Where local upheavals threatened more concrete national interests, the regime reacted swiftly, if not always successfully. When commoners, encouraged by the central uncertainty in early May, destroyed fences and trees in the Forest of Dean, a significant naval resource, Parliament itself instructed Gloucestershire's office-holders to restore order, and appointed a committee to preserve the Commonwealth's timber.[63] Although calm did not immediately return – at the end of May complaints of 'continual and frequent riots' were still coming in – Parliament had impressed its presence on the participants, and would show itself receptive to their legitimate grievances. In June a petition from the 'Commoners, Myners freeholders and other Inhabitants', who could plausibly claim to be resisting Protectoral innovations, was read and referred to the forests' committee. Redress was not precluded by Parliament's resolution, on 9 July, to uphold the enclosures in existence at its return; indeed, Parliament repeatedly ordered action to satisfy the petitioners.[64] Yet this resolve, together with the committee's apparent support for

---

61 *Journal*, 722, 745; WRO, Salisbury Common Council minutes G23/1/4, Ledger D, fos 115–16. The conflicts surrounding Colchester's charter were long ago chronicled in J. H. Round, 'Colchester and the Commonwealth', *EHR* xv (1900), 641–64.

62 Council to the high sheriff and JPs of Northumberland, 31 May, SP 25/98, fo. 8. The riot evicting Howard's tenants allegedly occurred on 2/3 May, and squatters were said to be still terrorising the neighbourhood: council to mayor and JPs of Canterbury, 1 June, ibid. fo. 10; MS Rawlinson C79, fos 30–1.

63 *Journal*, 648. Parliament was responding to an appeal from Major Wade, the local militia captain and official managing Dean's timber and foundries. The background and significance of these riots are lucidly analysed in A. R. Warmington, *Civil war, Interregnum and Restoration in Gloucestershire, 1640–1672*, Woodbridge 1997, 129–33, 158–60.

64 Daniel Furze to the navy commissioners, 30 May, *CSPD 1658–9*, 361; *Journal*, 670, 708, 726.

their opponents, sparked further troubles, carefully fostered by Royalist agita-
tors hoping – in vain – for substantial recruits.[65] These cost the commoners
any influence at the centre: Parliament had no sympathy for those suspected
of politically motivated unrest. By August, the counter-intelligence and
vastly expanded military presence that foiled Massey's plot had also subdued
the rioters in Dean.[66] Other forests proved less difficult to control – orders in
May to stop the purloining of deer and timber in Hampton, Saulry,
Whittlewood and the New Forest needed no repetition.[67]

More damaging to the Republic than the periodic disturbances in distant
Dean, which seldom reached the diurnals, was the protracted and increasingly well-publicised strife between commoners and the purchasers who were
attempting to enclose former crown lands at nearby Enfield Chase in June
and July. On first learning of this conflict, the council responded, as usual, by
ordering the Middlesex JPs to 'proceed according to law for quieting the
proprietors in their possession', and requesting Fleetwood to place troops at
their disposal if necessary.[68] But since these magistrates proved more sympathetic to the commons, the troubles continued, culminating in the arrest of
nine soldiers employed by the proprietors after they had fired on the multitude.[69] The escalating conflict began to assume political overtones, as both
sides petitioned Parliament and published charges and counter-charges of
disloyalty. Thus the purchasers sought to discredit the rioters by likening
them to the 'Irish Rebels' and accusing them of 'Declaring for CHARLES
STEWART', while the commons, in language reminiscent of the Levellers,
averred that they were defending their 'ancient Customs' against the arbitrary invasion of Cromwell's followers.[70] Newsbooks not only reported, and so
gave a wider currency to, these events, but joined the verbal fray themselves –
Politicus, with official restraint, endorsed the proprietors' version; the more
radical Weekly Post, though reserving judgement to Parliament, essentially
commended the inhabitants' attack on Cromwellian tyranny.[71] All parties

[65] Royalist hopes and encouragement of the rioters in July are apparent in Hyde's correspondence: Clarendon 62, fo. 120; 63, fo. 4. The latter letter, reporting that 13,000
commoners 'openly profess the Parliaments hard usage in supporting Major Wade will force
them to turn Cavaliers', illustrates their lack of political motivation.
[66] Though the Post reported that Col. Okey and 15 troops had gone to suppress hundreds
of rebels who had gathered in the Forest of Dean with 'great Concourse of people resorting
to them' (no. 13, 26 July–2 Aug., 105), Daniel Furze, the Commonwealth's shipwright at
nearby Lydney, writing on 1 Aug., reported no unusual disturbances: CSPD 1659, 65.
[67] Council to chief rangers, 30 May, SP 25/98, fo. 9.
[68] Council to Middlesex JPs, 1 June, ibid. fo. 10.
[69] The JPs arrested the soldiers rather than the rioters; their fitness to exercise authority
was consequently challenged by the proprietors in their petition, A RELATION Of the
Riotous Insurrection of divers Inhabitants of Enfield (broadsheet).
[70] Ibid. The commons' much longer manifesto was entitled A RELATION Of The
CRUELTIES And Barbarous Murthers . . . committed by some Foot-Souldiers and others . . .
upon some of the Inhabitants of Enfield.
[71] Politicus, no. 578, 7–14 July, 592; Post, no. 11, 19–26 July, 97.

acknowledged the gravity of the situation: Archibald Johnston, the council president, lamented the 'blood falling out between the souldiours and countrey people', while Royalists gleefully interpreted the disorders as the precursors of a general plebeian revolt in favour of monarchy.[72] Though this expectation was mistaken, the extraordinary publicity accorded these events clearly challenged the Commonwealth's claim to provide just and orderly government.

In response, Parliament firmly asserted its authority as arbiter. The conflicting petitions were referred to the experienced committee handling the Dean case, while a ban on 'all force and disturbance' was to be read in the parish churches; the latter were evidently still central to peacekeeping despite the rise of a sectarian world. When this prohibition failed to quench the smouldering embers entirely, the House not only reiterated the injunction to the sheriff and JPs to suppress 'riotous and unlawful assemblies', but summoned them to give an account of their proceedings.[73] Disorder only ceased when the sheriff, accompanied by twenty bailiffs and substantial reinforcements of horse, persuaded the rioters to disperse and await Parliament's decision. This demonstration of power succeeded in overawing the commoners, and creating some confidence in central arbitration. Royalist hopes that the conflagration would be rekindled as soon as the troops withdrew proved unfounded: some days after the sheriff's visit, a republican officer was relieved to report that the 'Country hubbub about Enfield Chase [was] still for the present'. Despite the anxiety that the disturbances had occasioned, Parliament had compelled the reluctant officials to restore order, and renewed respect for its authority and justice.[74]

Exceptional as its high profile was, the Enfield Chase affair illustrates some important problems faced by the republicans in the provinces. There was a real danger that commoners, emboldened by the advent of a seemingly weaker central government, would take the law into their own hands, and that JPs more sympathetic to their grievances than to the demands of that government would fail to subjugate them.[75] What is remarkable, however, is not the infrequent occurrence of such disturbances, but the relative ease with which they were usually suppressed. The experiences of Enfield and Dean also demonstrate the falsehood of monarchist claims that republican administration was anarchical, and that the provinces were in a state of simmering revolt. In fact, Parliament, assisted by the majority of local magistrates,

---

72 *Johnston diary*, 125. For the Royalist view see 'Miles' to Nicholas, 22 July, *Nicholas papers*, 173, and Brasy to Hyde, 15 July, MS Clarendon 62, fo. 120.

73 *Journal*, 721, 722. The officials delivered a satisfactory report two days later: ibid. 726.

74 Details of the sheriff's visit were published in *Politicus*, no. 579, 14–21 July, 607; Major Barton to Col. Saunders, 23 July, DRO, 1232 m/o, fo. 80.

75 Studies of the fenland disturbances of the 1640s and early 50s confirm the inclination of some local gentlemen to support rather than subjugate aggrieved commoners: see K. Lindley, *Fenland riots and the English Revolution*, London 1982, esp. pp. 255–6, and C. Holmes, *Seventeenth century Lincolnshire*, Lincoln 1980, 152–5.

succeeded in maintaining order almost everywhere. Not only the assizes but quarter sessions proceeded as usual; most citizens continued to go about their ordinary business. The general quiet was remarked by Ralph Josselin, minister of Earls Colne in Essex, who prided himself on his neutrality, yet, soon after the Republic's resurrection, was to be found praising God for 'outward mercies', and observing that, though sectaries were particularly overjoyed at the change, 'all are secure'. His diary entries thereafter are filled with normal activities – the apprenticeship of his son, the building of a little 'retiring meditating place' – until the rebellion in late July and August again thrust national affairs upon his notice. He then responded with a passionate concern for peace and the prevention of bloodshed, engaging in a day of prayer for these ends with a fellow minister.[76]

Josselin's anxious and completely unenthusiastic reaction to the rising exemplifies provincial attitudes far better than the inflammatory preaching of some Presbyterian clergy, or the unfounded optimism of certain Royalist agents. A majority even among the regime's ideological opponents preferred a disapproving detachment to the dangers of involvement in conspiracy and rebellion. As historians well know, the cry that 'Forty-one is come again' was a major motive for order after the Restoration.[77] Yet that same fear exercised an equally powerful brake on active disaffection in 1659. Meanwhile, a 'well-affected' minority rallied to Parliament's support, making it possible for it to implement necessary policies and subdue the threatened general insurrection. As their zealous loyalty more than counterbalanced the neutrality or passive disaffection of the rest, the Republic's ability to survive and provide effective government clearly did not depend on that elusive quality, 'popular support'. Only by alienating its faithful adherents, or provoking the majority to revolt, could the Commonwealth endanger its own survival. In governing the provinces, Parliament therefore pursued a delicate balance between encouraging the 'well-affected' and securing acquiescence from powerful, if unenthusiastic, local magistrates. Though this balance began to crumble as crisis gathered in late September, the republican achievement prior to that point should not be underestimated.

[76] *The diary of the Revd Ralph Josselin*, ed. E. Hockliffe (Camden Society, 3rd ser. xv, 1908), 129–30.

[77] Thus Jonathan Scott argues in his *Algernon Sidney and the Restoration crisis, 1677–1683*, Cambridge 1991, that the crisis of 1679–83 was a repeat of that of 1639–42, but recognises fear of a new civil war as an important reason for the different outcomes.

6

Towards a Republican Foreign Policy

These people promised ... that they would do glorious things in delivering the people from oppression and poverty ... as to make peace with Spain and to increase Trade and by minting all of the King of Spains bullion and many such things which now they take in and this makes many not so concerned for them as they were: Royalist intelligence, 23 May 1659.

This government leave no time to attend to any foreign business. They attend only to the conspiracy discovered and the risings: Giavarina to the Venetian Senate, 5 Aug. 1659.

These are that Power who managed so great ... a Warr with the Portugal, French and Dutch with admirable Success to the Honour of this Nation.. These were the Called, Chosen and Faithful of that Parliament and the very fine flower ... the chaff ... by many special Providences being ... sifted out: *A WORD OF SETTLEMENT*, Sept. 1659.

The distinction between domestic and foreign affairs, though analytically useful, is essentially artificial. This is particularly true where republics are concerned, as Machiavelli long ago observed.[1] Recent seventeenth-century scholarship has not only sought to situate the British Isles within 'the wider European religious and political complex', but has revealed the importance of interaction with that wider world in the development of English republicanism.[2] In 1649 the improvised Commonwealth was insecure and insignificant, facing ostracism, if not outright hostility, from an international community appalled by the regicide. By 1653 the Republic had attained general recognition and an active European role: Parliament's navies were fighting England's principal commercial rivals, the Dutch, while the warring superpowers, France and Spain, competed for its favour. Military and diplomatic success, contrasted with Stuart ineptitude, supported theories that republics, lacking selfish dynastic constraints, were superior to monarchies, both in efficiency and dedication to the national interest. Self-confident republicanism consequently gathered strength. In particular, Blair Worden has charted the growing influence on certain politicians, led by Neville, and

---

1   For a recent discussion of Machiavelli's dictum in relation to the English Republic see D. Armitage, 'John Milton: poet against empire', in Armitage, Himy and Skinner, *Milton and republicanism*, 206–25 at p. 207.

2   J. Scott, *England's troubles: seventeenth-century English political instability in European context*, Cambridge 2000, 14. Republicanism is, of course, only one aspect of this magisterial study – see esp. ch. xiii.

propagandists, especially Nedham, of a 'classical republican' ideology justifying an aggressive, expansionist foreign policy.[3] This was, in Milton's famous phrase, the moment when 'the English boasted they would build' a 'goodly tower of a Commonwealth' to be 'another Rome in the west'.[4] Such classical aspirations coexisted, and sometimes blended, with radical Protestant visions of liberating oppressed peoples everywhere from AntiChristian tyranny.[5] At the start of the 1650s, England's revolution was only the most dramatic episode to date in a series of wars and revolts shaking thrones throughout a Europe whose future might well prove republican.[6]

By 1659 immediate hopes of a crownless continent had suffered successive frustrations. The French monarchy had survived the Frondes, and emerged victorious over an exhausted Spain, with whom peace negotiations were underway. Though the Spanish Hapsburgs were declining, the Austrian branch, headed by the Holy Roman Emperor, still seemed to pose a serious threat to European Protestantism.[7] Meanwhile, a resurgent Swedish kingdom sought to enlarge its territories and dominate the Baltic. Britain's Commonwealth had become a quasi-monarchical Protectorate that aligned itself with France against Spain and Sweden against Denmark. These setbacks did not vapourise English 'republican confidence', as David Armitage has suggested; indeed, Cromwellian foreign policy inadvertently enhanced retrospective confidence in the Commonwealth's excellence. Disgruntled republicans saw in the Protector's 'sell-out' peace with the Dutch and 'anachronistic' war on a weakened Spain the cause of the general decay of English trade, and confirmation that any single person trusted with power would mistake or betray the common good. In speeches and writings, prose and poetry, the commonwealthsmen contrasted perceived Protectoral failures with the Republic's prowess and potential: by the time of the interruption, Thomas Scot fondly

---

3 A. B. Worden, 'Marchamont Nedham and the beginnings of English republicanism', in Wootton, *Republicanism*, 46–81, esp. pp. 48, 71–3; 'Classical republicanism and the Puritan Revolution', in V. Pearl, H. Lloyd-Jones and A. B. Worden (eds), *History and imagination: essays in honour of Hugh Trevor-Roper*, London 1981, 182–200; and 'Milton's republicanism and the tyranny of heaven', in G. Bock, Q. R. D. Skinner and M. Viroli (eds), *Machiavelli and republicanism*, Cambridge 1990, 225–45 at p. 226.

4 John Milton, *The Readie and Easie Way to Establish a Free Commonwealth*, 1660, 2. Milton's classical and Renaissance readings are well analysed in Armitage, 'Milton'.

5 On the importance of apocalyptic republicanism see Steven Pincus, 'England and the world in the 1650s', in Morrill, *Revolution and Restoration*, 129–47 at pp. 130–1, 136–7, and *Protestantism*, esp. pp. 18–20, 76–9 and ch. viii.

6 The 'wider European pattern of revolution', and the hopes that it fostered in English republicans, are analysed by A. B. Worden in 'Milton and Marchamont Nedham', in Armitage, Himy and Skinner, *Milton and republicanism*, 156–80 at pp. 172–3, and 'Nedham and English republicanism', 72–3.

7 John Dury, for example, stressed the menace of a long-standing, highly successful Austro-papal 'League for the Extirpation of the Protestant party': *The Interest of ENGLAND IN THE Protestant Cause*, 14.

recalled, 'we never bid fairer for being masters of the whole world'.[8] Yet rejection of the Cromwellian present did not only or even necessarily generate complacent nostalgia for past triumphs. Armitage has clearly shown how Cromwell's rise from within the Republic fulfilled Machiavellian forebodings that pursuing external conquests could lead to internal corruption, luxury, ambition and ultimately the loss of liberty to empire.[9] Some 'classical republican' thinkers in the 1650s consequently came to prefer a stable, defensive 'commonwealth for preservation' to a dynamic, expansionist 'commonwealth for increase', an agrarian polity modelled on Sparta to a commercial society resembling Athens.[10] Such distinctions, academic while the republicans were in opposition, would become more significant when they recaptured the helm of state.

In that event, the very force of the republican critique engendered considerable expectations. Parliament was heralded and welcomed back by a host of pamphlets celebrating its previous achievements abroad and predicting a reversal of the Protectorate's damaging policies.[11] Amidst such clamour, even the most insular MPs could not overlook the importance of foreign triumphs in the Commonwealth's rehabilitation. Yet since Parliament in 1659 had little obvious effect on the wider world, narrative histories, intent upon its downfall, resulting from a purely English crisis, have largely ignored the European context; ideological studies are equally silent on republican attitudes to foreign affairs after the clashes in Richard's parliament.[12] Hindsight finds support in contemporary criticism of a government preoccupied with internal problems at the expense of its external responsibilities. Ambassadors

---

8 *Burton diary*, iii. 112. For these republican responses see Norbrook, *Writing*, ch. vii, esp. pp. 309, 313–15, and Pincus, 'England', 143–6.

9 Armitage, 'Milton', passim, and 'The Cromwellian Protectorate and the languages of empire', *HJ* xxxv (1992), 532–55. The Machiavellian dilemma, and Harrington's unique solution, are also discussed in A. B. Worden, 'English republicanism', in J. H. Burns and Mark Goldie (eds), *The Cambridge history of political thought, 1450–1700*, Cambridge 1991, 443–75 at pp. 466–7.

10 The commercial/Athenian versus Spartan/agrarian dichotomy is the central argument of S. Pincus, ' "Neither Machiavellian moment nor possessive individualism": commercial society and the defenders of the English Commonwealth', *American Historical Review* ciii (1998), 702–36. Despite their differences, Armitage and Pincus both identify Milton and Harrington as exemplifying the anti-imperial/anti-commercial trends; aversion to luxury connects the two. Yet Pincus' distinction between 'classical', agrarian republicans and 'liberal', commercial ones is essentially artificial. Classical models varied, as he himself admits. It was perfectly possible to oppose imperialism/expansion and support commercial prosperity.

11 Among the most vigorous critiques of Cromwellian foreign policy and its ideological implications were [Slingsby Bethel], *A Second NARRATIVE Of The Late Parliament (so called)*, and J[ohn] S[treater], *The Continuation of this Session of Parliament, Justified*.

12 Hutton and Woolrych are silent on the subject. Less than one third of Davies's chapter on foreign relations concerns the Republic, and there is no general assessment of Parliament's policy. Pincus concludes his overview, 'England and the world', with the debates in Richard's parliament.

sometimes complained that Parliament and Council neglected their representations for pressing domestic concerns;[13] Royalists swiftly detected disillusionment arising from the Republic's failure to deliver instant tangible
benefits such as peace with Spain.[14] But what really happened when the
Protector's critics found themselves obliged to develop a positive approach to
international relations? Did they neglect problems, compromise principles, or
disappoint their adherents? To answer such questions, this chapter will
explore every dimension of the restored Commonwealth's foreign policy.

Personnel and principles

Parliament was no more indifferent to the outside world in 1659 than previously.[15] A cursory reading of the *Journal* shows that within a week of its
return, it had communicated its *Declaration* to the resident diplomats, and
received a detailed report on the international situation. During the next five
months, the House granted three formal audiences, and discussed external
affairs on no less than forty-three occasions, or at one-third of all its sessions.
Almost half of these debates occurred in late May and June, as the new
government established diplomatic relations and despatched representatives
to the Baltic; very few took place amidst the gathering crisis of the autumn.
There is, however, no simple correlation between domestic difficulties and
inattention to foreign questions. In early August Parliament found time,
despite the rebellion, to consider such pressing matters as the final ratification of the treaty of The Hague, the latest reports from the Sound and the
new credentials of the French ambassador.[16] September saw little international business of comparable urgency; the council continued to handle
the many routine diplomatic exchanges. The council's minutes and correspondence afford still more evidence of the time and thought that England's
rulers devoted to European politics. Throughout these official communications, and indeed the pamphlet literature, one theme consistently predomi-

---

[13] Thus Giavarina during Booth's rising, CSPVen., 54; Nieuport, on 3 Aug., reported that
the council itself had used the rebellion to excuse its inattention to his continual
complaints about piracy: SP 78/114, fos 335–6. Bordeaux, on 1 Aug., described Parliament
and council as wholly preoccupied with internal affairs: Guizot, *Histoire*, i. 467–8.

[14] See, for example, the Royalist newsletter in this chapter's epigraphs: MS Clarendon 61,
fo. 1.

[15] Parliament's dignified conduct of foreign affairs from 1649 to 1653 is described in
Kelsey, *Inventing a republic*, chs ii, iv.

[16] The *Journal* records 21 reports and resolutions on foreign affairs between 13 May and
30 June; in July and August there are 17 such references, including 5 between 2 and
16 Aug., the period of Booth's rising; for September and October there are only 5. Parliament sat on 128 days.

nated: safeguarding that elusive, but vital quality, 'the honour of this Commonwealth'.[17]

Defending the Commonwealth's reputation abroad presented a real as well as rhetorical challenge. Weak regimes invite foreign manipulation. In 1659 both the French and the Dutch hoped to profit from England's instability by extorting concessions from a government whose survival depended, they supposed, upon their support. Meanwhile, the English Royalists constituted a fifth column who lost no opportunity to denigrate the Republic to foreign powers and solicit their assistance. After Booth's defeat they redoubled their efforts, sending Charles Stuart to the scene of the treaty between France and Spain.[18] There was a real apprehension that the Catholic kings might, once reconciled, intervene to restore England's monarchy. Fear of invasion spanned the political spectrum from the militant republican who warned that France had a vested interest in resisting the 'Establishment of a Republick which . . . embraceth both the one and the other Hemisphere . . . and defieth the Universe' to the moderate Cromwellian who dreaded the transformation of 'this green, unsetled and distracted republique into another Sceen of blood and desolation'.[19] It was surely not timeserving alone that led former Protectoral ambassadors such as Whitelocke and Lockhart, who cared little for Parliament's fame and less for republicanism, into willing collaboration with their late opponents. Concern for national security and well-being transcended particular differences between the new rulers. To protect England from external interference, maintaining domestic order was necessary, but not sufficient. Parliament also needed to avoid all appearance of weakness and pursue an independent line in Europe.

Maintaining England's honour was, however, expensive. Effective diplomacy required the backing of a powerful army and navy, which consumed vast sums. The occupation of Scotland and Ireland represented a constant drain on the English exchequer, whose overstretched resources were depleted still further by the retention of Dunkirk, the continental foothold captured in 1658. Increased expenditure due to the Spanish war was, indeed, a significant source of the enormous debts inherited by the new government.[20] Though

[17] This phrase recurs frequently in the diplomatic correspondence, especially in Lockhart's despatches: for examples see SP 78/114, fos 322, 329; MS Clarendon 64, fos 16–19.

[18] The Royalist quest for foreign aid is well documented in the Clarendon manuscripts; Bordeaux, as a recipient of their attentions, gives an illuminating account in his correspondence: Guizot, *Histoire*, i. 381, 458, 453–4.

[19] Le White, *AN ANSWER To A LETTER*, 5; *FRANCE No Friend to ENGLAND. Or, The Resentments of the French upon the Success of the ENGLISH*, 16. Bordeaux reported that the ministers negotiating with him frequently expressed suspicions that Franco-Spanish intervention was intended: Guizot, *Histoire*, i. 430, 433, 412.

[20] By April 1659 the national debt stood at nearly £2 million; the annual deficit at more than £80,000. England was subsidising the armies in Scotland and Ireland to the tune of £12,200 per month. Total expenditure on the armed forces amounted to over £2.3 million *p.a.*, or 127% of existing revenue. These figures are derived from the financial reports to Richard's parliament and the Long Parliament: MS Add. 11597.

the republicans might, and did, blame Cromwell for the financial predicament, they could not ignore the practical implications. At least for the present, the Commonwealth could not afford expansion, even if all its leaders had wanted it. Yet precipitate withdrawal from Europe was unthinkable. A delicate course between the conflicting demands of economy, security and reputation was indicated. And Marten, Challoner and Neville, the 'classical republican' hawks of 1651–2, were not the men to steer it. Although the *Journal* records their participation in some foreign business, council minutes show that Neville and Challoner sat on comparatively few committees for external affairs, and were only moderately active.[21]

Management of diplomacy reverted instead to the godly Sir Henry Vane, a highly experienced negotiator.[22] Though sometimes classified as an 'apocalyptic republican', Vane saw Christ's earthly reign over the nations as 'extraordinary and very remote'; pending its establishment by divine power, he favoured the use of 'ordinary means'. These, in 1659 as in 1650, entailed exploiting foreign rivalries for the 'interest of England'.[23] Institutional sources reveal that he presented over two-thirds of the council's reports to Parliament, and served on a majority of the committees conferring with ambassadors.[24] That Vane was not merely the assiduous mouthpiece of the council, but a significant maker of policy, is confirmed by the diplomatic correspondence. It was to Vane that Lockhart addressed secret missives supplementing his official communications to the council; and Vane who, with Scot, was suspected of commissioning a secret agent to spy on Lockhart's proceedings.[25] Nieuport's master, John de Witt, singled out Vane as the one

---

21 The classical republicans were all included in Parliament's committee to give audience to the representative of Hamburg; Challoner was appointed to similar committees for the agents of Venice and, with Marten, Tuscany; Neville reported on procedure for Nieuport's audience, and was deputed to attend him, while Challoner reported one letter from Sweden, and was commissioned to draft another to the Venetian government: *Journal*, 685, 769, 793, 663, 736, 788. Council committee lists provide an approximate guide to participation in foreign affairs: Challoner and Neville each served on only 18%, or 7 of the 38 committees created in this connection. Of the 28 councillors who took their seats, 12 took little or no interest in foreign policy, serving on 5 committees or less; 13 were appointed to at least 8, of whom 3 were on 50% or more.

22 Vane's diplomatic career had begun nearly thirty years before, with employment on an embassy to Vienna; his differences with Marten in the early 1650s, and renewed control of foreign policy in 1659 are attested in Jonathan Scott, *Algernon Sidney and the English Republic, 1623–1677*, Cambridge 1988, 94–5.

23 Pincus, *Protestantism*, 19; [Henry Vane], *A Needful CORRECTIVE Or BALLANCE In Popular Government*, 7; *Original letters and papers of state addressed to Oliver Cromwell*, ed. J. Nickolls, London 1743, 40–1. That Vane's approach had not changed significantly since 1650 is apparent from the emphasis on England's interest in his speeches in Richard's parliament: for examples see *Burton diary*, iii. 384–5, 401.

24 Vane presented 15 of the 22 reports on foreign policy to parliament; he served on 20 of the 38 council committees, and chaired 9.

25 Lockhart addressed his additional letters jointly to Vane and his relative and patron, Fleetwood, but as the latter showed no interest whatsoever in foreign affairs, it was clearly

on whom the Dutch viewpoint must be impressed. Whereas Holland's repre-sentative listed all councillors who visited him, only Vane's name merited mention in the French dispatches. Bordeaux often praised his tact and civility; in June he observed that Vane seemed to be the 'principal minister of this regime'.[26]

Vane might dominate, but could not monopolise, the direction of the Republic's foreign policy. All his recommendations required the approval, first of the council, then the House, which occasionally challenged his judge-ment.[27] In August Bordeaux referred, significantly, to 'Vane and the others with the main direction of foreign affairs', implying that Vane's position was that of *primus inter pares*.[28] The identity of the others may be determined from the council minutes, which shed interesting light on the internal dynamics of the regime. As might be expected, Vane was assisted by his faithful parlia-mentary ally, Richard Salway, and, until their departure to the Sound in July, his brother-in-law, Sir Robert Honywood, and his talented republican admirer, Algernon Sidney.[29] The prominence of the indefatigable Thomas Scot, as chief of intelligence, is no more surprising than the frequent appear-ances of that admiralty expert, Colonel George Thompson.[30] The only coun-cillors whose workload in foreign relations equalled that of Vane, however, were the ex-Cromwellians Bulstrode Whitelocke and Archibald Johnston. Neither expressed independent opinions, but both made themselves extremely useful – so much so that Whitelocke was the council's first choice for the Sound mission, while Vane at least toyed with the idea of making the

Vane who benefited: SP 78/114, fos 304, 329. Though Scot was certainly spying upon Lockhart (a report from the spy survives ibid. fo. 288) the main evidence for Vane's in-volvement is a letter from Hyde of 11 Oct.: MS Clarendon 65, fos 62–3.

[26] De Witt to Willem Nieuport, 14 Oct., TSP vii. 764–5; Bordeaux to Mazarin, 16 June, Guizot, *Histoire*, i. 452. For additional praise of Vane see ibid. i. 457–8, 416, 410. After falling out with Vane in the autumn, Bordeaux recollected him as one who had 'intrigued to get the direction of foreign affairs': ibid. ii. 272.

[27] Parliament usually accepted Vane's reports without alteration; the only significant exception was his proposal that George Downing should continue as the Commonwealth's resident minister in Holland. The House initially refused, ordering the council to consider alternatives, and suggesting that godly republican MP, Col. Nathaniel Rich. When he declined, Vane proposed, and Parliament approved, a compromise whereby Downing would be temporarily accredited, pending the choice of a more suitable representative: *Journal*, 688, 699.

[28] Bordeaux to Mazarin, 22 Aug., Guizot, *Histoire*, i. 426.

[29] Salway, Honywood and Sidney served respectively on 12, 11 and 6 conciliar commit-tees, a considerable number, given the early departure of the latter two. Sidney's admiration for, and close collaboration with, Vane are illuminated in Scott, *Sidney and the English Republic*, 95–6, 100–2, 126–8.

[30] Scot appears on 11 committees, and was ordered to make 3 reports to Parliament. Thompson was also appointed to 11 committees, and appears 23 times in the council records, usually in connection with admiralty matters, though he was also deputed to send Lockhart the weekly occurrences.

horrified Johnston ambassador to France.[31] The eventual decision to retain the experienced and submissive Lockhart, together with the other diplomats nominated by the Protector, suggests that Vane had forged a working alliance of Cromwellians and republicans, at least where external affairs were concerned.[32]

But the council proceedings also reveal the importance of Lambert, who, alone among the generals, displayed a keen interest in foreign policy.[33] That interest was of long standing: as Oliver Cromwell's councillor, Lambert had vigorously opposed the Spanish war; most recently, in Richard's parliament, he had joined the republicans in recommending 'great care' to defend the 'interest of England' against potential encroachments by either the Dutch or Sweden.[34] In the new Council of State, Lambert soon proved his diligence in European business, reporting such significant items as the instructions for the plenipotentiaries in the Sound, or the latest representations from the Dutch and Swedish ministers. As a member of almost all the major foreign committees created before his expedition against Booth in August, Lambert inevitably worked in close association with Vane, with whom his name was often juxtaposed.[35] The partnership between these men thus existed long before the September crisis, and may well have owed much to their fruitful co-operation over external matters. The formative role of foreign affairs in reinforcing outlooks and alliances is suggested by the clear correlation, if no more, between the councillors most deeply engaged in such business and the most prominent civilians appointed to the future Committee of Safety.[36]

---

31 Whitelocke served on 25 committees, made four reports to the council and was entrusted with three to Parliament; his expertise on Swedish and German affairs was much in demand. Johnston was appointed to 23 committees, with special care of at least one, and four times reported progress. Despite this activity, Johnston's contemporary diary and Whitelocke's later memorials refrain from comment on foreign policy. For the proposals to send them overseas see Whitelocke, Memorials, iv. 351–2, and Johnston diary, 118.

32 Lockhart, following Thurloe's advice, hastened to submit to the new government. After exhorting his officers in Dunkirk to obedience, he returned to brief the council, and received new credentials: CSPD 1658–9, 340; TSP vii. 670–1; council minutes, 3 June; Journal, 682. Downing, in Holland, and Sir Philip Meadow, in Sweden and Denmark, were also reaccredited, though the latter's request to return was granted in August, after the plenipotentiaries arrived.

33 Of the other grandees in the council, Disbrow and Berry were nominated respectively to 9 and 5 committees, but evinced little concern for foreign policy. Fleetwood served only on the general committee for the 'discovery of all designes against the Commonwealth and managing Intelligence both forreign and domestique' created on 25 May.

34 Burton diary, iii. 400. For Lambert's opposition to the Spanish war see especially his arguments in the Protectoral council debate reproduced in Clarke papers, iii. 207ff.

35 Council minutes, 1, 21, 2 June. In all, Lambert was nominated to 13 foreign committees, or 46% of those created before his departure. This percentage under-rates Lambert's importance, since several committees were merely delegations to attend a particular ambassador for a specific purpose, and had no permanent existence. Lambert and Vane are juxtaposed on 7 of these committees.

36 Johnston, Whitelocke and Vane, who were, with Lambert and Thompson, the council-

Almost as illuminating as the managers of foreign policy are the many councillors who avoided much involvement.[37] These included not just infrequent attenders such as St John, Wallop, and Dixwell, but some of the most active and prominent members: Sir Arthur Hesilrig, Solicitor-General Robert Reynolds, Sir James Harrington, Edmund Ludlow, Valentine Walton, William Sydenham, John Downs and Lieutenant-General Charles Fleetwood.[38] It is impossible to escape the conclusion that there was an efficient division of labour within the council, whereby those not gifted, or uninterested, in diplomacy concentrated on other aspects of government. For Fleetwood it was the Army, for Walton the navy; for Ludlow a combination of Parliament, Army and Ireland. Downs specialised in finance; Reynolds focused on Ireland. Harrington and Sydenham were diligent MPs, while Hesilrig devoted himself to Parliament and the re-commissioning of the officers. Had he wished to challenge Vane's primacy in foreign policy, it is inconceivable that Hesilrig could not have done so. Though the tact befitting diplomats was hardly one of his more outstanding qualities, he was neither unfamiliar nor unconcerned with European questions. On four occasions the council selected him, as one who undoubtedly had the ear of the House, to report foreign correspondence.[39] But only in October, when tensions between the two men had almost reached breaking point, did Hesilrig invade the diplomatic realm by securing appointment alongside Vane to a committee to confer with Bordeaux.[40] It was, significantly, at this juncture that the latter first informed his government of Hesilrig's importance as 'head of the republican faction'.[41] But Hesilrig's habitual willingness to leave almost the entire conduct of the important area of foreign relations to Vane and his associates does much to dispel the legend that republican administration was character-

lors most active in foreign policy, would become the most prominent civilians on the Committee of Safety. The correspondence between collaboration over foreign policy and appointment to the committee is also apparent in Salway's case. The only councillor who does not fit this pattern is Sir James Harrington, who was as inconspicuous in the committee as he had been in foreign business.

[37] Some knowledge of foreign business was an inevitable concomitant of membership, since the whole council gave formal audiences to ambassadors, and discussed reports from its committees.

[38] With the exceptions of St John, Walton and Ludlow, who were named to 3, 4 and 3, all of these men were appointed to 2 foreign committees or less; Downs and Wallop do not appear on any at all.

[39] Council minutes, 8 June, 23 July, 8, 22 Aug.; he actually presented three. Hesilrig's familiarity with European affairs is evident from his speeches in Richard's parliament (see, for example, *Burton diary*, iii. 457–9), but he was clearly less interested than some of his colleagues.

[40] Council minutes, 1 Oct. The only previous foreign committee to which he had been nominated was that which drafted the instructions for the Sound plenipotentiaries in June.

[41] Bordeaux to Henri-Auguste de Brienne, 6 Oct., Guizot, *Histoire*, i. 477. Bordeaux had, of course, offered his analysis of the various factions in government much earlier, but this was the first time that he named Hesilrig as a significant leader, and rival to Vane.

ised by constant factional in-fighting. Instead of conflict, Hesilrig's behaviour suggests that there was, until the autumn, some consensus on diplomacy within the council, which could safely delegate implementation to the experts.

Peace with honour, not the 'prevention of universal monarchy', as Steven Pincus would have us expect, was the cornerstone of republican foreign policy in 1659.[42] Despite his personal distrust of French 'tyrannical princi-ples', Vane could truthfully assure Bordeaux that 'this regime only thinks of being on good terms with all neighbour states and of making the interior secure'.[43] His success in securing a consensus in favour of this course is unsur-prising, given its manifold advantages. If less glorious than a successful war, peace was also far less expensive, and less hazardous. Good relations with the major European powers would diminish the external menace to the Commonwealth, and give its rulers space in which to resolve pressing dom-estic problems. Peace was also likely to increase customs revenue and endear the government to suffering commercial interests – Herbert Morley was doubtless not the only MP to sympathise with urban constituents pleading 'generall poverty, decay of trade' due to 'losses by sea in the warres with Holland and Spaine'.[44] As for republican principle, Parliament's propagan-dists hastened to reconcile the demands of 'greatness' and 'preservation'. PEACE and not WARRE, the emphatic title John Harris bestowed on his comprehensive vindication of the Commonwealth, deplored Cromwell's 'War . . . with Spain' as more detrimental to 'the Trade of England' than 'all the Wars . . . since 1638'. Except in the case of 'unsufferable' provocation, 'peace with all Forraigne Nations' was the hallmark of a truly prosperous Commonwealth bent on 'advancing trade', contended the *Looking-Glass of England's Liberty*. With the vast expanse of the New World open, the same author argued that it would be immoral and imprudent to 'cast away our men . . . and treasure, and to impoverish and in danger our Commonwealth at home, in hopes only of enlarging our Dominions abroad'. Instead, the English Republic should assume the more prestigious role of European peacemaker, balancing the interests of its neighbours by 'Christian and civil addresses, mediations and interpositions [rather] than by the Sword'.[45] Such sentiments

---

42 Pincus, 'England and the world', 146. Pincus' analysis is based on what the republicans said in Richard's parliament rather than what they did when in power. Insofar as republican policy in 1659 was directed against any aspirant to universal monarchy, it was not Sweden or France but the Austrian empire, and that only as a distant, indirect goal.

43 *Burton diary*, iii. 489; Bordeaux to de Brienne, 21 July, Guizot, *Histoire*, i. 413.

44 Mayor, jurats and commonalty of Rye to Morley, John Fagg and William Hay, 30 Aug., Rye MS 47/161, fo. 1. Morley's sympathy was apparent in the readiness with which he im-mediately secured their relief from the additional burden of supporting a foot company: ibid. fos 2–4.

45 John Harris, *PEACE and not WARRE: Or The MODERATOR. Truly but yet Plainly, STATING the CASE Of The COMMON-WEALTH*, 21; *Speculum Libertatis Angliae Re restitutae*, 16–17. Other republican publications commending 'general peace' for the good

exactly mirror those of Hesilrig, who had exhorted Richard's parliament to 'do like Christians', counting it England's 'interest' and 'honour to redeem and reconcile' the warring Baltic powers. Even Neville had similarly counselled the last government to secure 'trade, the essential interest of state' by remaining 'umpire' instead of going to war.[46] Godliness, glory and material gain thus united to commend the pursuit of peace.

The Baltic

The obvious opportunity for peacemaking was, of course, the conflict between Sweden and Denmark, which threatened English access to vital naval supplies from the Baltic. Sweden, whose monarch Oliver Cromwell mistook for a Protestant hero, had hitherto been England's ally. Denmark enjoyed the backing of the Dutch, whose decision to send their fleet to the Sound had prompted Richard Cromwell's government to do likewise. This move had been vehemently criticised by the republicans, who supported Denmark, as the weaker power, and denounced the danger of war with the Dutch. Instead, they advocated diplomatic methods. These were not, in fact, neglected. In the Protectorate's last days, representatives of England, France and the United Provinces at The Hague agreed a treaty of mediation, whose terms would be enforced by the maritime powers in the event of Swedish or Danish refusal. Meanwhile, the Dutch and English fleets would remain in a state of armed neutrality, refraining from military assistance to their respective allies. At Parliament's return, this treaty had not been ratified, peace had not been imposed and the expiry of the period of neutrality was imminent. Action was going to be required of the new regime.

The restored Republic did not disown its predecessor's diplomatic initiatives. There was no 'sharp change in policy', as Jonathan Scott has contended,[47] but rather a more subtle transfer of sympathies from Sweden to the Dutch and Danes. Instead of recalling the fleet from its 'expensive attendances on other Princes' and repudiating the Swedish alliance, as some republicans advised, Parliament rapidly resolved to send its own plenipotentiaries to procure a peace based on the treaty of The Hague.[48] On 9 June the House approved the council's nominees: three MPs – Algernon Sidney, a

---

of trade include *Chaos; Twenty seven queries;* Bland, *Trade revived; The Good Old Cause Explained;* and William Ball, *LAW and STATE PROPOSALS Humbly Presented to the Supream Authority, the Parliament.* Pincus correctly emphasises the prominence of commercial republican arguments in 'Neither Machiavellian moment', but does not relate them to the Commonwealth's actual policy.

[46] *Burton diary,* iii. 457–8, 388, 392.

[47] Scott, *Sidney and the English Republic,* 124. This account ignores the fact that the Treaty of The Hague, to the terms of which the republicans stubbornly adhered, was negotiated before Parliament assumed the reins of power, though not ratified until July.

[48] *Chaos,* appendix; *Journal,* 670.

fervent republican admirer of Vane, Sir Robert Honywood, Vane's brother-in-law, and the merchant Thomas Boone, plus, perforce, Colonel Edward Montagu, the admiral on the spot. The latter, as a Presbyterian coaxed out of retirement by Cromwell, had no reason to welcome the Protectorate's demise; though he promised obedience, he did not attempt to disguise his lack of enthusiasm for the Commonwealth.[49] Despite rumours that the sailors under his command were better affected, Parliament could hardly dismiss him without definite proof of disloyalty.[50] An important, albeit unstated, function of the new envoys was therefore to watch Montagu, and provide reliable reports on the allegiance of the fleet.[51] Preparations for their departure, delayed by cash shortages, continued throughout the remainder of June.[52] The council entered into complex negotiations with the Dutch to revise and prolong the treaty of The Hague, and scoured the palaces for plate and other furnishings intended to impress the Commonwealth's magnificence on the foreigners entertained by its representatives. On 2 July the Speaker delivered their credentials and commissions. Two days later, the plenipotentiaries set sail, armed with secret instructions that reveal the breath-taking extent of the Republic's diplomatic ambitions. This mission was not just to resolve the immediate conflict, so preventing any 'one hand' from controlling the Baltic, but also to bring 'tranquillity to all those parts' by encouraging Sweden's bellicose monarch to redirect his energies against the Austrian Hapsburgs. The ultimate goal was a pan-Protestant alliance founded on 'a nearer Union and a more intimate Correspondence between this Commonwealth, Sweden and the United Provinces'.[53]

It was not the fault of the new ambassadors that peace, the vital prerequisite to these grandiose plans, did not ensue. Sidney's overbearing manner and impatience at time lost in 'tedious ceremonyes and disputes' certainly appealed to neither northern king. Yet there was, at first, a fair chance that

---

49 Edward Montagu to Lenthall, 27 May, MS Tanner 51, fos 69–70. In this letter Montagu readily admitted that the news from England 'filled [his] heart with fears and sorrow'; he rejoiced only that God had 'prevented disturbance and Combustions', and omitted any explicit reference to the new government.

50 Reports of republican enthusiasm in Montagu's fleet were published in *Scout*, no. 2, 29 Apr.–6 May, 16; no. 5, 20–7 May, 40; no. 7, 3–10 June, 54. The absence of official confirmation in *Politicus*, which hastened to announce the loyalty of the forces in Scotland and Ireland, suggests that reliable information for the fleet was lacking.

51 The Royalists, who themselves hoped to win over the fleet, not unnaturally saw this as the entire purpose of the mission, discounting the rhetoric of peacemaking. Thus Nicholas's correspondent reported that Sidney and the others were 'under pretence of reconsileing the two Kings, to worke upon the sea officers and . . . secure the navy': *Nicholas papers*, 153.

52 In a report from the council on 20 June, Hesilrig used the shortage of cash for the plenipotentiaries to urge speedy collection of arrears of revenue. Parliament promptly created commissioners for this purpose.

53 *Politicus*, no. 277, 30 June–7 July, 567, 576; 'A secret instruction to [the commissioners] upon their repair to the Sound', MS Sloane 4159, fos 198–9.

his unorthodox diplomacy might achieve Parliament's objectives.[54] Initial reports from the plenipotentiaries seemed promising. New commissions were distributed and the Engagement duly administered to Montagu and his officers, who proffered assurances of 'their fidelity to the Parliament and . . . their desires to make themselves as useful as may be'. Meanwhile a good understanding was reached with the Dutch admirals and commissioners, who reiterated their commitment to the treaty.[55] Encouraged by this news, the council on 27 July expressed the hope that a 'good issue' to the 'business of the Sound' was imminent.[56] Peace seemed even nearer in the embassy's next letters, which announced that Denmark, under Dutch pressure, had acceded to the Hague terms, and asked instructions on how to treat the Swedish king if he refused. Although the same despatches warned that the fleet now had supplies for less than a fortnight's stay, they did not advocate complete withdrawal. To salvage the summer's expenditure and protect Sweden and English interests from the Dutch and Danes, the plenipotentiaries instead counselled negotiation of a mutual reduction in the naval presence, whereby the English would leave fifteen ships until the end of September.[57] Parliament readily endorsed this scheme and dispatched a stiff letter notifying the Swedish monarch that he could expect no aid from England if he rejected the peace offered.[58]

The obduracy of Charles X of Sweden brought about the collapse of the negotiations. In a dramatic confrontation with Sidney and the other mediators, who were threatening joint naval action to enforce the treaty, the king resolutely declined English arbitration and defied the Dutch altogether.[59] To the bewilderment of the plenipotentiaries, his confidence that England would revert to the 'Cromwel's designe' once domestic tranquillity obviated the need to appease the Dutch appeared unshakeable. Even Parliament's letter, sent after the suppression of the revolt, did not convince him. By the time it arrived, Montagu and the English fleet had departed, taking with them the last hope that Charles might heed Sidney's fulminations. From that time forth, as Sidney grimly noted, the Swede 'never thought England would

---

[54] Algernon Sidney to the earl of Leicester, Copenhagen 13 Sept., in *Sydney papers*, ed. R. W. Blencowe, London 1825, 163. Sidney's attitude and his violations of diplomatic convention are thoroughly expounded by Scott in *Sidney and the English Republic*, ch. viii.
[55] Plenipotentiaries to the Speaker, 19/29 July, MS Tanner 51, fo. 98, and to the council, *TSP* vii. 708–10. Montagu noted the oath's administration and distribution of new commissions in his laconic diary, *The journal of Edward Mountagu first earl of Sandwich, 1659–1665*, ed. R. C. Anderson, London 1929, 43.
[56] Council to Lockhart, 27 July, SP 78/114, fo. 293.
[57] Plenipotentiaries to the council, 10/20 Aug., BL, MS Sloane 4158, fos 164–7.
[58] *Journal*, 768, 765. The letter itself does not survive, but Nieuport, whose authority was Vane, reported its contents on 26 Aug.: *TSP* vii. 734–5. His account is confirmed by the plenipotentiaries, who naturally received a copy: MS Sloane 4158, fo. 193.
[59] Plenipotentiaries to the council, 24 Aug./3 Sept., MS Sloane 4158, fos 170–1.

doe any thing against him'.[60] English influence on the settlement of the Sound diminished immediately. Though Sidney still cherished 'some expectations of concluding a peace', weariness is evident in the plenipotentiaries' last letter, composed on the 12 September. This confessed that there had been 'very small progresse' in the three weeks since the fleet left, and asked how much longer their mission should continue.[61]

But Charles X had grounds for his optimism. The fatal blow to Parliament's hopes of playing peacemaker came with the defection of Montagu, who sailed for home with the whole fleet on 23 August. Ostensibly, their departure was due to 'absolute necessitye for want of victualls'; Montagu excused his failure to leave fifteen ships on the grounds that they would not be safe from the Dutch, who had not yet received orders to withdraw an equivalent force. The explanation seems plausible, and indeed persuaded both the officers in council of war and the other civilian commissioners, Boone and Honywood.[62] Yet the matter is not so simple. By his own admission, Montagu had provisions for another month: the voyage to England took less than ten days. Sidney, who passionately contested the withdrawal, reported that fresh supplies for ships remaining were available, and that the Dutch were so anxious to retain English co-operation in the execution of the treaty that they offered to prove their trustworthiness by dividing their own fleet, obeying English orders or even providing hostages.[63] Montagu, who disliked and disbelieved the Dutch, flatly denied that it could be in the 'interest of England' for his ships to coerce Charles X, with whom he enjoyed cordial relations.[64] The timing of his departure, after the rising had begun,

[60] Plenipotentiaries, 12/22 Sept., ibid. fo. 193; Sidney to Whitelocke, 13 Nov., *Sydney papers*, 172.

[61] Sidney to Leicester, 13 Sept., *Sydney papers*, 166; plenipotentiaries to the council, 12/22 Sept., MS Sloane 4158, fo. 193.

[62] Montagu justified himself in a long letter to Richard Cromwell of 20 Sept. (MS Carte 73, fo. 312), and more briefly in a letter of 23 Aug. announcing his arrival to the council (MS Tanner 51, fo. 127). A detailed narrative, dated 29 Aug., is in his *Journal* at pp. 47–67. He was careful to emphasise the concurrence of his officers and fellow commissioners; his distrust of the Dutch was certainly shared by Vice-Admiral Goodson, who on 31 July asserted that only special providence had hitherto prevented an attack on the much smaller English fleet: *Clarke papers*, iv. 30. His ships had all reached the English coast by 1 Sept., when the council prepared a report for Parliament.

[63] Sidney to the council, 21 Aug., *TSP* vii. 731. Given the state of Anglo-Dutch relations, it is much more probable that these offers were sincere than that they concealed treacherous designs to 'possess or destroy' 15 ships representing a 'considerable strength of the English Nation', as Montagu suspected: *Journal*, 54. Sidney had established close relations with the Dutch commissioners, and so was well-placed to judge their intentions.

[64] *Montagu journal*, 62. Cordiality is also apparent from the jewels, including his picture, that Charles bestowed on Montagu, to which Pepys alluded in 1660–1: *The diary of Samuel Pepys, from 1659–1669*, ed. Richard, Lord Braybrooke, London 1879, 52, 69. Montagu himself recorded Charles's parting gifts of 'chains of gold and medals for every commander': *Montague journal*, 45. These, predictably, failed to soften Parliament's attitude: Guizot, *Histoire*, i. 475.

and before news of its defeat, supports the suspicion that he may even have contemplated intervention in English politics. Royalists had certainly tried to approach him beforehand; afterwards they claimed that he was planning to hold the Thames for the Stuarts, and that Sidney confronted him for this reason.[65] There is, however, no proof. In heated verbal argument, Sidney hinted that the proposed withdrawal was tantamount to treason, and berated Montagu for perpetuating the Protectorate's partiality towards a monarch who opposed the restored Commonwealth. But his written objections centred upon the damage that the fleet's departure would do to Parliament's foreign policy. Had he possessed any definite evidence of Montagu's disloyalty at the time, it is inconceivable that Sidney would not have disclosed it in the lengthy self-justification that he sent to the council. Such was Montagu's discretion that the only direct contemporary indication of his allegiance is the narrative that he addressed to Richard Cromwell, as Lord Protector, after he had satisfied the council, and retired into private life.[66]

Whatever his real motives, Montagu's unauthorised return demonstrated the capacity of divided counsels to thwart and embarrass the Republic. Nieuport at once protested that the 'sudden and unexpected withdrawing' of England's ships just as the moment for action approached would greatly encourage the opponents of peace, and urged the council to send the fleet back to execute the Hague agreement after revictualling. Bordeaux complained that he had been kept in the dark, and reproached the English government for not maintaining proper communications with the French, who were also mediators. The Swedish commissioners, no doubt ironically, thanked Parliament for permitting the fleet to stay so long, despite its inadequate instructions and failure to complete the business.[67] These reactions, though negative, at least presumed that the government was responsible for Montagu's action. But when, two weeks later, Parliament manifested its displeasure by instituting an inquiry, 'the coming home of the English Fleet without Orders' suddenly became headline news in the unofficial press, causing the Commonwealth's prestige at home and abroad to decrease still more.[68]

---

[65] This extravagant assertion was made by an unidentified Royalist in a letter to Charles II of 12 Sept. (MS Carte 213, fo. 301). For Royalist attempts to secure Montagu's help for the rising see the letters in CSP iii. 493–4, 497–8 and 565, and that of the agent Whetstone to Montagu himself (MS Clarendon 61, fos 280–1). In conversation with Pepys after the Restoration, Montagu admitted receiving the king's letters but did not claim to have intended action on his behalf: Pepys diary, 8 Mar. 1663, 146.

[66] Montagu journal, 62; MS Carte 73, fo. 312. Montagu afterwards stressed his allegiance to Richard, and disapproval of the change: Pepys diary, entry for 21 June 1660, 41.

[67] Nieuport to the council, 2 Sept., TSP vii. 737; Bordeaux to Mazarin, 8 Sept., Guizot, Histoire, i. 443; Swedish commissioners to Parliament, Sept., MS Carte 73, fo. 313.

[68] Journal, 779; Post, no. 20, 13–20 Sept., 161; WI, no. 20, 13–20 Sept., 153 (headlines). It was at this moment that Giavarina realised that Parliament was 'not over pleased' with Montagu's return: CSPVen., 72. The newsbooks had previously given little space to the

Faced with this predicament, the republicans did what they could to limit the domestic and diplomatic fallout. Nedham, editing the government newsbooks, boldly resorted to disinformation, announcing that negotiations with the northern kings were so 'well advanced by the care and prudence of our Plenipotentiaries' that the fleet's presence was no longer necessary; the subsequent inquiry he buried in a long list of Parliament's proceedings.[69] To escape further loss of face, the council publicly accepted Montagu's explanations, and protected him from Parliament's displeasure. Vane assured Bordeaux that, if Montagu's conduct had not entirely matched his orders, it nevertheless had the council's approval. This equivocation convinced the ambassador that the fleet had returned by government design, not the accident of the admiral's disobedience.[70]

But repairing the situation required action, not just rhetorical camouflage. The council's initial proposal, endorsed by Parliament on 2 September, was to implement the earlier resolution by sending back fifteen ships. A committee conveyed this reassuring decision to Nieuport, while commissioners hurried to meet Montagu and speed the revictualling. They found the fleet in poor condition, owing to sickness, damaged vessels and shortage of provisions; optimism faded as speedy solutions to these problems proved undeliverable.[71] By mid-September the council was obliged to report that, due to the 'extremity of the weather and the State of Victuals', the fifteen ships could not be ready so soon. As the season was nearly over, and the ships were to have returned in any case by the end of the month, it made sense to abandon the plan: on 22 September the plenipotentiaries were granted leave to return if they saw fit. Realism had compelled Parliament to concede that its endeavour to make peace had failed, and cut its losses.[72]

---

fleet's arrival: typical was the report that the fleet had returned because there was 'little occasion for their stay in those parts': *WI*, no. 18, 30 Aug.–6 Sept., 143.

[69] *Politicus*, no. 585, 1–8 Sept., 714; no. 587, 15–22 Sept., 739.

[70] Bordeaux to Mazarin, 8? Sept., Guizot, *Histoire*, i. 443. The council accepted Montagu's written report on 14 Sept., and questioned him no further. Scott therefore seems mistaken in asserting that 'the Council condemned Montague's departure unequivocally': *Sidney and the English Republic*, 135.

[71] *Journal*, 773; council minutes, 2, 3 Sept. The admiralty commissioners Thompson, Walton and Col. Thomas Kelsey were charged with the instructions to the fleet; they arrived by 6 Sept.: MS Carte 73, fo. 304. Goodson described the fleet's problems to them on 13 Sept.: ibid. fo. 307.

[72] Council minutes, 15 Sept.; *Journal*, 779, 785. In the event the plenipotentiaries remained for some months: Scott argues that they did not 'instantly lose the central negotiating position they had wrested': *Sidney and the English Republic*, 136. Nevertheless, from Parliament's – and indeed an international – perspective, the mission had plainly failed: *CSPVen.*, 87. The Dutch eventually resorted to unilateral action.

The United Provinces

Parliament pursued peace more successfully in relation to the United Provinces. At first, renewed conflict between the two republics seemed much more likely than a *rapprochement*. English republicans had, after all, repeatedly condemned the 'dishonourable' and 'disadvantageous' terms on which Cromwell had ended the war.[73] With the Commonwealth's return, the 1654 treaty, like all acts by usurping authority, became vulnerable to legal challenge, and rumours that Parliament's executive committee had actually pronounced it 'unlawful' were soon circulating.[74] Jealousy of the United Provinces' commercial predominance had been aggravated by their recent capture of trade routes closed by belligerent Spain. In Richard's assembly, Scot had emphasised England's 'irreconcileable quarrel' with Dutch trading rivals, whom he suspected of pro-Stuart designs, and predicted eventual war. Even Vane, who doubted Dutch enmity, complained that the 'Spanish interest . . . now mingles much in their counsels', and sardonically suggested that attacking them in the Sound would have been more useful than the actual assault on Jamaica. Out of doors, several republican pamphlets stridently denounced the Dutch 'water-Rat', and again demanded defensive action against this contemporary 'Carthage', now striving 'for the Mastery in Power and Commerce'. Cromwellian failure to enforce Parliament's provocative Navigation Act was particularly deplored.[75] The Sound crisis constituted a ready-made flashpoint. Vice-Admiral Goodson, on duty there, reported that the Commonwealth's restoration brought a 'long stoppe to affairs', due to Dutch uncertainty concerning their 'old antagonist our present Parliament'. A few days after Parliament's restoration the godly republican Nehemiah Bourne suspected the United Provinces of preparing war; Royalists confidently predicted that this republic would indeed assist Charles Stuart.[76]

---

[73] For examples of such condemnations see *Burton diary*, iii. 389–90, 457, 474.

[74] Information sent to Nicholas, 11 May, SP 18/203, fo. 6 (wrongly entered in *CSPD 1658–9* as an actual resolution of Parliament's committee, whose minutes do not survive). The nearest Parliament came to questioning the treaty was an order of 19 May to the council to consider how far the Commonwealth was committed to foreign war/peace by events during the interruption, but here the emphasis was on ensuring that wars had parliamentary sanction.

[75] *Burton diary*, iii. 394, 475, 401, 490; *A BAKERS-DOZEN of Plain Down-right QUERIES*, 6–7; *Trades destruction*, 4; *Excise anotomizd*, 8; F. B., *CONSIDERATIONS AND PROPOSALS . . . Touching the not Warring with SPAIN*, 1. Publications criticising non-enforcement of the Navigation Act include [Streater], *Continuation*, 11–12; *The CASE of Colonel MATTHEW ALURED*, 5, William Cole, *Severall PROPOSALS Humbly tendered to the CONSIDERATION of those in Authority, for the Ease, Security, & Prosperity of this Common-wealth*, 5–6; and *Scout*, no. 3, 6–13 May, 20. On the prior use and significance of comparisons with Carthage see Pincus, *Protestantism*, 92.

[76] William Goodson to George Monck, 31 July, *Clarke papers*, iv. 29; Bourne, 20 May, ibid. iii. 216; Broderick to Hyde, 23 May, MS Clarendon 61, fo. 15. Nicholas was still expecting the fleets to fight in July: *CSPD 1659*, 18.

In fact, the Dutch government rapidly resolved to avoid conflict, ordering its admirals to show 'all courtesy and kindness' to the Commonwealth's ships. Early contacts with England's new rulers encouraged hopes of establishing good relations. By 16 May, Vane was openly announcing that 'the Dutch and we are agreed . . . so that . . . all will be fair betweene us'.[77] Three days later the States-General issued Nieuport with new credentials assuring Parliament of their 'sincere intentions . . . to preserve, increase . . . and corroborate further the good friendship, correspondence, Union and Alliance between the two States and Nations founded on common interests of religion, of State, and of Commerce'. At his audience on 24 May, Nieuport expounded these senti-ments in an 'Elegant Speech', widely publicised by the newsbooks.[78] Such rhetoric, reviving former aspirations to closer political and economic integra-tion, was calculated to attract all English republicans who regretted, with Scot, the lost opportunity to bring the Dutch to 'oneness'. That goal united zealous Protestants, such as Vane, who had strongly supported Parliament's earlier attempts to achieve it by negotiation, and initially opposed war, with secularists such as Neville, who would have preferred conquest, but recog-nised its impracticability in present financial circumstances.[79] Reinforcing unification at home, directly or implicitly, was a rich vein of pro-Dutch propaganda, which counteracted the negative images. Such texts variously celebrated a people who had become 'Potent, Rich and Dreadful' through rejection of political and spiritual tyranny, contended that 'the World [was] wide enough' for their trade as well as England's, and counselled emulation rather than attempted elimination of Holland's successful commercial prac-tices. Differences of opinion among its supporters could thus work in Parlia-ment's favour, ensuring the feasibility of its policy.[80] The council, replying to Nieuport on 26 May, expressed an ardent desire to lay 'a firm foundation . . .

---

[77] Journal, 653; Mordaunt to Hyde, 16 May, MS Clarendon 60, fo. 553. War had been trig-gered in 1652 by the Dutch refusal to show proper courtesy to the Commonwealth's ships.
[78] MS Sloane 4158, fo. 162; MS Clarke 31, fos 126–7. Brief accounts of Nieuport's speech for 'Amity and Peace' appeared in most newsbooks: for examples see Moderate Informer, 19–26 May, 16; Weekly Account, 25 May–1 June, 8.
[79] Burton diary, iii. 111. The best account of Anglo-Dutch negotiations in 1651–2 is Pincus, Protestantism, chs iii, iv. Vane's initial opposition to war is better documented in Scott, Sidney and the English Republic, 94, and Worden, Rump Parliament, 313–14. Bordeaux clearly perceived that Vane was 'much inclined towards the Dutch': Guizot, Histoire, ii. 273. Neville articulated his views in Richard's parliament (Burton diary, iii. 389–90, 391) and was prominent in the early conferences with Nieuport; Royalists observed that he favoured 'firm union' with Holland: MS Clarendon 63, fo. 4.
[80] William Cole, A ROD FOR THE LAWYERS, 15–16; Chaos, appendix; Speculum, 17. See also The Good Old Cause Explained, 3; Peter Chamberlen, A SCOURGE For A DENN Of THIEVES, 5, 8; LILBURNS GHOST, 8; ENGLANDS SETTLEMENT, upon the Two solid foundations of The Peoples Civil and Religious LIBERTIES, 11, 31. Pincus has shown that the impact on popular opinion of an upsurge of negative portrayals of the Dutch in 1651–2 played an important part in frustrating Parliament's diplomatic efforts to preserve peace: Protestantism, ch. iv.

of a lasting peace and nearest union'. As they used near-identical language to describe the projected tripartite alliance with monarchical Sweden, it is improbable that England's leaders in 1659 envisaged as comprehensive a conjunction as that proposed in 1653, which the Dutch had rejected as entirely alien to their federal republicanism. Details, however, never reached discussion.[81] In subsequent exchanges the Dutch proposed, and the English resolved, that union would be negotiated by a special embassy led by some 'considerable member of the government'. Vane's name was suggested in the summer, but he declined to leave England at this critical juncture. There the matter effectively rested.[82]

Union was the ultimate objective, deferred by mutual consent until the resolution of more urgent practical problems.[83] Besides England's support for Denmark in the Sound, the Dutch desired redress for merchants whose vessels had been seized by English captains holding Swedish letters of marque. Nieuport inundated the council with memorials about these 'piracies', and received a sympathetic response. Such cases went to the admiralty commissioners, with orders to do justice 'according to Law and with all expedition'; several ships were released.[84] But the republicans were well aware that the Dutch were not the only sufferers. Sweden's representatives countered with similar accusations, while injured English merchants and mariners complained that Nieuport had dismissed their losses with the remark that 'ambassadors are for the affairs of their own countrymen and not for others'. The council, determined that justice must be bilateral, requested compensa-

---

[81] *TSP* vii. 676. On the 1653 proposals see Pincus, *Protestantism*, ch. viii. The Dutch would scarcely have rekindled hopes of union if they had expected a revival of these unacceptable terms. The secret instructions to the Sound commissioners afford the main clue to English intentions: these enjoined attempts to persuade the Dutch that supporting a Swedish attack on Austria was 'the best means of laying a lasting foundation of friendship' between the two republics: MS Add. 4159, fo. 199.

[82] *TSP* vii. 677, 682–3, 751. On 1 July Bordeaux reported that Vane's enemies had nominated him in a bid to distance him from England's constitutional debates; a week later he noted that Vane's party had blocked the scheme: Guizot, *Histoire*, i. 399, 459. On 8 July Sir John Chiesley in Scotland received news that his friend Johnston and Vane 'wer chosen to go Ambassadors to Holland, but that he had refused to go': *The diary of Andrew Hay of Craignethan, 1659–1660*, ed. Alexander Reid (Scottish Historical Society 1st ser. xxxix, 1901), 74. In fact, neither Parliament nor council formally nominated Vane, but he may well have been considered, and made his views known in debates at this time. There is a clear parallel between this proposed embassy and that of Strickland and St John in 1651.

[83] Thus de Witt's late September letter urging the necessity of a high-level English mission to negotiate union also stressed the prior need to resolve the piracy issue and mitigate the damaging effects of Montagu's return: *TSP* vii. 751.

[84] For a typical case and result see the council minutes, 21 July, 7 Sept. Nieuport also complained of the unlawful seizure of Dutch ships on 27, 30 May, 1, 15, 21 June, 27 July, 11, 26 Aug., 15 Sept. Besides commending cases to the admiralty court, the council ordered the customs commissioners and the commanders in Dunkirk to take 'special care' to prevent any English subjects from sailing against the Dutch, and to release any Dutch ships brought into Commonwealth ports as prizes: council minutes, 10, 12 Aug.

tion for these petitioners from the States.[85] To prevent future depredations and ensure 'free passage' for merchant ships, negotiations began for a joint proclamation against piracies, envisioned as a perpetual law forbidding the subjects of either nation to accept foreign commissions. Enough progress had occurred by September for de Witt to anticipate a 'good issue' shortly, but English insistence on free access to the Dutch East Indies delayed agreement indefinitely.[86] The republicans thus did not sacrifice the interests of English merchants to secure good relations with 'our brethren the Dutch'.[87] Rather, they meant such an alliance to produce the genuine advantages for English commerce that the Dutch themselves had promised.

The same independence characterised Parliament's approach to negotiations with the United Provinces over the Sound. Here the two republics shared an interest in stopping either Scandinavian power from restricting entry to the Baltic. England's new rulers were quite willing to pursue equal trading rights for both nations, and to co-operate in mediation by exerting pressure on Sweden. But when the Dutch tried exploiting the Commonwealth's restoration to rewrite the treaty of The Hague along lines more favourable to Denmark, the English proved unexpectedly uncompliant. To Nieuport's flattering intimation that the Parliament 'so wonderfully restored to the government of the three united nations' could not want to dispute such trivial details with the States-General, the council firmly replied that these matters had been settled at The Hague, and were no longer open for discussion. Parliament ratified the original treaty with only minor amendments.[88]

Dutch hopes of reaping 'great advantage' from the English Republic[89] suffered a further blow when the fleet returned from the Sound. This setback made no difference to Parliament's pro-Dutch policy: Sidney still cherished hopes that the mediation would facilitate a 'neare alliance between the United Provinces and England', while Bordeaux remarked the English authorities' constant inclination 'to maintain a complete agreement between

---

[85] Petition of Thomas Stevenson, mariner of Whitby, CSPD 1658–9, 386. The council demanded reparation for this petitioner from Nieuport on 23 June. In September de Witt insisted that the Dutch were complying with such requests and releasing English ships taken as prizes: TSP vii. 751.

[86] Council minutes, 27 July, 10, 12 Aug., 6, 12 Sept., 5 Oct.; de Witt to Nieuport, 2, 23 Sept., TSP vii. 736, 751.

[87] Chaos, appendix.

[88] Nieuport to the council, 14 July, and council reply, 15 July, TSP vii. 696–8. The changes Nieuport proposed were far from trivial, since they would have changed the entire basis of the Hague settlement from the Treaty of Roskilde of 1658 to the 1645 Treaty of Bromsebro, which took no account of recent Swedish conquests, and so would have been much better for Denmark.

[89] This apt description of Dutch policy towards the republic came from the Royalist Lord Inchiquin, in a letter of 21 May: SP 78/114, fo. 256.

the two republics'.[90] The council assured Nieuport that they had acted with 'all faithfulness', and were as committed as ever to the pacification of the North. Yet the 'notorious contravention' of the treaty was undeniable, as Sidney had foreseen. Since the promised naval co-operation was no longer forthcoming, the Dutch condemned the summer campaigning season as a complete waste of time and money. De Witt claimed that this disappointment had occasioned a 'general indignation of the inhabitants' of Holland against his anglophile policy. To dispel their distrust, Parliament should at least redeem its word by declaring against Sweden, as the refuser of the peace. Without such a declaration, and a properly enforced convention against piracy, he threatened that the States would not proceed to a 'further alliance with England'. And without such an alliance, de Witt warned that the English Commonwealth would soon 'suffer a very great shipwreck'.[91]

De Witt's comments reflect Dutch bewilderment and annoyance at England's persistent refusal to defer to their wishes, as became the junior partner in the alliance. The English republicans, far from meekly accepting their inferiority and waiting for guidance, harboured secret designs to draw Holland into a grandiose Protestant scheme of their own. According the United Provinces the deference they desired would have been inconsistent with the honour of the Commonwealth, whose diplomacy aimed at 'necessary, equal and like advantages' for both states.[92] The Dutch constantly overestimated the value of their support, which they judged indispensable to the survival of a government struggling to surmount domestic difficulties. Parliament undoubtedly found Dutch goodwill useful. Early recognition from the United Provinces, as a major European power, gave the new regime 'great reputation', and encouraged lesser states to initiate diplomatic relations.[93] The much publicised readiness of the Dutch Republic to proceed towards a nearer union further enhanced Parliament's prestige, and helped counter English reactionaries' claims that a hereditary monarch was essential to the formation of foreign alliances.[94] During the emergency of Booth's rising, the States-General forbade the transportation of Royalists in Dutch ships, and so impeded their plans somewhat.[95] Notwithstanding these benefits, and the hopes of greater commercial and political gains, the friendship of Holland

[90] Sidney to Leicester, 13 Sept., *Sydney papers*, 168; Bordeaux to de Brienne, 26 Sept., Guizot, *Histoire*, i. 476.

[91] Nieuport to the States-General, 16/26 Sept.; de Witt to Nieuport, 23 Sept./3 Oct., 14/24 Oct., *TSP* vii. 744, 751, 764–5.

[92] The council stated this aim in an answer to Nieuport, 28 June, ibid. vii. 690–1.

[93] Hyde to Mordaunt, 25 May/4 June, *CSP* iii. 480. The Venetian senate instructed their ambassador to follow the Dutch example in deciding whether to recognise the new regime: *CSPVen.*, 31. Sweden, Denmark, Portugal and the Hanse towns hastened to extend recognition in the wake of Nieuport's audience.

[94] For such claims by Royalists see *Interest of England*, 4, 9, and [John Evelyn], *An APOLOGY for the ROYAL PARTY*, 11.

[95] Sparkes to Hyde, Middelborough, 1 Sept. n.s., MS Clarendon 64, fo. 5.

was far from essential. When shipwreck did indeed befall the English Republic in October, its cause was not the cooling of Anglo-Dutch relations, but an internal crisis that the United Provinces could hardly have prevented.[96]

France

France, like its northern neighbour, expected deference from the English Republic, but did not obtain it. Anglo-French relations were, however, considerably less cordial than those with Holland. While the Dutch courted the new government with flattering expressions of regard, the French ostentatiously remained aloof. As Mazarin, unlike de Witt, had nothing to gain from the change, he instructed Bordeaux to sustain France's ally, the Protectorate. Although the ambassador did his best to foster Cromwellian resistance to the Republic, he utterly failed to make good his later boast that France was 'the only one capable of preventing its establishment'.[97] After confirmation that the armies in Scotland and Ireland had submitted, Bordeaux abandoned his secret intrigues with Thurloe, and advised his government to recall him or recognise Parliament, the sole visible authority. This step the French crown was patently reluctant to take, despite warnings that prolonged hesitation might result in the ignominious expulsion of its ambassador. Not until 20 June, six weeks after Parliament's return, and more than a month after the Dutch extended recognition, did it issue new credentials. Meanwhile Bordeaux, like other diplomats awaiting accreditation, was admitted to informal conferences with the council, in which he offered ingenious excuses for the delay, and disingenuous assurances of goodwill. It is hardly surprising that these did not eliminate 'distrust . . . of [French] aversion against the new regime'. To the English republicans, France was triply suspect as a Catholic monarchy closely connected with both the Stuarts and Cromwells. Mazarin's obvious unwillingness to institute formal diplomatic relations not only affronted Parliament's dignity, but fuelled fears that the French were playing for time, and would attack the Commonwealth as soon as they had finalised peace with Spain.[98]

---

[96] Nothing short of successful military assistance on the scale of 1688 could have enabled the Dutch to save Parliament, and this de Witt certainly did not contemplate.

[97] Bordeaux's letters related his obedient efforts to subvert the Republic by offering Richard Cromwell French money and military assistance: Guizot, *Histoire*, i. 380–2, 383–4, 388–9, 405.

[98] Bordeaux first counselled recognition in an express sent on 24 May, after the submissions of the Cromwell brothers and Nieuport's audience; two days later he reiterated this advice, outlined his excuses for the delay, and warned that expulsion was possible if new credentials did not appear in reasonable time. This letter and the next, on 5 June, clearly explained republican suspicions: ibid. i. 402–3, 456–8, 436–7.

In a climate of such fear and suspense, the eventual presentation of Bordeaux's credentials provoked a major diplomatic incident. At first, it seemed as if tensions would be defused by a formal audience, during which he would publicly communicate French respect for Parliament. That body accepted his credentials on 24 June and, as its manner was, deputed three MPs to attend him to an audience scheduled for the next morning. Though he had twenty-four hours' notice, Bordeaux excused himself at the last moment on the grounds that the ceremonies were identical with those accorded the Dutch ambassador. France, as a superior state, should receive greater distinction: more carriages, more soldiers, more MPs, preferably of higher rank. Parliament should at least replace Whitelocke, who had also headed the delegation attending Nieuport. Instead of acceding to these demands, the House abruptly cancelled the proceedings without sending formal notice to the ambassador.[99] France had certainly done nothing to merit preferential treatment. The official letter of credence was decidedly lukewarm: whereas the States-General and the Swedish king paid fulsome compliments to the new rulers, Louis XIV did not congratulate Parliament, but professed only his 'good Affection . . . at all tymes to the Nations which compose your Republique'.[100] As some MPs pointed out, the new credentials did not actually appoint Bordeaux ambassador, but assumed that he already held this rank under that illegitimate government, the Protectorate. Distrust of France was openly voiced in debate; many saw in Bordeaux's objections a specious pretext for hostility.[101]

The controversy over this audience reveals much about the restored Republic's conduct of foreign relations. Parliament would not swallow an insult to the Commonwealth's honour, or yield to intimidation. Bordeaux,

[99] *Journal*, 693. The next day's entry has no record of the cancellation, a sure sign that Parliament was offended. When an audience was deferred, the usual practice was to send notice by the master of ceremonies – cf. the treatment of the Portuguese ambassador, ibid. 710, 714. Bordeaux noted the omission of this formality in the justification of his conduct composed on 27 June: Guizot, *Histoire*, i. 404–7. He claimed that he had requested, and been promised, superior treatment when he presented his credentials to the council. There is, however, no evidence that the council made such a recommendation and was over-ruled. In arranging the audience Parliament clearly followed standard procedure, which became controversial only when Bordeaux began to object.

[100] Louis XIV to 'the Parliament of the Commonwealth of England', MS Tanner 51, fos 78–9; cf. the States-General, which professed its affection for the 'Parliament of the Republic of England' (MS Sloane 4158, fo. 162), and Charles X's address to the 'most excellent and illustrious rulers, our good friends and confederates of the Republic of England, Ireland and Scotland': *Journal*, 692.

[101] Bordeaux reported the criticisms of his credentials, suspicions of France and the council's subsequent refusal to address him as 'excellency', the correct title for an ambassador, in his letters of 27 June and 1 July: Guizot, *Histoire*, i. 406–7, 398–9. There is no republican narrative of the dispute; the only English account comes from a Royalist, who accurately records Bordeaux's objections, but exaggerates Parliament's displeasure, inventing radical egalitarian messages which were certainly not sent: SP 78/114, fo. 273.

who naturally refused to believe that he had given just cause of offence, contended that Parliament should rescind its resolutions, and hinted that a proper concern for its own safety should lead it to conciliate the mighty power of France. By declining to do any such thing, the English proclaimed 'the pride of this regime' to all Europe. So formidable was this stance that Bordeaux hastened to assure Mazarin that the Republic was not dangerous; its behaviour was explicable only by dismissing the majority of MPs as 'extravagant enough to forget . . . their own interest'. Sir Henry Vane he excepted from this number, and the incident is, indeed, a good illustration of Vane's diplomacy. Unlike his colleagues, Vane neither badgered the French ambassador to back down, nor insinuated that his intransigence implied Louis XIV's intention to champion his Stuart cousins, nor threatened that Parliament would henceforth negotiate exclusively through Lockhart, its representative in France. Rather, he treated Bordeaux with his usual civility, continued to consult him over the Sound, and encouraged the search for compromise which proceeded on both sides of the Channel throughout July. Parliament, according to Vane's confidential disclosures, desired nothing better than good relations with France.[102] As Mazarin deemed it expedient to remain upon terms with the *de facto* English government, a breach was averted. The French court granted Lockhart an especially civil reception, and this, together with Bordeaux's reaccreditation as ambassador *extraordinaire*, enabled Parliament to make concessions without losing face.[103] After careful consultation with the council, ceremonies fully 'answerable to the Amity and honor this Commonwealth bears to the French Crown' were agreed. At the eventual audience on 22 August, Bordeaux enjoyed the escort of two earls, a knight and two more files of musketeers than Nieuport had received.[104] Mutual protestations of respect and goodwill marked the occasion. French recognition, following Lambert's decisive victory over the domestic insurgents, helped build the English Republic's reputation in Europe.[105]

[102] Bordeaux to Mazarin, 27 June, 1, 19 July: Guizot, *Histoire*, i. 405–8, 398–9, 410.

[103] The positive effect of Lockhart's reception on Parliament's attitude is clear from Bordeaux's letters of 7 and 21 July (ibid. i. 392, 412) and the council's reply to Lockhart of 24 July, SP 78/114, fo. 293. Lockhart himself promoted good relations by assurances that if either 'rational grounds of interest' or 'firm promises' could be trusted, Mazarin had no hostile intentions towards the Commonwealth; he urged the council to take 'kind notice' of Bordeaux, whose 'truth and sincerity' in relating English events 'to the advantage of the Commonwealth' he applauded – mistakenly, since Bordeaux never failed to report signs of the Republic's weakness: ibid. fos 302, 309–10. Mazarin evidently concealed these details from him.

[104] Accounts of the audience were sent by the council to Lockhart and Bordeaux to Mazarin on the same day: SP 78/114, fo. 351; Guizot, *Histoire*, i. 425. Bordeaux noted his new credentials' arrival on 8 August; four days later Parliament received and referred them to the council, which conferred with him on the arrangements: *Journal*, 757, 762; Guizot, *Histoire*, i. 421–2.

[105] Thus Bordeaux's audience, together with Booth's defeat, caused even Giavarina to reverse his opinion of the Republic's chances of survival. Though he cynically, and inaccu-

Despite public professions of solidarity at the audience, the course of Anglo-French relations did not run smoothly afterwards. Rumours that France had permitted Charles Stuart to pass through on his way to the peace negotiations in the Pyrenees reignited republican fears of a Franco-Spanish plot to restore him. By mid-September Bordeaux acknowledged that Royalist boasting gave some grounds for alarm, but suspected Vane of magnifying the external danger in order to 'intimidate and retain those who oppose his designs'. Given the growing divisions within the English government, this suspicion is not altogether unfounded. Internal unity certainly mattered more than French cordiality to Vane, whose progress from principal advocate of good relations to the foremost exponent of distrust may be traced in Bordeaux's reports. The ambassador retaliated by taxing Vane with his failure to maintain proper consultation with France over the Sound since the fleet's return.[106] The council, in its turn, adduced further grievances: the moneys still owing to the regiments that Cromwell had lent to France, and the latest restrictions on merchant ships lading at French ports. Friction over these issues did not, however, imply that Parliament was about to abandon its pacific policy. Early in October the council readily assented to Bordeaux's request for a formal audience, and gave such a positive hearing to his proposals to renew the alliance of 1655, as a sign of goodwill, that he departed with the impression that fears of French duplicity had receded again. Vane and his associates were, as the Frenchman realised, far too politically adept to risk embroiling England in a new war just when peace was most needed.[107] If they had any conscious design to use French affairs to divert Parliament from the gathering domestic crisis, they failed utterly. Though the House discharged urgent foreign business as conscientiously as ever, it would not allow itself to be distracted: on 11 October, days before the second interruption, it heard Salway report on Bordeaux's proposals, and sanctioned the recall of Lockhart before resuming its deliberations on the Army petition.[108] As Lockhart's return would leave Bordeaux the only official intermediary with France, it is unlikely that the English government was harbouring serious misgivings as to Mazarin's immediate intentions.

---

rately, asserted that Bordeaux had delayed audience until the outcome of the rising became known, he hastened to follow the French example by delivering his own credentials: CSPVen., 61, 64.

106 Bordeaux to Mazarin, 8, 19, 26 Sept., Guizot, Histoire, i. 443–4, 439–40, 476–7. This was the moment when Hyde produced his 'way how ye Kings of Spayne and France may . . . establish the King of England without warr and with very litle or noe charges': 16 Sept., MS Clarendon 64, fos 187–9.

107 Council to Lockhart, 5 Sept., SP 78/114, fo. 367; Bordeaux to Mazarin, 3, 10 Oct., Guizot, Histoire, i. 482–4, 486–8. Bordeaux's audience with the council took place on 4 Oct., the day after his request was reported. In his speech he asserted that Charles Stuart had passed through France without Mazarin's knowledge, and reaffirmed his government's friendship for the Commonwealth.

108 Journal, 795.

Spain

The termination of Lockhart's embassy in October not only marked a new stage in Anglo-French relations, but also removed any lingering prospects of an early peace with Spain. The failure to negotiate such a peace in five months at first sight seems one of the most conspicuous proofs that republican foreign policy was ineffectual. Parliament's return in May had generated universal expectations of a speedy end to the war. Ambassadors and Royalists anticipated that Parliament would rapidly make terms with Spain; loyal newsbooks proclaimed Spain's eagerness for good relations with the Commonwealth; merchants whose livelihoods had suffered hastened to renew their petitions against the conflict.[109] These expectations had a firm basis in the new government's known inclinations. In opposition, the republicans had consistently condemned Cromwell's 'costly and dishonourable war' as contrary to the 'public good', and affirmed solidarity with injured commercial interests.[110] In power, they manifested no ambition whatsoever to continue hostilities, which remained in abeyance, at least on land, throughout their ascendancy. Confirmation that Parliament's general policy of peace extended to Spain comes not just from Vane's conversations with Bordeaux, but from the correspondence of Thomas Scot, who deplored the origins and conduct of the conflict, and professed 'the same inclinations for a . . . Perfect Understanding betwixt Spain and this Commonwealth which I have ever expressed'.[111] There is no reason to suspect the republicans of insincerity. Apportioning blame was, unfortunately, much easier than concluding peace. The difficulties were the opposing pressures shaping English foreign policy, and unforeseen obstruction by Spain.

The problem of the Spanish war most clearly illustrates the tension between the twin imperatives of peace and honour. However satisfying, denunciations of the Protector's policy would not miraculously restore the *status quo ante*. Much as they might dislike it, the republicans had to grasp the nettle of the Cromwellian legacy. Scot aptly summed up the new government's position: 'though we have not contributed to this war yet being now

---

109 CSPVen., 25, 28; Guizot, *Histoire*, i. 375, 390–1; MS Clarendon 61, fos 1, 120, 268, 271; *Nicholas papers*, 130; *Post*, no. 3, 17–24 May, 17; *WI*, no. 7, 14–21 June, 56. The 'Humble Petition of the Merchants trading to the Dominions of the King of Spain', presented to Parliament on 26 May, and referred to the council, was probably almost identical with the petition of the same title presented to Richard's parliament, and published at large. Bethel estimated that the Spanish war had cost England 705 ships, worth £2.3 million, and another million in lost exports: *Second narrative*, 54–5.

110 *Burton diary*, iii. 457, 490, 314, 474.

111 A truce suspending the fighting on land had come into effect at the beginning of May, and continued with Parliament's approval throughout the following months. Ludlow's narrative emphasises Parliament's concern for peace, and unwillingness to sanction 'any act of hostility' against Spain: *Ludlow memoirs*, ii. 97. For Vane's assertions to Bordeaux see Guizot, *Histoire*, i. 413, 484; Scot to Joseph Bamfield, 21 June, MS Clarendon 61, fo. 286.

left charged upon our account we shall not conclude dishonourably what they began improvidently'. Far-sighted politicians of all persuasions perceived that this outlook made an instant resolution of the conflict improbable and injudicious. John Streater, justifying Parliament, argued that the war tending 'to the destruction of Trade . . . must now be defended for the honour of the Nation'; the *Faithful Scout* reproduced his warning, while the moderate Cromwellian author of *Twenty-seven Queries* cautioned readers to patiently leave the present rulers 'to their best understandings to effect' the 'general Peace with Spain' which they 'in part held forth'.[112] The Commonwealth could not hazard its reputation in Europe by betraying an excessive anxiety to make peace. Rather, its representatives endeavoured to convince foreign powers that England, though preferring friendship with all, was quite indifferent to the continuation of the war.[113] To add plausibility to these assertions, Parliament gave a gracious welcome to the Portuguese ambassador, who entreated confirmation of the Cromwellian alliance against Spain. Though they evaded a commitment so fatal to the prospects of peace, the council carefully considered his proposals, and instructed both Lockhart and the Sound plenipotentiaries to defend Portuguese interests insofar as these did not impede the other business entrusted to them.[114] By September even Bordeaux had realised that those in charge of foreign affairs valued the political and economic advantages of peace much less than they feared the 'dishonour' of surrendering the territorial gains of the war.[115]

The ultimate answer to sceptics who supposed that the English Republic must be desperate for peace was the lofty detachment with which Parliament waited for Spain to make the first move. The prerequisite of any settlement was the opening of a channel of communication. This proved surprisingly difficult. England had not been included in the main treaty between France and Spain negotiations for which had begun on the frontier in the Pyrenees. Lockhart had received peace overtures from leading Spaniards in Paris during his last embassy for the Protectorate, but the change of government curtailed this initiative before serious discussions could start.[116] Contrary to popular

---

112 Scot to Bamfield, 21 June, MS Clarendon 61, fo. 286; S[treater], *Continuation*, 13; *Scout*, no. 3, 6–13 May, 20; *Twenty seven queries*, 6. For a Royalist who soon reached the same conclusion see MS Clarendon 61, fo. 1.

113 See, for example, Lockhart's speech to Don Luis, in which he assured the Spaniard that Parliament's desire for good relations sprang 'not out of the least apprehension of the issue of a war, but out of their love to peace in general': MS Clarendon 64, fos 16–19. Bordeaux reported similar statements by ministers in England: Guizot, *Histoire*, i. 413, 489.

114 The Portuguese ambassador had audience on 14 July, with the same ceremony accorded Nieuport (*Journal*, 718); the instructions to English diplomats are in the council minutes, 29 June, and the council's letter to Lockhart of 28 July in SP 78/114, fo. 295.

115 Bordeaux to de Brienne, 26 Sept., Guizot, *Histoire*, i. 476–7.

116 That the Spanish approached Lockhart in Paris is clear not only from the correspondence of alarmed Royalists (SP 78/114, fos 241, 246, 252) but from Thurloe's letter informing Lockhart that, due to the officers' decision to recall Parliament, no commission to negotiate a peace could be sent: *CSPD 1658–9*, 340.

belief, the Spanish crown evinced no immediate enthusiasm for renewed amity with the Commonwealth, and seemed to credit its Royalist allies, who portrayed the new regime as inherently unstable and inconsiderable.[117] Unless and until these representations were exploded, Spain would not risk a formal diplomatic mission. Instead, the Spanish sought to keep their options open by sending a secret, and so repudiable, agent to discover English dispositions to peace. This move was blocked by the republicans' refusal to treat with anyone lacking proper accreditation.[118] Nor would the English government endanger its honour by a direct approach to Spain. Deadlock ensued. The Venetian resident shrewdly observed that it might be broken by a 'princely mediator'. Louis XIV was the obvious candidate for this role, but in the delicate state of Anglo-French relations could not be relied on to smooth England's path to peace.[119] Parliament's solution was to send back Lockhart, officially as ambassador to France, actually in the hope that Spain might renew the offers of the spring.

Despite its end in failure, Lockhart's mission achieved two of its main objectives. First, the English Republic made contact with the Spanish government at the highest level, in the person of Don Luis de Haro, Mazarin's counterpart in the frontier negotiations. Second, Lockhart contradicted Royalist propaganda, and communicated Parliament's general inclination to peace on 'reasonable terms' consonant with the 'honour and safety' of the Commonwealth.[120] Only in the all-important task of discovering Spain's exact intentions, and the 'likelyhood . . . of any progresse towards a peace', was Lockhart less successful.[121] Although Don Luis received him with 'extraordinary demonstrations of courtesy', and confirmed that Spain blamed not Parliament but Cromwell's 'injustice and ambition' for the war, he offered

---

[117] The Royalist endeavours to influence Spanish attitudes to the Republic may be traced in the correspondence of Hyde and Sir Henry Bennet, the Stuart representative in Spain.

[118] Scot spelt out the objections when writing to his agent in Paris on 21 June: a 'letter without a Superscription, addressed to Mr. White' gave the council no 'sufficient ground' to proceed to renew amity with Spain, desirable though this was: MS Clarendon 61, fo. 286. The presence of Spain's agent incognito was known to both Giavarina and the Royalists: CSPVen., 31; Nicholas papers, 135.

[119] Giavarina to the senate, 20 May, 3 June, CSPVen., 25, 31.

[120] Lockhart's original instructions do not survive, but the importance of these objectives is clear from the extant correspondence. On 8 Aug. Lockhart assured the council that he would obey instructions to use 'all wayes . . . to make some entrance into and get some knowledge from a discourse with the Spaniard', and announced that a meeting with Don Luis on 'equall terms' was imminent. On 24 July the council had reminded Lockhart of the danger that 'false reports both at home and abroad' were employed 'to provoke to an attempt against this nation'; he in turn related his efforts to discredit such reports, and asserted that neither Mazarin nor Don Luis believed them: SP 78/114, fos 322–3, 293, 302, 304.

[121] Council to Lockhart, 8 Aug., ibid. fo. 324. The council and its representatives reiterated the demand for exact information at least twice during the following month: ibid. fos 362, 367.

no more than vague reciprocal assurances of his government's desire for 'peace and friendship with all their neighbours'. The request for an unequiv-ocal definition of the Spanish position he deflected by urging the necessity of consulting his master in Madrid, who would then send a qualified negotiator. As Lockhart's visit coincided with the rebellion in England, it is probable that, as he suspected, Don Luis's reticence sprang from concern to learn the outcome before committing his government.[122] Lockhart himself was hampered by the fact that he had no powers to treat, and no specific proposals to present: the purpose of his embassy was to 'lay the foundation . . . of a peace' the precise terms of which Parliament had yet to decide. The council undertook to provide 'such further instructions . . . as shall be fit' as soon as Lockhart could report 'any further answer or application' from Don Luis. That left the initiative squarely with the Spaniards, who declined to take it, even after the news of Booth's defeat. Don Luis told the Royalists that he had received Lockhart under the misapprehension that he brought some 'great proposition', and was empowered to conclude an agreement. Once the truth was revealed, Spain lost interest. By early October Giavarina had heard that the Spanish king opposed peace with England, and that Lockhart was now accorded a 'very cold reception'. In view of Spain's refusal to co-operate, there was little to gain by continuing his mission.[123]

Republican determination that Spain should be the first to propose peace not only stemmed from zeal for the Commonwealth's honour: it also reflected the confusion of competing priorities. Bordeaux detected a division between, on the one hand, those MPs who wanted a rapid settlement based on a return to the previous state of affairs, and, on the other, those in control of foreign policy, who feared the humiliation and potential danger of tamely aban-doning Cromwell's conquests. Vane definitely held the second view; Hesilrig probably subscribed to the first, since he had inveighed against the immo-rality of 'seeking after the dominion of Spain, which was none of ours', and dismissed radical dreams of destroying AntiChrist by a 'fleshly sword'.[124] Many zealous Protestants did, indeed, invest English possession of Dunkirk

122 Lockhart narrated his audience with Don Luis to the council on 22 Aug., and to Fleetwood and Vane on 1 Sept.: CSP iii. 544, 549–50.
123 Lockhart to the council, 8 Aug., and council to Lockhart, 5 Sept., SP 78/114, fos 322–3, 367; Bennet to Hyde, 6 Sept., MS Clarendon 64, fos 79–80; Giavarina to the senate, 7 Oct., CSPVen., 77. Direct evidence of the republican reasoning behind the decision to recall Lockhart is lacking, due to the disappearance of his last letters and any account of the debates in council and Parliament.
124 Bordeaux noted these differences in letters of 27 July, 22 Aug. and 26 Sept., identifying Vane as one of the second group: Guizot, Histoire, i. 418, 426, 476. Hesilrig is unlikely to have changed the views he outlined in February: Burton diary, iii. 457–8. Vane's attitude probably resulted from a superior grasp of the strategic/honorific implications of aban-doning Dunkirk rather than from religious enthusiasm for conquest. His theology emphasised passivity more often than the pure use of the 'sword still in the hands of Gods people', whom he warned against attempting to achieve 'the fleshly glory of Christs King-dom' by violence: Meditations, 381, 310. An interesting, though not wholly convincing,

with apocalyptic significance, as the first stage in the fall of Babylon. John Canne, the Fifth Monarchist editing the official news until mid-August, advocated the spread of Reformation light to this stronghold of Roman Catholicism, 'the saddest, the maddest Religion'. The Quaker Edward Burrough, recounting his own efforts to preach there, waxed still more enthusiastic, prophesying that the English Army should rescue all Europe from 'the weight of Romes Idollatry', together with the prevailing political 'tyranie and grievous oppressions'; he particularly exhorted vengeance on Spain and Italy. To retreat from Dunkirk would thus constitute a betrayal of Protestantism and radical republicanism that would further reduce the regime's credibility with its adherents among the sects.[125] But sober reasons for retaining the town were also advanced by its English occupants. Lockhart, as governor, implored Parliament to 'keep Dunkirk wherein the honor and interest of England is so much concerned'; his deputies echoed this appeal, admonishing the council not to despise the gift of providence but to 'secure our footing in the continent of Europe, lost ever since Queen Mary's days and now regayned'. Such a foothold would, they reasoned, be 'a goad in the sides' of future enemies. Dunkirk therefore had strategic as well as religious and honorific value.[126]

Advocates for the retention of Jamaica also emerged. Merchants trading with the West Indies volunteered to invest in its colonisation if Parliament would constitute them a company with a monopoly on the region's commerce, and supply the necessary ships. This enterprise, they forecast, would either 'induce the Spanyard to make such an equall peace as may be agreeable to the welfare of this Commonwealth', or else sustain the war at 'Litle charge and great advantage to the English Interests'. Evidently, commercial interests were not united in support of peace, despite the preponderance of propaganda ascribing the decay of trade to the war.[127] The merchants' project, together with the 'fair proffers' of the Portuguese, was sufficiently attractive to strengthen doubts as to the advisability of peace at any price. Colonel Thompson, relating these events to Lockhart, urged him

---

reading of the *Healing question* as a reaction against the imperialist 'Western Design' is Armitage, 'Cromwellian Protectorate', 544–5.

[125] *PI* (no. 187), 25 July–1 Aug., 616–17; Edward Burrough and Samuel Fisher to Gerrard Roberts and Thomas Hart, 28 May, FHL, MS Portfolio I, fo. 107; Edward Burrough, *A Visitation & Warning PROCLAMED And An Alarm Sounded in the Popes Borders*, 29–30.

[126] Lockhart to Parliament's committee of safety, *Journal*, 657; Cols Lillingston and Alsop to the council, 15 Aug., *TSP* vii. 729. The reasoning was sound; Downing's protest that the restored monarchy's sale of Dunkirk to France would lead to England ceasing to be 'considerable indeed' in Europe was abundantly fulfilled: Scott, *England's troubles*, 313.

[127] 'A Proposition for the Erecting a West India Company and for the better securing the Interests of this Commonwealth in America', MS Egerton 2395, fos 87–8. The merchants emphasised the potential benefits to English trade. On the background and remarkable scope of their proposal see Robert Bliss, *Revolution and empire: English politics and the American colonies in the seventeenth century*, Manchester 1990, 68–71.

to ascertain the minimum conditions acceptable to the Spanish, so 'that this State may steare their affairs accordingly, and not Ingage too far to retract'. The implication was plain: if Spain would cede its lost territories, peace would be judged most advantageous; if not, there was a real possibility that the war might continue.[128]

By deliberate indecision, justified by the need for reliable information on Spain's attitude, Vane and his associates long maintained an uneasy harmony within the government on the issue of peace. It was not unrealistic to expect that Spain might offer the Commonwealth favourable terms; that it did not do so was no fault of the English republicans. New counsels, beginning with Lockhart's recall, were adopted when it became evident that Spanish views would not be disclosed without sacrifice of the Commonwealth's dignity. These counsels, however, were overtaken by the internal crisis of the autumn. To judge policy in the preceding months a failure, merely because it did not end the war, is to miss the fact that peace was not Parliament's sole, nor yet its highest, priority. Rather, it had to be weighed against the conflicting demands of security and prestige. The republicans sought peace, but would not sue for it to England's dishonour.

Minor powers

The twin imperatives of England's honour and interest, subject though these were to differing interpretations, determined the Republic's handling of foreign affairs. Selection was essential, since there were so many calls on the time available. At the top of the agenda were those areas that most affected English welfare: the Spanish war, the Sound crisis and relations with those powerful and potentially hostile neighbours, France and the United Provinces. More remote states received proportionately less attention. Parliament scrutinised all credentials, but did not itself grant audience to the envoys of powers deemed inferior. Representatives of Hamburg, Tuscany and Venice were referred to committees; those of Sweden, Denmark, Holstein and Poland, to the council.[129] That body listened courteously, albeit infrequently, to these diplomats, made occasional gestures of goodwill while they stayed,

---

128 Thompson to Lockhart, 29 Aug., SP 78/114, fo. 362. The West Indies merchants first petitioned the council on 8 July; on 25 Aug. that body created a committee, including Thompson, to consider their proposals for a West India company that would furnish men and provisions for the state's ships in return for 80% of the profits from the war. Thompson explained that the attraction of this offer lay in its promise to save, and even make, money for the Commonwealth. The council did not, however close with it while a more advantageous peace remained possible; in October the scheme was still under discussion.

129 *Journal*, 685, 793, 769, 689, 701–2, 686. The Polish ambassador had not yet received new credentials, but wrote to Parliament to protest at the arrest of his interpreter on suspicion of being an Irish-born Catholic priest.

and pledged the 'Continuation of all friendly respect' when they departed.[130] Stimulated by Whitelocke, the council did display a fleeting concern for the affairs of northern Germany in the early summer, when it appointed various committees to confer with the German diplomats, and recommended the ongoing employment of England's agent in Hamburg. This report foundered amid more urgent matters, and never reached Parliament. With rebellion imminent a month later, the council regretfully informed Lubeck's deputy that it had no leisure to return a 'particular definite answer' to his proposals before he left England; though Whitelocke was instructed to prepare a 'general answer', interest in Germany lapsed thereafter.[131] But official replies seldom invoked domestic pressures to excuse inaction; where delay was necessary, soothing promises of further deliberation were preferable to anything resembling an admission of inadequacy. Giavarina's sneers at Parliament's inattention to 'all private affairs especially those of the foreign ministers' were based largely on hearsay, since he had few personal dealings with the regime.[132] In general, Parliament was careful to treat ambassadors with the consideration befitting their rank and the Commonwealth's honour.

For all this cordiality, neither advances nor affronts from minor powers evoked much response from the English Republic, which had little business of its own to transact with their agents in London, and hence little to gain from the expenditure of valuable time.[133] Thus Sweden's emissaries got scant

---

[130] This was the council's farewell message of 12 August to the representatives of Poland and Hamburg; gestures of goodwill included the prompt release of the Polish interpreter, the removal of restraints on the horses of the Venetian and Holstein residents and the licence granted to the former to import currants duty-free: council minutes, 21 June, 30 July, 3 Aug., 16 July, following Parliament's order, recorded in *Journal*, 717. The infrequency with which the affairs of minor European states occupied the council's attention is evident from its minutes which mention the envoys of the Hanse towns, Holstein, Poland and Venice on only a handful of occasions. There is an obvious contrast with the major powers: Nieuport had 29 consultations with the council or its committees, while even Bordeaux, who was far less anxious to negotiate, had 9. Due to the Sound business, Sweden and Denmark received attention disproportionate to their status, with 17 and 9 consultations respectively.

[131] Council minutes, 26, 31 May, 1, 17, 21 June, 12, 22, 28 July. Whitelocke was extremely prominent in these committees: on 21 May he announced the arrival of Lubeck's envoy, with business that could not wait for new credentials, while he was given care, as the only MP, of the committee for that envoy's farewell audience on 28 July. An order of 25 June had instructed him to use his 'interest and endeavours' to gather news from Hamburg and Lubeck.

[132] Giavarina to the senate, 23 Sept., *CSPVen.*, 73, a statement supported by asserting that the Portuguese ambassador had sought audience in vain. Even if true – there is no other evidence – this did not prove that the English government was neglecting foreign ministers: the council's minutes reveal that it had appointed a committee to confer with the Portuguese only four days earlier, on 19 Sept. Giavarina's personal experience was limited to the controversy over his own audience, in which English ministers employed the 'pretext of other affairs', but only in private conversations: ibid. 70.

[133] Where Parliament did have business to transact, as in the case of the Baltic powers, it preferred to approach their rulers directly through its own agents.

sympathy, since they were offering nothing comparable to the glittering prospect of the Dutch alliance; the Portuguese ambassador was kept on perpetual
tenterhooks while the question of peace with Spain hovered in the balance.
Conversely, envoys whose masters did not address new credentials to Parliament were civilly used, and sped on their way with the government's
blessing.[134] When Giavarina, emulating Bordeaux's tactics, declined his audience with a parliamentary committee on the ground that this procedure
disallowed the Venetian claim to great power status, he provoked a minimal
reaction. Speaker Lenthall, to whom he addressed his complaint, assured him
that Venice was 'greatly esteemed by parliament', though he undermined this
consolation by the inaccurate assertion that all foreign diplomats received
equal treatment. Other ministers held out 'hopes of satisfaction' in private,
but were silent in public. The council did not trouble to arrange a compromise; Parliament itself showed no sign of retreat or offence.[135] The contrast
between this unconcern and the furore over Bordeaux's audience is explicable by the fact that Venice, unlike France, was so far from menacing
England's security that it was actually more anxious than its agent to conciliate 'so great a parliament'. Its letter of credence was as laudatory as the
vainest MPs could have wished: the Senate not only affected to 'rejoice at . . .
the establishment of the republic' but even declared that it would 'welcome
any opportunity' to manifest its former 'cordial disposition' towards 'the
sovereign power of England . . . for which we would desire all prosperity'.[136]
Hence Giavarina's antics inspired none of the fear and suspicion that had
been aroused by Bordeaux. The English Commonwealth could ignore the
pretensions or importunities of distant and inferior European states with

---

134 This was the case with the envoys of Poland (council minutes, 1, 12 Aug.) and
Courland (Journal, 769); the latter had related his plight in a letter to Lenthall: MS Tanner
51, fo. 129.
135 Giavarina detailed his reasons for refusing audience, and English responses, in letters
of 2 and 9 Sept., CSPVen., 66–7, 70. No progress occurred in the remainder of that month;
on 7 Oct. he reported his determination to resist Parliament's reputed intention to give less
distinguished audiences to residents who lacked the title of ambassador: ibid. 78. Institutional sources reveal no such resolutions; whatever private discussions took place, the
council made no attempt to formally negotiate a compromise. It did, however, entrust
Giavarina with copies of Parliament's letters requesting his government to secure the
insane earl of Arundel (council minutes, 4 Oct., ibid. 78). These illustrate Parliament's
desire to remain upon terms with Venice without reversing its resolves anent the audience.
136 Venetian senate to Parliament, 18/28 June, ibid. 36–7. That Giavarina was more
hostile to the English Republic than his government appears from his delay in presenting
his credentials, in which he imitated Bordeaux rather than the Dutch, Swedish and Danish
representatives specified in his instructions: ibid. 32. When Parliament's letter concerning
Arundel gave the Venetian authorities the opportunity they craved, they immediately
transmitted the request to the magistrates in Padua; though the latter were reluctant to
surrender Arundel without his relatives' consent, the necessity was removed by the news of
the October coup: ibid. 82–3, 85, 87, 95–6.

impunity. And in this, it resembled major powers of every political complexion.

What then was uniquely 'republican' about the restored Commonwealth's foreign policy? Its basic principles – 'interest' and 'honour' – were, of course, shared by all English patriots. 1659, however, saw a reversal of the regressive trend to subsume these national concerns in an individual or dynastic interest, and their reconnection, instead, with collective models of government.[137] Thus the *Scout* assured its readers, within days of Parliament's return, that a Commonwealth 'never maketh War Defensive or Offensive but it is simply for the profit of the Whole', and contrasted this commitment to the common good with princely wars fought for a 'Distinct Interest' to the people's detriment.[138] The great difference between 'Monarchy' and a 'Republick', another author explained, was that the latter metamorphosed England from a merely 'considerable Country' into one 'formidable to all the Earth'. Patriotic longings for prestige and prosperity also underpinned poetic depictions of the future British republic as 'Europes darling', enriched with 'Gold and Pearl'.[139] Beyond such general themes, there was no single 'republican' approach to international affairs; rather, differing views of the meaning, relative importance and practical implications of England's twin goals competed for influence inside and outside the government.

In the difficult circumstances of 1659, defensive counsels predominated. Facing domestic unsettlement and near-bankruptcy, it is not suprising that the reinstated Republic opted to be a 'commonwealth for preservation', eschewing dangerous and costly expansion, at least for the time being. A majority opinion favouring honourable peace soon emerged in Parliament and the press, and this set the tone for relations with all European neighbours. Closely linked with peace in republican minds was the promotion of national prosperity by means of trade, an object universally commended.[140] No more

---

[137] On this trend under Cromwell, and the early Republic's efforts to make itself 'a vehicle for national identity', see Norbrook, *Writing*, 293–8, 308–9.

[138] *Scout*, no. 3, 6–13 May, 21. The editor was quoting, without acknowledgment, from Streater's description of the three excellencies of a free state: *Continuation*, 15. The *Scout's* didactive plagiarism is discussed in more detail in ch. 8 below.

[139] *France no friend*, 16; *Chaos*, prefatory poem.

[140] Even Milton would make this connection, celebrating 'peace . . . plentiful trade and all prosperitie' as benefits of a settled republic, and attacking the 'vain and groundless apprehension that nothing but kingship can restore trade': *Readie and easie way*, 11, 17. Pincus' argument that Milton categorically 'rejected commercial society' ('Neither Machiavellian moment', 714–15) therefore needs qualification: Milton commended trade and its role in enhancing national wealth; what he feared was luxury, the pursuit of materialism/excessive consumption to the exclusion of more essential values, such as 'religion, libertie, honour'. Hence his suspicion of merchants and admiration for agrarian commonwealths. *Chaos* voiced a similar suspicion of overmighty merchants, yet supported trade and banks in particular. Differences between those republicans who embraced and those who distrusted commercial society thus seem to have been far less clear-cut than Pincus allows.

than in its first session were Parliament's decisions determined by particular mercantile interests, as Robert Brenner has alleged.[141] Yet the republicans in 1659 did express the desire to secure 'free commerce' from the Sound to the East Indies, and showed little interest in protectionist advice; instead, they sought closer ties with England's great trading rivals, the Dutch. The impulse behind this policy now, as at the beginning of the decade, was overwhelmingly ideological, based on shared republicanism, and, above all, shared Protestantism. Pincus' conclusion that by the late 1650s 'common interest rather than confessional similarity had become the basis for foreign alliances' therefore seems premature, resting upon a misleading dichotomy. Contemporary perceptions of England's interest *vis-à-vis* potential allies – or indeed enemies – were inevitably influenced to a greater or lesser extent by confessional identities as well as narrowly political or economic considerations. In aspiring to unite European 'Protestants . . . now miserably divided to the endangering of the totall ruin of that profession', the leaders of the English Republic were actuated by solidarity with suffering co-religionists as much, or even more than the need to defend 'national sovereignty' against the remote menace of the Austrian emperor's candidacy for the universal monarchy.[142]

Although Parliament's performance on the international stage in 1659 did not match the splendour of its earlier exploits, it none the less merits recognition. The Commonwealth neither returned to the perilous isolation of 1649, nor succumbed to any external menace, but rapidly attained recognition and recommenced activity in European affairs. French and Dutch attempts at manipulation were successfully resisted, and costly additional entanglements avoided. Despite the Swedish and Spanish unco-operativeness that thwarted particular aims, English prestige abroad suffered little reduction. That would come later. It was not the republican, but the monarchical Restoration that resulted in England's ambassadors lamenting the loss of the 'respect and observance' to which they had become accustomed.[143]

Nor did a foreign policy that failed to deliver dramatic immediate gains undermine the Commonwealth's standing at home. Republican commentators usually accepted that the Protectorate's legacy could not be undone overnight, and showed more tolerance to delays in foreign than domestic business. Though Parliament could not comply with all the conflicting advice offered by its supporters, the latter did not abandon it on that account. One indication of relative satisfaction with the conduct of international

141 Robert Brenner, *Merchants and revolution: commercial change, political conflict and London's overseas traders, 1550–1653*, Princeton 1993. Brenner's argument that the economic interests of London's 'new merchants' determined the early republic's relations with the Dutch is disproved by Pincus, *Protestantism*.

142 Pincus, 'England and the world', 146–7; 'A secret instruction', MS Sloane 4159, fo. 198; cf. Dury's unusual fusion of desire for Protestant unity with preventing the 'future prevalency of the *Austrian* absoluteness': *Interest*, 15.

143 This comment by Downing is quoted, with other evidence of England's post-Restoration decline in prestige, in Scott, *England's troubles*, 312.

affairs is the general absence of criticisms concerning it after the second inter-ruption, when Parliament found itself accused of failing the common good in almost every possible way. This silence doubtless reflects the conspicuous diplomatic role of politicians that the Army esteemed, especially Vane, Lambert and Whitelocke. Yet Vane's pre-eminence should not obscure the credit due to other councillors, and the working consensus established in Parliament itself. MPs were not ostriches buried in the sand of domestic poli-tics, but active champions of England's reputation and advantage in a wider world which daily demanded their time and resources. Parliament's consis-tent defence of these vital issues, and the Republic's dignity, represented a solid, if unspectacular, achievement.

7

A Greater Britain

Poor Scotland lyes desolate without law, justice, government, or settlement of public or privat interest, religious or civil. I admire their casting Scotland and Irland in that confusion that they will not regrayte the breach of this Parliament: Archibald Johnston, diary entry, 4 Oct. 1659.

The Union . . . settled by the prowess and prudence of the Parliament is so completely perfected that . . . it hath made those several Countries one Nation, which the premised Roman course being observed, may so remain . . . while the Sun and Stars run the same course: M. H., *The History of the Union of . . . England, Wales, Scotland and Ireland.*

I have pressed divers of the Councell of State, even unto wearinesse, and had not a confusion of busyness and a more important application to their own preservation diverted them from such distant occasions, I doe believe I should have provoaked them to have supplyed you: Thomas Povey to Governor Doiley of Jamaica, Oct. 1659.

Early modern historiography has recently seen the welcome rise of a 'new British history'.[1] Although this approach has repudiated insular nationalisms, especially the 'anglocentricity' once dominant, in order to emphasise 'interaction' of the various inhabitants of the 'Atlantic archipelago', a central theme remains the 'reactions' of peripheral peoples to the 'growth of the English state' that ultimately became 'Britain'.[2] An important stage in this process was, of course, the mid seventeenth-century 'war of the three kingdoms', culminating in the forcible creation of a non-dynastic, 'new British polity' by Cromwell and the English Commonwealth. Historians have exposed the Christian and classical imperatives driving British union, together with the latter's fundamental contribution to the innovative notions of an expansionist, sea-borne 'empire' that helped inspire the Protector's initially disastrous attack on the Spanish West Indies.[3] Analysis of the high

[1] Useful introductions to this subject are the essays in B. I. Bradshaw and J. S. Morrill (eds), *The British problem, c. 1534–1707: state formation in the Atlantic archipelago,* London 1996, and G. Burgess (ed.), *The new British history: founding a modern state, 1603–1715,* London 1999.
[2] J. G. A. Pocock, 'The Atlantic archipelago and the war of the three kingdoms', in Bradshaw and Morrill, *British problem,* 172–92 at p. 172; Morrill, 'Preface', ibid. p. vii.
[3] D. Hirst, 'The English Republic and the meaning of Britain', *Journal of Modern History* lxvi (1994), 451–86 at pp. 464–9; Worden, 'Nedham and English republicanism', 73–4, and 'Classical republicanism'; Armitage, 'Cromwellian Protectorate', 533–4.

costs, financial and political, of maintaining a supranational state has even generated argument that 'the British problem brought down the republic almost as surely as it did the Stuart monarchy'.[4] To test such conclusions, this chapter will explore the largely uncharted British – and indeed, imperial – dimension to the restored Republic of 1659.[5]

The 'near absence' of an explicitly 'British self-perception' that historians have remarked among seventeenth-century Englishmen holds true for this year.[6] Parliament ruled a composite state officially known as 'the Commonwealth of England, Ireland and Scotland', though it also comprised the North American and West Indian colonies, together with the continental foothold, Dunkirk.[7] With the collapse of Cromwellian pretensions to overlordship, the title 'Great Britain', famously adopted by King James in 1603, and provocatively revived by the Scots to proclaim his grandson in 1649, again became the near-exclusive preserve of the Stuarts' adherents.[8] Against their depictions of a conventionally 'Royal Ile' might be set William Sprigge's salute to the 'sun of prosperity that in the dawning of a Free state . . . hath once more . . . displayed its Golden beams upon our British Islands'. The poem preceding the republican discourse boldly christened *CHAOS* went further, conceiving the 'Queen of Islands, Britain' in millennial terms, as a 'glorious Throne' for Christ; the text advocated 'one Law' for '*Great Britain* . . . heretofore divided into many, but now . . . incorporated into one Commonwealth'.[9] Yet the rarity of attempts to appropriate 'Britain' for the Republic surely reflects revulsion from this name's long-established monarchical – and recent Protectoral – associations as much as 'rooted English chauvinism'.[10]

4   Hirst, 'English Republic', 486.
5   Davies, the only narrative historian to address the subject, provided brief and colourless accounts of Scotland and Ireland, but ignored the colonies. National histories do cover the period, but their primary focus is local administration. See F. D. Dow, *Cromwellian Scotland, 1651–1660*, Edinburgh 1979; T. C. Barnard, *Cromwellian Ireland: English government and reform in Ireland, 1649–1660*, Oxford 1975, and now Clarke, *Prelude to Restoration*.
6   Scott, *England's troubles*, 15.
7   The order of the subordinate commonwealths was sometimes reversed in foreign credentials, petitions and newsbooks following Protectoral precedent.
8   Examples of pro-Stuart usage in 1659 include *Bibliotheca regia, or The Royal Library containing such papers of His late Maiesty King Charls, the second monarch of Great Britain, as have escaped the ruines of these times*; *Forraign and Domestick PROPHESIES . . . Foretelling . . . His Highness arrival to the Government . . . of Great Britain*, and *The Army mastered, or Great Brittains joy*. One clue to the spuriousness of this text's superficial republicanism is its use of this phrase. Earlier attempts to connect Cromwell with 'Britain's empire' are described in Hirst, 'English Republic', 468–9.
9   *The Honest Patriot*, 12; [Sprigge], *Modest plea*, 48; *Chaos*, preface, 6. *France no friend*, the only other republican text to use the phrase 'Great Britain', pointedly associates it with kingship.
10 Hirst traces Commonwealth and Protectoral failure to 'exploit purposively the new order' made possible by the British conquests to this cause: 'English Republic', 470. It was, significantly, the Royalists who in 1659 recounted the myth of Brute, the supposed origin for the name Britain. See, for example, the Welsh mystic Arise Evans, *Rule from heaven*, 1ff.

150

Disinclination to use the signifier 'Britain' did not imply disinterest in the dominions thus signified. Whatever their previous failings on this head, the Commonwealth's rulers in 1659 evinced much pride in, and derived considerable propaganda dividends from, British conquests.[11] These last not only undergirded the praises heaped on the 'renowned victorious Parliament' but ranked equally with European achievements as visible signs of the efficacy, even superiority of republics.[12] Thus Streater, in a single sentence illustrating 'the Power, Vigour and Excellency of a *Councel* of a *Free People*', recalled Parliament's successful management of both the British campaigns and the Dutch war. Henry Stubbe found matter in republican victories for a triumphal ode *Ad late Dominantem Angliam*. Even a loyalist who denied the inherent supremacy of any constitutional form composed a *History of the Union* that ascribed the incorporation of Wales, Scotland and Ireland into 'one Commonwealth with England' to Parliament's prudent use of Roman methods as well as the 'unanimous valour and constant circumspection of the English', and prophesied the united polity's permanence in the high-flown language of Virgilian epic.[13]

Nor did the English patriotism so prominent in the propaganda prevent the Republic's defenders from simultaneously imagining what was, in effect, a 'British' identity. The *History of the Union* blithely asserted that English, Welsh, Scots and Irish had actually become 'one Nation', distinct from 'all forraign Foes' by use of a 'common speech'. John Rogers contended that in 'our Free-State' Protestant England and Scotland 'are both one and in a far better capacity both for PRESERVATION and INCREASE to deal with an Enemy than under the King'.[14] Mutual assistance against linguistic and religious outsiders was but one of many benefits predicted for all Britain's inhabitants. Neo-Leveller and Quaker Edward Billing pleaded for a just union allowing free trade between 'three Nations' made 'equally alike . . . so the long-talkt-on common-weale may no longer continue to be a particular Wealth'. Other republican voices also urged that 'England, Scotland and Ireland' could and should 'be not only called but become a Commonwealth',

[11] Republicans often expressed pride in their management of the conquest of Scotland and Ireland: for examples from Richard's parliament see *Burton diary*, iii. 98 (Hesilrig), 473 (Scot); iv. 144 (Sir James Harrington), 178 (Vane).

[12] *Humble representation of divers well-affected . . . of Westminster*, 2. Even where Scotland and Ireland were not explicitly mentioned, claims that this Parliament had been uniquely 'victorious by a constant series of gracious Providences' instantly recalled, and gained credence from, these conquests.

[13] S[treater], *Continuation*, 11; M[ichael] H[awke?], *The History of the Union of the four famous kingdoms of England, Wales, Scotland and Ireland* (composed in 1659, but published early in 1660), preface, 80, 109, 137–8. Stubbe's Latin ode is printed at the beginning of this history.

[14] H[awke?], *History of the Union*, 137–8, preface; Rogers, *Diapoliteia*, 28. *Chaos* also stressed linguistic similarity, though slightly more cautiously, asserting that all Britons understood, even if they could not speak, 'the same language', i.e. English (p. 6).

and advocated inclusion of the periphery in 'all the priviledges, rights and immunities' of the future constitution. Such appeals for a genuinely inclusive union, transcending national differences, reveal that at least some English radicals were criticising exploitative Anglocentrism to a degree that went well beyond the condescending 'benevolence' that was so central in 'England's "British" ideology'.[15]

In proposing reform of the existing relations among the 'British' peoples, English radicals were not indulging in utopian speculation, but responding to a climate where change suddenly seemed imminent – yet never actually arrived. The politicians who regained power in 1659 were expected to replace the Cromwellian settlement, whose legal and political imperfections they had vehemently criticised while in opposition, with a constitution better suited to a republic. Hopes that 'union would be a short business' ran so high at first that various interested parties, especially from Scotland, hastened to make their views known. By October, however, Archibald Johnston, the solitary Scottish councillor, was deploring what he saw as English carelessness towards both subordinate commonwealths. After the interruption, MPs were accused of selfishly keeping the 'whole Nations of Scotland and Ireland without any Civil Judicature' simply to prolong their own session.[16] Contemporary dissatisfaction with Parliament's failure to achieve a united state providing tangible benefits to peripheral subjects is undeniable. Scots and Irish were not the only sufferers: Thomas Povey, an advocate of Jamaican interests, also lamented the government's inattention to 'distant occasions'.[17] But were the charges of neglect, deliberate or otherwise, justified? Can the problems be traced to 'shortsightedness and chauvinism', as some scholars have suggested?[18] How did the republicans respond to the challenge of ruling the territories whose acquisition had so much heightened the Commonwealth of England's prestige in Europe? Answering such questions requires a closer examination of Parliament's dealings with all its remote dominions.

Furthest from Westminster were the English colonies in America, an exchange of letters with which took between two and four months. Though trade with Virginia and Barbados was the most valuable to England, the restored Republic esteemed each of these settlements an integral 'part of this Commonwealth'.[19] This was, after all, the regime that had revolutionised the nascent empire by claiming 'a new legislative supremacy', reducing recalci-

---

15 E[dward] B[illing], *A MITE OF AFFECTION, Manifested in 31. PROPOSALS, Offered to all the Sober and Free-born People, Tending and tendred unto them for a Settlement in this the day of the Worlds Distraction*, 10; *A Common-wealth or NOTHING*, 3; *Speculum*, 18. On the importance of benevolence, see Hirst, 'English Republic', 462.

16 *Baillie letters*, iii. 430; *Johnston diary*, 140; *A CONFERENCE BETWEEN Two Souldiers*, 12–13.

17 Thomas Povey to Governor Doiley of Jamaica, Oct., MS Add. 11411, fo. 21.

18 As Hirst, 'English Republic', 453.

19 Council circular to plantations in New England, Virginia and the Carribean, 6 June, SP 25/98, fo. 14.

trant colonies to obedience, and effectively nullifying their royal charters.[20] In 1659 Parliament's immediate priorities were to revive its own authority and ensure local order. Just six days after their readmission, MPs passed resolutions for the 'administration of Justice' and 'preservation of the Jurisdiction of the Parliament in the foreign Plantations'. As implementation was, incongruously, entrusted to the overburdened Committee of Inspection into the Treasuries, little was achieved until the creation of the Council of State, which was instructed to 'promote the good of all Forreigne plantations'. The council in turn delegated this duty to a committee, whose first task was to prepare a circular letter, to be sent with Parliament's *Declaration* to New England, Virginia and the Caribbean. This communication aimed to impress the new government's supremacy upon these far-flung subjects, who were exhorted to acknowledge the 'good providence of God' in Parliament's restoration, and 'rejoyce among such as beare good will to this Commonwealth'. At a more practical level, the smooth functioning of local administration was ensured there, as in England, by continuing the powers of existing officials until further notice. The council commanded them to execute good laws, and promised to show 'due regard and Care' for the colonies' welfare.[21]

This promise was no idle civility from a government preoccupied with other problems. Colonial affairs consumed conciliar time on some eighteen occasions in the succeeding months. A few of these instances entailed direct action: on learning of the illegal minting and transfer of silver to Maryland, for example, the council immediately decreed the arrest of the Catholic proprietor, Lord Baltimore, and revived plans for legislation prohibiting the export of bullion. The majority, however, involved the committal of petitions ranging from trading proposals to applications for positions and attacks on colonial authorities. These petitions were processed slowly but surely: three Quakers, whose complaint against Boston's magistrates was not presented until October, got no relief; George March, who had delivered his denunciation of the governor of Christopher's island in June, obtained an order for the return of his confiscated property in September. The volume of business confronting the colonial committee may be inferred from the expansion of the membership from the original six to twelve in mid-June, and nineteen, or almost all the active councillors, in October, and from the consignment of Jamaica to a separate committee in August.[22]

---

[20] Bliss, *Revolution*, 61. Bliss discusses the revolutionary impact of Parliament's first session in ch. iii.

[21] *Journal*, 650; *A&O* ii. 1274; council minutes, 30 May, 6 June, SP 25/98, fo. 14. The Barbadians responded positively, reporting on 9 Sept. that they had published the Declaration, and anticipated that the 'Supreme Authority' would 'retain the native lustre and beauty of government': *Calendar of state papers colonial America & West Indies, 1574–1660*, ed. W. Noel Sainsbury, London 1860, 476.

[22] Council minutes, 4, 5 Oct. (Maryland, Boston Quakers), 7 June, 21 Sept. (Christopher's); petitions in the other two categories were considered on 9 June, 8 and 18 July, 25 Aug. and 26 Sept. Some petitions on colonial matters were probably directed to the

Of all England's transatlantic possessions, it was, indeed, Jamaica, the latest and least settled, that received the greatest individual attention. Far from repudiating Cromwell's controversial conquest, the republicans gathered information on its problems and potential. At the end of July Parliament responded to a petition from the 'well affected Officers and soldiers', and a report on their condition, by ordering payment for the forces stationed there, provision for their dependants at home, and an investigation into the means of making the island 'most serviceable'. Domestic political considerations, in the form of the need to convince the Army of Parliament's care, doubtless influenced these votes. The council did scrape together a month's pay for the soldiers, and a quarter of the sum owed to wives and widows, but considered Jamaica's usefulness only obliquely, under the general heading of West Indian trade, and arrived at no conclusion regarding its future. Although this irresolution was mainly due to the uncertainty over the Spanish war, the lack of recent, accurate information also played a part. The last Jamaican letters, announcing large profits, were written at the end of April, and took over two months to reach England.[23] Without further 'particular Intelligence', the West Indies investor Thomas Povey, who ceaselessly lobbied the council on Jamaica's behalf, admitted that his task was more difficult; nevertheless, he contrasted the Republic's concern for this outpost with the Protectorate's effective abandonment of it as an 'unprofitable, remote and hopeless consideration'. But for the 'confusion of busyness' and more 'important application' to self-preservation, he believed that the council would have provided the necessary supplies. Crisis at home, however, inevitably took priority over 'distant occasions'.[24]

Slow and unverifiable communications from all its remote dominions exposed Westminster to misrepresentation and manipulation by local interests. The council appreciated these hazards, and proceeded cautiously. Thus it declined to accept March's biased account of affairs on Christopher's without reservation; rather, it made the recovery of his estate conditional upon the findings of a commission to investigate the charges and the revenue owed from the island since 1648. This effectively suspended the execution of its judgement indefinitely, since Parliament was interrupted before the council could nominate the commissioners and a new governor. Nor could Parlia-

---

committee rather than the council following an order to this effect of 14 June. The committee was expanded on 13 June and on 8 Oct.; Jamaica, formerly a joint province with the admiralty commissioners, received a separate committee on 2 Aug.

[23] *Politicus*, no. 581, 28 July–4 Aug., 631; *Journal*, 740–1. There are nine explicit references to Jamaica in the council minutes, more than triple the number for any other plantation, but most concern the needs of the forces there. Warrants for the payment of the garrison and dependants were ordered on 18 Aug.; by 19 Sept. a second report was ready for Parliament but not presented amidst the crisis. Abstracts from the last Jamaican letters survive in MS Tanner 51, fo. 82; these reported the capture of a Spanish vessel carrying 40 tons of cocoa and the seizure of money and plate worth £4,000.

[24] Povey to Doiley, Oct., MS Add. 11411, fos 21–2.

ment follow advice to ensure that other colonial governments consisted of 'knowing publike spirited men', since the responses of these authorities to its *Declaration* reached England too late for it to take any action.[25] Distance therefore restricted the actual impact of the republicans on the New World to an extent that all their diligence could not overcome in the brief time at their disposal.

The lion's share of time and resources was, of course, bestowed nearer home. Dunkirk, situated just across the English Channel, presented no problems of communication. Quite the contrary. Colonels Lillingston and Alsop, deputising for Governor Lockhart, bombarded Whitehall with all too frequent appeals for assistance. These commanders espied dangers everywhere: outside the walls, from Spanish, French and Cavalier forces, and inside, from the garrison itself, whose loyalty was strained by the acute shortage of pay and provisions. In their anxious view, the town would never withstand a siege without reinforcements and repairs to the fortifications.[26] All this would require large sums of money, which the English treasury could ill afford, and the republicans were, predictably, reluctant to expend. Isolated on the European mainland, Dunkirk was certainly vulnerable, and claimed more attention relative to its size than any other territory. It was then with reason that some MPs considered the town 'more trouble than it was worth'; the colonels on the spot lived in constant dread that Parliament would decide to discard it altogether.[27]

Although the new regime had no immediate plans to evacuate Dunkirk, it was slow to appreciate the scale of the problems there. Initially, attention focused almost entirely on securing the allegiance of the English garrison. Speculation that Lockhart, as a faithful Cromwellian, would hold the port against Parliament was rife. To avert such a disastrous affront to the Republic's prestige, the temporary executive committee at once sent letters enjoining obedience and representing the change as positive: material needs would be satisfied and the Good Old Cause fulfilled by the ideals set forth in Parliament's *Declaration*.[28] The danger of defection was, in reality, largely

[25] Such advice, with particular regard to Virginia and Barbados, came from Bland, *Trade revived*, 11, and Cole, *Severall proposals*, 5.

[26] Fourteen letters from the colonels to the council or influential government members between May and September are in *TSP*; this total far exceeds extant communications from Scotland or Ireland. The tone of desperate entreaty was set by the very first, written to Fleetwood on 6 May, which lamented the great cost of living and repairing the defensive works, complained that letters beseeching supplies had gone unanswered, and announced that after 'many streights' to provide weekly subsistence for the soldiers, the colonels had reached their wits' end: *TSP* vii. 668.

[27] Bordeaux to Mazarin, 26 Sept., Guizot, *Histoire*, i. 476. The colonels' dread is evident from their reiteration of the case for Dunkirk's retention in one third of the surviving letters. Though seldom discussed in Parliament, Dunkirk claimed the council's attention on 53 days. Ireland and Scotland, by contrast, occupied the council on a mere 22 and 28 days respectively.

[28] Such speculation was common among the Republic's enemies: for examples see the

imaginary. Though some of Lockhart's officers murmured against the change, Dunkirk was untenable without financial aid, and would be little threat to England in the unlikely event that he sacrificed his patriotism so far as to sell the town to France or Spain.[29] In fact, Lockhart was eager to ingratiate himself with Parliament, and returned post-haste to oversee a smooth transfer of power. His zeal impressed not only Alsop, who composed a glowing account of his superior's speech exhorting the officers to the 'strict performance of their duty', on the grounds that the national interest in Dunkirk was 'still the same', but even a disappointed Royalist, who thought him 'hartily connected to the Parliament' or dissembling 'very cunningly, so that he is verily believed to be so'. The committee's letter, in Alsop's opinion, produced 'very much satisfaction' among the officers. Lockhart duly reported their gratitude for its favour and complete concurrence with the rest of the Army, together with his own readiness to yield the town to representatives of the 'supreme power'. Within a fortnight of Parliament's return, Mercurius Politicus triumphantly announced the 'unanimous consent' of Lockhart and the regiments in Dunkirk to the change of government.[30]

The consent so carefully engineered by Lockhart concealed a distinct lack of self-denying devotion to the Republic on the part of the soldiery. Cracks in their loyalty became public knowledge six weeks later, when the official newsbooks, which began by ignoring the trouble, had to counter the wild rumours circulating with the admission that there had been 'some little late disorder', swiftly subdued, among the garrison. This was an understatement. The council classified the disturbance as a 'mutiny' grave enough to merit Parliament's direct notice. According to the only eyewitness account, from Lillingston and Alsop, the soldiers, frustrated by the non-appearance of their pay, and possibly manipulated by Royalist secret agents, had formed a 'distemper or combination' to seize their officers and plunder the town. Only the 'prudence and diligence' of the officers, who had discovered the design at the eleventh hour, prevented its execution; once assured that their commanders would intercede for the redress of their grievance, the soldiers meekly reverted to a 'peaceable and settled condition'.[31] The authors had a vested

---

Royalist letters in MS Clarendon 60, fos 503, 563, and Giavarina, CSPVen., 16. The committee's letter does not survive, but its contents may be deduced from the colonels' responses, cited below, and the similar message to Monck: Clarke papers, iv. 9.

[29] Bordeaux accurately appraised Dunkirk's situation on 16 May: Guizot, Histoire, i. 381. Evidence that some officers, including Alsop, initially expressed dissatisfaction was presented to Parliament's commissioners: MS Rawlinson A65, fos 17–25.

[30] Alsop to Fleetwood, c. 17 May, TSP vii. 671; Royalist report to Hyde, Dunkirk, 3/13 June, MS Clarendon 61, fo. 93; Lockhart to parliament's committee, 17 May, TSP vii. 670; Vane's report, Journal, 657; Politicus, no. 567, 12–19 May, 448.

[31] Politicus, no. 277, 30 June–7 July, 567; council minutes, 23, 27 June; colonels to the council, MS Tanner 51, fos 85–6 (this letter is undated, but must have been written after 18 June, when Lockhart left Dunkirk, and before 23 June, when news of the mutiny reached the council).

interest in magnifying the officers' ability and fidelity, at a moment when recommissioning by Parliament had just commenced, but this story cannot be dismissed simply as a convenient fiction. Its emphasis on the common soldiers' dissatisfaction tallies with other letters, in which the colonels bewailed the 'many [who] . . . make money their cause', because 'not so well principled as becomes good men to be'. Whatever the outlook of their fellows in the British Isles, the greater part of the garrison at Dunkirk had indeed become a 'meer mercenary army'.[32]

The overt insubordination and impatience for money of the regiments in Flanders came as a shock to a government confiding in Lockhart's lavish assurances of support, and conscious of its own diligence. Far from neglecting Dunkirk, the council had devoted a significant amount of time to fulfilling the pledge to meet its many needs. A committee established for this purpose compiled a lengthy shopping list, based on advice from Lockhart and the other officers. The council concentrated on assembling those items essential to the garrison's survival, and managed to ship a two months' supply of cheese and biscuit, together with powder, matches and other military provisions from the public stores, plus £3,000 for repairing the fortifications.[33] Arrangements for the soldiers' remuneration were not forgotten, but occupied a lower rung in the ladder of priorities. Not till mid-June, the week before the mutiny, did the committee receive orders to find 'some solid way' of providing 'constant payment' for the garrison, and produce a report leading to the issue of £1,600 for the first month. Lockhart therefore returned empty-handed, as far as the soldiers were concerned; in their commanders' view, it was this disappointment, plus his departure again to France, that unleashed their resentment.[34]

Parliament's initial reaction to the disturbance was all that Lillingston and Alsop could have wished. Relief at the restoration of order inspired a letter thanking the officers for a 'real Demonstration' of their 'faithfulness to this Commonwealth', and promising 'special care' to provide for the garrison. Instant monetary aid was forthcoming: in addition to the £1,600 already on the way, £4,000 was allocated from the £15,000 advanced by the East India Company.[35] Encouragements of this type might alleviate the emergency, but were no substitute for long-term solutions. Now alerted to the gravity of

---

[32] Colonels to [?] Walton, 23 Aug., *TSP* vii. 732. A similar letter to the council of 4 Aug. represented the soldiers as 'much troubled and discontented' for want of money: ibid. vii. 720.

[33] Council minutes, 25 (committee created), 26 (the list, containing 55 items), 27, 30, 31 May, 2, 6 June. As might be expected of a committee the primary business of which was military, the most prominent members were Lambert and Disbrow, though Vane also presented occasional reports.

[34] Council minutes, 13, 14, 18 June; colonels to council, MS Tanner 51, fos 85–6. Lockhart had secured reimbursement of £1,700 he had expended on the garrison.

[35] *Journal*, 696; council to colonels, 28 June, SP 25/98, fo. 21 (this letter was officially approved by Parliament the next day).

Dunkirk's problems, the republicans perceived the need for closer investigation by individuals without axes of their own to grind there. As soon as it heard of the mutiny, the council had ordered the Army officers in its midst to propose a 'fit and able person' to go over; two days later it approved Lieutenant-Colonel Pearson and Colonels Ashfield and Packer. Their instructions comprehended not only inquiry into military matters and the recent troubles, but the disposal of moneys, and regulation of public revenues and civilian officials. Particular scrutiny was reserved for the officers: any denounced as 'disaffected or of uncivill or prophane behaviour' were to be reported. So perished any hopes that Parliament's commendation would result in automatic renewal of commissions. Lillingston and Alsop, sensing that their jobs were in jeopardy, spent much of the summer defending their own and their subordinates' integrity against malicious accusations.[36]

The mission of Ashfield, Packer and Pearson achieved some, but not all, of its goals. As senior officers, the council's representatives and the bearers of the £4,000, they succeeded in raising morale by declaring Parliament's concern and their own willingness to act as intermediaries, making known their fellow soldiers' needs at Westminster. Visible testimony to the garrison's submission and satisfaction with 'their old masters' appeared in the loyal addresses 'unanimously signed' under the watchful eye of the commissioners before being presented to the House and published in *Politicus*. The best evidence of the Republic's popularity in Dunkirk came from Alsop's regiment, which not only admired the 'special providence' that had restored Parliament to perfect 'the Peace and Settlement' in which it had formerly made 'great Progress', and vowed to support it against 'Kingly power', but also returned thanks for its care in sending all the supplies that could reasonably be expected in its 'short time of settlement' and commissioning 'honourable Persons' to examine conditions. Having secured such affirmations, it is no surprise that the commissioners departed in the belief that the forces had been pacified by their assurances, and that the situation was likely to remain 'very well and quiet'.[37]

Faith in the future tranquillity of Dunkirk was strengthened by the investigation into the mutiny. This uncovered no trace of the Royalist infiltration feared by the council and local commanders. Lack of pay was accepted as the principal cause. To prevent a resurgence of discontent, the commissioners recommended provision for arrears, a 'constant supply' of money, and an

---

36 Council minutes, 23, 25 June; instructions to commissioners, ibid. 29 June. The commanding colonels defended themselves in letters to Pearson and the council in August: *TSP* vii. 730, 729, 722–3. Allegations of disaffection and immorality against several officers, including Lillingston and Alsop, survive in the commissioners' papers: MS Rawlinson A65.

37 Richard Ashfield, Willaim Packer and John Pearson to the council and Fleetwood, *TSP* vii. 712, 695; Pearson to Monck, 15 July, *Clarke papers*, iv. 118. The addresses from the five regiments in Dunkirk were presented on 27 July; that from Alsop's was reproduced in *Politicus*, no. 580, 21–8 July, 621–2.

equality with the regiments in England. A significant share of the blame was, however, allotted to those officers who alienated their men by 'not taking that care of them as might have been expected, and as they found from their officers' in Britain. In a private letter to Monck, Pearson exclaimed in pious horror at the discovery of 'grand inquities', including 'drunkenness, dreadful swearing, uncleanness, [and] money coining'. Not least among the commissioners' responsibilities was the enforcement of discipline. Though the official newsbooks emphasised their strictness by reporting the court-martial of a captain for inebriety and false mustering, Pearson claimed that they corrected offenders with a 'very tender hand', and encouraged the 'many very good and substantial officers' by all means, including support for the speedy dispatch of the new commissions to end uncertainties. Godliness and good affection to the Commonwealth among both the garrison and the largely Catholic populace might be promoted by sending out 'painful and learned preachers', and an 'honest, godly, faithful and able' resident governor. The latter proposal made good sense, given Lockhart's frequent absences and the feeble grasp on the reins of Lillingston and Alsop.[38]

As military men themselves, the commissioners were most competent in handling military matters. Adept at conciliating the garrison and assessing the fortifications and magazine, they found the details of civil government baffling. For this the genuine complexity of Dunkirk's customs was partly responsible: the intricacies of the excise, for example, might have puzzled the most brilliant of administrators. But the commissioners' bewilderment was also their own fault, since they declined offers of assistance from the local authorities, whom they distrusted, and then complained of the shortage of well-informed, English-speaking officials. This conduct alarmed the town dignitaries, who feared a design to have Dunkirk 'governed after the English manner', and entreated Lockhart's intervention to uphold their privileges, as guaranteed by the articles of surrender. The commissioners did, indeed, counsel a greater degree of English control over those civil officers elected annually, but they also warned that any changes, especially in the distribution of taxes, would cause 'grievance and offence' if imposed without magisterial assent. Pearson's initial forecast that the town would happily contribute £16,000 *per annum* to the costs of the English occupation proved hopelessly unrealistic. In their report to the council, the three commissioners owned that they had suspended their endeavour to regulate the revenues after discovering that two-thirds belonged to the magistrates, who were considering independent negotiations with Parliament.[39]

---

[38] Ashfield, Packer and Pearson to the council, *TSP* vii. 712–14; *PI*, 25 July–1 Aug., 616–17; Pearson to Monck, 15 July, *Clarke papers*, iv. 118. Three more officers were eventually cashiered for drunkenness by the council's committee, on Pearson's recommendation: *CSPD 1659*, 150.

[39] Commissioners' report to the council, and detailed account of revenue, *TSP* vii. 712–14, 714–19; Peter Faulconnier, bailiff of Dunkirk, to Lockhart, 18 July, ibid. vii. 699–700; Pearson to Monck, 15 July, *Clarke papers*, iv. 118.

Such negotiations proved unnecessary. After the ceremonial attestation of its authority in the presentation of the regimental addresses on 27 July, Parliament paid scant heed to its continental outpost.[40] The summer rising supervened, displacing Dunkirk from the political forefront to which the mutiny had briefly brought it. Thus the underlying problems survived the passing of the immediate crisis. Already, at the end of July, Lillingston and Alsop were again 'in very great streight for money for . . . weekly subsistence'. Anglo-Dutch *rapprochement* exacerbated this predicament, since orders to show 'all Offices of friendship' to the Dutch by restoring ships seized by Commonwealth subjects and forbidding foreigners to sell their prizes there deprived the garrison of valuable customs revenue, and so heightened unrest among the soldiery.[41] With available resources fully committed to the campaign against Booth, the council had little help to spare for Dunkirk. In August it bluntly informed the colonels that a 'large Supply' was impossible, and advanced only a meagre £1,160 to cover a month's pay for the officers.[42]

The improving situation in England by late August enabled the council to give Dunkirk more attention.[43] Steps were taken to implement several of the commissioners' recommendations. Lockhart remained governor, but Lillingston and Alsop's deficiencies were counterbalanced by appointing two colonels to command his regiments and take overall charge of the garrison during his absences. With few exceptions, the officers received their new commissions. Another source of discontent was removed by granting the forces at Dunkirk equal status with those around London, the best paid section of the Army, and resolving to replace the foot regiments after one year's service. The council arranged fresh supply contracts, and assigned another £8,000 from the excise for the soldiers' pay. It also decided to send an able minister as chaplain, though the post was still vacant in October. Meanwhile, the committee for Dunkirk was instructed to examine the vexed questions of revenue and the articles of surrender. Although it had not resolved these issues by the time of the second interruption, the council was plainly beginning to look beyond the garrison's material needs to explore the long-term viability of English rule.[44]

---

[40] After this point Dunkirk required Parliament's attention exactly once, on 16 Aug., when commissions for the officers serving there were approved: *Journal*, 760.

[41] Colonels to council, 29 July, TSP vii. 711; council to colonels, 12 Aug., SP 25/98, fo. 105. The colonels were responding to the previous week's orders to protect Dutch property: due to 'extreme necessities' and the soldiers' 'mutinous temper', they had been unable to prevent the sale of a Dutch ship brought in by a Swede, which had yielded £2,000 in customs. They subsequently pleaded the difficulty of handling such contentious matters, being 'out of our element': TSP vii. 721.

[42] Council to colonels, 16 Aug., SP 25/98, fo. 133.

[43] In the six weeks after Booth's defeat, Dunkirk occupied the council on 17 occasions; most involved discussing the committee's reports. Though Dunkirk featured in the council minutes 13 times in the preceding six weeks, these mainly entailed answering appeals from the colonels, who believed, with some justification, that Dunkirk was being neglected.

[44] Council minutes, 16, 25, 30 Aug., 2, 7, 10, 20, 28, 29 Sept., 1, 8 Oct.

Dunkirk exemplifies both strengths and weaknesses of republican govern‑ ment outside England. The failings are conspicuous: chronic shortages of pay and provisions afflicted the garrison, while the controversy over the town's retention inhibited the development of schemes for its integration within the Commonwealth. Yet Parliament did achieve its primary ambition, the estab‑ lishment of its own authority. This success owed much to the diligence of the council and Army officers in dealing with the plaints of local commanders, and diverting scarce resources to meet the most urgent needs, especially in the aftermath of the mutiny. The mission of Ashfield, Packer and Pearson demonstrates not only the regime's ability to rise to an emergency, but its good sense in seeking the accurate information that would lay the ground‑ work for any future settlement of this unfamiliar region. Autumn saw the introduction of some administrative reforms, and the projection of others. Sustained attention to Dunkirk was, however, always difficult, and at times, impossible. In light of the multiplicity of other business, foreign and dom‑ estic, the marvel is not that Dunkirk's problems remained unresolved, but that they received the council's notice as often as they did.

Control of Scotland and Ireland, unlike Dunkirk, was essential to the defence of England and the integrity of the Commonwealth itself. Here, too, the Army was crucial. The conflicts of the previous two decades had abun‑ dantly proved the potential of rebellion on the periphery to destabilise the central government. Despite, or even because of, the pacification achieved under the Protectorate, those who had failed to hinder Parliament's return at Westminster hoped to unseat it by fresh upheavals in the British provinces.[45] Neither General Monck, an able ex‑Royalist elevated by the late Protector to the supreme command in Scotland, nor the energetic lord lieutenant of Ireland, Henry Cromwell, renowned for his conservative sympathies, was expected to rejoice in the change. As spontaneous enthusiasm from the subjugated Scots and Irish was still more improbable, the Republic's establish‑ ment would depend on the attitude of the substantial Army detachments stationed there. Parliament lost no time in seeking their support. On its very first day, the House ordered Fleetwood, as commander‑in‑chief, to transmit its *Declaration* to Ireland and Scotland. Accompanying that key statement of Parliament's aims were letters from the temporary Committee of Safety, which enjoined 'care and vigilance' on the officers, and pledged the new regime to 'care for the supply of the affairs there'.[46] This was a considerable commitment, for the pay of the forces in Scotland and Ireland was even deeper in arrears than that of those in England.[47] While awaiting replies, MPs

---

[45] Amongst those who nursed such hopes were Giavarina (CSPVen. 16, 28, 35), Bordeaux and Thurloe (Guizot, *Histoire*, i. 429, 374, 379, 380–1, 384) and various Royalists. For examples see MS Clarendon 60, fos 503, 563; 61, fos 289–90; MS Carte 213, fos 238, 256.
[46] *Journal*, 646; committee to Monck, 10 May, *Clarke papers*, iv. 9. Henry Cromwell, writing to Fleetwood on 24 May, acknowledged receipt of a similar missive: TSP vii. 674.
[47] The first report from the Committee for Inspection estimated the combined debt to the

exuded confidence that the distant forces would endorse the decisions made by those at London. This calm demeanour, backed by the numerous precedents for such concurrence, impressed even some hostile observers with the unlikelihood that the Commonwealth would be toppled by disunion within its Army.[48]

The response from the Army in Scotland was swift and satisfactory. Even before tidings of the change reached Edinburgh, Monck had advised Fleetwood of the 'quiet state' of his forces, and their preference for the Long Parliament. Thereafter, his officers confirmed that the recall of this Parliament, the 'best expedient for curing . . . distempers', had 'anticipated [their] desires', since they, too, had progressed from nostalgia for the 'Divine Presence', through repentance for self-interested backsliding from the 'Good Old Cause', to a firm resolve to fulfil the early engagements to secure the 'just liberties of the whole people' and remove 'all oppression and every heavy intollerable yoke'. But this Army's enthusiasm for the new regime knew fewer bounds, at least on paper, than that of its southern counterpart. Where the latter stopped short at vague regrets for the past and prayers for a future blessing on Parliament's counsels, the 'unanimously practical' officers in Scotland urged the General Council to take an 'effectual course' to reach a 'good understanding' with the civil power 'so there may be no more dashing in pieces' or irregular dissolutions, and advised Parliament to adopt such congenial precautions against 'Ambitious spirits' as limited powers for and careful scrutiny of the persons entrusted with military responsibilities. Unlike the fifteen-point *Humble Petition* of the officers in England, the official address from Monck and his council not only offered MPs the warmest congratulations on their 'happy Restauration to the Government', but confined its requests to uncontentious generalities: provision for the Cromwells and completion of the 'work of Reformation' by countenancing 'sincere professors' of 'Godliness' and securing 'native Rights and Liberties' in a 'Free State' ruled by the 'truly Godly and Conscientous'. Gratified by such deference to its wisdom, the House on 18 May ordered immediate publication and an answering 'letter of good acceptance and thanks'.[49] By printing this address, and two others to the General Council, the government advertised its

---

forces in Scotland and Ireland by March 1659 at £464,955, about twice the amount owing to those in England: *Journal*, 659–60. By September, the pay of the army in Ireland was 14 months in arrears: MS Dep. C159, fo. 176.

[48] Thus Bordeaux perceived the government's confidence, the precedents for Army unity and English xenophobia as good reasons for the French to refrain from intervention unless war between the armies in England and Ireland actually broke out: Guizot, *Histoire*, i. 380–1.

[49] *Journal*, 647, 658; Monck and his officers to Fleetwood and the General Council, 12, 10 May, printed in *Politicus*, no. 568, 19–26 May, 456–7, 461; *Letter . . . from the Officers . . . in Scotland*, 3, 4; cf. the English Army's *Humble petition*, which not only specified the income to be allotted to Richard Cromwell and his mother, but presumed to suggest the form of the future constitution.

strength in Scotland and the unity of its Army, to the delight of friends and disappointment of enemies. While the godly Nehemiah Bourne rejoiced in the seemingly miraculous 'ful and . . . Ample concurans' of the entire northern army in favour of 'the ould Parliament And A Commonwealth', Bordeaux concluded that republican feeling was strongest in these regiments, and even Giavarina eventually had to acknowledge the daily arrival of 'fresh assurances of adherence'. Though optimists persisted in suspecting that these were fabrications, sober Royalist hopes of Monck receded before the mounting evidence of his submission.[50]

Monck was, indeed, at pains to win Parliament's trust. Through both official letters and private contacts with such well-placed individuals as Whitelocke, he worked to retain command of an efficient army under his personal control.[51] The tone was set by his prompt reply to the executive committee, in which he applauded the delegation of national security to 'persons of soe eminent worth and integrity', and promised the 'greatest care and vigilancie'. Through a routine report on rumoured Royalist intrigues, the general discreetly underlined his ability to keep the Scots in 'good order'. Maintaining this desirable state of affairs depended, he pointed out, on a 'seasonable provison' for his soldiers, currently 'very unanimous and in as good a temper as [he had] known them'. For evidence of high morale, he pointed to the ready welcome accorded the Commonwealth in his officers' recent address. So began a fruitful correspondence with the committee and its successor, the Council of State, which appreciated Monck's usefulness, and rapidly ordered the release of funds to his forces, of whose 'good affections' it took grateful note.[52]

Agreeable as it doubtless was to the republicans, the fervent loyalty expressed by the army in Scotland did not, as Monck may have expected, place it above suspicion. Despite their own advice to nominate only the trustworthy, the actual recommissioning process dismayed the officers there, as elsewhere.[53] Tensions surfaced early in June, when Monck requested

[50] Nehemiah Bourne, 20 May, *Clarke papers*, iii. 215–16; Bordeaux to Mazarin, 19 May, Guizot, *Histoire*, i. 386; Giavarina to the senate, 27 May, *CSPVen.*, 28. A week earlier Giavarina had inclined to the view of those who doubted the authenticity of Monck's letters: ibid. 25. A sober Royalist evaluation is supplied in an anonymous report of 20 May, MS Clarendon 60, fo. 563.

[51] Whitelocke fondly recalled receiving letters 'of high compliment' from Monck, who not only accorded flattering recognition to his prominence in the construction of the Union, but requested his intercession on behalf of some officers: *Memorials*, iv. 352, 359. Monck also solicited favours from Vane (MS Clarke 267/1, fo. 75) and other powerful individuals involved in nominating officers (MS Add. 21245, fo. 146).

[52] Monck to the committee, 17 May, *Clarke papers*, iv. 10; council minutes, 31 May; council to Monck, 26 May, SP 25/98, fos 3–4.

[53] The distress that the purge could cause officers in Scotland is apparent in the letters of John Baynes, stationed at Leith, whose oft-expressed fears that false accusations from secret enemies at the centre might cost him his own place before he could exonerate himself were heightened when he saw comrades losing commissions 'who I thought might deserve them,

non-interference with his officer corps on his guarantee of their 'faithfulness to the present Government'. For Parliament to have granted such an exemption would have been both inequitable and potentially explosive, given the murmurings at the purge amongst the officers in England. In an answer drafted by Hesilrig and approved just three days after the controversial vote for all commissions to be signed by the Speaker, Parliament flatly refused to relinquish its prerogative to judge who would 'be truly and really faithful', and thereby demonstrated its impartiality to the whole Army. Though this exchange spawned fresh rumours of a breach, relations in fact improved significantly afterwards. Conciliation was the keynote of Monck's next letter, in which he denied any intention to protect the 'Scandalous or disaffected', and meekly presented himself as an obedient, unassuming professional soldier, whose 'great principle' was ever to 'reverence the Parliaments Resolutions in Civil things as infallible and sacred'. The House, for its part, had no wish to alienate so capable and respectful a general, whom it accepted at his own valuation as a 'faithful servant' even as it reproved his presumption.[54] Having asserted the principle of parliamentary authority, it was prepared in practice to permit him, like the other grandees, a considerable influence over appointments.[55] But the glaring contrast between Monck's dutiful subjection and the more grudging acquiescence of Fleetwood, Lambert and Disbrow had ominous implications for the future, since it strengthened doubts as to Army unity, taught distrustful MPs to regard the regiments in Scotland as the most reliable, and so paved the way for Hesilrig's fateful confidence in Monck during the autumn crisis.

The allegiance of the Army in Ireland remained doubtful longer, since it greeted the change more slowly and less warmly than did the other forces. Radical hopes for a revival of the 'good old cause' certainly rose with the news that Richard Cromwell's parliament had been dissolved, but whereas Monck's officers actively sought to impress the republican solution on their comrades at London, Henry Cromwell induced his divided subordinates to adopt a 'waiting frame to see what God or our superiors would command'. Silence left

not knowing any thing of miscarriage in them': MS Add. 21425, fos 131, 61, 66, 96. A full account of changes to these regiments is in Massarella, 'Politics of the Army', 594ff.

54 Monck to Lenthall, 2, 18 June, MS Tanner 51, fos 72, 88; Parliament to Monck, 10 June, *Journal*, 680. Rumours that Monck and the 'ruling rebels' were about to fall out over the issue of commissions reached Giavarina and Nicholas by late June: CSPVen., 35; CSPD 1659, 5, 18.

55 Monck's power over nominations is clear from correspondence of the Baynes family, clients of Lambert. Thus John Baynes was as much alarmed by Monck's coolness as the threat from unknown enemies: MS Add. 21245, fo. 61. Though John kept his place, the importance of having the general's support is plain from Robert Baynes's failure to transfer from his Yorkshire captaincy to a majority in Monck's regiment. Averse to the intrusion of an outsider favoured by Lambert, and desirous of the 'privilege of chusing his own officers', Monck politely rebuffed the family's overtures, and successfully lobbied influential politicians for promotion of the senior captain: ibid. fos 146, 136, 138.

space for conflicting speculation. Parliament received comfortable intelligence from 'old Officers' in Ireland, who professed solidarity with the Army in England and affirmed the eclipse of conservatives. The Republic's adversaries, who dreamed of a Stuart–Cromwellian conjunction, avidly swallowed stories that the lord lieutenant was fortifying Dublin, arresting antagonistic councillors, or even hanging Baptists.[56] In fact, he had merely forbidden 'unlawfull Assemblies' and the circulation of seditious papers intended to 'divide the good People . . . or alienate them' from the Protector. This proclamation, issued upon receipt of the first, confused reports that only a faction of the London officers favoured the Long Parliament, Henry later plausibly excused as an exercise in peacekeeping, directed against Royalist plotters. Resistance to the rest of the Army, once the true situation had been clarified by Fleetwood's letter and Parliament's *Declaration*, was both unfeasible and undesirable. Relaying these documents to his council of officers, Henry Cromwell enjoined resignation to providence, but checked a proposal for a 'free and affectionate Declaration of their engaging themselves for . . . the Good Old Cause', on the grounds that this might seem 'too like a capitulation'. Instead, he chose commissioners to report to Fleetwood and the General Council on the best way to bring stability and 'general satisfaction to the whole nation'.[57]

Despite an undertaking to 'continue in a peaceable disposition', this course, so different from Monck's readiness to join his officers in addressing Parliament directly, caused consternation behind the scenes at Westminster. In public, Archibald Johnston preserved the confident facade, writing to assure Scottish friends that Ireland had submitted and 'all things [were] . . . lik to be peaceable'; in his private diary he recorded misgivings as to 'Lord Henrys dark letter and present obedience'. To onlookers of all political persuasions a strange ambiguity distinguished Henry Cromwell's stance from that of the Protector's other commanders for over five weeks after Parliament returned. If he accepted the Commonwealth, why the delay in acknowledging it? If not, why did he retain his offices and refrain from declaring against it? Though late May saw glowing accounts of his submission in some newsbooks, the government organ *Politicus* published only a guarded statement that Ireland was quiet, its army 'resolved upon a compliance' after the failure of attempts to 'misrepresent' English events.[58] Not surprisingly, the

---

56 Henry to Richard Cromwell, 23 May, *TSP* vii. 674; *Journal*, 647. For the rumours circulating see especially MS Clarendon 60, fo. 503; *CSPVen.*, 17; and Guizot, *Histoire*, i. 379, 386.

57 *Scout*, no. 5, 20–7 May, 38; Henry to Fleetwood, 23 May, 15 June, *TSP* vii. 674, 685. His reply to the committee on 18 May, to which both these letters allude, has not survived, and was not copied into his letter book. Details concerning the commissioners and the proposals that they brought may be found in Clarke, *Prelude*, 34ff.

58 *TSP* vii. 674; *Johnston diary*, 116, cf. the summary of his letters in *Hay diary*, 27; *Politicus*, no. 568, 19–26 May, 464, cf. the stories in the *Scout* and *Moderate Informer* for the same week; Hyde to Villiers, 10/20 June, *CSP* iii. 500.

regime's enemies refused to credit such a 'formal compliance'. Some poured oil on the flames by publishing pseudo-republican condemnations of the commissioners as a calculated insult to the majesty of Parliament.[59] Royalist conspirators lured Sir George Booth into their net with promises that his Cheshire base would not be threatened from nearby Ireland, yet even they were increasingly exasperated by Henry's 'dullness' and 'pendulous' outlook.[60]

Republican disquiet over Ireland was much allayed by the commissioners' arrival. Instead of imposing conditions or negotiating exclusively with Fleetwood, as some anticipated, they assured the council of their army's 'unanimous and ready concurrence' with the course taken to restore 'the Commonwealth to its former state of Freedom'.[61] Ever more favourable accounts of the Irish situation in *Politicus* culminated in the publication of a brief address presented to the House on 27 June. This announced the 'humble, hearty and free submission' of the Army in Ireland to the change effected by 'the good hand of Providence', and its 'great expectations' of harvesting the 'good fruit' formerly yielded by this government, especially in the field of those 'high concernments of Peace and Liberty as Men and Christians'. Though they reminded MPs of the need to consider Ireland's 'Union with England', these officers explicitly renounced specifics as inappropriate in the context of submission. Hence their address, unlike those from the other armies, requested only that Henry Cromwell might receive the favour befitting 'a branch of that stock which God hath made so eminently instrumental in the service of these Nations'. Residual loyalty to their commander moved these officers to ascribe the tardiness of their approach to Parliament to Ireland's remoteness rather than the opposition that he had maintained until mid-June. By that point the lord lieutenant had received certain news of his brother's acquiescence and his own impending displacement; he therefore wrote letters recognising the Commonwealth and relinquishing his authority before it could be reft from him.[62]

---

[59] *Irelands ambition taxed*, also published as *Ambitious tyranny*. This tract's uniquely extravagant celebration of parliamentary authority and extremely violent attack on the commissioners, and by extension all supporters of the Protectorate in Ireland, suggest that its true object was to drive a wedge between Westminster and Dublin by provoking Parliament to wrath and showing conformist new English landowners that their gains were insecure. Such a division would have done much to overcome the major obstacle to a general anti-republican coalition in Ireland: fear that a Stuart restoration would nullify the conquerors' profits.

[60] Barwick to Hyde, 3 June, MS Clarendon 61, fos 289–90. Mordaunt reported the assurances given Booth, and his discouragement at their disproof: *CSP* iii. 516–18.

[61] Council minutes, 31 May. No formal discussion of the commissioners' proposals occurred; Royalists Orlando Gee and Edward Rawdon reported that the commissioners had returned without action because Parliament had not received them as negotiators, or considered their proposals: HMC, *Third report*, appendix 88; *Rawdon papers*, 195.

[62] *Politicus*, no. 276, 23–30 June, 540. The same number reproduced Henry Cromwell's curt letter of 22 June surrendering the government to Parliament's representatives. He had withdrawn his objections to an address from his officers by 15 June, the date of a longer

The contrasting responses of the armies to its return strongly influenced Parliament's immediate handling of the two provinces. In Ireland, Henry Cromwell's ambivalent behaviour necessitated an unequivocal assertion of Parliament's authority. Once assured that he lacked his army's backing, the republicans acted swiftly. On 7 June the House resolved that Ireland should again be ruled by commissioners rather than 'any one person', fixed the number at five, and summoned Henry to Westminster. As the council warned that the commissioners could not be 'suddenly dispatcht', Parliament authorised the interim transfer of the government to the two already in Dublin, William Steele and Miles Corbet, experienced administrators who had served in the same capacity from 1650 to 1654. Protectoral councillors, yet opponents of Henry Cromwell, these men gladly supplanted him, promising to discharge their new responsibilities 'with all faithfulness and diligence'. Meanwhile, MPs busied themselves with a bill to define the commissioners' powers and apply all previous legislation of the Long Parliament to Ireland. This measure, which Aidan Clarke has aptly described as an 'explicit exercise of English legislative supremacy', took much longer to enact than first anticipated. Read twice on 9 June, and referred to a committee instructed to report 'with speed', it did not become law until 7 July. The delay was due partly to the pressure of other business, which led the House to defer relevant reports on at least two occasions, but partly to contention over the proposed commissioners. Though William Steele, John Jones, Robert Goodwin and, later, Matthew Thomlinson, earned instant approval, other nominees were rejected. Miles Corbet's reputed corruption made him a particularly controversial choice: in a thin House, Hesilrig and Sidney narrowly defeated his candidacy. That decision was overturned the next week, when Parliament approved him with the proviso that he should return to explain the state of Irish affairs after three months, the period set to the commissioners' authority. A last minute attempt to add Edmund Ludlow, now reinstated as commander of the forces in Ireland, caused another close division won by Hesilrig, who championed the formal separation of the military from the civil power.[63] Thus Parliament replaced Henry Cromwell with a legal civilian government dominated on paper by its own members, and supported by a general who could be relied upon to enforce the changes in the officer corps.[64] So confident were the republicans of their hold on Ireland by the end of July that they recalled regiments thence to subdue the English rebellion.[65]

---

letter of acquiescence which he asked Fleetwood to report to the House or communicate privately as he saw fit: TSP vii. 685. Fleetwood chose the latter option.

[63] Clarke, Prelude, 57; Journal, 674, 683–4; William Steele and Miles Corbet to Lenthall, 22 June, MS Tanner 51, fo. 84; Journal, 678, 692, 699, 674, 707; council to the commissioners, 30 July. MPs technically predominated in the commission (3/5) but the aging Goodwin never departed to Ireland.

[64] Details of the changes, especially Ludlow's purge, are in Clarke, Prelude, ch. iii.

[65] The republicans' readiness to withdraw troops from Ireland contrasts with their concern to recruit to full strength the forces in Scotland, where they feared a 'correspondency'

In Scotland, where the seemingly trustworthy and undoubtedly competent Monck could safely be left in control, Parliament had little need and less inclination to upset the *status quo*. Such disruption as occurred was the incidental result of the delegitimation of the central government at the lapse of the Cromwellian Union. Fears of insurrection were unfulfilled: Monck punctiliously executed the council's commands to forestall trouble by securing leading Royalists, and soothed Lowland gentlemen made nervous by rumours of marauding 'moss troupers' in the Highlands.[66] Under the Army's keen surveillance, local order was largely undisturbed.[67] Confirmed in office until further order by the act of 11 May, Scottish JPs and sheriffs, like their English and Irish counterparts, functioned as usual until July, when Parliament stripped sheriffs of the power to decide civil cases. This, together with the lapse of the central courts at the Protector's fall, provoked loud complaints of the 'Hurt and prejudice Sustained by the Subjects of Scotland for want of Justice'. In the interest of stability and satisfaction with the Republic, Monck himself urged redress of the Scots' grievances, and thereby persuaded many of his 'tenderness and impartiall judgment of the condition of [their] poor nation'.[68] Parliament regarded the suspension of the judiciary as a temporary inconvenience, desired by the Scots' own deputies in order to hasten the perfection of the Union agreed in 1652.[69] Pending the enactment of that

between disaffected Scots and the English rebels: SP 25/98, fos 88, 92. Though compliant, Parliament's representatives in Ireland did not advise the reduction in the forces available to them: *Ludlow memoirs*, ii. 110.

[66] Council to Monck, 14 July, and Monck to local commanders, 29 July, *Clarke papers*, iv. 28. On these rumours, and Monck's reassurance of the gentry, see *Hay diary*, 55, 58, 65. Colourful accounts of a new Royalist rebellion in the Highlands reached some London newsbooks in the summer, but there is no confirmation in any official source. At the end of August Monck did inform the council of the gathering of some 'Rogues . . . in the Highlands to steal Cattle', but estimated their numbers at less than 200, and was confident that he could disperse them: MS Tanner 51, fo. 113.

[67] The persistence of order and stability at the local level, despite the 'legal chaos' occasioned by the change of government, is the conclusion of the only published study of Scotland in this period, by Dow, who assigns most of the credit to the Army: *Cromwellian Scotland*, 231–47.

[68] *A&O*, ii. 1272; *A DECLARATION Of the Parliament . . . July 7*; MS Clarke 31, fos 226–7 (a list of grievances). Monck's sympathy for the Scots is well-illustrated in his letter to the council of 5 July: HMC, *Ninth report*, appendix ii, 445. The judgement is that of the Resolutioner cleric James Sharpe, whose faction Monck had cultivated during the Protectorate's last years: *Register of the consultations of the ministers of Edinburgh*, ed. W. Stephen (Scottish History Society, 1930) ii. 188.

[69] The 'Humble Address of such of the Deputeis as did in the Yeir 1652 consent to the uniting of Scotland in on Commonwealth with England . . .', presented to Parliament on 24 May, requested and was generally blamed for the suspension of all courts and civil government except as 'necessarie for preservatioun of the peace and management of the revenues': John Nicoll, *A diary of public transactions and other occurrences chiefly in Scotland, 1650–1667*, Edinburgh 1836, 242–3. It is, however, unlikely that Parliament's curtailment of the peculiar powers of Scotland's sheriffs was directly inspired by this address, which had been quietly shelved by the council nearly two months previously; rather, this decision

Union, the Scots were arguably worse off than the Irish, since they lacked not only justice but a lawful civilian authority.

In other ways, however, the Scots were definitely the more favoured nation. Even godly inhabitants of Ireland got little say in their future settlement, and no share in the Commonwealth's present management.[70] Representatives of various Scottish factions exploited contacts with MPs, Army officers and clerics to obtain not only a hearing for their views but a measure of influence at Westminster. Most successful, in the short-term, were the Protesters or Remonstrants, who had opposed Charles II, and now bid fair to regain their old status as England's trusted allies.[71] Parliament speedily decided to include one or two Scots among the ten councillors who were not also MPs: both candidates seriously considered were Protesters. At Vane's suggestion, the choice fell on Johnston of Wariston, esteem for whose principled opposition to Richard Cromwell's recognition in the Other House outweighed qualms arising from his reputed zeal for Presbyterian uniformity.[72] This appointment gave Scotland a voice at the highest echelons of government, and England another diligent minister. Assiduous in his attendance, Johnston was soon voted president, and marvelled to find himself preferred to Cromwell's former seat.[73] His wonder was not mere vainglory. The unprecedented spectacle of a Scotsman superintending the 'greatest affairs of state' amazed and alarmed contemporaries of both nations.[74] Wariston's advancement predictably aroused envy and indignation in hostile compatriots, but

should be seen in the light of July's debates on the question of conforming Scottish to English law.

[70] Petitions from godly residents of Dublin and later Limerick got thanks but had no discernible effect on policy: *Journal*, 695, 722. After the dissolution of Richard's parliament Ireland had no formal and little informal representation at Westminster.

[71] Some of the Scots' extensive connections and intrigues with prominent English individuals may be traced in Johnston's diary and in the letters of his arch-enemy, Sharpe. On 27 May he noted that the 'honest pairty of Scotland', i.e. the Protesters, were now 'in good repute heir', but feared that their differences would, as formerly, undermine this standing: *Johnston diary*, 116. Sharpe worked hard to combat the Protesters' claims 'that their party are only fitt to be trusted at home because of their principles disposing them to a commonwealth way': *Register of the ministers*, 189.

[72] Parliament had adopted the notion of including at least one Scot by 14 May, when it elected most councillors; the other candidate was Swinton. The appointment was announced on 16 May. He learned the circumstances of his nomination from Vane and other MPs: *Johnston diary*, 112–13.

[73] Ibid. 116–17, 121. Johnston attended 84% of all council meetings, more than any other councillor (the nearest rivals were Scot, at 76%, and Vane, at 72%). As an outsider, he, unlike most of his colleagues, had no other responsibilities; this, together with his diligence, made him an attractive candidate for the chair. He first presided on 3 June.

[74] The only possible parallel is the election of the Scottish radical Sir James Hope to the Nominated Parliament's Council of State in July 1653, though Hope never presided, and was dropped after three months. On Hope's career see Arthur H. Williamson, 'Union with England traditional, union with England radical: Sir James Hope and the mid-seventeenth-century British state', *EHR* cx (1995) 303–22.

some of his allies were almost equally critical of his 'so great concurrence with the English'.[75] A xenophobic minority in the House denounced him as 'a spye, a stranger . . . so unfit in this ticklish tyme to be on their Counsel', and subsequently objected strenuously, and ultimately successfully, to his re-election as president when Englishmen were available. Where the regime's public relations in England were at stake, the Scotsman's strong accent and deficiencies as an orator negated his usefulness as a compliant figurehead. To Johnston's own relief, Whitelocke replaced him in the chair for the crucial exposition of Parliament's *Declaration* against the rebels to the City magistrates.[76] Johnston's nationality thus made him as much a liability as an asset to the republicans. That they did not take the easy option of excluding all Scots from the political process is some token of their sincere commitment to Union.[77] To consider his appointment an inconsequential sop to importunate Scots or the rhetoric of representative rule is to overlook its true importance as a harbinger of the future, a small but significant step towards the ideal of Scottish participation in a united polity.

Johnston himself took his role as Scotland's mouthpiece only too seriously.[78] A man of intense but volatile emotions, he swung from extravagant delight at

[75] *Hay diary*, 42, 145. Despite their friendship, Hay's initial reaction (p. 34) to news of Johnston's elevation was disbelief. More radical Scots attacked his appointment by invoking republican principle: A *LIVELY CHARACTER of some Pretending Grandees of SCOTLAND To the good old cause*, published in June, stressed Johnston's unfitness for the council on the grounds of his compliance with Oliver Cromwell, corruption and antipathy to the republican cause. From the other end of the political spectrum, Sharpe quietly sought to discredit Johnston in the eyes of England's rulers: *Register of the ministers*, 180–1, 189.

[76] *Johnston diary*, 113, 130. Whitelocke officially succeeded Johnston as president on 5 July. He noted that the council would have been content to let him continue, but that 'som of the House woundred that I was putt in the chaire as President as if they had not an Inglishman for it': ibid. 123. Nevertheless, he deputised occasionally, then continuously from 18–27 July. On 8 Aug. the council again voted him president for two weeks, but Whitelocke replaced him for the morrow's address to the City. The question was finally settled on 16 Aug. when the council resolved that members should take turns to preside for two weeks in the order in which they were listed in the act. In theory, this permanently excluded Johnston, since the council's authority would expire long before his turn, as one of the last named, arrived; in practice, he still sometimes substituted for the current president.

[77] In Richard's parliament the republicans had, of course, demanded the removal of Scottish MPs pending a lawful union, a goal achieved with the fall of the Protectorate. A few had, however, gone further. Most notably, John Hobart had questioned the validity of any union, and traced all the Protector's infringements on English liberties to illegal Scottish involvement in England's institutions. It would have been easy and, in some quarters, popular to exclude the Scots, just as the Irish. Johnston's appointment, enshrined in statute, was unquestionably legal.

[78] Before taking his place, he prayed that he might serve God's 'interests in al the three nations, and particularly . . . thes in Scotland whom I alone in this Counsel doeth represent'; thereafter, he frequently reminded his colleagues that he was 'but one heir to remember them of Scotland', and urged that country's business upon them: *Johnston diary*, 113, 118.

the prospect of serving his country to bitter disillusionment at the first setbacks to his designs. Letters home boasted of his importance. Diary entries, intended at least in part to exonerate him before posterity, bewailed his inability to do any good and the vanity of his exalted station – an 'airy, windy, shadowy hour of presiding without real advantage fed but my phantasy'. For this disappointment he blamed not his own unrealistic expectations – he hoped to rush through a settlement acceptable to his party – but the cunning machinations of more skilful and less caring politicians: 'pity my simplicity preyed upon by subtility of uthers'.[79] Such laments, born of impatience with English unwillingness to accord top priority to Scots affairs and accept his opinions thereon without question, exaggerated his own impotence and inexperience. Twenty years in the Covenanting movement had hardly left him a political innocent. True, the presidency was a position of more prestige than power. But as one of the committee for Scottish administration, Wariston was well aware that he possessed a real, if restricted, capacity to shape policy. Fear of being 'less regarded in busines of consequence to Scotland' overcame his scruples at signing arrest warrants for English suspects in August. Earlier that month he had procured permission for Edinburgh to collect its assessment by a 'more equall, easie and insensible' method, and received that city's 'humble and heartie thanks for his singular caire'.[80] A seat on the council afforded him unique opportunities to impress his vision of the Union upon the republican leadership. His efforts had some effect on the outcome: the Scots, at least, attributed the abandonment of the toleration clause to his closely reasoned protests, written and verbal.[81] Johnston was not therefore the negligible quantity that his dissatisfaction moved him to depict, but the single most influential Scot.

[79] Ibid. 118, 122, 127–8. In contrast to the frequent pessimism of the diary, written to justify his actions and possible martyrdom in the eyes of 'my children and friends and any uther that shal ever by providence see' it (p. 123), Johnston's letters emphasised the magnitude of the affairs on which he was employed and the influence that he wielded. Not until October, with the Union Act imminent, did he confide to his friends his 'fears that nothing shall go right in reference to Scotland': *Hay diary*, 150.

[80] *Johnston diary*, 132; council to Monck, 15 Aug., *Clarke papers*, iv. 42; *Extracts from the records of of the burgh of Edinburgh, 1655–1665*, ed. Marguerite Wood, Edinburgh 1940, 161. This was not the first time that he had helped his countrymen: on 23 July he noted that he had 'got somthing doen for the poor fishers in Scotland': *Johnston diary*, 127. Council proceedings attest his prominence in Scottish matters: see the minutes for 31 May, 14, 16 July, 29 Aug., 15 Sept.

[81] Johnston was well-placed to discover what was happening in Parliament and deluge his colleagues with written and spoken remonstrances. His diary records several such endeavours, while a paper against the proposed toleration clause, which is almost certainly his, survives in *Clarke papers*, iv. 50–5. Not only the admiring Hay, but otherwise hostile Resolutioners William Row and Robert Baillie credited him with blocking this measure: *Hay diary*, 124; *The life of Robert Blair, minister of St Andrews . . . with continuation of the history of the times to 1680, by his son-in-law, Mr William Row, minister of Ceres*, ed. Thomas McCrie, Edinburgh 1848, 338; *Baillie letters*, iii. 430.

Though they listened, and sometimes followed his advice, the republicans wisely refused to concede control of Scottish policy to Johnston or his associates, who lacked authority to speak for Scotland as a whole.[82] The Protesters' initial dominance was more apparent than real, and, in any case, lasted little more than a month. From mid-June onwards Parliament's approach to the Union consistently radiated its resolve to be independent, yet considerate, of all local groups. No longer were negotiations confined to the deputies selected in 1652, of whom only a vociferous handful were present. On 25 June the council instructed the committee drafting a new act to consult the 'persons from Scotland' at London; two months later Parliament created a subcommittee expressly to hear anyone concerned in the bill.[83] Anxious for the united Commonwealth to be as widely recognised as possible, English republicans actively encouraged input from Scots of contrasting political and theological outlooks. Vane and Scot, interrogating the Revd James Sharpe, delegate of the majority 'Resolutioner' or pro-Stuart faction in the Kirk, on rather flimsy charges of conspiracy, seized the opportunity to solicit his views on the 'way most acceptable to Scotland'. Sharpe observed that Union would serve either 'the interest of the whole' or 'the ends of a party', but declined to descend to specifics, except in the ecclesiastical sphere, where he strongly advised the English to confer with 'all parties' before making any innovations. Despite his reluctance to assist, Sharpe supposed that he had made a good impression, since the councillors had treated him with 'very much civility, speaking in the latter end very kindly and insinuatingly'. Evidently, the government was loath to offend even Scots of dubious loyalty. Much more did it welcome overtures from those few who celebrated Parliament's God-given commitment to the 'glorious work' of settling 'Rights and Liberties' throughout its dominions. Edinburgh's Independents, Quakers and Baptists, who pleaded in these terms for the abrogation of Scotland's intolerant laws, received thanks for their 'many good expressions', and the sympathetic assurance that the Union would match Parliament's solicitude for their welfare and that of 'the whole Nation'. To Presbyterian consternation, the petition was published in *Politicus* with editorial comments celebrating its significance, as the first Scottish approach 'to any Power in England' since the 'late Troubles'. Yet the separatists, for all their enthusiasm for English rule, secured no monopoly for their model. Parliament's reply proclaimed its ambition to establish a Union that would safely accommodate all interests.[84]

---

[82] Their enemies never tired of pointing this out. Sharpe, for example, lost no time in warning a sympathetic councillor that Johnston was the 'head of a faction', not a genuine representative of Scotland: *Register of the ministers*, 180.

[83] Council minutes, 25 June; *Journal*, 768–9. The deputies' address to Parliament indicates that they expected to resume their former role as sole intermediaries; Whitelocke's report to the House shows that they were, at first, the only ones consulted: ibid. 681.

[84] Sharpe described this interview on 28 May: *Register*, 184. The Edinburgh petition, with Parliament's answer, was reproduced in *Politicus*, no. 580, 21–8 July, 623. Wariston, 'troubled' by this positive response to sectaries, predicted that it would 'mightily provoke [the

Such a comprehensive goal, necessitating extensive consultation, put paid to early plans to achieve a 'speedy settlement' for Scotland along the lines laid down in 1652, but was not as unrealistic as it may appear.[85] Given the high cost of the occupation and the parlous financial position, it made both political and economic sense to invest time in seeking a solution sufficiently satisfying to the Scots to justify a substantial reduction of the military presence.[86] Scottish rejection of a voluntary Union with England was far from inevitable: north of the border, as discerning politicians realised, a deep reservoir of commitment to the idea of 'Britain' waited to be tapped.[87] Indeed, the first calls for a new Union after Parliament's restoration came not from English reformers but from those Scots determined to disprove pessimistic predictions that the new government would be 'so taken up with [England's] affairs . . . as matters relating to us will not be much minded'. Late in May a harassed Vane remarked that 'diverse [Scots] who are here do move us about it. We find they are not all of a mind'.[88] Therein lay the nub of the problem. Essentially, two contrasting concepts of Union were proposed. The first, favoured by Johnston and his patron, the marquis of Argyll, envisaged Scotland as an inferior but 'distinct republick' run by the Protesters, with an independent Kirk and legal system, and representation at Westminster proportionate to its share of taxation.[89] The alternative, cogently advocated by Robert Pittilloh and other nonconformists, centred upon the extension to Scotland of 'those Gospel priviledges that the truly godly in England contend

Presbyterians] in Scotland': *Johnston diary*, 128. The Edinburgh presbytery countered by issuing A *Testimony and Warning* against a petition that designed 'the overturning of the ordinances and truth of Christ in this Church' (title).

85 This phrase was used by the council in a letter of 28 May, notifying Monck of its progress in executing Parliament's orders, given ten days previously, to prepare a Union bill on the 'Grounds formerly declared': SP 25/98, fo. 8; *Journal*, 658.

86 On the damaging costs of occupation to England, and the Scots' superior dedication to 'Britain' see Hirst, 'English Republic', 476–8, 485–6.

87 The Scots had sought some form of 'confederal union' with England since 1639–40. On the origins of this objective, and English negative reactions see J. S. Morrill, 'The Scottish National Covenant in its British context', in his *Nature of the English Revolution*, 91–117, and 'Three kingdoms and one commonwealth? The enigma of mid-seventeenth century Britain and Ireland', in A. Grant and K. Stringer (eds), *Uniting the kingdom?*, London 1995, 170–90; and D. Stevenson, 'The early Covenanters and the federal union of Britain', in R. Mason (ed.), *Scotland and England, 1286–1815*, Edinburgh 1987, 163–81.

88 It was Sharpe who predicted, wrongly, that Parliament would have no time for Scotland. He reported Vane's remark and his own observation of certain Scots' endeavours to 'improve the opportunity of this late change for the interest of their party': *Register of the ministers*, 179, 184, 187. The reopened question of union with Scotland is conspicuously absent from the reforming agendas of most English pamphleteers.

89 Sharpe summarised the Johnston–Argyll model on 28 May: ibid. 185. Scattered references in the diaries of both Johnston and Hay corroborate his account. Extreme Protesters, such as James Guthrie, rejected any formal union, and demanded that England surrender Scotland to them completely, and trust godly unity to prevent any further threat to English security.

for and expect'. Contradictory local laws, covert persecution and the Kirk's coercive power would cease, and English oversight continue indefinitely. From the ashes of Scotland's autonomy a more unified and righteous commonwealth was expected to arise.[90]

That Parliament could not choose swiftly between these divergent models of Union was partly due to the answering chords that each struck among the English. Assimilation appealed strongly to patriots convinced that England's laws were 'worthy to govern the world', and should accordingly be extended to Scotland, leaving only 'particular customs . . . consonant to reason'. Radical egalitarians who censured existing law waxed still more enthusiastic about incorporating Scots and Irish with the English into one reformed polity, with 'the same Laws usages customs and manners'. Endowing the benighted periphery with the blessings of English laws and liberties had a benevolent appearance attractive to many MPs, especially those convinced that godly solidarity should over-ride national differences.[91] It also had the merit of consistency with the regime's previous engagements, at a moment when renewed fidelity to the glorious past was much prized. Scottish dissenters were not the only ones who argued that England's 'faith and credit' were at issue.[92] Sir Henry Vane, as commissioner to Scotland in 1652, had pledged Parliament's protection to everyone who lived 'soberly and christianly'; he now restated the Republic's commitment to 'countenance and encourage all who feared the Lord under whatsoever form'. Such a stance was, of course, anathema to rigid Presbyterians in general, and the Protesters in particular. Vane's emergence as their most influential opponent within the government may be charted in Johnston's diary: in June, complaints that Vane was 'loath to favor us or admitt of the proviso for religion' replaced early hopes of his collaboration; by the time of the Edinburgh petition, he had,

---

90 'Humble Petition . . . of some well-affected persons in Edenburgh and other places', *Politicus*, no. 580, 21–8 July, 623; Robert Pittilloh, *THE HAMMER of PERSECUTION: Or, the Mystery of Iniquity, in the PERSECUTION of many Good People in SCOTLAND Under the GOVERNMENT Of OLIVER . . . Disclosed with the Remedies thereof.* This urged Parliament to make appointments in Scotland by the advice of the 'congregated churches', 'moderate godly Presbyerians', experienced English judges and Army officers; it also has strong millennial overtones.

91 H[awke?], *History*, 112–13; John Turner to Fleetwood, 16 Nov., MS Sloane 4165, fo. 43; cf. *Speculum*, 18. On the attractions of benevolence and the general appeal of union to the godly see Hirst, 'English Republic', 461–5.

92 Pittilloh, *Hammer*, 8. In addition to the pledges of Parliament's commissioners, Pittilloh invoked the desire to deliver godly Scots from AntiChrist professed by the Army at Musselburgh in 1650. It is no coincidence that this declaration, with its prayer that 'those who fear the Lord in England and Scotland may become one in the hand of the Lord' (*A Declaration of the English Army . . . to the People of Scotland . . . Aug. 1 1650*, 7) was reprinted late in April, just as the soldiers reconsidered past engagements and returned to the 'Good Old Cause'.

from Johnston's perspective, become 'very froward and untoward and humorous about the busines of Union'.[93]

Yet comparative devolution also found prominent supporters in England. The opposition of some MPs to Johnston's presidency reflects ongoing reluctance to build integrated institutions empowering the alien Scots, still often perceived as 'an indigent, rude and illiterate Nation', to interfere in English affairs.[94] Devolution not only appealed to such insular prejudice, but held out the greatest probability of realising the ideal of consensual incorporation which had inspired the original decision to offer Union rather than compulsory annexation, and was still cherished by many republicans.[95] Recent debates in Richard's parliament had revealed that certain common- wealthsmen were uneasily conscious of smouldering Scottish resentment at the conquest and its sequel. John Hobart went so far as to expose the gulf between the magnanimous rhetoric and the fictitious consent forcibly extracted in 1652, and demand that Scotland be allowed every liberty 'consistent with the Public Safety', including a separate legislature, subject only to English veto. Henry Neville similarly reasoned that the Scots should retain their own laws, 'not have Englishment [sic] imposed upon them by letters to enslave them and us too'.[96] But the supreme exponent of the constitutional – and practical – dangers of involuntary anglicisation to both nations was James Harrington, who devoted ten of his APHORISMS POLITICAL to the subject. Regarding the Scots, unlike the Welsh, as an unassimilable 'forraign interest', he warned that mingling them with the English in the 'same standing Councils' would either destroy liberty in the minority commonwealth, or produce perpetual conflict, if each were equally represented. Integration of two such disparate legal systems was impossible without armed force incompatible with the very notion of 'Union as it is vulgarly discoursed of'. Harrington's alternative was a 'just League', whereby Scotland would remain a 'province' but 'enjoy her own Laws, her own Government, her perfect Liberty' at minimum expense to England. Such an outcome would please not only Scots objecting to subjugation but Englishmen who feared that Scottish 'participation in all Magistracies and Offices' of a single polity would reduce their liberties as well as their opportunities for advancement.[97] Residual Scotophobia and republican principle thus combined to commend a federal approach.

---

93 *Register of the ministers*, 183; *Johnston diary*, 122, 126.

94 *Panthalia*, 33. 1659 also saw the reprinting of the violently anti-Scottish *A Perfect Description of the people and countrey of Scotland*. Anti-Scottish prejudice was not confined to Royalists; on its previous manifestations in this Parliament's history, and before, see Williamson, 'Union', 306–7, and Hirst, 'English Republic', 470–1.

95 For the shift from annexation to union in 1651–2, and the classical overtones of that policy, see Hirst, 'English Republic', 460–1, and Worden, 'Classical republicanism'.

96 Hobart, speech 'Against the Scots sitting to Vote in the English Parliament' 21 Mar., MS Tanner 51, fo. 35; *Burton diary*, iv. 188. Ludlow and Scot also questioned assumptions that the Scots were genuinely reconciled to their lot: ibid. iv. 173, 136.

97 Jame Harrington, *APHORISMS POLITICAL*, 5–6. Henry Stubbe agreed that incorpo-

Jettisoning incorporation for a looser British federation was an extreme course to which Parliament never seriously inclined. The risks to England's security would have been grave – as Lambert pointed out, there was no guarantee that the Protesters could suppress disaffection among the majority of their countrymen if the Army withdrew.[98] Moreover, the Republic's reputation would undoubtedly have suffered from renunciation of the long-standing and lately renewed commitment to Union. So imperative did it judge the performance of this obligation that the House set aside time for the bill every week throughout the summer rising.[99] Harrington's assault, in late August, on the prevailing tendency to put provincial Union 'first, which is naturally last', was unmistakably aimed at Parliament's apparent determination to give Scotland's settlement precedence over England's. Disapproval of such inverted priorities was shared by some MPs: observing their careless demeanour in early autumn, Johnston worried that Union would be altogether laid 'asyde until the government be settled first heir'. He was mistaken. Despite occasional resolves to consider nothing but finance, security and the future constitution of England, Parliament never dropped and seldom deferred the weekly debates on Scotland.[100]

These sessions saw gradual progress towards a compromise. Late in September Johnston himself reported that 'the Act of Union is neer closed'. Gone were the clauses most offensive to Presbyterians, for the conforming of Scots to English law and the toleration of peaceable Protestant dissenters professing 'faith in God by Jesus'.[101] Also omitted were the Protesters' provisos confining the Union to civil matters and guaranteeing the 'free excercise ... with Christian moderacion' of the doctrine and discipline of the established Church.[102] Scotland's representation remained virtually un-

---

ration of either Ireland or Scotland, but especially the latter, would necessarily be 'destructive to the English Liberties': *A LETTER To An OFFICER of the ARMY Concerning a SELECT SENATE*, 62.

[98] So Lambert responded to Guthrie's appeal for Scotland's liberation: *Johnston diary*, 116. Sharpe drew the same conclusion: 'if England would leave Scotland, we would soon find if the Remonstrators should hold the power long': *Register of the ministers*, 185.

[99] The new Union Act received its first reading on 27 July, its second three days later. The House considered it in Grand Committee on 2, 6, 10, 13 and 19 Aug., twice a week, therefore, during the period of the rebellion. Thenceforward, it debated the bill every Friday.

[100] Harrington, *Aphorisms*, 7; *Johnston diary*, 135, entry for 6 Sept. Only twice did Parliament ever postpone the Friday debate – once, on 23 Sept., the day that Hesilrig unveiled the Derby petition – and again on 7 Oct., when MPs, preoccupied by the crisis, decided to resume after two weeks: *Journal*, 785, 792.

[101] Johnston to Chiesly, summarised in Hay, *Diary*, 150. As the text of the bill is not extant, the main sources for its contents are Johnston's letters and diary. That the toleration clause considered in the summer was essentially that of the Protectorate's first constitution is the contention of *Some Sober ANIMADVERSIONS ... Upon A Testimony and Warning, emitted by the Presbytery of Edenburgh* (p. 8). It is possible that anti-Cromwellian sentiment, as well as concern to conciliate the Presbyterians, contributed to its defeat.

[102] *Clarke papers*, iv. 55. Had Johnston won acceptance for these provisoes, he would

176

altered, at 6–7 per cent of the whole. Though the act failed to prescribe this proportion for taxation, MPs did acknowledge the 'injust inequality' of the Scottish tax burden, and spoke of abating it in the new assessment.[103] Much as he regretted the rejections of his counsel, and resented English tendencies to treat Scotland as a conquered 'province', Johnston, at least, was ready to accept Union on these terms. His criticisms increasingly shifted from the bill itself to the preparations to send commissioners to manage the civil government, and judges to staff the winter sessions. Here he detected persistent designs to make 'the lawes of Ingland . . . the reule of our justice in Scotland' by replacing Scots with English lawyers, and 'men of interest . . . especially Presbyterians' with 'men above ordinances', or sectaries.[104] Strict enforcement of the commissioners' instruction to ensure that all office-holders met the qualifications decreed by Parliament on 9 May would have had this result: few Scottish Presbyterians, however able and God-fearing, could claim to 'have given Testimony of their love to all the People of God and their faithfulness to the Cause of this Commonwealth'. But was strict enforcement intended? To the radicals' disgust, there had been no wholesale purge of conformist judges and magistrates in England, where the qualification was already in effect; plans to retain Johnston in some judicial capacity suggest a similar flexibility with regard to Scotland.[105] The proposal to appoint equal numbers of Scots and English judges, instead of a majority of the latter, militates against Johnston's suspicion that his countrymen would be excluded to facilitate the subversion of their legal system. As Pittilloh pointed out, English judges had acquired considerable experience of Scottish law in the past six years; their continued presence could help to prevent prejudiced verdicts, particularly against the separatists.[106] As a further check on militant

certainly have proclaimed his victory to his correspondents. His failure to do so, together with his forebodings as to the future, indicate that the English reaction remained as negative as when he first proposed them: *Johnston diary*, 125–6.

[103] *Johnston diary*, 136. Scotland's assessment was currently £6,000 per month, or 12% of the total for the three nations. Hence Johnston's concern to diminish it to the level of representation, which had been slightly reduced from the Cromwellian 7.5% (30/400) to the 'sixteenth part', or 6.25%, in August: ibid. 131. Instead, the new assessment bill proposed to double it but grant a 50% abatement, effectively making no change.

[104] Ibid. 141–2, 136, 143. Though he never praised it, Johnston's acceptance of the revised union bill of the autumn is apparent from his indignation at the delays in passing it (p. 138), and contrasts with his flat rejection of the first draft in July (p. 124).

[105] The commissioners' instructions survive in MS Egerton 1048, fos 176–80: the third and fourth articles applied the qualification of 9 May to Scotland's universities, schools and corporations. At the time of the interruption, Wariston's colleagues were considering whether to make him a judge or continue him as clerk register: *Johnston diary*, 142–3.

[106] *Hay diary*, 167, entry for 19 Oct; Pittilloh, *Hammer*, 13. English judges had constituted a majority on both civil and criminal benches for much of the Protectorate, and restrained Scottish partiality to some extent: D. Stevenson, 'Cromwell, Scotland and Ireland', in J. S. Morrill (ed.), *Oliver Cromwell and the English Revolution*, London 1990, 149–80 at p. 176.

Presbyterianism, the commissioners had orders to promote Gospel preaching and the 'Power of the true Religion and holiness' rather than the Kirk, and protect only the salaries of ministers 'well-affected to the Commonwealth'.[107] Thus the projected administration of Scotland would have afforded dissenters some recompense for the deletion of formal safeguards from the Union Act.

Other aspects of that administration were less controversial. Most of the commissioners' duties required little discussion in council, since they dealt with commonplace matters of finance and security.[108] A few also reflect a wider concern for Scotland's well-being. Johnston could have rejoiced in the injunctions to preserve the peace, so that the people might have 'right and justice duly administered', and to give 'all due encouragement' to 'trade and commerce . . . manufactures and the fisheries' whose interests he had espoused. Instead, he moaned that Scotland lay 'desolate without law, justice, government, or settlement'.[109] Quite oblivious of his inconsistency, he censured the English now for neglecting Scottish problems, now for pressing on with solutions that fell short of his own.[110] Neither reproach was deserved. The republicans' dedication to settling their northern dominion is evidenced by their diligence in seeking advice and attending to its affairs amidst ever more difficult circumstances. By the time of the interruption, the House had read the commissoners' instructions once, sanctioned new public seals for both Scotland and Ireland, and wanted only the council's nominations of commissioners and judges to complete the legislation.[111]

While Parliament made considerable progress towards Scotland's settlement, the future of Ireland was relatively neglected. As an English dependency of far more ancient date than Scotland, its integral place in the Commonwealth was taken for granted – symbolically, the restored Republic's great seal reverted to the design of 1651, depicting only England and Ireland. Reconquest and the redistribution of its lands had, in the opinion of its new rulers, made it 'now more than ever an English plantation'. Ireland's exact constitutional position, however, was undefined. Though the republicans

---

[107] MS Egerton 1048, fo. 176. The language of this instruction echoed Parliament's original commitment, in its October 1651 *Declaration . . . concerning the settlement of Scotland*, to promote the glory of God.

[108] Eight of the nineteen tasks assigned the commissioners were financial, involving improvements in tax collection, distribution and accounting, the reduction of expenditure and the recovery of alienated revenues. A further two concerned security: appropriate restraints, including exclusion from office, on persons 'opposing the present Government' or 'any ways dangerous'. Allegations of carelessness, on the ground that all the instructions passed 'without reading them one over togither' (*Johnston diary*, 136) were exaggerated: one clause was recommitted, two more added, and all read a second time before their report to Parliament was agreed: council minutes, 15, 20 Sept.

[109] Instructions to commissioners, articles 5, 14; *Johnston diary*, 140.

[110] For examples see *Johnston diary*, 127, 136.

[111] *Journal*, 791–2. The MPs on the council did meet to consider nominations. Some candidates were discussed by the Grand Committee on 7 Oct., but only the number, 5, and proportion of MPs, 2, were fixed: council minutes, 5 Oct.; *Johnston diary*, 141–2.

recognised the need for a formal incorporation – Vane, in Richard's parliament, had even suggested that this should precede that of Scotland – no promises bound them, and few petitioners importuned them to accomplish it. It is not, therefore, surprising that they failed to prioritise it. The House did contemplate the possibility of a joint Union bill for the British provinces in August, but soon discarded the notion.[112]

Such energies as MPs could spare for Ireland were primarily directed towards the settlement of confiscated lands upon the English soldiers and investors to whom they had been pledged. The Cromwellian distribution, like all actions since April 1653, had lost its legal force, plunging the property of thousands into jeopardy. Justice to early creditors, the expediency of preserving stability in the plantation and hopes of profiting from any surplus moved Parliament to plan a new act. Ambitious revision rather than simple confirmation of the earlier ordinance was intended. With government approval, the London-based 'Committee of Adventurers for Lands in Ireland' advertised for applications from those who had either not previously claimed, or received poor quality lots.[113] On 6 July the adventurers presented their petition, and the council introduced a bill; both were referred to the same committee, which had agreed some amendments by 18 July. Despite appeals from the commissioners to send it 'with all possible speed', consideration of the measure did not resume until after the rising, on 17 August. Several clauses were added, but a morass of individual claims and counter-claims impeded the bill's passage. Seven debates and exactly one month later, the House set a deadline for the reception of petitions and provisos, and scheduled the introduction of the engrossed bill for 3 October. An early casualty of the autumn crisis, the Irish land settlement never recaptured Parliament's full attention.[114]

Concentration on the high-profile issue of confiscated lands long diverted Parliament from other foundations of order. In Ireland, like Scotland, justice was effectively suspended. JPs and sheriffs could act locally, though not all were willing to do so; the courts remained closed during the summer term, so

---

112 The Commonwealth's new great seal, enacted on 14 May, bore the maps and arms of England and Ireland, whereas the Protectorate's had added Scotland's: Irish commissioners' instructions to Ludlow, 17 Oct., MS Stowe 185, fos 136–40. Vane's speech is in *Burton diary*, iv. 114. The Army's is the only extant petition to touch on the theme of union with Ireland. *Politicus*, no. 583, 11–18 Aug. reported that Parliament was discussing the union of Ireland as well as Scotland; on 9 Sept. MPs decided not to comprehend Ireland in the bill: *Journal*, 775.

113 *Journal*, 657, 682, 706. The pressing need to stabilise the plantation was eloquently set forth by Ludlow and John Jones: MS Tanner 51, fo. 93. The 'Committee for Adventurers' advertised in *Politicus*, no. 567, 12–19 May, 445.

114 *Journal*, 706, 707; Ludlow and Jones to Parliament, 19 July, MS Tanner 51, fo. 93; *Journal*, 761, 763–4, 767, 770, 774–5, 778–9, 780. Forgotten on the appointed day, the Irish land bill last surfaced on 5 Oct., when it was deferred for another week: ibid. 792.

neither civil nor criminal trials could proceed.[115] Stressing the 'great Detriment' inflicted by the vacuum at the centre on 'the Publique Revenue and . . . every Mans private Concernment', the commissioners urged the 'speedy erecting of Courts'. The fate of their letter seems to exemplify republican dilatoriness where Ireland was concerned: dated 17 August, it was not referred by the council until 8 September, and only reached the House on 5 October.[116] Yet Parliament could react swiftly when speed was most necessary to conserve its authority: the reminder, in early September, that the commissioners' term of office was about to expire elicited an immediate act renewing their powers for six months. Thus Ireland was never left without 'legal government', as some historians have asserted.[117] The confusion there, as in Scotland, arose by default, not design. By October Westminster had begun to inquire into the 'obstructions' encountered by its agents 'in the Execution of [their] trust'. Convinced that change was coming, the commissioners proposed solutions centring upon the thorough anglicisation of the legal system, the protection of English property from Irish depredations, and the expansion of their powers to cover corporations, the judiciary and the customs and excise.[118] As a similarly comprehensive jurisdiction was planned for Scotland's commissioners, while the tide of opinion favouring the export of English law ran even more strongly in Ireland's case, these recommendations were not unrealistic. Had Parliament survived to receive them, it would doubtless have remedied Ireland's disorder in due course.[119] Britain's problems were not inherently insoluble.

The shadow of the interruption has distorted subsequent impressions of republican government in the British dominions by magnifying short-term disruption and minimising long-term initiatives that did not reach fruition. Hindsight, together with the dominance of Archibald Johnston's jaundiced perspective, has fostered an image of deliberate neglect and maltreatment which is far from the truth.[120] Parliament's immediate goal was certainly to

---

[115] On the lack of justice, and consequent disruption, see Clarke, *Prelude*, 79–80. Not all inhabitants were dissatisfied with the situation – the Quaker William Morris joyfully observed that 'scandalous and persecuting Magistrates . . . now begin to droop . . . as if their end . . . were near': *To the supream authoritie*, 3.

[116] The letter is summarised in the council minutes, 8 Sept., and *Journal*, 792.

[117] *Journal*, 773; Davies, *Restoration*, 243; Barnard, *Cromwellian Ireland*, 23. Clarke does note the renewal of the commissioners' powers, but buries it without comment in the middle of a paragraph on the estates bill: *Prelude*, 84. The error of earlier historians arises from Firth and Rait's omission of the duplicate act from their collection.

[118] Irish commissioners' instructions to Ludlow, 17 Oct., MS Stowe 185, fos 136–40, and letter to the council, 5 Oct., MS Dep. C159, fo. 189. Ludlow and Steele, at least, were sure that Parliament was about to create courts: *Ludlow memoirs*, ii. 125.

[119] As Parliament had approved the commissioners' earlier suggestions for the forms of commissions of oyer and terminer, gaol delivery and decision of civil causes in Ireland, and referred the question of courts and judges to the council (*Journal*, 764, 792), it is probable that it would have heeded their latest proposals.

[120] Thus Davies uncritically adopted Johnston's lament on Scotland's desolation as an apt

reinstate its authority and ensure that the periphery remained safely subordinate. In this it succeeded admirably, having secured the respectful assistance of the armies there. And such success was vital: revolts by the forces in first Scotland, then Ireland, would do much to undermine the next regime, the Committee of Safety, and with it the Republic. But Scotland and Ireland, unlike Dunkirk and the colonies, were much more than adjuncts to be run for England's benefit: their ultimate destiny was admission to all the privileges of a united Commonwealth. If this policy had emerged from 'contingency and crisis' in 1651–2, it was pursued in 1659 from conviction consequent upon mature consideration as much as blind fidelity to the past.[121] Disputes, differences, delays and distractions should not obscure Parliament's determination to effect a lasting union, or, in Scotland's case especially, its actual progress towards this end. Well might MPs accused of achieving nothing during their brief months of power retort that the acts for Scotland's union and Ireland's settlement 'took up a very great deal of time' because they were 'very long . . . and of great weight . . . and not to be slightly passed'.[122] The restored Parliament of 1659, even more than the Nominated Assembly of 1653, 'offered a serious chance for new directions' leading to 'genuinely multinational institutions'.[123] That these were never attained owed less to shortsightedness or lingering national prejudice on all sides than to the Commonwealth's failure to establish itself. And that failure, in turn, resulted from a crisis at the centre, in which peripheral issues played little part.

conclusion to his brief summary of Parliament's Scottish policy: *Restoration*, 225. More recently, Hirst has judged the 'restored Rump's' dealings with the Scots in 1659 'one-sided' and 'cynical', solely on the basis of Johnston's testimony: 'English Republic', 453.

[121] By 1659 coherent visions of the united Commonwealth had developed: most systematic was Hawke's lengthy *History of the Union*.

[122] *True relation of . . . the case between . . . Parliament and the officers*, 6.

[123] This verdict on the Nominated Parliament is that of Williamson, 'Union', 322.

8

Identity Asserted:
Visions and Vindications of the Republic

I shall observe . . . the happiness of a Commonwealth, even in this one instance of the liberty of Printing . . . as it satisfies the impulse of the spirit of those that write, and contents the Reader and puts him in hopes and thoughts that we are free men, because our mouths are not stopped: so it may (if they please) give great light to the Parliament: *Margery Good-Cow . . . Or a short DISCOURSE shewing That there is not a Farthing due . . . to Old Oliver*, May 1659.

Here's no Obscenity, Scurrility, Sedition, or Calumny . . . to corrupt thy sober mind, or cause thee to abuse . . . thy precious time . . . as in the swarmes of foolish and rediculous Pamphlets that shamefully are permitted to fly up and down with uncliped wings, tending rather to debauch . . . and divide the minds of men than any way to compose us to the reception of those sounder . . . principles . . . that may . . . reduce and happily establish us in a just and equitable . . . constitution of a real Commonwealth: *Speculum Libertatis Angliae Re restitutae*, July 1659.

Men, yea very honest men, are too apt to be surprised with every overture for setling this distracted State, and I fear many have unwarily suckt in the poyson of this Pamphlet (*The Interest of England Stated*) . . . This age is very pregnant of projects; everybody hath a fling at the State: and set their wills aworking to hammer out a Government . . . every Book-sellers Basket and Shop hath some new thing to shew for a Popular Government: *The Grand Concernments of ENGLAND ENSURED*, Oct. 1659.

Historians have long recognised the qualitative and quantitative importance of the print output of 1659. Hutton notes the 'great commotion in the London press' and the 'vigour' of 'republican pamphleteering'; Aylmer pronounced 1659 'one of the vintage years for radical tracts', while Zagorin, adapting Dryden's famous phrase, judged it 'republicanism's *annus mirabilis*'.[1] An explosion of controversial print did, indeed, accompany the Republic's restoration. London bookseller George Thomason collected eighteen pamphlets in April, forty-eight in May, and an astonishing sixty-seven in June; of the 255 tracts and broadsheets that he acquired between the dissolution of Richard's parliament and the expulsion of its successor, nearly

---

[1] Hutton, *Restoration*, 47, 121; G. E. Aylmer, *Rebellion or revolution? England, 1640–1660*, Oxford 1986, 192; Zagorin, *History of political thought*, 155.

two-thirds were republican in outlook.[2] Encouraged by the relative freedom of the press, and inspired by the political uncertainty, newsbooks and pamphlets pressed upon public notice expedients ranging from monarchy to theocracy, from a resurrected Leveller programme based on the 'ancient fundamental' constitution of England to Harrington's elaborate schemes for a bicameral republic derived from classical and foreign precedents.

Historians have not done justice to this diversity, nor appreciated the cogency of conservative arguments; instead they have focused upon radicalism, in general, and within that upon certain strands to the neglect of others.[3] Thus Harrington has been studied in depth by historians of political thought, while the ideas of Quakers and Fifth Monarchists have received some analysis in histories of these movements.[4] Other godly republicans, with the partial exception of Sir Henry Vane, have been almost entirely overlooked. Christopher Hill asserts that the Levellers had become 'indistinguishable from Harringtonian republicans', while Woolrych relegates their resurgence to an ineffectual 'radical fringe'.[5] These omissions, together with hindsight, have distorted historical interpretations, fostering negative conclusions. Hutton asserts that there is 'an air of limpness, of intangibility about many of the republicans of 1659', and that their former 'fervour and determination' were 'now breathed by the Quaker tracts'. Scott opines that this year's writings demonstrated the 'variety and vitality of republican discourse rather than its capacity for continued development'. Zagorin saw in the 'babel of argument and controversy' the signs of 'anarchy', and maintained that the republican 'opportunity had passed' long ago, since 1649 was the 'moment when the free commonwealth should have begun to take shape'. Davies, too, thought the variety of ideas indicative of the divisions that destroyed the Commonwealth: representing its adherents as 'engrossed' by 'Utopian ideas', he insisted that 'they had only to read each other's proposals

---

[2]   During these months Thomason collected 69 texts written by the conservative enemies of the regime, 25 theological and other miscellaneous items, and some 161 works by radicals of various kinds, though only 92 of these directly advocated political changes. These figures do not include the newsbooks, which were overwhelmingly republican, at least outwardly. At least 45 additional radical tracts, including numerous Quaker items, were published in this period, but not added to Thomason's collection.

[3]   The conservative argument and its importance is discussed in ch. 1 above.

[4]   On Harrington see especially J. G. A. Pocock's 'Introduction' to *The political works of James Harrington*, Cambridge 1977, and Blair Worden's more recent analysis, 'James Harrington and *The Commonwealth of Oceana*, 1656', in Wootton, *Republicanism*, 82–110. For the contributions of Quakers and Fifth Monarchists see Reay, *The Quakers*, and Capp, *Fifth Monarchy men*.

[5]   Christopher Hill, *The experience of defeat: Milton and some contemporaries*, London 1984, 32; Woolrych, 'Good Old Cause', 159. Woolrych discusses Vane's *Needful corrective* in 'Introduction', 104–6.

to see how far apart they were', and so perceive the vanity of their hopes for a settled republic.[6]

But the epigraphs that head this chapter reveal that republican optimism was not founded upon ignorance of the multitude of contrasting views. *Margery Good-Cow*, written amidst the first raptures attending Parliament's return, extolled the absolute 'liberty of Printing' as a clear sign of a 'true Commonwealth'; celebrating the 'world of new inventions communicated by the Press' since the abolition of monarchy, the author looked forward to still greater advances now that the Protector's fall had broken the latest 'Bands of darkness' enslaving the people's understanding. Other republicans soon apprehended the dangers of complete freedom of expression. *Liberty's Looking-Glass*, published in July, not only highlighted the damage done by the multitude of rival pamphlets by likening them to 'swarmes' of insects pestering the people, but tacitly criticised the failure to curb their circulation. *The grand concernments of England* similarly feared the vulnerability of even 'honest men' to the blandishments of such Royalist propaganda as the *Interest of England Stated*, now in its second printing.[7] Yet these writers were equally convinced of their ability to refute contrary arguments, and instruct readers in the 'sounder principles' that would, if implemented, produce a 'real Commonwealth'. Never had the prospects of a 'happy settlement' seemed brighter: with Parliament receiving 'Models, Representations, Petitions, Proposals', and spending days debating the future form of government, it is hardly surprising that every hopeful writer hastened to cast his 'mite' of advice into the 'Treasure of Common Good'.[8] Confidence in the power of ideas to shape opinions, and hence events, had seldom been greater, or more justified. The print debates were not abstract intellectual exercises, but struggles in deadly earnest that had profound consequences for the moment from which they sprang. To rightly understand that moment, it is essential to examine republican publications in their original context, evaluating their complex contribution, offensive and defensive, to the Commonwealth cause. It will then become apparent that, far from symbolising the inevitability of failure, radical pamphleteering exhibited a creativity and vitality that reflected the Republic's real potential to succeed.

6 Hutton, *Restoration*, 122; Scott, 'English republican imagination', 51; Zagorin, *History of political thought*, 154–5, 163; Davies, *Restoration*, 95, 92.
7 *Margery*, 3–4; *Speculum*, 3; *Grand concernments*, 3, 43.
8 *The PEACE-MAKER: Or Christian Reconciler*, 1; *No RETURN To MONARCHY; & Liberty of Conscience SECURED, Without a Senate . . . in a way most agreeable to a COMMONWEALTH*, 3. See also titles such as B[illing], *Mite of affection*, and *The poor mans mite*.

The 'Good Old Cause' and the revival of competing newsbooks

The intimate connection between the Republic's fate and printed ideas was first demonstrated, in the spring of 1659, by the agitation for the 'Good Old Cause' that played such a substantial part in the Army's decision to abandon the Protectorate and recall the remnant of the Long Parliament.[9] As censorship crumbled with Richard Cromwell's government, republicans seized the initiative, producing a stream of pamphlets and petitions urging soldiers to revert to their ancient allegiance. Important as 'emotional exhortations' to forsake the Cromwellian 'apostacy' undoubtedly were, positive justifications of Parliament were far from the 'thin' and 'tedious contentions' that Woolrych depicts.[10] Rehabilitating the reputation of the 'Good Old Parliament', so much tarnished by its expulsion in 1653, was a crucial strategy. Recalling the wisdom and virtue that had characterised its earlier administration, republicans dismissed allegations of corruption and self-perpetuation, and insisted that this government alone was 'truly legitimate and of English Right'. Since the people's rights were inextricably intertwined with those of Parliament, 'the . . . natural Head of our Country', nothing less than its return could satisfy their expectations and produce a lasting settlement, based on first principles.[11] Thus such a restoration was not, as Scott has alleged, a symptom of the 'practical poverty of the political imagination': rather, it was an essential step forward to the reformed Republic of the future.[12]

Closely linked with the campaign for the 'Good Old Cause' was the return of competitive journalism. In 1655 all but the official newsbooks, *Mercurius Politicus* and the *Publick Intelligencer*, had been suppressed. As these now preserved an uneasy silence, reporting only foreign events, former rivals sensed an opportunity to profit from the demand for domestic news and promote the cause of the Commonwealth.

First into the field was the *Faithful Scout*, which reappeared on 29 April, replete with the rhetoric of the most prominent republican pamphlets, reproduced sometimes with, more often without, attribution. The didacticism of this newsbook was plain from the opening declaration of its mission 'as well to turn the Pen into Prayer, that GOD would be pleased to discloud these gloomy Dayes with the Beams of His Mercy, as to present you with the Transactions and Affairs of both States and Commonwealths'. From the very first page, readers were taught to admire the 'progress' of the 'Honourable Council of Officers' with the republican agenda, identified as 'the National Interest, for the establishing . . . a Commonwealth and restoring the People to their

---

[9] The classic account of this agitation is Woolrych, 'Good Old Cause'.
[10] Ibid. 151.
[11] *To the Officers and Souldiers . . . The humble Petition and Advice of divers well affected to the Good old Cause, Inhabitants in and about Southwark*, 5; *Declaration of the well-affected.*
[12] Scott, 'English republican imagination', 51. The forward-looking nature of calls to restore this Parliament has been rightly emphasised in Norbrook, *Writing*, 398.

just Rights and Priviledges'. Extracts from the *Humble Representation* of Westminster's 'well-affected' inhabitants clearly explained the next steps towards these goals: the immediate expulsion from office of all enemies of the 'Good Old Cause', however high their rank, and the recall of 'that Renowned Long Parliament', with whom the Army had engaged to defend the 'Government as then established without King or House of Lords'. Carefully omitted were the less complimentary lamentations and bitter attacks on 'the advancement of a private personal Interest in stead of the Weal publick' of its source. The *Scout* reprinted only those passages that promoted positive action, recalling that the 'glorious presence' of God had manifested itself in Parliament's 'Counsels and Armies' through their assertion of the 'Liberties of the People', 'provision for the Souldiers', and, supremely, their constant victories; and it prophesied similar blessings upon a prudent, self-denying return to 'that Way'.[13] Thus the editor cultivated both Cromwellian grandees and republican leaders. His advocacy of the Commonwealth succeeded so well that the *Scout* not only survived but found an expanding market, further exploited by the revival, less than three weeks later, of its Tuesday version, the *Weekly Post*.[14]

Though the *Scout* and the *Post* continued to disseminate republican views, other consequences of the liberated press augured less well for the new regime. At first unofficial newsbooks protected themselves and made the most of the moment by imitating the *Scout's* loyalist tactics. Even the Royalist John Crouch, in the early numbers of *Mercurius Democritus*, combined ribald nonsense and foreign news with serious excerpts from the Army's *Declaration* of 2 May, the petition of the 'well affected to the *Good old Cause*' in Southwark, and an attack on Prynne's 'Scandalous Libel to the Commonwealth'. Subsequent issues abandoned such sops to republican *gravitas*. Reviving the tradition established by *Mercurius Fumigosus* prior to its suppression in 1655, *Democritus* replaced news headlines with doggerel verse, adopted the subtitle 'A Perfect Nocturnal' and devoted itself to a scurrilous and nonsensical parody of the regular diurnals.[15] The reappearance of

---

13 *Scout*, no. 1, 22–9 Apr., 1, 6–7; cf. the *Representation of divers well-affected persons of . . . Westminster*.

14 Hutton is therefore mistaken in asserting that the *Scout* was 'wound up' after Canne became editor of *Politicus* and returned as the Army's newspaper after the October dissolution (*Restoration*, 45–6, 72): it continued, under various names, throughout the year.

15 *Mercurius Democritus Communicating Faithfully the Affairs both in City and Country, with most observable Occurrences from Forreign Parts*, no. 2, 26 Apr.-3 May, 14–16. The next issue became *Mercurius Democritus or a Perfect NOCTURNAL Communicating many strange Wonders Out of the World in the Moon, the Antipodes. . . . Published for the right understanding of all the Mad-merry People of Great Bedlam*. This title obviously echoed *Mercurius Fumigosus, OR THE Smoking Nocturnall, Communicating Dark and hidden News out of all Obscure Places in the Antipodes. . . . For the right understanding of all the Mad Merry People in the land of Darkness*. *Fumigosus* had succeeded an earlier *Democritus* in 1653, which in its turn had assumed *The Man in The Moon's* mantle. On the distinctive style of these newsbooks see J. Raymond, *The invention of the newspaper: English newsbooks, 1641–1649*,

Democritus in unadulterated form exemplified the growing confidence of the Republic's enemies, who launched an increasingly strident challenge to its authority. *Democritus* itself was relatively harmless: Crouch loudly declined 'to intermeddle with State affairs', and reserved explicit ridicule for Prynne, insignificant figures such as the radical bookseller Livewel Chapman, and the 'time-serving Excisemen and Lawyers' execrated by radicals and conservatives alike.[16] But *Mercurius Pragmaticus*, the next Royalist newsbook to resurface, was much less innocuous. Commencing with the lines *'What Monster's this? stand back, the Good Old Cause, That hath destroyed the Fundamental Laws'*, it proclaimed an unambiguous, if satirical, message of condemnation.[17] In this, it was at one with numerous pamphlets already circulating. The very success of the 'Good Old Cause' in undermining the Protectorate had provoked a strong reaction among Royalists and, especially, Presbyterians, who took advantage of the relaxation of press controls to denounce and then reinterpret the radical understanding of this motif, before moving on to comprehensive denials of the Commonwealth's legitimacy and expediency.

Parliament's self-defence: censorship

At first sight, England's new rulers seemed to be doing little to defend their authority against the onslaught of conservative propaganda. Friends and foes alike exclaimed at Parliament's inaction. In June Army newsletters complained that 'desperate books' expounding 'another Good old Cause' were 'suffered to go abroad without question'. A Royalist posing as a Commonwealthsman informed his masters that 'ungodly pamphlets do so daily poison the Good Old Cause that I fear its falling to the ground'; Giavarina represented the 'extraordinary and unbridled licence in writing and publishing' as an unmistakable sign of the new regime's weakness.[18] Republican writers sneered at 'poor pamphleting Opponents', dismissing their 'pestilent Libels' as the products of 'weak corrupted Judgments and discontented minds', yet paid unwitting tribute to their subversive potential. Though the *Weekly Intelligencer*, in mid-June, announced that the government was 'now taking a course to suppress' the 'many Pamphlets laden with as

Oxford 1996, 180–3, and D. Underdown, *'The Man in the Moon*: Levelling, gender and popular politics, 1640–1660' (Ford Lecture 1993), published in *A freeborn people: politics and the nation in seventeenth century England*, Oxford 1996.

[16] *Democritus*, no. 5, 31 May–7 June, 33, 34, 36; no. 8, 14–21 June, 50.

[17] *Mercurius Pragmaticus* (20 June), 1. This publication, unlike the earlier serial under this title, lacks most of the defining characteristics of a newsbook identified by J. Raymond in *Making the news: an anthology of the newsbooks of revolutionary England, 1641–1660*, Moreton-in-the-Marsh 1993, 16–18: it had neither dates nor number, and may have been intended as a single pamphlet. Similar Royalist satirical attacks included *Several new cheats* and *England's changeling*.

[18] *Clarke papers*, iv. 21; MS Clarendon 61, fo. 101; *CSPVen.*, 29.

much impudence as ignorance', no drastic measures followed, and reactionary tracts continued to proliferate with impunity.[19] Introducing *Panthalia*, his Royalist *roman-à-clef*, Richard Brathwait contrasted the 'keen and eager Talons' of the Protector's 'Statizing Censors' with the relaxed approach of 'a prudent re-assembled Synod, which made their constant care for constitution and conservation of a Republick, their sole interest'. John Rogers also sensed a deficiency: condemning 'the Liberty which loose pens or tongues take to traduce . . . our Worthies . . . to the prejudice of the State and hinderance of them in their Publick faculties', he urged Parliament to follow the example of 'all . . . orderly and well-settled Governments' in restraining the 'unjust, unlawful License of Slandring'.[20]

Appearances to the contrary notwithstanding, Parliament was by no means indifferent to the threat from 'Unlicensed and Scandalous Books and Pamphlets'. An act of 1649, revived with amendments in 1653, had prescribed penalties for the writers, printers and sellers of such literature, procedures for discovery and destruction and a comprehensive regulation of printing to prevent its future production.[21] In 1659 this legislation was neither repealed nor forgotten. Faced with the rising tide of subversive publications, the council gave serious attention to its responsibility to execute the laws against them. On 15 June Thomas Scot, as chief of intelligence, was ordered to employ 'all legall meanes' to discover and suppress 'seditious and libellous bookes and pamphletts', and punish the 'Offenders'. The council promised to refer 'any defect' that Scot found in the law to Parliament for amendment. Though the House, following Harlow's revelations in July, ordered the introduction of a bill to prevent the 'publishing or spreading of false Rumors and scandalous Reports', the lack of progress, together with the absence of any recommendation from the council, usually so sensitive to security needs, suggest that the existing statutes were judged adequate.[22]

Enforcement, not lack of legislation, was the real problem, and this is extremely difficult to evaluate. With typical exaggeration, Giavarina claimed that 'nothing [was] suppressed', yet successfully suppressed books, by definition, gain little publicity. Evidence of Scot's diligence in detecting at least some of those engaged in illicit book production does exist: on 12 July the council issued a warrant for the committal of one Alexander Aspinwall, arrested on 'suspicion of being the Author and disperser of severall dangerous

---

19 A COMMONWEALTH, *And Commonwealths-men Asserted and Vindicated*, 1, 8; *WI*, no. 7, 14–21 June, 49–50. Thomason collected more conservative tracts in June than in April, May and July put together.

20 [Brathwait], *Panthalia*, 'Advertisement to the judicious Reader'; Rogers, *Diapoliteia*, 97–8. Though Thomason did not acquire this text until 20 Sept., the prefatory epistle is dated 14 July, and Rogers stated that most of it had been written before the rebellion.

21 The 1649 and 1653 Acts for regulating printing are reprinted in *A&O* ii. 245–54, 696–9.

22 Council minutes, 15 June, MS Rawlinson C179, fo. 73; *Journal*, 725. The Harlow incident is discussed in ch. 3 above.

and seditious libells & pamphletts'. The fortuitous survival of the examinations of both Aspinwall and his printer amongst the Clarendon manuscripts reveals that Scot had actually uncovered a particularly dangerous conspiracy.[23] Through a clever combination of Leveller rhetoric and the conservative critique of the 'pseudo-Parliament', the pamphlets in question, *Timely Advice* and *The SOVLDIERS Alarum Bell*, incited the Army to 'perfect Libertie as Free-born People' by revolting – the goal, the restoration of its late Protector, Richard Cromwell. The council's efficient enforcement of the law in this case may be deduced from the fact that Cromwellian propaganda attracted little attention from contemporaries, and even less from historians, who have seldom or never admitted that the Protectorate remained the preferred alternative of at least some of Parliament's opponents.[24] More conspicuous was the republicans' failure to stop the printing and circulation of Presbyterian and Royalist polemic. Yet here, too, the council's role in deterring sedition may have been underestimated. Aided by informants, the committee for examinations in August pursued the printers and distributors of Booth's declarations, and such 'scandalous pamphlets' as *Pragmaticus* and *A Pair of Spectacles*.[25] It is surely not coincidence that *Democritus* ceased to appear at this time, and that the attempts to revive *Pragmaticus*, first in June, and then, more seriously, in September, proved abortive. Royalist journalism in 1659 was, and remained, a shadow of its former self. Enjoying the sunshine of government favour, republican pamphlets and newsbooks easily predominated: conservative writings constituted less than one-third of the massive accession to Thomason's collection during this period.[26] After the summer emergency, the council reiterated its determination to improve the regulation of printing, instructing a committee to study proposals from the Stationers' Company and all relevant acts and ordinances.[27] It is, of course, impossible to ascertain the quantity of seditious material that would have appeared under an indifferent or completely incompetent government. Nevertheless, the remarkable contrast between the restricted counter-revolutionary output under the confident republicans of the spring and summer and the avalanche of subversion that greeted their second, far feebler, administration in the winter indicates that the first council's performance, though imperfect, was not altogether ineffectual.

[23] *CSPVen.*, 24 June, 37; council minutes, 12 July, MS Rawlinson C179, fo. 165; MS Clarendon 62, fos 76, 141–2.

[24] *Souldiers alarum*, 3, 5; *Timely advice*, 6. Thomason did not collect these pamphlets, and most contemporary observers did not remark their hopes to restore Richard; the ambassadors were rapidly convinced of the hopelessness of his cause, and were impressed, instead, by Royalist aspirations: *CSPVen.*, 10, 22, 37–8; Guizot, *Histoire*, i. 374–5, 380–1, 388–9. After his resignation, Richard vanishes from all the major historical narratives.

[25] Some examinations and information concerning the printers and stationers involved in disseminating these pamphlets survive in MS Clarendon 64, fos 70–1.

[26] For the derivation of this proportion see n. 2 above.

[27] Council minutes, 10 Sept., SP 25/79, fos 129–30.

Parliament's self-defence: ceremonial and declarations

Even at their most effective, repressive measures offered only a negative and incomplete solution to the problem of seditious publications. Much more significant was the campaign to vindicate the Commonwealth before citizens and foreigners by disproving hostile arguments and demonstrating its greatness. Though the 'failure to forge a republican culture that erased . . . images of kingship' has attracted historical criticism, Parliament in fact devoted considerable attention to recreating and disseminating a positive image.[28] From the moment when the reassembled MPs solemnly processed from the Painted Chamber to the House, following the Speaker and that potent symbol of their authority, the mace, Parliament insisted upon its dignity, reviving the iconography and ceremonial developed to display the splendour of the republican state from 1649 to 1653.[29] Continuity at the administrative centre was affirmed by the early order for the making of a new great seal according to the 'form of the last . . . made by authority of the Parliament'. The result almost exactly replicated the 1651 seal, realistically depicting the members assembled in dignified, yet vigorous, debate on the obverse, and the maps and arms of England and Ireland on the reverse. Only the inscription had changed, from the originally controversial 'in the third year of freedom by Gods blessing restored', to the uncontentious, pious legend 'God with us 1659'. On the day of the new seal's introduction, its predecessor, described only as that 'last in use', was deliberately broken in the House, in a dramatic demonstration of the invalidity of its owner's government. MPs consistently refused to recognise the Protectorate, referring to Richard simply as 'the oldest son of the late Lord General', and never lent the least countenance to allegations that their authority had been at all impaired by the six-year 'interruption'.[30] In dealing with foreign diplomats, Parliament proved as strict as ever about proper credentials, not only refusing to accept those addressed to the Protector but suspiciously examining the new ones for the least signs of disparagement. Thus Bordeaux could represent the members' dissatisfaction with his credentials as a major factor in the breakdown of his intended audience in June, and expressed exasperation at 'the pride of this regime, which

---

[28] Kevin Sharpe, ' "An image doting rabble": the failure of republican culture in seventeenth century England', in K. Sharpe and S. Zwicker (eds), *Refiguring revolution*, Berkeley, Ca. 1998, 25–55 at p. 26. Such arguments, focusing on the narrowly visual, take no account of the important role of newsbooks and oral culture in relaying republican representations.

[29] The procession was reported in *Politicus*, no. 566, 5–12 May, 424. The development and significance of iconography and spectacle in this Parliament's first session is analysed at length in Kelsey, *Inventing a republic*, chs ii–iii, and more briefly, from a less positive perspective, by Barber, *Regicide*, ch. vi.

[30] *Journal*, 647, 654, 655. Parliament also ordered new seals for the council and courts. An engraving and description of the 1659 seal is in George Vertue, *Medals, coins, great seals and other works of Thomas Simon*, London 1780, 40–1, plate xxiv; the new motto had previously appeared on the Commonwealth's coins. See frontispiece.

... is quite extraordinary'.[31] Audiences, when granted, remained impressive spectacles, following the rigid protocol previously devised to that end. Typical was Nieuport's reception on 24 May: with the House beautified by a Turkey carpet, the Dutch ambassador was escorted to a special chair by the master of ceremonies and the serjeant with the mace, and made a speech announcing the 'real affections of the States General and their Compliance with this Commonwealth', during which all present uncovered whenever either government was mentioned. Such ceremonies, duly recounted in the loyal newsbooks, sought to communicate the grandeur of the Republic and its high repute with foreign states to a wide public.[32] An important new ritual, related in detail by both *Politicus* and its competitors, was, of course, the delivery of commissions to officers from the Speaker, in a vivid demonstration of the subordination of the military to the civil power.[33]

But the inculcation of a positive image at home required more than the resurrection or invention of stately forms, which had contributed to the anxieties that culminated in the charges of corruption and self-perpetuation hurled by the radicals in 1653.[34] Six years later, even the keenest advocates of Parliament's return found it expedient to excuse its 'great miscarriages and mal-administrations' on the ground of 'human weakness'; some went so far as to warn MPs to repent, not repeat, their 'great failings'.[35] To succeed, it was imperative to dispel such misgivings and show that the new regime was, indeed, committed to fulfilling the 'Good Old Cause'. Although Parliament, unlike the Army, never hazarded its dignity by acknowledging past mistakes, it took every opportunity to justify itself by its public pronouncements. Top priority on the first day was the issue of a *Declaration* on the 'wonderful providence of God in restoring this present Parliament to the Exercise . . . of their trust'. This emphasis on divine providence, rather than the Army's instrumentality, averted recriminations and resonated well with recent propaganda. Recalling the 'eminent favor and mercy of God' that had graced their earlier government, the members announced that they, as the people's legitimate 'Representatives', were determined to 'apply themselves to the faithful discharge of the trust reposed in them'. Thus they confirmed their adherents' confident claims that they would rule as 'faithful and careful Trustees' for the

---

[31] *Journal*, 662; *CSPVen.*, 28, 36; Guizot, *Histoire*, i. 405, 408. This episode is analysed in ch. 6 above.

[32] *Journal*, 663; *WI*, no. 4, 24–31 May, 26–7; cf. *Moderate Informer*, 19–26 May, 16, and *Politicus*, no. 568, 19–26 May, 463.

[33] *Politicus*, no. 570, 2–9 June; cf. *WI*, 7–14 June, 43. The latter's editor excused the detail by pleading 'the novelty of it . . . the first Commissions that ever were immediately delivered into the hands of the Officers by the Speaker'.

[34] On the mixed reactions to republican stateliness see Kelsey, *Inventing a republic*, esp. pp. 54–5, 58, 73–4.

[35] *Representation of divers well-affected persons of . . . Westminster*, 2; *Some REASONS Humbly Proposed to the Officers . . . for the speedy Re-admission of the Long Parliament*, 5; *Declaration of the well-affected*.

people's benefit.[36] In explaining its intentions, Parliament again employed the reassuring rhetoric of the 'Good Old Cause'. It promised a Commonwealth settlement on a 'foundation' that would 'secure the property and Liberties of the people . . . both as Men and as Christians' without a single person or House of Lords, and the vigorous 'carrying on of the Reformation so much desired'; the objective was a 'Godly and faithful Magistracy and Ministry to the Glory and praise of our Lord Jesus Christ', and 'the reviving and making glad the hearts of the upright'. Further testimony to these righteous ambitions came forth on 9 May, when MPs voted to entrust office only to able men 'fearing God and such as have given Testimony of their love to all the people of God and their faithfulness to the Cause'.[37] An insistence upon godliness was clearly central to Parliament's self-authentication. Not only did it harmonise well with the saints' demand for the 'vindication of God's glory', but it firmly distanced its government from the accusations of self-interested corruption that had not only clouded its past reputation, but latterly had been used so tellingly against the Protectorate.[38]

In the campaign to restore Parliament's reputation, the *Declaration* of 7 May was fundamental. Quoted repeatedly by republican propagandists, this document set the tone for all the congratulations that followed. On 13 May a petition from the Hertfordshire 'adherents of the good old cause' admired the indescribable 'goodness of God in calling together this Renowned Parliament', and praised the promises of the 'late worthy Declaration'. Thirteen days later a similar group from Buckinghamshire announced their 'grateful resentment' of the 'honorable resolutions' contained therein, and applauded the 'Providence which [had] wonderfully appeared' in restoring the members to the 'trust wherein [they] were always successful and prosperous'. Early in June 'well-affected' Kentishmen claimed that the *Declaration* for 'the Liberties of the people both as men and Christians' had 'filled [them] with hope', and looked forward to 'the reality of . . . righteous Actions'. Wiltshire's loyal inhabitants professed 'great rejoycing and satisfaction' upon reading the *Declaration*'s rejection of monarchy and aristocracy, and hoped that the members' 'last works' would be 'best', so that posterity might remember this as 'the most famous and memorable Parliament that ever engaged for the Liberties of England'.[39] When returning thanks for these addresses, Parliament

---

36 *Declaration of the Parliament*, 7 May; *Declaration of the well-affected*.

37 This vote was published in *Politicus*, no. 566, 5–12 May, 429.

38 Canne, *Seasonable word*, 3. Canne both reminded MPs of the need to disprove the old charges against them, and denounced the Protectorate as a 'snare' protecting only '*Turncoats and Time-servers . . . Men of corrupt minds who suppose that gain is godliness*' (p. 1). On the general use of the rhetoric of corruption against the Cromwellian establishment see Woolrych, 'Good Old Cause', 152–3.

39 The Hertfordshire and Buckinghamshire addresses were printed in *Politicus*, no. 567, 12–19 May, 442, and no. 569, 26 May–2 June, 470–2; those from Kent and Wiltshire were printed as separate broadsheets, *To the Supreme Authority . . . The hearty Congratulations and humble Petition of thousands of well-affected Gentlemen, Freeholders and Inhabitants of . . .*

frequently reiterated its good intentions, and advertised its progress. Extending the familiar metaphor of the *Declaration* to emphasise achieve-ments to date, the Speaker informed the Hertfordshire delegation of the members' resolve to build on 'the Foundation upon which they now stand . . . if it please God to set the Topstone as formerly they have laid the Founda-tion'. Two weeks later a Baptist petition received answer that Parliament, having considered some matters already, was 'seriously upon' settlement 'in the name, but also in the nature of a Commonwealth'.[40] These phrases, underlining Parliament's commitment to fulfil expectations, were rapidly noted and exploited by those seeking acceptance for their proposals. In this way, the rhetorics of Parliament and supporters played to one another. The Buckinghamshire address prefaced specific requests with an appeal to 'pro-ceed speedily to settle a Free State or Commonwealth in nature as in name', while a Quaker exhorted MPs to 'follow [the Lord] fully (as you have said) to lay the Top-stone upon that foundation' by settling the people 'in their Rights and Liberties in Persons and Estates'.[41] Parliament's creative dialogue with its adherents enabled them to affirm their loyalty yet also communicate their diverse views of the future settlement. By projecting an image vague in details, but crystal-clear in essential principles, Parliament, like the propa-gandists of the 'Good Old Cause' before it, sought to unite the broad spec-trum of republicans beneath the banner of its authority.

Defending the existing Republic: the newsbooks

No medium was more important in regularly broadcasting the positive image of the Republic to a national audience than the newsbooks. Of these, *Politicus* and the *Publick Intelligencer* had for years been the most prosperous and influ-ential. Claiming to provide all significant foreign and domestic news, authen-ticated with the seal of government approval, attractive as a forum for all manner of advertisements, the privileged newsbooks enjoyed all the advan-tages of a long-established circulation and habitual readership. Nor did those blessings cease with the return of competition: one rival editor openly lamented the obstinate credulity of readers 'whose concentrical eyes and implicite faith have been so long fixed on and guided by the various *Political* Observations of that old Planet (or wandring Star) Mercurius'.[42] Quick to perceive the importance of ensuring that such influence was wielded by reli-able hands, Parliament within a week asserted its own control, and illustrated its zeal for righteousness, by replacing the 'infamous and scandalous' editor,

Kent, and *To the Supreme Authority the Parliament . . . The humble Petition of divers well-affected inhabitants of the County of Wilts.*
40 *Politicus*, no. 569, 26 May–2 June, 470.
41 R. H., *Good Old Cause briefly demonstrated*, 4.
42 *Occurrences*, 28 June–5 July, 10.

Marchamont Nedham, a consistent Cromwellian since 1653, with the loyal Fifth Monarchist John Canne, who had just published a tract rejoicing in the 'late Revolution' and offering godly counsel to the members.[43]

Under Canne's editorship, *Politicus* continued to provide the authorised version of events, blandly reproducing the 'daily Notes' extracted from the *Journal*, which omitted all references to individual MPs and divisions.[44] The resultant reports constituted detailed, authentic evidence of the republicans' daily attention to public business, calculated to disprove any lingering suspicions of laziness and self-interest.[45] Accounts of days of humiliation and days of thanksgiving manifested Parliament's godliness, while reprints of declarations and published resolutions, the latter sometimes distinguished by official black letter, attained a wider currency through the pages of the newsbook.[46] But *Politicus* also contained specific propaganda, advertising the new government's virtues, and the loyalty of its subjects, by reproducing the most congratulatory petitions, together with the answers. The presentation of petitions followed formal procedures that dramatised both Parliament's authority and its accessibility. Through the descriptions in the newsbook this spectacle, like the receptions accorded ambassadors, lived again. On these occasions, as almost every other, Canne made no comment, leaving the narrative to speak for itself. Indeed, so limited was his imagination, or so strict Parliament's control, that, though possessed of decided opinions, he never ventured to express them in the official news, confining his observations to an apology for continuing to use the pagan names for the days of the week, and, during the emergency of the rebellion, a diatribe against the Royalists.[47] Whereas Nedham, in 1650–2, had defended the Republic in a series of dazzling editorials, his successor did not raise, let alone resolve, the burning political questions of the day.[48] Instead, the official newsbooks sought to preserve the semblance of normality by exact adherence to the established pattern: *Politicus* remained the government's impassive mouthpiece.

---

[43] *Journal*, 652; *True catalogue*, 75; Canne, *Seasonable word*, 1.

[44] That Parliament released an official daily extract of its proceedings is plain from a later controversy in which Canne accused Nedham/*Politicus* of lacking 'a *Pair of Spectacles to read daily Notes of Parliament where these Words are Verbatim*': An *Exact Accompt*, no. 55, 6–13 Jan. 1660, 592.

[45] After the second 'interruption' in October, when precisely these charges were brought by the Army, Parliament's supporters could triumphantly point to the evidence of the 'Diurnals', insisting that 'every Book of our Weekly Intelligence [will] witness against [the Army] as very Lyers': *Northern qveries*, 5.

[46] See, for examples, *Politicus*, no. 569, 26 May–2 June, 470; no. 580, 21–8 July, 620; no. 581, 28 July–4 Aug., 632; no. 584, 18–25 Aug., 688; *PI*, no. 197, 3–10 Oct., 777; *Politicus*, no. 576, 23–30 June, 537 (resolution to continue tithes).

[47] *PI*, 4–11 July, 572; 25 July–1 Aug., 624.

[48] Nedham's remarkable contribution to the development of republican ideology has attracted much historical analysis. See, especially, Worden, 'Nedham and English republicanism', and 'Milton and Marchamont Nedham'.

The relative insipidity of the government organs gave competitors a golden opportunity to pose as the Republic's champions, not simply recounting the news but fulfilling the vital task of educating an obstinately conservative people to be good commonwealthsmen. For some, the didactic purpose was little more than the self-interested attempt of unauthorised rivals to demonstrate their loyalty to Parliament by echoing the rhetoric of its radical supporters. Thus the *Moderate Informer* and the *Weekly Intelligencer* declared England the 'land of wonders', and pronounced the Army's restoration of Parliament 'as great a blessing as a wonder, [which] will crown their memories with a serener Glory than all their Conquests'; the *Weekly Account* hailed MPs as 'those worthy Patriots', and claimed their sanction for its 'faithful and impartial Account'.[49] But the newsbooks with the most highly developed sense of their polemical purpose, and the greatest enthusiasm for the restored Commonwealth, were its earliest defenders, the *Scout* and the *Post*. Not content to celebrate the merciful providence which had revived the Republic, these newsbooks constantly depicted events at Westminster as evidence of Parliament's 'large progress into the Publique Affairs', and enlivened factual reports by interposing italicised comments – thus the presentation of articles of impeachment against officials guilty of embezzlement was greeted by the exclamation '*O that Justice and Equity may be speedily executed*'.[50] Such remarks taught readers to perceive Parliament's decisions in the unifying light of a wider campaign to enact reforms, making the relatively mundane details of daily business meaningful and accessible to those bemused by the lengthy, unsystematic reports of *Politicus* and the *Public Intelligencer*.

Nowhere was the didacticism of the *Scout* and the *Post* more apparent than in the decision to commence with editorials that freely adapted sources ranging from republican to Presbyterian and Royalist to promote an attractive vision of the Republic. At first sight, the results seem to consist of a random compilation of the most colourful rhetoric available, but though these editorials lack the sophistication and order of Nedham's writing, they were both cogent and coherent. The remarkable ability of the *Scout*'s editor to construct a consistent political message from a discordant array of tracts clearly emerges from comparing his adaptation of two mutually hostile authors: William Prynne, the most prolific Presbyterian polemicist, and James Harrington, the prominent republican theorist. True to their usual habit of suppressing intelligence embarrassing to the government, the official newsbooks ignored Prynne, setting an example followed by almost all competitors. The editor of the *Scout* and the *Post*, by contrast, made a deter-

---

[49] *Moderate Informer*, 12–18 May, 1; *WI*, no. 2, 10–17 May, 10; *Weekly Account*, no. 1, 25 May–1 June, 2. Pamphlets portraying this Parliament in such language include [Bethel], *Second narrative*, 11; *To the officers the humble petition . . . of Southwark*, 5; *Letter from the officers in Scotland*, 3.

[50] *Scout*, no. 3, 6–13 May, 24; *Post*, no. 3, 17–24 May, 24.

mined attempt to exploit Prynne's notoriety to promote these newsbooks. In May striking headlines announced Prynne's declaration against the government, and his attempted invasion of the House, which certainly qualified as exciting news. In early June the *Scout* and *Post* printed undated and unattributed extracts from a lively new account of his confrontation with MPs nearly a month before.[51] These were advertised with headlines promising the actual speeches made by republican leaders Vane and Hesilrig, as well as Prynne's answers. Interested readers unable or unwilling to buy one of Prynne's lengthy pamphlets were thus encouraged to substitute the compressed account of these newsbooks.[52] Evidently, the drawbacks of printing old news from a hostile source were outweighed by the capital to be made from a rare opportunity to enliven the dry facts from Westminster by incorporating inside information about the members.

Quoting Prynne was commercially profitable, but politically dangerous.[53] By conceding so much publicity to a prominent public enemy, the *Scout* not only risked Parliament's censure but exposed readers to the infection of his views. To prevent either result, the editor repeatedly decried Prynne's distorted vision of the Commonwealth and its rulers. Thus his passionate charges of conspiracy to establish 'Anarchy, Oppression and Tyranny' were confounded by the cold light of rational observation: 'obvious it is that the Parliament and Army endeavoureth nothing more than the preservation of the *Peoples Rights*'. Though Prynne's impudence was certainly remarkable, his obstinate addiction to monarchy was dismissed as hopelessly inappropriate for 'this Juncture of Settlement, where most prudent and serene Spirits are now steering . . . the Commonwealth to bring her to the Haven . . . of a Free State'. When the rebellion interrupted the smooth progress towards this harbour, the editor blamed the 'great Impression' made by Prynne's papers 'upon the hearts of many, tending much to Insurrections' instead of the unity necessary to preserve the nation from foreign enemies.[54]

Such condemnation is not surprising, given the pressing need to defend the Republic against Prynne's attacks. More remarkable is the simultaneous attempt to detach conservative readers from Prynne by exploiting common principles. The same issue of the *Scout* which denounced his disloyalty began

---

[51] See *Scout*, no. 3, 6–13 May; no. 6, 27 May–3 June; *Post*, no. 6, 7–14 June, using excerpts from Prynne, *Narrative*, 9–11. The editor would make similar commercial capital by recounting Prynne's strange dream of Cromwell on the night of his death: *Post*, no. 7, 14–21 June, 54–5; *Scout*, no. 9, 17–24 June, 88.

[52] As the full text of Prynne's *Narrative* ran to nearly 100 pages, the highlights provided by the *Scout* and the *Post* made its most dramatic moments accessible to a much larger audience than the original.

[53] A clear indication of the profits to be made from Prynne's notoriety is his broadsheet *The New Cheaters forgeries, detected, disclaimed*, published in May, in which he threatened to prosecute those who for 'their own private lucre have printed sundry illiterate Pamphlets in my name to cheat the People'.

[54] *Scout*, no. 4, 13–20 May, 26; no. 6, 27 May–3 June, 43; no. 15, 22–9 July, 109.

with an excerpt from his *Mola Asinaria* reproaching the 'self-seeking Man who unconcerned to the publick Good, regards onely his private Interest'. Such individuals were accused of barbaric ingratitude to their country, and exhorted to venture their all for the 'publick Interest', rejecting the specious pretences of tyrants to defend religion and liberty as 'Machiavilian Tricks and political Cheats'. Thus far Prynne could be used, with only minor modifications to spare the grandees inclusion in his criticism of Cromwell, in order to commend the republican virtues of liberty and sacrificial patriotic service against tyranny and indifference to the public welfare. But where Prynne summoned the apathetic English people to rebel to restore the legitimate and benign rule of the Stuarts, the editor of the *Scout* was careful to show that his premises actually tended to the opposite conclusion. True patriots should perceive that they had been liberated from Cromwellian oppression, and were now at last 'returning by the good Hand of Providence into a happy and Free State, the most purest Government under Heaven, where all things (we hope) will be duly weighed in the Scales of Equity and Justice'.[55] Editorial ingenuity could make even Prynne the basis of a lesson in republican values.

The engagement of the *Scout* and the *Post* with Prynne's ideas also illustrates the renewed interaction of journalism with the wider world of print controversy, showing that newsbooks could become active participants, not simply the passive recorders of the most sensational happenings.[56] While Prynne's conservatism invited, even required, condemnation, the treatment of Harrington reveals a rather more subtle relationship between controversial literature and the newsbooks. Unlike Prynne, Harrington is never named in the *Scout* and the *Post*; the editor neither supported nor criticised his complex constitutional blueprint. Instead, he trod a cautious middle course. At times, he adapted short passages from Harrington to make rather different polemical points. Thus an editorial of the *Post* in late May summoning all Cromwellians to follow the late Protector's example of submission reproduced Harrington's account of the Romans' rapid conversion to popular government once Brutus had imposed an oath against monarchy. Safely detached from Harrington's insistence that free elections under his Commonwealth would automatically produce representatives who would abjure monarchy, this history supplied a convenient classical precedent to support the efficacy and necessity of a new oath of allegiance to the existing English Republic.[57] To avoid offending readers with Harringtonian sympathies, the editor was quick to exploit the

---

[55] Ibid. no. 6, 27 May–3 June, 41–3, using Prynne, *Mola asinaria*, 1–2. Though one of the works condemned in *The new cheaters forgeries*, this was published in Prynne's name, and widely attributed to him; if spurious, it was certainly an excellent imitation of his style and sentiments.

[56] Interaction had precedents: Nedham's republican editorials of 1650–1 had addressed most of the constitutional arguments presented by the pamphlets of the time. The extent and explicit nature of the *Scout's* engagement was, however, unequalled by the other newsbooks of 1659, while the plagiaristic tactics were genuinely innovative.

[57] *Post*, no. 4, 24–31 May, 30–1; cf. James Harrington, *A DISCOURSE upon This Saying:*

ideological common ground. The *Scout's* fifth editorial consisted of highlights from the conclusion to Harrington's latest *Discourse*, which exhorted readers to 'endeavour the well ordering of a Free Commonwealth' with 'all prudence and fervent imploration of GOD's gracious Assistance', and prophesied the natural disappearance of parties within seven years of its establishment. By omitting Harrington's specifics, the *Scout* was left with an optimistic call to action, which could inspire godly republicans of all shades of opinion. But the chief attraction of this extract was probably the opening entertainment, a detailed description of the cat compelled to make green sauce in the Roman carnival. Where Harrington argued that each member of the rightly ordered Commonwealth would be as helpless as the cat to do anything but perform his proper function, the editor saw a vivid, exotic illustration, which might awaken the interest of anyone scanning the front page, and impress those unaware of its provenance with the newsbook's originality. The appropriation of this passage from Harrington, a major but far from wholly sympathetic figure, suggests the growing confidence of the editor, and his sense that a wider range of texts could be exploited to convey a republican message in a colourful and entertaining style.[58]

Important as the *Scout's* efforts at indoctrination were, its accomplishment was necessarily limited. The editor might, and did, ransack the latest defences of the regime to provide specific 'Reasons' for the rejection of Richard's Protectorate, the excellence of a free state and the evils of government by a single person. Such explanations simplified major republican arguments for the benefit of a wider audience, and afforded additional publicity to the original pamphlets. Thus the third number of the *Scout* openly advertised 'an excellent Piece, entitled *The Continuation of this Session of Parliament Justified*', and devoted much space to summarising it.[59] The unnamed author was actually John Streater, with whom the *Scout's* editor was clearly engaged in a common enterprise – seeking to rouse a genuinely popular republican consciousness.[60] But the few pages of the newsbook could not hope to address the complexities of political controversy. The greatest service of the *Scout* and other ostentatiously loyal newsbooks to the republican cause was not the originality of their arguments but their enunciation of basic principles, and favourable depiction of Parliament's daily government. In the ideological realm, the *Scout's* achievement, though remarkably creative, remained dependent upon the prior output of other writers.

The Spirit of the Nation is not yet to be trusted with Liberty; lest it introduce Monarchy, or invade the Liberty of Conscience, 8.

[58] *Scout*, no. 5, 20–7 May, 33–4, citing Harrington, *Discourse upon this saying*, 13.

[59] *Scout*, no. 4, 13–20 May, 31; no. 3, 6–13 May, 20–1.

[60] On Streater's endeavour to develop a popular classical republicanism see Smith, 'Popular republicanism', and *Literature and revolution*, Yale 1994, 196–9.

Defending the existing Republic: the pamphlet literature

The brunt of the burden of defending the Commonwealth against its detractors was borne neither by Parliament, nor the newsbooks, but by the host of unpaid polemicists who rushed into print. Battle had been joined even before Parliament's restoration: in April Rogers, for example, had vehemently attacked Prynne and Baxter's 'late Books and Pamphlets' designed to 'delude the poor plain people' by 'sinister and Sophisticated Reports . . . of the Good Old Cause'. Conflict intensified thereafter due to the urgent need to strengthen the fledgling Republic by diffusing loyalty and demolishing the dangerous reasoning of its assailants. In July Rogers introduced his latest, much longer, pamphlet as a 'most necessary Vindication' of the 'True Cause of the Commonwealth' and the 'Honour' of its 'most worthy Members' from the 'Venome and Vilification' of latter-day 'Gunpowder plotters'.[61] Although the tactics employed by the regime's defenders varied considerably – Rogers's dramatic invective, laced with corporeal metaphors, bore little resemblance to Streater's skilful invocation of the 'best Rules of Law, Reason and just-preserving *POLICIE*' – their basic arguments for Parliament's legitimacy and expediency were remarkably consistent.[62] Between them, Rogers, Streater and their allies produced a coherent case for the Commonwealth, which developed the themes of the 'Good Old Cause' into a comprehensive answer to counter-revolutionaries. As it not only reveals the vigour of republicanism, but was expressly designed to promote the positive image of Parliament, that case merits further examination.

To prove the Republic's legitimacy, it was essential to justify its revolutionary origins. In 1649 these had caused considerable embarrassment to many of Parliament's apologists. Francis Rous and Anthony Ascham had tacitly admitted the Commonwealth's illegality by contending for the necessity of submission to a *de facto* government sanctioned by providence, however improper its rise to power.[63] In 1659 such modest arguments resurfaced only in self-consciously moderate attempts to detach Presbyterians from their Royalist allies. Thus one refutation of *SIR GEORGE BOOTH'S LETTER* professed indifference to forms of government and insisted that obedience to Parliament, as 'the higher powers . . . ordained of God' and 'the only visible Supreame Authority . . . under whom we may lead a peaceable

---

61 John Rogers, Mr. *PRYN'S Good Old Cause Stated and Stunted 10 years ago*, 2; *Diapoliteia*, title, 1.

62 S[treater], *Continuation*, title.

63 Francis Rous, *The lawfulnes of obeying the present government*, and Anthony Ascham, *Of the Confusions and Revolutions of Government*, both published in 1649. On the uses of *de facto*-ist theory in the early Republic see Scott, 'English republican imagination', 39–40; Barber, *Regicide*, 187–90, The classic analyses of this phenomenon are J. M. Wallace, *Destiny his choice: the loyalism of Andrew Marvell*, Cambridge 1968, and Q. R. D. Skinner, 'Conquest and consent: Thomas Hobbes and the Engagement controversy', in G. E. Aylmer (ed.), *The Interregnum: the quest for settlement*, London 1972, 79–98.

and quiet life', was infinitely preferable to the horrors of a new civil war. Yet even this author dismissed Booth's criticisms of Parliament's insufficient numbers and oppressive policies, and denounced the design of 'Idolatrous Papists . . . superstitious prelates, and . . . old prophane, conquered Cavaliers', to restore the 'insuportable yoak of slavery' as doomed to founder upon the rock of divine disapproval. Rather than meddle in such unrighteous schemes, Presbyterians should gratefully acknowledge that the English had already become 'the freest people under the heavens . . . possest . . . with the blessed Gospel . . . in the greatest libertie . . . that ever was'. In this triumphant analysis, Parliament's manifest godliness and commitment to the 'Countrys rights and liberties' outweighed any doubts regarding its legal title to rule.[64]

Few of the Commonwealth's partisans in 1659 even admitted the possibility of such doubts. To the simple identification of the 'Good Old Cause' with the 'Good old Parliament' in the early propaganda succeeded increasingly sophisticated vindications of Parliament's authority. These represented the revolution as the ultimate, even the inevitable fulfilment of the cause – the moment when 'the True Good Old Cause first contended for' appeared 'in a better excrescence of Beauty and Perfection'.[65] Against all too plausible Presbyterian charges of force, fraud, innovation and betrayal of the declarations and covenants of the 1640s, republicans insisted that the parliamentary cause was not, and never had been, identical with the former government of 'King, Lords and Commons'. Rather, the 'whole Cause' had always been 'comprehended' in the assertion of 'The Liberty of the People', by whose authority and for whose benefit the old regime had existed. Therein lay the fundamental continuity. As representatives of the sovereign people, the faithful Commons retained the right to jettison king, lords and even the majority of their fellow MPs when these authorities began to pursue arbitrary power or 'their own particular interest' at the expense of the public good. The destruction of 'King, Queen, Prince, Lords and Kingdom in their political capacity' was therefore, as Henry Stubbe boldly remarked, 'not a disgrace, but an indearment of the Good Old Cause'.[66]

To substantiate such radical claims, it remained imperative to root them in a particular interpretation of English history. Some republicans provided detailed narratives of the progression of the cause to maturity in the 1640s, with telling reminders that even Prynne had applauded such important stages as the expulsion of the Royalist MPs and the successive incursions of the

---

[64] SIR GEORGE BOOTH'S LETTER . . . Together with An Answer . . . invalidating the said Reasons, 6, 3, 19, 9.

[65] Rogers, Pryn's Good Old Cause, 9. Rogers's use of this rhetoric does not imply that he was a Platonist; he inclined towards Aristotle more than any other Greek philosopher and explicitly criticised those who disturbed the Commonwealth with 'perplexed Platonian speculations': Diapoliteia, 105.

[66] S[treater], Continuation, 7–8; Harris, Peace, 27–30; H[enry] S[tubbe], The Commonwealth of ISRAEL, or a brief Account of Mr Prynne's Anatomy of the Good Old Cause, 2.

Commons upon the traditional privileges of an obstructive sovereign and upper house.[67] By dwelling on the constant 'design' of the Presbyterian members to hinder 'the carrying on of the Good Old Cause and . . . privately Insinuate poysonous Counsel', it was easy to justify their seclusion from public life as 'professed and avowed enemies to the Free-State and GOOD CAUSE'.[68] But champions of the 'Free-State' also invoked a more distant past to intimate that the conservatives' ancient constitution was itself a fraud, founded not upon popular election but 'the craft . . . and sinister contrivances of aspiring persons': well before the civil wars thousands weary of the 'Oppression and Slavery under Kings, Lords and Bishops' had longed to recover their liberties by 'reinvesting the Supream Authority in the Peoples Representatives in Parliament'. Republican history therefore challenged reactionary allegations that the Long Parliament had abrogated the law that protected both the rights of traditional authorities and the lives and property of subjects. According to Nedham, the removal of those 'excrescences of Arbitrary power', the royal prerogative and peers' privileges, had actually established the 'ancient Laws Municipal' that defined the people's 'Rights, Liberties and Priviledges'. By asserting that the 'inward line of Righteousness' followed by the adherents of the cause was superior to the 'letter alone of the old Laws' made for 'the interest of a single Person', Rogers similarly concluded that the revolution had preserved 'all good Laws' in their 'equity, sence and meaning'.[69]

Conscious that English history alone, however skilfully interpreted, was an inadequate defence of 1649, republicans simultaneously appealed to the higher principles of reason, nature and divine law. Rogers derived the cause from the triple foundation of the 'Law of God, of Nature, and . . . the fundamental Rights and Reason of this Nation'; Stubbe declined to enter the antiquarian debate with Prynne on the ground that 'Truth, Reason, Honesty and foundations upon nature' made the 'cause not only better but older than any plea from musty records and concessions extorted from Tyrants'.[70] Reviving the pleas of *salus populi* and magisterial accountability so prominent in the first justifications of the Republic, Streater maintained that allegiance was always conditional upon protection, and that a king false to his trust was 'no other but as a *Wilde Beast*, which Nature hath instituted to be destroyed'. To meet objections that this principle contravened the supremacy of the rule of law, he insisted that 'upon War and Change of Government Necessities of State must and ever did over-rule' the ordinary laws applicable only to indi-

---

[67] Examples include Rogers, *Pryn's Good Old Cause*, 5–7; J[ohn] S[treater], *A SHIELD Against the Parthian Dart*, 3–5, and, especially, Harris, *Peace*, 1–18.

[68] S[treater], *Continuation*, 11; Rogers, *Diapoliteia*, 7.

[69] *The Good Old Cause Explained, Revived, & Asserted and the Long-Parliament Vindicated*, 2; [Nedham], *Interest*, 39; Rogers, *Diapoliteia*, 67. At this point Rogers was, as he freely admitted, indebted to the argument of Vane's *Healing question*.

[70] Rogers, *Pryn's Good Old Cause*, 11; S[tubbe], *Common-wealth of Israel*, 9.

viduals in peacetime, and ridiculed monarchists' obsession with legal precedent, enquiring sardonically whether 'so high proceedings as these so many
vast Interests' could 'be made parallel and determined by the Example of a
Case of Thomas Mouse and William Frog . . . nothing to the purpose in hand'.
Not content to assert the 'real necessitie' for the revolution, Nedham made
an ambitious effort to convince Royalists and Presbyterians that their own
principles proved the dissolution of the ancient constitution of government
by the king's resort to war and subsequent defeat. Citing conservative authorities ranging from the famous Dutch jurist Grotius to the leading Presbyterian
divine Richard Baxter, he reached the radical conclusion that by the 'Law of
God, Law of Nature and the Law of the Land' only the existing Parliament, as
the 'victorious part' that had not betrayed the 'Fundamental Law of the
Constitution', was 'legally qualified to sit'. In his attacks on the pretensions of
the secluded MPs, Rogers, too, made much of the dissolution of the former
constitution, arguing that the vital disjuncture between the 'Free-State and
an Enslaved; the Commonwealth and a Kingdom' proved that they, as
members only of the 'defunct House of COMMONS' had no right whatever
to sit in the 'Commonwealth Parliament'.[71]

But the vindication of Parliament's legal authority in 1659 required more
than the restatement of the case for the initial revolution: it was equally
necessary to address the challenges that had arisen since 1649. Recent
attempts by Prynne and Baxter to blacken the English Republic's reputation
by blaming a Spanish–Jesuit conspiracy for its creation provoked a furious
reaction from Rogers, who descried the vast gulf separating the 'clandestine'
plots and 'wicked Anarchy' pursued by the Papists from the 'godly Commonwealth' intended by the indisputably Protestant Parliament that had
executed 'open justice . . . for peace and publick safety . . . the ends of
Government'. Less passionately, but perhaps more effectively, Henry Stubbe
adroitly turned Prynne's own method of reasoning against him:

> Bellarmine too is for Monarchy, and saith it is the BEST of Governments; so
> says Mr Prynne . . . you see that by his argument, Mr Prynne . . . is a Romish
> Jesuit . . . the Pope is principally against Toleration, so is Mr Prynne, Ergo he is
> an errant Papist.

Like Rogers, Stubbe defended Parliament's religious policy against Presbyterian aspersions, denying that the concession of a 'just and innocent Toleration' implied any design to destroy Protestantism.[72] Amidst the summer
crisis, Nedham reminded Presbyterians that they themselves profited from

---

71 S[treater], *Continuation* 8; *Shield*, 7–8; [Nedham], *Interest*, 30, 34–7; Rogers, *Diapoliteia*,
1, 7–8.
72 Rogers, *Pryn's Good Old Cause*, 4, and *Diapoliteia*, 27–33; S[tubbe], *Common-wealth of
Israel*, 8, 2. Stubbe argued at length for the 'Lawfulnesse and necessity of an universal Toleration', as the basis of England's Commonwealth, in *An ESSAY In Defence of the GOOD
OLD CAUSE*.

this latitude, contrasting the 'large immunities and enjoyments' that they currently possessed with the probable persecution that they would suffer under the 'Ranting Episcopacie' designed by the Royalists. Parliament's 'late memorable votes' to maintain tithes, augmentations and the ministry afforded writers courting conservatives ample evidence of its commitment to the 'Reformation of Religion' and its magnanimity towards Presbyterian opponents. At least one republican tried to turn the tables on Prynne by arguing that he himself had succumbed to Catholic deceits by consenting to lay 'the foundation of this last Sedition, which smells more of the Jesuit than any of the rest, being more cunningly designed . . . and universally spread'. Whatever their particular perspectives, all Parliament's defenders felt driven to assert the absolute incompatibility of its beneficent government and the Jesuits' malicious ambitions.[73]

Much more damaging to Parliament's authority than the shady, unprovable charges of Jesuit manipulation was, of course, the memory of the members' ignominious expulsion by Oliver Cromwell and the Army in 1653. To refute claims that this constituted a 'dissolution', republicans not only cited the 1641 non-dissolution act, but insisted that Parliament, as the 'Supream Power of the People', must necessarily be incapable of dissolution without its own consent. As Cromwell possessed no 'lawful power' except 'what he derived from them', his rebellion could only 'interrupt', not destroy, the rightful government, which might return whenever the obstructing force was lifted. All legislation during the interval must therefore be technically 'void and null', and all assemblies purporting to supersede the true representative nothing but illegal 'Conventions' serving the interest of a single person 'to the Ruin, the disturbance, and unquiet' of the nation.[74] The participation of some MPs in these assemblies, or even Cromwell's government, could not invalidate their just rights, or constitute a retrospective agreement to dissolve, since they acted only as individuals who sought, in many instances, to 'gain an opportunity to struggle for recovery of their freedom'.[75] Against allegations that Parliament's removal and subsequent restoration by the Army proved that it was no more than a cloak for 'the meer power . . . of the Sword', republican propagandists were at pains to demonstrate its independent authority. Taking their cue from their masters in the House, they elevated the role of providence above the instruments, hailing Parliament as the 'most immediate Authority set up by God which hath been in our days'.[76] Streater stressed the fact that the officers had publicly 'Acknowledged their

---

73 [Nedham], Interest, 12, 16; Grand concernments, 36–7, 28–9. See also the Answer to Booth's letter, 21–3, and A VINDICATION of That Prudent and Honourable Knight, Sir Henry Vane, from the LYES and CALUMNIES of Mr. Richard Baxter, 19.

74 S[treater], Continuation, 12; [Nedham], Interest, 39–40; S[treater], Shield, 11–12.

75 Harris, Peace, 32; [Nedham], Interest, 40–1.

76 Rogers, Pryn's Good Old Cause, 14; A WORD OF SETTLEMENT In these Unsettled Times. Containing Some Necessary Encouragements for the Well-affected, 3.

Errour', and returned to a dutiful submission to the 'Judgement, Wisdom and Authority' of the members, who had displayed their superiority by assuming the power to issue commissions, so reversing their humiliation at Cromwell's hands. Though Streater, like others before and after him, condemned the military intervention of 1653 as the moment when 'the Good Old Cause was Eclipsed, and . . . turned . . . to a *Barbarous Cause*', he was careful to promote the reconciliation by heaping the blame upon Cromwell's deceits, and admiring the manifest self-denial of the Army's repentance.[77]

Far from demonstrating Parliament's illegitimacy, the six-year 'interruption' became the pre-eminent advertisement for the expediency of its government. In 1659 all the arguments advanced against monarchy in defence of the first Republic reappeared, with this difference: it was less necessary to mine foreign precedents or the fading memory of England's kings when the Protectorate afforded such a rich vein of concrete, immediate illustrations of the evils of government by a single person. Thus Streater reinforced his theoretical account of the inconveniences of monarchy by recalling the 'visible miscarriages' of Oliver Cromwell's reign. The arbitrariness of the major-generals, 'unusual courts', unlawful imprisonments and, supremely, the war on Spain 'to the destruction of Trade and all Manufacture', all exemplified the irregularities of a single person, whose interest was necessarily distinct from and opposed to the 'Interest of the Publike'. Cromwell's apostasy constituted a clear warning that no individual, however meritorious, should be entrusted with 'absolute power'; the continuation of a government 'loaded with so much absoluteness and contradictions' could only have caused a new civil war or the return of the even less deserving Stuarts. To illustrate the expensive oppressions of Cromwell's tyranny, John Harris provided an ironic list of its 'advantages', foremost among which were the 'honourable and advantageous peace' with the Dutch and the 'glorious' Spanish war; even tax cuts he portrayed as a means to increase the national debt and alienate the people from their representatives. Others denounced the Protectorate as 'a Government distastful and abominable to God and good men', guilty of persecuting the godly and destroying national prosperity by 'covetous designs'.[78]

Against the dark backdrop of the material and moral deficiencies of monarchy, Stuart or Cromwellian, shone the excellencies of a Commonwealth, set forth in dazzling colours by its supporters. Six years had brought little change in the abstract arguments for the Republic's superiority. Echoing earlier vindications, Streater contended that a Commonwealth must be 'the most Natural and best sort of all Governments', while Rogers, like Nedham before him, saluted a free state as the form 'more pleasing to God than any other . . . because of the Common good and impartial distribution of justice

---

[77] S[treater], *Shield* 15, and *Continuation*, 12.
[78] Idem, *Continuation*, 13, and *Shield*, 22; Harris, *Peace*, 21–23; *Good Old Cause explained*, 5.

and emulation in mens minds to Virtue'.[79] But Parliament's defenders in 1659 demonstrated the practical validity of these principles by extensive invocation of its former 'Heroick and Worthy Acts'. Thus Harris acclaimed the members as those 'on whose Councills and actions so perfect an Impress of the power and owning of God was engraven', and instanced their achievement in laying the 'foundations of justice, freedom and security to all persons'. Amidst the anxieties of August, another writer encouraged the well-affected by recalling that the 'present Authority', as 'that Parliament which God so wonderfully raised . . . and honoured', had formerly 'subdued the Malignant party . . . removed many grievous Yoaks', and 'managed' foreign wars 'with admirable Success'. Extolling 'the Power, Vigour and Excellency of a *Councel* of a *Free People*' after 1649, Streater celebrated not only Parliament's military triumphs but its economic promise, hailing the Navigation Act as 'the Glory and Top of their great Advice', which would have made 'England . . . the most happy and most rich People this day upon . . . Earth'. Such rhetoric gave all subjects, whether covetous or godly, reasons to admire the Republic in general, and Parliament in particular, as the only government 'free to that work of equally respecting all interests'.[80]

The contrast between the self-interestedness of monarchy, in every guise, and the self-denial of republics was fundamental, since it explained the relative misery and prosperity of subjects in terms of the respective corruption and virtue of the rulers in each form. Republican propaganda constantly projected the image of Parliament's integrity, lauding MPs as 'faithful Patriots', 'Honourable Worthies', 'the Called, Chosen and Faithful' or even 'Persons of the most incomparable wisdom, worth and abilities'.[81] Lest these should appear mere high-sounding titles, writers endeavoured to substantiate their claims by every possible means. Some provided personal testimony – Harris professed that his motive was a 'real knowledge of many of the Gentlemen and of their aym in the general' not a 'principle purchased by Reward'; Rogers used his acquaintance with individual members, especially the much vilified Vane, to demonstrate that they were 'not wicked Livers but very excellent examples . . . of Peace and Holiness'.[82] But Parliament's former achievements and recent pronouncements afforded still clearer evidence of both its willingness and its ability to fulfil hopes of future blessing. Against allegations of incompetence, Streater insisted that the members who had 'shewed themselves able in the service of the Commonwealth' by their

---

[79] J[ohn] S[treater], *Government Described: Viz: What Monarchie, Aristocracie, Oligarcie, And Democracie is*, 4; Rogers, *Diapoliteia*, 121; cf. Nedham, *The Case of the Commonwealth Stated*, 1650, 93.

[80] *Good Old Cause explained*, 4; Harris, *Peace*, 26; *Word of settlement*, 1; S[treater], *Continuation*, 11–12, 14.

[81] Harris, *Peace*, 37; *Word of settlement*, 1; Rogers, *Diapoliteia*, 15.

[82] Harris, *Peace*, 38; Rogers, *Diapoliteia*, 21. Foremost among Vane's detractors was the Presbyterian Richard Baxter, who had recently attacked him in both *A Key for Catholicks* and the preface to his *Holy Commonwealth*.

management of its wars were the 'only persons . . . fit . . . to settle the Nation', while Nedham exhorted the Army to 'make much' of a Parliament that possessed the 'most experience in the work'.[83] To dispel the more damaging doubts regarding its intentions, Harris argued that 'the present Parliament . . . that have so frequently declared for it, so zealously contested against Tyranny . . . and remain so solemnly engaged . . . to accomplish it', must be 'the most likely persons to establish a Government upon the most equal principles of Freedom'. Another writer hopefully highlighted the absence of any evidence of parliamentary backsliding: 'of their performance . . . we have not as yet had, and . . . perswade ourselves we shall not at any time have any cause to doubt'. In such ways, republican polemicists sought to persuade both impetuous radicals and conservative sceptics to a 'free and voluntary or at least an Acquiescent submission and obedience' to Parliament's government.[84]

Yet broad arguments for Parliament's wisdom and virtue offered only an inadequate, since partial, reassurance; it was just as necessary to address the specific charges hurled by its enemies. Of these, none was more harmful than self-perpetuation, the mainstay of the early justifications of its removal in 1653, and the persistent fear of some radicals, particularly Fifth Monarchists and Harringtonians.[85] To counter such suspicions, Parliament's propagandists made much use of the vote of 6 June to dissolve by 7 May 1660. Streater dismissed demands for an earlier dissolution as 'unreasonable', and Nedham admiringly observed that the year was 'short enough . . . considering the greatness of their work, and the opposition like to be against them'.[86] Instant miracles were not feasible; far from falsifying its promises, the time spent in deliberation actually proved Parliament's dedication to the national welfare. Thus Streater excused the absence of immediate improvement on the grounds that 'they must Consult all Interests, and equally preserve all Parties; which is a Work worthy of their Care and Wisdomes, and will take up time', and accused his Royalist adversary of jumping to premature conclusions: 'the End Crowneth all Noble Actions, and . . . he cannot yet make a Judgment of the Event of Affairs'. Others cited debates and resolutions to show that Parliament had already embarked upon the great work of 'endeavouring to remove the Oppressions, Tyrannies and sore Evils'; one writer hopefully interpreted even the decision to continue the hated excise for another three months as a 'very important sign' that MPs were planning an investigation that might result in its repeal.[87] But Parliament's defenders did not just plead

---

83 S[treater], *Shield*, 12; [Nedham], *Interest*, 26.
84 Harris, *Peace*, 36–7; *A commonwealth, and commonwealths-men asserted*, 9.
85 For the Harringtonian outlook see, especially, *THE ARMIES DUTIE*, which used Parliament's temptation to become perpetual legislators as an object lesson in the dangers of an assembly with both 'debating and determining power'; Fifth Monarchist suspicions were manifest in the warnings of texts such as *Invisible John made Visible*, and the rehearsal of the condemnations of 1653 in *Fifth Monarchy . . . Asserted*.
86 S[treater], *Shield*, 6; [Nedham], *Interest*, 27.
87 S[treater], *Shield*, 12, 11; *The New Lords Winding-Sheet*, 4; *Grand concernments*, 34.

for patience and praise progress to date: they also advanced a coherent explanation of the problems that exonerated the members from all blame. From the lack of settlement, to the Royalist menace, to the decay of trade and heavy taxes, every difficulty could be traced to the 'unparallel'd Usurpation' and misgovernment of the Cromwells.[88] So convenient a scapegoat was the Protectorate that Parliament itself contemplated a declaration comparing the state of affairs at its interruption and restoration; though its plans were delayed by fiscal complexities, and eventually curtailed by the more pressing need to issue a declaration against Booth, nothing hindered its propagandists.[89] Idealised representation of 1649–53 allowed them to reconcile their case for the Republic's excellences with the real problems that persisted after that form returned in 1659.

As national problems were inherited, not created by Parliament, so their continuance was, in the republican analysis, extraordinary and temporary, due not to 'the nature of the Government . . . nor . . . the Wills of the present Governors' but the opposition that they faced. Nedham censured the 'folly . . . of Malcontented persons and parties'; Harris insisted that it was a 'necessary duty incumbent upon the Parliament to keep an Army' to 'ballance the discontents of honest men', while another writer dryly warned the people that they were unlikely to 'procure their happiness by reviling and reproaching . . . the chief Rulers'.[90] Discrediting the revilers was, of course, a promising method of rescuing Parliament's reputation from their aspersions, and the people from their deceits. Though a few writers, chiefly those professing most moderation, mildly asserted that the 'fair proposals' of MPs 'ought . . . to be believed . . . rather than any private men, who would perswade us that our Governors do not intend really what they . . . pretend', others vehemently assaulted the gainsayers. Prynne was naturally a prime target: republicans not only refuted his reasoning and ridiculed his 'Monstrous *Title-Pages*' and 'abhominable frightful Margent', but chronicled the deterioration of his character through the contrast between 'his former Laborious and praiseworthy works' and his 'last depraved writings, in which he hath laid aside his Reason and only exerciseth his Passion'. In addition to a sustained attack on Prynne, Rogers attempted to undermine Baxter's prestige by pointing out the contrast between his reputed sanctity and his unChristian conduct in bringing 'most scandalous, scurrilious and untrue' charges against 'the Lords dear servants and Commonwealths friends', the illustrious repub-

---

88 *Grand concernments*, 31. For other comparisons of this kind see especially *Word of settlement*, 2–3; Harris, *Peace*, 33–4; *Short discourse*, 3–4.

89 For the rise and progress of this declaration see *Journal*, 661, 693, 738, 748.

90 [Nedham], *Interest*, 20; Harris, *Peace*, 34; *Twenty seven queries*, 3. The same argument was deployed against the rebels in *AN ANSWER of some if not all the CITIZENS of London & Freemen of ENGLAND, To a Paper entituled An Express from the Knights and Gentlemen now Engaged with Sir George Booth*, 6.

lican leaders.[91] But the object of even the strongest censure of the regime's detractors remained their reclamation: Rogers hoped for a settlement that would satisfy the 'the sober minded . . . of ALL Judgements (whether they follow Mr Prynne . . . Mr Baxter . . . Mr Harrington . . . or us)'. In his brilliant pamphlet, *Interest will not Lie*, Nedham appealed to every group, but especially Royalists, Presbyterians and neutrals, to join in a 'cordial close with the present Parliament', as the certain way to attain 'the rich benefits of a State of Freedom'.[92] Faith in these benefits, and the real possibility of reaching them through Parliament's mediation, constituted the cornerstone of the case for its government so insistently argued in the pamphlet literature.

Imagining the future Republic: common themes

Explicit advocacy of the existing government accounted for only a fraction of the print output. Republicanism was not purely, or even mainly, defensive: much more important was the offensive, the creative endeavour to imagine and delineate the future, to dispel conservative derision by demonstrating that an English free state was feasible. Those who fervently acclaimed the 'great and incomparable advantages' that England already enjoyed of course looked forward to the still more marvellous blessings of a settled republic, and usually had their own positive prescription for obtaining them. Rogers, for example, vindicated Parliament in order to recommend his concept of a 'Christian Commonwealth in a Theocratick constitution', offering MPs and councillors explicit, though respectful, instruction from the vantage point of his own distinguished credentials as a 'faithful Servant to Jesus Christ, his Cause and the Commonwealth'. Disinterested propaganda simply did not exist – Nedham, lacking Rogers's claim to the moral high ground, submitted few specifics on the future settlement to avoid jeopardising his personal quest for renewed favour. Unlike Nedham and Rogers, many writers, including the influential Harrington, had little or no interest in celebrating the interim Republic; their visions of its successor nevertheless made a vital contribution to the wider campaign to rescue the Commonwealth from the 'disadvantagious imputation of a Novelism, unpractised and impracticable'.[93]

Although its government daily disproved such imputations, Parliament was careful never to pose as a permanent solution to the constitutional dilemma, and welcomed constructive advice. Viewed superficially, the outpouring of republican print seems diverse both in matter and manner: varying in length from six- or eight-page pamphlets to larger volumes containing a hundred or more, tracts ranged in style from lists of queries to

---

[91] *An Answer of some . . . citizens*, 5; *The CHARACTER or EAR-MARK of Mr. WILLIAM PRINNE*, 3; S[treater], *Shield*, 5; Rogers, *Diapoliteia*, 14–15.

[92] Rogers, *Diapoliteia*, 93; [Nedham], *Interest*, 20.

[93] *Word of settlement*, 5; Rogers, *Diapoliteia*, preface; *Commonwealth . . . asserted*, 2.

specific refutations to prophetic outpourings, from general treatises to disquisitions on particular topics. The obvious differences and disputes encouraged monarchists to dismiss republicanism as intrinsically chaotic, ever debating but incapable of resolving. But the apparent eclecticism of republican thought can be reduced to a competition between three basic visions of the future settlement: the Harringtonian, the theocratic and the neo-Leveller or 'ancient fundamentalist'. These models were dominant influences, not uniform categories into which every text can be neatly slotted. Boundaries remained fluid, and each pattern contained individual variations, shaped by and shaping the others. Beneath the rich complexity of ideas lay a bedrock of shared principles and attitudes that included much more than the belief, identified by Norbrook, in the possibility of recovering a 'sublime simplicity' whose 'ultimate institutional form . . . was still in the process of being discovered'. Hence 'the republicans' is a meaningful, not 'misleading shorthand' for these thinkers. As this common ground has been largely overlooked by hostile contemporaries and historians entranced by the spectacular arguments, it is essential to explore its extent before surveying the contrasting visions.[94]

The republican consensus was rooted in experiences and perceptions of the past. Commitment to Parliament through the furnace of civil war and revolution had forged a strong sense of common identity and purpose, which lingered despite the rising political and religious differences after 1649. In his influential *Healing Question*, first published amidst the uncertainties of 1656, and now reprinted, Sir Henry Vane had skilfully invoked this memory to support his argument for the transcendent unity of the 'good Party' as a 'Society by themselves', distinguished from 'all Neuters, close and open Enemies and deceitful Friends or Apostates' by their fidelity to the 'good cause' of 'just natural Rights in civil things and true freedom in matters of conscience'. With the great stumbling block of the Protectorate swept away on a tide of enthusiasm for the 'Good Old Cause', the lasting reunion for which Vane had pleaded seemed on the verge of attainment. Far from a 'parrot-cry' or 'substitute for thought', as Woolrych would have it, that famous slogan was a convenient shorthand for the ideals shared by all constituents of the 'good party', who echoed Vane's uncontroversial definition even as they unfolded its implications.[95] Harringtonians defended the people's right to 'freedom of their consciences, persons and estates', Quakers pleaded Parliament's promise that 'everyone shall have their free liberty, first as an English man, secondly as a Christian', while Levellers revived their old cry for 'Legal Fundamental Liberties, as well Religious as Civil'. Stubbe categorically insisted that 'LIBERTY, *civill and spiritual*, were the GOOD *old cause*'; Rogers not only paid extravagant homage to the role of *A healing question* and its

---

94 Norbrook, *Writing*, 397.
95 [Vane], *Healing question*, 1656, 8–9, 3; Woolrych, 'Good Old Cause', 160.

author in the near-miraculous 'Recovering . . . of this poor ISLAND', but himself epitomised its eirenicism: though highly critical of their proposals, he none the less embraced Harrington and his disciples, in marked contrast to Prynne and Baxter, as 'Friends' and allies in the Commonwealth.[96]

Communication and mutual respect among such diverse individuals was possible because republicanism was more than an idealised memory of the revolutionary past, in which Harrington had not shared: it was also founded upon present allegiance to particular principles. Whether they asserted its absolute superiority or merely its particular suitability to England, all republicans by definition believed that a 'Commonwealth' without single person or peers was the only government capable of a just and equal provision for the 'common good' of all interests. Though much more than anti-monarchism was involved, kingship was by no means 'irrelevant to republicanism', as certain historians have suggested.[97] Whereas the Healing question, in deference to Cromwellian sensibilities, had conceded the bare possibility that one man or a few might provide a 'righteous government' securing freedom, pamphleteers in the more open climate of 1659 flatly denied that liberty could subsist under any other form. Stubbe argued that, since all men were born 'equally free . . . to make a Monarchy best, you must introduce such a disparity as that one may transcend as God' – a manifest impossibility; in his view, the inevitable results of this government were 'Wickedness and Ignorance universal'.[98] Another godly republican treasured 'freedom in our Estates, Liberties and Lives as men, and true Christian liberty in matters appertaining to faith' as 'the most precious blessings . . . which we shall as certainly be deprived of under Monarchy as we may hopefully enjoy them under a Commonwealth'. Harrington similarly contrasted the inevitable 'suppression of civil Liberty, and in that of Liberty of Conscience' under monarchy with the protection of these advantages inherent in the 'True Form of a Democracy'.[99]

Though Harrington's argument stemmed from the specific need to persuade the godly that they would be safe in his republic, his assertion of the inseparability, even identity, of the secular and spiritual dimensions of liberty

---

[96] Armies dutie, 11; Hubberthorn, Real cause, 7; Panarmonia, 1; Stubbe, Essay, preface; Rogers, Diapoliteia, 41, 93.

[97] Pincus, 'Neither Machiavellian moment', 707. Worden contends that republicans were 'only rarely . . . uncompromisingly opposed to kingship': 'English republicanism', 446–7. If so, 1659 is the great exception. It seems more likely that post-Restoration repression encouraged a move away from outright denunciations of monarchy. Scott has convincingly demonstrated that the theoretical distinctions some writers drew between 'monarchy' and 'tyranny' made no difference to their practical anti-monarchism: England's troubles, 302ff.

[98] [Vane], Healing question, 16; Stubbe, Essay, preface, and MALICE REBUKED, Or A CHARACTER Of Mr. Richard Baxters Abilities. And A VINDICATION Of . . . Sr. HENRY VANE, 41.

[99] Word of settlement, 5; Harrington, Discourse shewing that the spirit of Parliaments . . . is not to be trusted, 4, 5.

was far from unique. The Leveller William Bray was equally convinced that 'where civil liberty is intire, it includes liberty of conscience', and *vice versa*, since both were 'the inseparable RIGHT of the people'.[100] Still more emphatically, the Quaker George Bishop maintained that 'the right of freedom of Conscience is a civil Right', and that 'a free mind, and a free speech and a Free State go together'.[101] From Fifth Monarchist railings against 'Tyranny in the Civil and Antichristianism in the Ecclesiastical' realms to the Levellers' critique of 'absolute Monarchy and persecution for Conscience', would-be architects of the Commonwealth constantly integrated civil and religious aspects of freedom.[102] Ardent republican convert William Sprigge thoroughly learned this lesson, commenting that spiritual and civil liberty 'seem so link'd and twisted to each other that what conduces to the security of one, hath no small tendency to the establishing of the other also'. The insistence that 'wheresoever there is a Free-state . . . Liberty of Conscience is inviolably preserv'd' casts some doubt upon the contention of J. C. Davis that 'in language and substance, civil and religious liberty did not march, if they marched at all, to the beat of the same drum'.[103] In the republican thought of 1659, arbitrary power was the antithesis, as a 'free Commonwealth' was the preservative, of 'both the Branches' of the one 'true freedom'.[104]

But the republicans of 1659 were also united by the conviction that liberty was, as yet, imperfect. Much had been accomplished by the initial revolution, and the more recent removal of the Protectorate, with its dangerously conservative tendencies. Estimates of progress varied. At one extreme, Canne exclaimed happily that 'the Earthquake is begun', and in an elaborate analogy likening the ancient constitution to a filthy and frog-infested pond insisted that 'something is already done in cutting a new channel, and drawing the

---

100 William Bray, *A Plea for the Peoples Good Old Cause, Or The Fundamental Lawes and Liberties of England Asserted*, 10
101 George Bishop, *MENE TEKEL, Or The Council of Officers of the Army Against The Declarations &c. of the Army*, 30. Read in context, Bishop's earlier statement that the Good Old Cause was 'chiefly Liberty of Conscience' indicates not an indifference to political forms that separated religious from secular republicans, as Norbrook has suggested (*Writing*, 397), but rather awareness that conscience was the aspect of liberty most threatened. Once Parliament embraced its defence, Bishop continues, 'the *Liberties* of the *Nation* . . . with the *Liberty* of *Conscience* were bound up and joyned together as two *lovely Twins* that cannot be divided but with the *mutual* Suffering, if not the *Dissolution* of each other': *Mene Tekel*, 4.
102 *Fifth Monarchy*, 49; *Panarmonia*, 12. Only John Canne seriously contemplated the possibility that the twin elements of liberty might be separated, warning Parliament not to give exclusive attention to 'Civil Rights', but he was motivated by concern for Christ's sovereignty rather than religous liberty *per se*: *Seasonable word*, 4–5.
103 [Sprigge], *Modest plea*, 18–19; J. C. Davis, 'Religion and the struggle for freedom in the English Revolution', *HJ* xxxv (1992), 507–30 at p. 514.
104 This metaphor, indicative of organic union, was used by Vane in *Healing question*, 8. Though Worden, following Harrington's misunderstanding, has asserted that Vane, unlike Harrington and the Levellers, did not see 'religious liberty as the natural ally of civil liberty' ('*Oceana*: origins', 135–6), these elements were as inseparable in Vane's thought as in anyone else's; the differences arose on the practical question of how best to secure both.

Waters to . . . a free Commonwealth', leaving behind 'the Weeds and Mud of Tyranny and Idolatry'; at the other, the incarcerated Leveller James Freeze complained that despite the severance of the 'head of Royalty', 'the members of Tyrannie' were 'suffered to flourish and still to bear the poysonous fruits of Slavery and destruction'.[105] Whatever their appraisal of the present, republicans agreed that much work was still required to conform the 'nature' of the 'free Commonwealth' to its 'name'. Residual oppressions and 'old rotten and obsolete foundations' inherited from monarchy needed to be cleared away, and a new constitution constructed on the pure basis of just and equal principles.[106] Though priorities and prescriptions diverged at this point, republicans concurred in looking to Parliament to deliver the desired settlement. Some did so with unqualified enthusiasm, others with greater misgivings: Quakers, Levellers and Fifth Monarchists were particularly given to reminding MPs of their past failings, and warning that only genuine repentance could avert disaster.[107] The majority, however, were prepared to accept Parliament as arbiter, directing their proposals with expressions of appropriate submission to its wisdom.[108] Republican tracts reiterated the scriptural maxim that a 'Nation divided against itself cannot stand', and pleaded for unity. Reverting to the revered trope of self-denial, they summoned 'all Persons and Interests' to deny themselves for 'the general good' by acceding to 'the Judgment of the *Parliament*, in regard it is not possible to have such a *Government* as shall suit with Every man's Mind'. Henry Stubbe set an example of personal willingness to 'acquiesce in . . . the determinate resolutions of the Good people . . . whatsoever my sentiments are I shall never esloign my self from the common interest'.[109] Optimism regarding the future Commonwealth was quite undimmed by the recognition of present differences, which were not expected to outlive its establishment. Republicans of almost every stamp shared the confident hope that the perfection of liberty in the eventual settlement would sooner or later restore prosperity and convince the entire nation of the "Justice and Excellency of this Government'.[110]

---

[105] AN INDICTMENT Against TYTHES: By John Osborne . . . Likewise a QUERY to William Prynne. By JOHN CANNE, preface; Freeze, Out-cry, 4.

[106] ENGLANDS SAFETY in the LAWS Supremacy, 10; Commonwealth . . . asserted, 3.

[107] Examples of each include Bache, Few words; H. N., Observation; and Canne's Seasonable word.

[108] For such expressions see, especially, Long Parliament-Work, (if they will please to do't) For the Good of the COMMON-WEALTH, 12 (Leveller); Humble petition of divers well-affected persons, 12 (Harringtonian); and Rogers, Diapoliteia, esp. pp. 76, 88 (theocratic).

[109] Twenty seven queries, 8; Stubbe, Essay, preface.

[110] Twenty four queries, 8, 7. For similar optimism from very different perspectives see H. N., Observation, 8; Englands safety, 8; James Harrington, Pour enclouer le Canon, 3; and Hubberthorn, Real cause, 6.

Imagining the future Republic: the Harringtonians

Of all visions of the future settlement, none was more influential or more highly systematised than that of James Harrington, whose ideas, first published in *The Commonwealth of Oceana* in 1656, had gained a significant following. Quantities of historical ink have been expended by J. G. A. Pocock and others on the precise provenance and meaning of this work's complex ideas and obscure terminology.[111] Yet the practical dimension of Harrington's enterprise has less often been appreciated.[112] In 1659 he and his supporters, anxious to exploit the moment, clearly expounded the principal features of his constitution in a series of brief pamphlets designed to dispel charges of incomprehensible utopianism. The supreme example of the transformation of Harrington's approach was his *Aphorisms Political*, which reduced to ten pages of concise reasoning the political theory that had filled hundreds in *Oceana*.

At the heart of Harrington's thinking remained an unbounded faith in the power of 'stated Laws or Orders' to establish an everlasting 'equal Commonwealth', and a correspondingly limitless distrust in a government by men without such orders. Saintly claims to rule Harrington himself dismissed on the ground that their only result would be an inequitable oligarchy or tyranny that actually contravened Mosaic precepts for the people to choose all magistrates; his disciples issued still more strident condemnations of the 'blasphemous arrogancy of such as rule without laws', and the folly of entrusting liberty to 'good men', who must remain frail and corruptible, and whose succession could not be guaranteed.[113] To cure the 'base itch of the narrow Oligarchy' that he detected in Army and Parliament, Harrington prescribed the exact 'Orders' required for a 'popular Government rightly balanced'. These centred upon the indirect election of a bicameral legislature by the entire nation, including those determined enemies of a Commonwealth, the Royalists and Presbyterians. The smaller assembly, known as the 'Senate', was to represent the 'wisdom' of the nation, with the exclusive right to debate legislation; the sole function of the larger, representing the people's 'interest', was to vote for or against the Senate's propositions. As a precaution against the perpetual power of any individuals, annual elections were to replace one-third of each assembly, while the executive was to be separate from and accountable to the legislature.[114] Though he insisted that his Commonwealth would necessarily tolerate religious differences, Harrington attempted

---

111 Thus Pocock devotes nearly half of his 'Introduction' to Harrington's political works to *Oceana*, and less than a fifth to the nine short tracts published in 1659–60.

112 A partial exception is Worden, who traces some of the ways in which Harrington and his followers, especially Neville, sought to adapt his ideas to practical political argument: 'Oceana: origins', 126ff.

113 Harrington, *Discourse upon this saying*, 3–4, 1–2; *Armies dutie*, 14.

114 Harrington, *Discourse upon this saying*, 13, 7–10; *Humble petition of divers well-affected*, 7–9.

to reassure conservatives by arguing that it would maintain a 'National Religion' with an 'endowed Ministry', since to do otherwise would violate the liberty of the majority.[115]

But Harrington offered more than a set of specific orders to be implemented: he also insisted on the viability of his republic. Challenging those who claimed that this form of government must be at best impracticable, at worst anarchic, Harringtonians contrasted the stability and prosperity of foreign commonwealths, ancient and modern, with the 'civil war and sedition' experienced by monarchies, including England.[116] Confusion was, in Harrington's analysis, the inevitable characteristic of a people without properly balanced orders: hence he and his adherents dilated upon the current unsettlement. Typical was the *Humble Petition* presented to Parliament on 6 July, which commended the Harringtonian remedy by bewailing the 'bad effects of long continued distractions, in the ruines and decayes of Trade' and ascribing all the blame to the fact that England, unlike every other people changing their government, had 'no fundamental Constitutions of any kind duly setled'.[117] Against assertions that foreign precedents were irrelevant, since England was congenitally unsuited to anything except her divinely sanctioned ancient monarchy, Harrington's followers deployed his formidable historical argument that forms of government are contingent upon the balance of property, which had shifted irrevocably from king and lords to the English people. As providence had presided over the transfer, a free Commonwealth securing the 'common and equal interest' was no sacrilegious 'Novelty' but the only pious and practical possibility. A zealous Harringtonian could therefore convict counter-revolutionaries on their own charges of 'repining and dissatisfaction at the Providence and Prudence of GOD', of preferring 'Anarchy' to the duty to 'yeild their compliance or assistance to . . . that Basis of Government which even GOD and Nature have laid amongst us'. With the Republic's foundation so powerfully supported, and no alternative capable of prospering, all that remained – in the Harringtonians' view – was the relatively straightforward task of 'building . . . agreeable Superstructures'.[118] The heady combination of providentialism and economic determinism in Harrington's theory afforded his followers strong motives for optimism.

Though they adhered to the essentials of his constitution with remarkable uniformity, Harrington's disciples proved more willing than their master to modify some of its accidentals to meet critics half-way. In response to fears that assemblies elected without political restrictions would instantly restore monarchy and persecution, Harrington, supremely confident in the

---

115 For this argument see, especially, Harrington's *Aphorisms*, 2–5.
116 *A Common-wealth or nothing*, 2; Harrington, *Discourse upon this saying*, 3, 4, 7, 8, and *Aphorisms*, 9.
117 *Humble petition of divers well-affected persons*, 3–4.
118 *Commonwealth . . . asserted*, 3–4, 7.

constraining power of the economic orders, offered no more tangible safe-guard than an oath of loyalty to the Commonwealth. The July petitioners, by contrast, recommended supplementary 'Expedients' for the effectual trial and execution for treason of anyone proposing to betray liberty. Still nearer to the mainstream of practical politics was A MODEL Of a Democraticall GOVERNMENT, which specified qualifications for voters and representa-tives that would exclude all Royalists who had not given 'signal testimony of their good affections', and even suggested that the senate should be the existing Parliament, recruited and subject to rotation. This version of Harrington's constitution found favour even with that inveterate parliamen-tarian, Sir Arthur Hesilrig.[119] Amendments to assuage the alarm raised by Harrington's assertion of absolute liberty of conscience were also introduced: the July petition, for example, denied toleration to all non-Christian reli-gions and prohibited the 'publique exercise' of Catholicism or any other 'pro-fessedly Christian' faith based on a foreign interest. In their decision to address Parliament directly, the petitioners also deviated from the method of Harrington, who made little mention of that body, preferring to target his published writings at a general audience, or, occasionally, the Army.[120] Harringtonians did, however, share his narrowly political focus: apart from the gestures towards commercial welfare in the July petition, and an equally tactical prediction in The Armies Dutie that 'such a settlement of Libertie would transforme the manners of the people', they displayed little interest in wider national problems.[121]

Imagining the future Republic: theocracy

Advocates of theocracy, lacking the cohesion that allegiance to one man's theory gave the Harringtonians, were much more diverse. From Quakers and Fifth Monarchists to 'godly republicans' such as Vane and Rogers, all those in this camp looked primarily to Scripture as the authoritative source of ideas and rhetoric. What distinguished their visions of the future government was not faith in precise constitutional mechanisms but a preoccupation with righ-teousness in both the system and its operators. Magistrates 'fearing God and

---

[119] Harrington, Discourse upon this saying, 8; Humble petition of divers well-affected persons, 10–11; A MODEL Of a Democraticall GOVERNMENT, Humbly tendered to Consideration, by a Friend . . . to this COMMON-WEALTH, 8–9, 4. A manuscript note on the Bodleian copy states that Hesilrig brought this text into the House in September.

[120] Humble petition of divers well-affected persons, 9. Harrington aimed A discourse upon this saying at the officers; in Valerius and Publicola: Or, the true FORM Of a Popular Common-wealth, published in November, he complained of the futility of approaches to Parliament. He did petition its 'Committe for the Government', but a petition addressed to the House was never presented by the members to whom he entrusted it (pp. 26–7).

[121] Humble petition of divers well-affected persons, 3, 5; Armies dutie, 28. The Model similarly proposed a Council for Trade, but did not elaborate on the idea.

hating covetousness', a qualification drawn directly from the biblical account of the inauguration of the Jewish commonwealth, were demanded in works as various as Rogers's great polemical treatise, appeals to Parliament from Quakers Edward Burrough and Ambrose Rigg and the major Fifth Monarchist manifesto delineating the *Kingdom of Christ, In opposition to the BEAST'S*.[122] Vane's *Needful CORRECTIVE* to Harrington grappled with the problem of devising a structure that would make the people 'holy as well as free' another godly republican observed that though 'good rules' were 'needful' and might 'greatly avail', a settlement on the 'right Basis of good Government' was impossible 'till Christ reveal himself in our Rulers, as the Corner-stone of the whole building, teaching them to deny themselves and naturally to take care of the Common-weal'. Confidence in the possibility of substituting the perfect wisdom of Christ as 'Political King and Civil Legislator' for the selfish dictates of human authorities was, indeed, the ultimate foundation of every theocratic scheme.[123]

Millennarian hopes of Christ's immediate reign characterised all theocratic republicans, whose optimism was fed by a powerful application of biblical prophecy to recent history. Providence, in this view, was not Harrington's remote superintendent of natural processes equally operative in foreign or pagan spheres, but the active director of events unique to a Christian, English context – 'a cloude going before us daily, to instruct us . . . but . . . blinding those who oppose . . . that Commonwealth of Israel which the Lord will erect'.[124] Scrutiny of the past could therefore reveal, and enable the godly to further, the divine purpose for the future kingdom. Thus Vane's *Healing question* had urged reunion in order to 'uphold . . . this blessed cause and work of the Lord, that has already come this far . . . in its progress to its desired and expected end, of bringing in Christ . . . as the chief Ruler amongst us', while Burrough based his exhortations on former deliverances yielding 'good expectations that the Lord will suddenly so appear as to free us from future oppressions'. The New England minister John Eliot, announcing that Christ had 'now come to take possession . . . making England first in that blessed work of setting up the Kingdom', presented his *Christian Commonwealth* as an aid to the saints in their duty to be 'wise and discerning of the times to know what Israel ought to do in this great work'. For the Fifth Monarchists, Canne used precedents, especially the Army's declarations, to demonstrate that the true meaning of the 'Good Old Cause' was '*NO KING BUT JESUS*', and

---

122 Rogers, *Diapoliteia*, 62; Burrough, *To the Parliament . . . councel*, 4; Rigg, *Oh ye heads*, 8; *Fifth Monarchy*, 50–2.

123 [Vane], *Needful corrective*, 3, 9; *Short discourse*, 8.

124 Stubbe, *Essay*, preface, using the metaphor from Exodus xiii.21; xiv.20. This view was, of course, an offshoot of the conventional Puritan understanding of providence, on which see A. B. Worden, 'Providence and politics in Cromwellian England', *Past and Present* cix (1985), 55–99. What distinguished the theocrats was their belief in the imminence of Christ's kingdom, and their duty to hasten it.

admonished Parliament to act accordingly.[125] Canne's emphatic negative shows how the theocratic understanding of past events not only channelled future hopes, but also fear lest the divine purpose be frustrated by the revival of what providence was plainly discarding. In the political realm, monarchy must be rejected; in the ecclesiastical, tithes and a national religion imposed by the civil government must be opposed. To complete the work of destroying such remnants of the 'Antichristian Tyranny and bondage', and secure the sovereign rights of Christ over conscience, not only Quakers but Vane, Stubbe and the Fifth Monarchists concurred in calling for the magistrate's exclusion from this sphere: his commission was merely to preserve 'external Rights and Liberties'.[126] Though they shared Harrington's commitment to liberty of conscience, the radicals' very different understanding of providence thus led them to exactly the opposite conclusion on the method of securing it.

Indeed, theocratic visions of the future settlement reflected not only a broad consensus but the contrasting perceptions and priorities of their various exponents. At one end of the spectrum were the strict Fifth Monarchists, who equated the 'Fifth Monarchy or Kingdom of Christ' with the exclusive reign of his representatives, the saints. Negatively, their programme required the thorough 'destroying of Antichrist and his interest', which extended beyond the political realm to include, as Canne observed, the 'carnal Church, Ministry, Worship and Government, with all the corrupt Laws of the Nation'. The biblical letter was the vital balance in which existing laws and institutions were weighed and found wanting; those who mistrusted the Fifth Monarchists' condemnation of the 'Tyrannous Law' were referred to specific lists of the 'Laws expressly contrary to Scripture'. The positive corollary was, of course, the demand for the 'Laws and Directions of the Word . . . not only in Church-Government . . . but also in . . . all affairs in the Commonwealth'. Convinced of the 'sufficiency and perfection of the Scripture', Fifth Monarchists disdained all 'human Polities and platforms of Government' as untrustworthy inventions whose final ruin was imminent.[127] Instead, they preached the blessings of a 'vigorous and thorow Reformation' dictated by the divine commands and implemented by the 'restored Ordinance of Magistracy' foretold in prophecy. No doubts as to the possibility of discerning God's order diminished their ardour: John Eliot, for example, advertised his Scripture-based model as that whereby the angels were

---

[125] [Vane], *Healing question*, 21; Burrough, *To the Parliament . . . councel*, 3; John Eliot, *The Christian COMMONWEALTH: Or, The Civil Policy of The Rising Kingdom of Jesus Christ*, preface; Canne, *Seasonable word*, 5.

[126] [Vane], *Healing question*, 5–7; Stubbe, *Essay*, 12–35; R. H., *Good Old Cause briefly demonstrated*, 7; Burrough, *To the Parliament . . . councel*, 6; *Fifth Monarchy*, 52–3.

[127] Christopher Feake, *A BEAM OF LIGHT Shining In the midst of much Darknes*, 58; Canne, *An indictment*, preface; *Fifth Monarchy*, 51; Eliot, *Christian Commonwealth*, preface.

governed, and looked forward eagerly to the 'heaven upon earth' that would succeed its universal application.[128]

The Fifth Monarchists in 1659 offered only extravagant rhetoric, not a systematic account of the anticipated kingdom. Eliot's was the only constitutional blueprint, and did not appear until late October; despite its universalist claims, it failed to transcend the gulf between the English and the converted Indians for whom it had been designed. Rather than devise comprehensive schemes, the Fifth Monarchists, newly returned from the political wilderness, concentrated on vindicating their reputation for sanctity, and hence their claim to power. Years of opposition to Cromwell after the defeat of their hopes in 1653 had left them branded a 'discontented, giddy, fanatick Munster-spirited people'. Their latest pamphlets therefore adduced a mass of evidence that they had, in fact, been the only 'faithful friends to the Cause' during the 'great Apostacy'.[129] To the imputation that they were ignorant anarchists, better at 'pulling down . . . than building up', Fifth Monarchists replied that the corruption of existing structures more than justified their destruction; and they stressed the superiority of 'Proposals grounded upon Scripture' in securing 'equal and impartial justice to every one' in their 'persons and proprieties'. Recognising Christ as the invisible 'Head of the State' was, they insisted, no less feasible now than it had been during the Jewish theocracy, or still was in the government of the Church; nothing but a 'righteous Settlement' on this basis could provide stability 'in this hour of distraction'.[130] Thus Fifth Monarchists attempted to compensate for the lack of a comprehensive theory, and make practical politics out of their millennarian commitment.

In rhetoric and substance Quaker political ideas closely resembled those of the Fifth Monarchists. Quakers, too, saw in the Protector's downfall the end of the 'dark night of Apostacie', and the dawning of a moment of apocalyptic expectancy – 'the Lord Jesus Christ (with thousands of his Saints) rides on gloriously . . . treading down all Rule and all Authority (contrary to him)'.[131] Like the Fifth Monarchists, they vigorously denounced the 'Antichristian yoke of bondage', demanding the repeal of 'all unrighteous Laws' and the removal of 'oppression, tyranny and injustice', particularly tithes, oaths and the national ministry.[132] Some Friends were equally interested in proving their own fitness to rule, insisting, albeit without lengthy histories, that they, too, had 'waded through hazards and hardships in times of difficulty and

---

128 *Fifth Monarchy*, 52–3; Eliot, *Christian Commonwealth*, preface.
129 *Fifth Monarchy*, 1–49; *True catalogue*, passim; Feake, *Beam of light*, 2–57.
130 *Fifth Monarchy*, 49, 53, 50.
131 Burrough, *To the Parliament . . . councel*, 7; R. H., *Good Old Cause briefly demonstrated*, 13. Similar expressions were used by William Morris in his testimony *To the supream authoritie*, 3–4, and John Hodgson in the title of his *Love, kindness and due Respect*. On Quaker hopes at this moment see also Reay, *The Quakers*, 82–3.
132 R. H., *Good Old Cause briefly demonstrated*, 9; Burrough, *To the Parliament . . . councel*, 7; Morris, *To the supream authoritie*, 2.

danger for the promoting the *good old cause*', and that their righteousness exceeded that of their neighbours.[133] But there were important differences. Eager as they were for virtuous magistrates, Quakers evinced no interest in the 'Fifth Monarchy' or the rule of the saints as such. Instead, they championed the rights of all 'free-born people' to be a 'free Nation', in language reminiscent of the Levellers.[134] Burrough, for example, advised Parliament to produce an 'equal and just government' through consultation with the 'ablest and soberest . . . of each . . . profession' – Presbyterians, Independents, Baptists, Quakers and 'all sortes of men'.[135] Those Friends who considered constitutional issues in any detail echoed the Leveller call for annual elections and accountability.[136] Nor did Quakers share the Fifth Monarchists' literal approach to Scripture; far from demanding the blanket imposition of Mosaic law, Burrough asserted that all human law should be 'grounded upon the law of God, pure reason and equity'.[137] Although Quakers have been credited with outdistancing all other groups on the 'road to the New Jerusalem', they were, in fact, no more enthusiastic, and certainly no more creative than anyone else. While they might, as Burrough famously declared, anticipate 'a New Earth, as well as a New Heaven', they provided no clear map.[138] On the rare occasions when they descended from the clouds of apocalyptic rhetoric, Quakers offered few positive proposals, and even these were largely borrowed from the Levellers. The overlap between Quaker and Leveller thinking is not surprising, given the fact that many Levellers had by 1659 converted to Quakerism. In so doing, they were not retreating to quietism, as has often been supposed. Rather, they found in the Quaker movement a common desire for liberty and equity, and a congenial base for political activism.[139]

Though Quaker and Fifth Monarchist radicalism has secured for them a place in the limelight, the most constructive thinking in the theocratic camp was, in fact, that of the 'godly republicans', especially Sir Henry Vane and his great admirers, the ex-Fifth Monarchist preacher John Rogers, and the young Oxford intellectual, Henry Stubbe. Desiring as much as any Fifth Monarchist

133 Morris, *To the supream authoritie*, 11; Hubberthorn, *Real cause*, 4.
134 For this terminology see, especially, Burrough, *To the Parliament . . . councel*; Hubberthorn, *Real cause*; Rigg, *Oh ye heads*; B[illing], *Mite of affection*. As Billing was a former Leveller, his indebtedness to such thinking is not surprising.
135 Burrough, 'To the Parliament', MS Rawlinson D397, fo. 17.
136 Ibid. fos 6, 9; idem, *A DECLARATION To all the WORLD of our FAITH: And what we believe who are called QUAKERS*, 4–5.
137 Idem, *A declaration*, 4.
138 Hutton, *Restoration*, 121–2; Burrough, *To the Parliament . . . councel*, 3.
139 Quaker political activism has been stressed by Reay, but the Leveller input has not been widely recognised. John Lilburne's own conversion has frequently been seen as typifying the Levellers' retreat from the activism of the 1640s. On the common radical demand for equity as well as liberty see M. Goldsmith, 'Levelling by sword, spade and word: radical egalitarianism in the English Revolution', in C. Jones, M. Newitt and S. Roberts (eds), *Politics and people in revolutionary England: essays in honor of Ivan Roots*, Oxford 1986, 65–80.

a government with foundations 'laid . . . firm and deep in the Word of God, bottomed upon that Corner-stone the Lord Jesus', these men were by no means deaf to all voices but Scripture.[140] Instead, they attempted to channel the various currents of republican thought into a workable synthesis that might find acceptance with both the godly and others, especially the Harringtonians. The essence of their prescription was the *Healing question*'s definition of the sovereign people, upon whom the Republic was to be based: the 'whole body' of 'faithful ones, adherents to the Cause'.[141] In 1659 this solution seemed realistic, recognising as it did the ungodliness and hostility of the majority of the nation, while appealing to the widest possible basis for the new government. Rogers eagerly advertised it as the upright middle course between the 'two extreams' represented by Harrington and the 'rigid Fifth Mon. man', who endangered the cause by their respective reliance upon a 'meerly Natural' and a 'meer Religious' right. Godly republicanism could claim to incorporate the best of both.[142]

Faced with the popularity of Harrington's constitution and the resurgence of Fifth Monarchist enthusiasm, Vane, Rogers and Stubbe adopted quite different tactics to commend the godly republican solution. Vane's *Needful Corrective or Ballance in Popular Government* took the form of a letter to Harrington, and courted his supporters by professing the greatest admiration for his 'humane Prudence', and an intention not to 'oppose but rather countenance the essentials' of his model by perfecting 'the principles of true freedom'. After an abstract analysis of the origins of government, Vane addressed the major objection brought by the godly against Harrington: the problem of compelling 'the depraved, corrupted and self-interested will of man in the great Body which we call the People' to 'espouse their true publick interest'. As nothing short of an 'extraordinary effusion of [the] Spirit upon all flesh' would make the nation 'truly free' to 'use the power of its own will in providing for its own Government', it would be wise to confine 'the right and priviledge of a free Citizen', at least temporarily, to the regenerate and those qualified by their 'tryed good affection and faithfulness to common Right and publick Freedom'.[143] This limited electorate was to choose a 'Ruling Senate' and 'Representatives' to sit as a single assembly – another major deviation from Harrington, despite the superficial resemblance of the names. Vane was careful to retain the appearance of moderation, praising the 'degree of

---

140 [Vane], *Corrective*, 9.
141 [Vane], *Healing question*, 10–11, 17, quoted in Rogers, *Diapoliteia*, 45, 76, 87 and incorporated into the title of his *Mr Harrington's Parallel Unparallel'd . . . Wherein it appears, Neither the Spirit of the People, nor the Spirit of men like Mr. R, but the Spirit of God, of Christ, of his People in Parliament and Adherents to the Cause, is the fittest for the Government of the Commonwealth.* Stubbe paraphrased Vane's dictum, arguing that a Commonwealth must be limited to the 'honest and faithful party', the 'good people which have adhered to the Good Old Cause': *Essay*, preface.
142 Rogers, *Diapoliteia*, 59–60.
143 [Vane], *Corrective*, 1–2, 5–6, 7–8.

Freedome very desirable' that might result from Harrington's system even as he pressed the merits of his alternative as 'the most exact platforme of the purest kind of popular Government, and that which hath its . . . first pattern in the Word . . . in the practise of Israels Commonwealth'. Such emphasis upon the 'Divine Institution' of this constitution was, of course, calculated to appeal to the godly, whose sensibilities were also soothed by Vane's insistence that 'true godliness' must be valued despite the prevalence of the counterfeit variety. But Vane also went further than the Fifth Monarchists in bridging the gap between the mundane and the millennial, urging the necessity of 'ordinary means' while insisting that they could lead to still greater things: the 'perfect day' when the 'publick sentence and judgment of such a restored People . . . in their Assemblies . . . may not so much be the judgment of Man, as of the Lord himself, their King'. Thus the *Corrective* presented a godly republic as an attractive and eminently practical alternative.[144]

In contrast to Vane's studied moderation and subtle promotion of a new constitution, Rogers vindicated the 'Theocratick or godly Commonwealth' by direct polemic. Although he censured extreme Fifth Monarchists for their blindness to 'the natural Rights and freedom which people have to choose their Representatives', and gave lukewarm assent to Harrington's dictum that any faction 'for Saints meerly as Saints and for none but such whom they so account (excluding men as men) are dangerous', Rogers retained considerable sympathy for his erstwhile colleagues, insisting that those who were 'gracious and meek' deserved preferment, not ridicule.[145] To convince such individuals that their aspirations would find fulfilment in the godly republican *via media*, he contended for government by the 'most holy, able, wise, pious and qualified persons', insisting that this was a righteous and realistic option – 'not that they should be all such, or none but such (for that we cannot expect) but to do our best to find some such . . . and that the highest principles have the highest places'. This was, of course, an open challenge to Harrington's maxim that 'good orders' would make 'good men'. On this issue, Rogers firmly aligned himself with the loyal godly, arguing that Harrington had grossly underestimated human depravity in general, and that of the Commonwealth's enemies in particular. Adapting Harrington's notorious carnival image, Rogers scornfully dismissed, as 'a pretty toy (for fools to play with)', the supposition 'that frames (of mens making) can keep [the Royalists] in, like Cats; when the Laws of Gods making cannot hold them, without new hearts'. Insistence on the wisdom of Scripture and the 'distinguishing mercies' of providence was his cogent objection to a constitution enfranchising all parties; Rogers, like Baxter before him, denounced Harrington's underlying philosophy, alleging that a model based on 'Principles Paganish or Popish, fetch'd from Athens or from Venice', could not possibly be

---

144 Ibid. 8–9, 10, 2, 7.
145 Rogers, *Diapoliteia*, 59, 76–7, 123.

'adequated' to a 'Christian Commonwealth', and would, in fact, benefit only the Catholic interest.[146] To persuade even ungodly republicans of the folly of such a system, Rogers cited the classical authorities that Harrington so much prized: Aristotle, and the experiences of Greek city states, underscored the injustice of a rotation that would regularly expel 'the most publick Spirited Worthies'.[147]

Instead of Harrington's 'unequally Equal Commonwealth', Rogers celebrated the virtues of a government founded on 'Christian principles' yet incorporating the best of ancient wisdom. While he prescribed no precise constitutional structures – though he did condemn Harrington's bicameral system as a monstrous betrayal of the cause – Rogers set forth the general advantages of theocracy.[148] Chief among these was the achievement of a 'most certain and perfect . . . balance', uniting 'all parts in . . . order, symmetry and service' and distributing 'an exact justice and freedom'.[149] Such classical harmony would arise from universal recognition of the 'Publick, Pious and Pure Reason' of this form of government: citing Cicero, Rogers optimistically maintained that 'men as men, as well as Saints are the Subjects of and may be restored unto' this reason. Thorough education in the 'true and genuine Principles of a Christian Commonwealth' was the means; and though Scripture endorsed the principle of instruction, all the detailed recommendations for the curriculum came from Aristotle. Rogers's indebtedness to ancient wisdom was equally apparent in his account of the moral reformation that would follow the settlement of a theocratic republic: recalling that even pagans such as Cicero had recognised this form as the 'best Polity with respect to piety', he declared that 'Virtues [would be] excited [and] . . . Vices detested in no kind of Popular Government like to a Christian Commonwealth'. Merit, not money, would determine access to office in this righteous system: in language that closely mirrored Nedham's republican editorials, Rogers called for the opening of a 'wide and welcome door . . . to . . . those Persons who climb up into the Chair of honour and dignity . . . by steps of publick virtue, wisdom, fidelity, fortitude and ability'. To show that this 'Rule' was also 'highly exemplified in the holy Scriptures', he added the curious precedent of the 'worthies' promoted by godly Jewish kings, particularly David. To Rogers the 'Theocratical polity' or 'unquestionable Reign of Christ on earth' was the perfect fulfilment of both Scripture and classical republicanism.[150]

Unlike other godly republicans, Stubbe did not emphasise the ultimate

---

146 Ibid. 66, 74, 77, 79. Baxter had brought exactly the same charges against Harrington in the 208th aphorism of his *Holy Commonwealth*, a work with which Rogers, of course, was also engaged.
147 Rogers, *Diapoliteia*, 77, 75, 65–6, 82.
148 Ibid. 66, 72.
149 Ibid. 93–4, 120, 114.
150 Ibid. 106, 107–10, 121, 112, 123.

millennium.[151] Though he, too, presented Israel's commonwealth as 'our pattern' in significant respects, he denied that divine prescription constituted this a 'Theocracy'. Not saints but those superior intellects, the Harrington-ians, were Stubbe's targeted audience in the preface to his *ESSAY in Defence of the GOOD OLD CAUSE*. To overcome objections to an 'Unequall Commonwealth' based on the 'good party', he took Vane's complimentary strategy a stage further. Effacing himself as 'too inconsiderable to add any thing to those applauds which the understanding part of the World must bestowe upon [Harrington]', Stubbe acclaimed the latter's model of 'an equal Commonwealth' as 'that whereunto we ought and may prudentially grow', refrained from criticising its injurious tendency to treat 'equally men of different qualifications', and admired his followers' 'supererogating tendernesse . . . for the liberty of those who would have deprived them of theirs'. But where Vane and Rogers stressed popular unregeneracy, Stubbe's case against the mechanical efficacy of orders rested on a sophisticated under-standing of self-interest. The realisation that 'men do not pursue what is really their interest, but what seems so to them' enabled Stubbe to expose Harrington's main weakness, and predict inevitable turbulence on the part of an enfranchised people 'unconvinced of their interest . . . not instructed in, yea averse from a Republick'. Mere instruction would not suffice – unlike Harrington or Nedham, Stubbe acknowledged that it was not yet 'the interest of all nor of an infinity . . . to promote a Republick'. Restricting full participa-tion to the 'honest and faithful party, leaving the residue so much liberty as they are now capable of' was therefore an equitable as well as feasible solu-tion. Against Harringtonian criticism of reliance on the 'goodness' of any men, Stubbe marshalled biblical, classical and contemporary precedents to show that a senate composed of 'our patriots', and 'ruling purely for the good of the people . . . to enstate them in a perfect freedom' could not possibly degenerate into 'Oligarchy'.[152] Stubbe's *Letter . . . oncerning a Select Senate* developed this theme, and is unique among godly republican texts in formu-lating precise constitutional principles and proposals to transform them into a settlement.[153]

---

[151] Stubbe did, however, share their view of providence, portraying recent history in apoc-alyptic terms, as an 'Age that . . . hath been all Miracles', revealing the 'true anointed ones of the Lord': *Malice rebuked*, 1ff. The difference in emphasis owed much to the difference in readership.

[152] Stubbe, *Essay*, preface. Stubbe's sincere admiration for Harrington contrasted mark-edly with his contempt for his other target, Baxter, whom he derided as 'no Scholar at all, not skilled in Latin, Greek or Hebrew, nor versed in Ecclesiastical history or philosophy. But a meere Glowe-worme in literature, who borrowed his luster from the darknesse of the night'. Stubbe used his superior scholarship to demonstrate the absurdity of Baxter's argu-ments against a tolerant, democratical commonwealth.

[153] Stubbe, *Letter . . . concerning a select senate*. Stubbe's constitutional proposals were heavily influenced by Harrington; completed on the day of the interruption, they came too late to influence Parliament's debates.

Imagining the future Republic: the ancient fundamentalists

The most far-reaching visions of the future, recommending not just political structures for imposition or oppressions for demolition but comprehensive reforms in areas as diverse as the law, poor relief, trade, universities and local government, came from the 'ancient fundamentalists', or new Levellers. Though Scripture and Harrington influenced many of them, the members of this group adhered to no individual's theory, and exhibited little or no interest in the millennium; they had differing priorities and even conflicting views on significant issues such as the relationship between civil and ecclesiastical power, some writers advocating a national Church with or without tithes and others echoing the theocrats' call for the magistrate's complete exclusion from this sphere.[154] What distinguished their proposals from others was their tendency to draw their main inspiration from myths of 'the antient and fundamental Government' long obscured by monarchical corruptions, and so revive the Leveller demand for the 'ancient birthrights' of 'free-born Englishmen'.[155] This vision of the constitution had the obvious advantages of antiquity and suitability to the English people: it rebutted the monarchist argument that a commonwealth must be an impossible, alien novelty by a historical narrative showing that kings had actually been the truly injurious innovators. With their 'freeborn English' rhetoric, ancient fundamentalists enlisted patriotic sentiment and criticised Harrington's outlandish schemes. Even some who sympathised with him asserted that the readiness of an 'English way of a Commonwealth' obviated the necessity for a 'new pattern' from Venice; others, such as William Bray, denounced the dangerous folly of importing foreign notions when England had 'GOOD ANCIENT LAWS' and 'righteous Fundamentals already laid, better than which we none can lay'.[156] The unnamed author of CHAOS advertised the simplicity and practicality of his immensely detailed model by exploiting the contrast with Harrington's elaborate and exotic obscurities: after promising that there would be 'no hard or strange Names, nor unknown Titles', the subtitle concluded that 'if it must be so, that Cats shall provide Supper, here they shall do it suitable to the best Palats, and easie to digest'.[157] The ostentatious rejection of new and foreign influences by the 'ancient fundamentalists' was not, however, a simple result of Leveller sympathies: it also reflected the

---

154 Qualified support for tithes was expressed by *Speculum*, 14; a major exposition of the radical view was *Lilburns ghost*, 2–3.

155 *Englands safety*, 9; *Speculum*, 4–5.

156 *Grand concernments*, 24; Bray, *Plea*, 10.

157 *Chaos*, title. This writer did, however, present the creation of his English republic in heroic terms drawn from classical epic, an aspect elucidated in Norbrook, *Writing*, 400–1.

'providential nationalism' that had characterised the early Republic's self-presentation.[158]

In their plans for restoration of the legendary English commonwealth the ancient fundamentalists were nevertheless heirs of the Leveller movement. Not only did they demand the decentralisation of justice and the repeal of 'tyrannical' laws: the essence of their platform was government by successive, annual parliaments, with powers limited by a written constitution spelling out unalterable 'fundamental laws' guaranteeing liberty of conscience and a republican form. Like the Levellers, they proposed that this constitution, variously described as the 'Agreement of the People', the new 'Magna Charta', or the 'Model of Civil Government', be presented to the sovereign people for subscription, in order to secure its ratification as the supreme law.[159] But where the first Levellers had been relatively naive political optimists, giving little thought to the practical institution of their government or the probability that the overwhelming majority of the people would refuse the 'Agreement', their successors in 1659 were nothing if not hardheaded realists. Systematic thinking was a speciality of *Chaos*, which offered six easy stages to the recreation of the ideal commonwealth, covering almost every imaginable aspect of the settlement; though the author modestly described it as a 'rough draft . . . shewing the facility of doing what is by all men so much desired', he boasted that it could be implemented in less than seventy days. Others expressly tackled the problem of disaffection, recommending not only indoctrination, especially of children, in 'the principles of a Free State', but qualifications disfranchising those who had not actively supported the cause. If 'the people' were identified with the 'well-affected', *Panarmonia, Or The Agreement of the People Revived*, insisted that the subscribers would easily form a majority. Far from being 'low-key and defensive', as Hill has alleged, the new Levellers of 1659 confidently sought to demonstrate that their far-reaching programme was practicable.[160]

Consideration of the discrete, and often competing elements of the pamphlet literature may be essential, but it obscures the creativity and variety of republican thought. Individuals did not necessarily conform to doctrinaire moulds labelled 'Harringtonian', 'Leveller' or 'theocratic', but remained free to devise new syntheses including aspects from each. Such liberty is apparent in the case of William Sprigge, whose *Modest Plea For An Equal Common-wealth*

---

[158] On the 'anglicism of republican culture' in 1649–53 see Kelsey, *Inventing a republic*, 211–14.

[159] *Panarmonia*, 4; *Speculum*, 6–8; Samuel Duncon, *SEVERAL PROPOSALS Offered by a Friend to Peace & Truth to The Serious Consideration of the Keepers of the Liberties of The People of England, In Reference to a SETTLEMENT Of Peace and Truth*, 3. The classic statement of this political programme by the first Levellers was the third *Agreement of the Free People of England*, issued by Lilburne, Overton, Walwyn and Prince from the Tower in May 1649.

[160] *Chaos*, appendix; *Lilburns ghost*, 8, 5; *Panarmonia*, 10–11; Hill, *Experience of defeat*, 32.

Against Monarchy reflects widespread reading and fits neatly into no category.[161] As a godly zealot, Sprigge was very receptive to theocratic influences. Like Rogers, he advocated a 'Holy Commonwealth', in which office would be entrusted to only the able 'Saint' who had given 'so good . . . a testimony, that if ever he prove Apostate, a black brand of perpetual infamy may rest upon him'. Quoting with approval the Hull Fifth Monarchists' petition for government by the 'holy just righteous Laws of the great and wise God our rightful Lawgiver', Sprigge agreed that the moral and judicial laws of Moses should remain 'the Rule and Standard for Civil Governors'. Sprigge's biblical literalism, however, was tempered by the claim that 'the Equity of them is written in mens hearts by Nature'; unlike the Fifth Monarchists, he was very interested in 'the order both of God and Nature'. In this he resembled Harrington, from whom he also imbibed specific concepts such as the 'equal Rotation' and the theory that the transfer of landed property had created 'a natural and strong vergency towards a Commonwealth'. Other aspects of Sprigge's thinking were closer to the ancient fundamentalists. Not only did he adopt their commitment to 'fundamental Constitutions' and their nationalistic rhetoric, declaring that 'the free born people of England', who had broken 'the more ancient Norman Yoke', must now be capable of enjoying liberty, but he also shared their concern for a wider range of national problems, and recommended similar solutions. Thus he urged relief of the poor by the creation of workhouses, and reform of the universities to eradicate 'the ill principles of Tyranny and Presbytery'. Yet Sprigge's pamphlet was more than a miscellaneous assortment of the ideas of others; rather, he had a personal agenda and a unique theory to promote. As a younger son himself, Sprigge added an 'Apology for younger brothers' in which he reasoned that the 'Tranquillity of the Commonwealth' could only be ensured by according them their 'natural right' to an equal share in the inheritance.[162] More interesting is the way in which he developed well-known themes into a coherent argument that nothing less than the extirpation of all 'interests' opposed to the 'one common interest' would produce a permanent settlement. Sprigge offered a detailed critique of three 'irreconcileable Antagonists': those familiar radical targets, the 'Mercenary Lawyers' and 'National Clergy' and, more surprisingly, the 'Hereditary Nobility'. In his analysis, the much-publicised religious differences were actually 'inconsiderable'; the clash of material interests with that of the Commonwealth was the fundamental problem. Giving his own materialist twist to the prevailing optimism, Sprigge predicted that 'were these [interests] once cancelled . . . the other of

---

161 Sprigge's pamphlet, though fascinating, is not unique in this regard; there are others that do not conform to one of the three categories.
162 Sprigge's entry in R. Greaves and R. Zaller (eds), *Biographical dictionary of the British radicals in the seventeenth century*, Brighton 1982, iii. 196–7, confirms that he was, indeed, a younger son. A passionate, and surely personal sense of grievance informs his discussion of the subject.

Presbyterians and Independents, Quakers and Baptists would soon vanish or at least make little noise'.[163]

While his idiosyncratic vision of the future reflects republican creativity, Sprigge's account of his ideological progression illustrates the persuasive power of the case for the Commonwealth. From a 'passive . . . compliance with the present Power', as ordained by providence, he had reached the conviction that 'some Governments [were] more pure, refined and less prone to corruption than others', and that monarchy, in particular, was 'diametrically opposite to, and inconsistent with the true liberty and happiness of any people'. Though he rehearsed the standard intellectual arguments, Sprigge was no armchair theorist, but a passionate crusader for the republican faith. Presenting his own 'Map of the Commonwealth' as a 'few bunches of Grapes' to correct those who hankered for the 'old constitution' and raised 'an evil report . . . on the Land whither we are travelling, as if it were a Land of Confusion and not of Peace and Liberty', he modelled himself on the faithful spies, and implored England not to imitate the rebellious unbelief of ancient Israel. Instead, he entreated the nation to follow Parliament, as 'the Captains that first lead us out of Egypt', and himself set an example of respectful submission to the wisdom and authority of the members, 'our Master-builders, which through the blessing of God have never miscarried in any of their Heroick Undertakings'.[164]

Sprigge's pamphlet, published in late September, exemplifies not only the fluidity of alignments but also the enthusiasm for both the present and future Commonwealth that continued to motivate almost all republicans. Concentration on Harrington, whose detachment was exceptional, has encouraged excessive historical estimates of the 'distance between republic and republicanism': though Worden has opposed them, 'republicanism' in 1659 could actually function simultaneously as 'criticism' and 'endorsement of the English republic'. Complaints of 'chaos' or 'anarchy', from republican writers, were usually partisan devices designed to commend particular prescriptions by obscuring progress to date. Thus Rogers warned Harringtonians that it was 'dangerous to insinuate that the Parliament are Setled on no Foundation of Government as well as Erroneous', and insisted that the members had already made a good beginning. Optimism was therefore justified. As a substantial consensus united republicans, their hopes of a settlement satisfying all parties in the main were far from fantastic. The creative, self-assured, carefully crafted republicanism of 1659 had much greater potential than its infant predecessor of 1649, described by Worden as an 'improvisation, triumphant by default, unconvinced and largely unprofessed'. What destroyed the promise of the English Republic was not irreconcilable ideological conflict,

[163] [Sprigge], *Modest plea*, dedicatory epistle, 34, 74, 26–7, 5, 87, 89, 11, 42–4, 48, 58, 79–81.
[164] Ibid. 1–4, dedication, 90.

but a sudden and, to many, unexpected political crisis that redirected the energies of its supporters from constructive proposals to bitter recriminations. In sharp contrast to the virtual silence of April 1653, the massive outcry that greeted Parliament's second 'interruption' in October 1659 demonstrated that confidence in its authority had been only too well restored.[165]

---

[165] Worden, 'Oceana: origins', 138; Rogers, Diapoliteia, 70–1; Worden, Rump Parliament, 173–4

9

The Crisis of the Autumn

The insolence of the Parliament and the ambition of their Commanders cannot long agree, but some schisms will fall out: Hyde to Mordaunt, 9 Sept. 1659.

The place, the face of this Congregation seem to mee to have written upon them *Union, Union Union* . . . *of Parliament, City, and Armie:* which *Union is the foundation of marriage* . . . let no man put asunder . . . no man, no Devill, no Jesuit: Nathaniel Holmes, *A SERMON Preached before the Parliament . . . Oct. the 6th.*

To quarrel with the army, before the constitution was settled, and measures taken to woo the political nation, would be suicide. Yet that is just what the Rump proceeded to do: Woolrych, 'Introduction', 98.

Disaster overtook the Commonwealth on Thursday 13 October 1659 when the Army once more interrupted Parliament. Events seemed, at last, to have vindicated conservative opponents, who had from the first prophesied, and promoted, a repetition of the rupture of April 1653. This chapter will argue that, though memory and personality differences played a part, the collapse of the parliamentary Republic was not the predetermined outcome of inveterate hostility or suspicion, but a near adventitious consequence of changing circumstances.

Determinist explanations of the catastrophe have found favour with historians. The Royalist Edward Hyde insisted at the time that Parliament's 'insolence' and the officers' 'ambition' must soon produce 'schisms', and later advanced the same interpretation in his famous *History of the rebellion.* Among modern scholars, Davies has claimed that 'the relations of the army and parliament were still inimicable [*sic*]', and that 'unsolved problems had already provoked a crisis which the rising merely postponed', while Woolrych maintains that 'the defeat of Booth's rising removed the one serious check on the worsening relations between the army grandees and the Rump'.[1] Divisions, in these accounts, are primarily attributed to malice and ineptitude on Parliament's part, since the Army has been largely exonerated from contemporary charges of insatiable ambition. Worden suggests that 'the rumpers . . . in 1659 devoted themselves to the pleasures of revenge', and so rendered the officers' disgruntlement entirely understandable. Woolrych prefers to emphasise the members' incompetence, asserting that they had 'learnt noth-

---

1 Hyde to Mordaunt, 9 Sept., *CSP* iii. 560–1; Davies, *Restoration*, 144; Woolrych, *England without a king*, 45.

ing' from the interruption, but proceeded to commit political 'suicide' by alienating the Army; Davies, similarly, contended that 'the Rump . . . entirely failed to appreciate its peculiar position' of dependence on the soldiers' allegiance.[2] Parliament's folly, coupled with the insuperable distrust that stemmed from its past humiliation, thus produced a perpetual conflict that led inexorably to its downfall.

Although these assessments afford an attractive, since intelligible, clue to the labyrinthine complexities of 1659, their oversimplifications raise more questions than they resolve. Founded upon the assumption that MPs, as a body, were unthinking and the reconciliation of the spring insincere, most explanations of the crisis ignore the substantial evidence for the successful establishment of a working partnership between the Army and the restored Parliament. When Nathaniel Holmes, preaching the thanksgiving sermon only a week before the debacle, hailed the triple 'Union . . . of Parliament, City, and Army', he was not just indulging in a flight of rhetorical fancy, but celebrating a real alliance that had so far withstood considerable pressure for its collapse. For many of his auditors, and the more numerous readers of the newsbook accounts of the 'mutual congratulations' exchanged at the banquet that followed, the crisis came as a great shock.[3] The breach was not, at first, expected to be permanent: early reports avoided recriminations, smoothing over differences by representing the difficulty as a 'Misunderstanding', and predicting that Parliament would soon return.[4] To understand why militant counsels triumphed suddenly, and permanently, over moderation, it is essential to re-examine the sequence of events after Booth's rising without the distortion of determinism.

The decisive defeat of the rebellion left Parliament in a much stronger position than before. Enthusiastic republicans acclaimed the victory as fresh proof of the divine blessing upon its wise counsels, and the corresponding curse of the Stuarts; damaging counter-blasts from the now demoralised Royalist and Presbyterian writers virtually ceased.[5] Even the habitual sceptic Bordeaux remarked that Parliament 'appears in a great confidence, with some foundation'.[6] Irksome security measures were relaxed, while disbandment of the costly new militia and volunteer forces began. Sequestration of rebel property, together with the new bill for a £100,000 assessment, held out some hope of alleviating the financial problems. By exposing enemies, the insur-

---

[2] Worden, *Rump Parliament*, 340; Woolrych, *England*, 44; Davies, *Restoration*, 109.

[3] Holmes, *Sermon*, 37; *PI*, no. 197, 3–10 Oct., 777; *Post*, no. 23, 4–11 Oct., 186.

[4] *Occurrences*, no. 30, 11–18 Oct., 392; *A Particular Advice*, no. 31, 14–21 Oct., 399–400; *A DECLARATION OF THE PROCEEDINGS Of the Parliament & Army*, 7.

[5] Such republican responses include *An answer of some . . . citizens*, 7; *A Bloudy FIGHT Between the Parliaments Forces, and Sir GEORGE BOOTH'S*, 5; *Politicus*, no. 584, 24 Aug.–1 Sept., 688; *PI*, 15–22 Aug., 674; Rogers, *Diapoliteia*, 122. In the six weeks that followed Booth's defeat, Thomason collected only 4 conservative tracts, as opposed to 47 in the previous 3 months.

[6] Bordeaux to Mazarin, 25 Aug., Guizot, *Histoire*, i. 470.

rection offered new opportunities, not only to demonstrate republican justice, through the trials for which the council was gathering evidence, but to cement Parliament's authority at the grassroots by weeding out disaffected magistrates. The ending of the emergency also gave Parliament greater leisure for diplomacy, Scotland and Ireland.[7] On 22 August Bordeaux, who had been suspected in some quarters of deliberately waiting on the outcome of the rising, finally received audience, with 'nothing omitted . . . that might represent a magnificent respect'; the Venetian representative hastened to submit his own application for audience.[8] Success had visibly enhanced Parliament's prestige, at home and abroad, and in so doing increased the self-assurance of the members, who were more determined than ever to defend their authority against all opposers.

Victory did not, however, create harmony. Quite the contrary: it raised new problems and reduced the necessity for unanimity. Within two weeks of the tidings of Booth's defeat, the members divided sharply over the best means of safeguarding their authority in future. As the rebellion had revealed treacherous inclinations on the part of some officers in the ordinary militia and even a few MPs, Sir Arthur Hesilrig urged the imposition of a new engagement of loyalty to 'this Commonwealth' against any single person, and pushed it through two readings.[9] When, three days later, this oath was presented for subscription by the members, Hesilrig met vehement resistance from Sir Henry Vane. On 7 September Archibald Johnston heard that 'the greatest heats that could be in words' had passed between them; ten days later the Royalist Secretary Nicholas gleefully relayed reports that they had almost come to blows. Though hostile observers frequently attributed Vane's opposition to Fifth Monarchist fears of abjuring the kingship of Christ, there were few Fifth Monarchist sympathisers among the members; as a whole Parliament was 'mightely devyded' over the oath.[10] A more compelling reason to reject the new engagement was almost certainly its undoubted tendency to divide and discourage the 'well-affected' in the Army and the provinces. Fifth Monarchists were likely to refuse, and Quakers certain, as were any who apprehended that it might commit them to the imperfect interim Commonwealth at the expense of the better constitution that they desired. The experience of resistance to the oath required of councillors, judges, JPs and other officials in the spring hardly augured well for its successor; the grandees, in particular, had then announced conscientious objections and, according to

---

[7] These are discussed in chs 6 and 7 above.

[8] *WI*, no. 16, 16–22 Aug., 128; *CSPVen.*, 40–1, 64.

[9] *Journal*, 774. The Engagement arose in the context of Parliament's regulation of the ordinary militia, which was to replace the disbanded new militia. The most notoriously disloyal member was Peter Brook, captured in the rebellion.

[10] *Johnston diary*, 134–5; MS Carte 213, fos 313, 301; Guizot, *Histoire*, i. 445. Johnston gives no reason for the furore; the Royalists and Bordeaux stress Fifth Monarchist principles.

Bordeaux, actively supported Vane now. Troublesome to 'tender consciences', oaths were equally notorious for their failure to bind the unprincipled. Whatever his exact reasoning, Vane secured a compromise: the engagement was not subscribed but referred to a committee, where it rested pending a decision on that other controversial issue, the government.[11]

The spectacular clash over the proposed engagement has traditionally been treated as a symptom of the inevitable resurgence of deep-seated factional strife over the future shape of the government that had been momentarily muffled by the emergency. Davies went still further, highlighting republican irresponsibility by stating – inaccurately – that Vane's quarrel with Hesilrig took place at the time 'when the need for unity was greatest'.[12] But such representations overlook the close collaboration, even esteem, between these men until this juncture, and obscure the contingent nature of the incident.[13] Though this Parliament had a history of resorting to engagements in moments of stress, there was nothing programmatic about Hesilrig's decision to introduce one at this point, or Vane's implacable opposition – he had, after all, raised no audible objection to the similar requirement in the spring.[14] The issue of the government, supposedly the real bone of contention, occasioned no such uproar: despite their differences, MPs had debated it amicably on six days during the past month, and quietly proceeded, on 8 September, to appoint a committee to prepare a constitution.[15] Nor were coherent factions led by Vane and Hesilrig visible in the acrimonious debate of 6 September: Johnston learned that 'Nevil and uthers' were not only committed to neither, but actually 'jeering at their division and taking advantage of it'.[16] The true significance of the dispute was twofold. As the first quarrel to become public knowledge, it diminished Parliament's standing with outsiders, and afforded monarchists the encouraging intelligence that two important leaders were at odds.[17] More seriously, it left a legacy of antago-

11 *Journal*, 774; *Johnston diary*, 135; Army newsletter, 10 Sept., MS Clarke 31, fo. 213.
12 Davies, *Restoration*, 146. For other determinist interpretations of the quarrel see Hutton, *Restoration*, 63, and Worden, 'Introduction', 110.
13 Vane and Hesilrig had collaborated at least since Richard's assembly, where their closeness had led one dissatisfied member to accuse Hesilrig of trying 'to make himself and Vane the great Hogen-Mogens to rule the Commonwealth': *Burton diary*, iv. 221. Hesilrig there praised Vane's perceptiveness and administrative skills: ibid. iii. 442–3. Their partnership in this Parliament is considered in ch. 3 above; most recently, they had jointly interrogated Booth.
14 Vane had, however, avoided taking the oath or declaring its tenor himself, a point considered more fully in ch. 3 above.
15 *Journal*, 747, 752, 760, 766, 769, 771, 774, 775. August's debates on the government had seen nothing like the clashes between Vane and Neville in June.
16 *Johnston diary*, 135.
17 Thus Nicholas rejoiced that 'its certain that Sir H Vane and Hasslerig do not agree': MS Carte 213, fo. 313. Until news of the quarrel reached him, Hyde had bracketed these two leaders together, regretting the Royalists' inability to persuade Lambert 'that his interest will be better provided for . . . under the King than under Sir H Vane and Sir A Hesilrig': CSP iii. 561.

nism and suspicion that survived the submergence of the specific issue. Divisions followed in the House much more frequently in the remainder of September, and even started to occur in the council, where they had previously been almost unknown.[18] On major political and religious questions, members of the government began to cluster around opposite poles represented by Hesilrig and Vane. Bordeaux detected a conflict between 'true republicans' and an uneasy coalition of millennarians and ambitious ex-Cromwellian officers; Johnston agonised between the two, lamenting that Hesilrig's 'party is mor for ordinances and against Quakers, but less for godly men; and Sir Henry Vane mor for godly men but lesse for ordinances'. Johnston's perplexity, confided to his diary as late as 3 October, illustrates the ongoing fluidity of the situation, and the difficulty of the decision that faced individuals.[19]

That a pattern aligning Vane and the grandees against Hesilrig began to develop was not, of course, the simple consequence of the Engagement controversy. Background, temperament and principle were also significant. Johnston's dilemma demonstrates the ongoing distance between Vane's esoteric antiformalism and Hesilrig's more conventionally clerical Christianity. Such contrasting religious views had contributed to their conflicts in Parliament's previous session, and now resurfaced with the issues of toleration and ecclesiastical settlement.[20] Political preferences also separated them. Whereas Hesilrig inclined to a modified version of Harrington's constitution, Vane envisaged a commonwealth requiring voluntary co-operation from all those eligible to participate. He therefore pursued consensus in practice as well as theory, extending recognition and trust to repentant ex-Protectorians, whose supreme representatives were, of course, the senior officers, especially Lambert, with whom he had established good relations. Diplomatic and conciliatory, Vane's personality exactly suited the role of eirenical republican apologist. Though Hesilrig had participated in the endeavour to win the Army, proclaiming his forgiveness of those guilty of the 1653 expulsion, he never forgot that ambitious officers might again menace the civil authority.[21]

---

[18] There were 9 divisions in the remaining three weeks of September, as opposed to 3 in the month preceding that point. The first council division had occurred on 30 Aug.; a second followed on 13 Sept. In general, however, council decision-making remained consensual.

[19] Guizot, *Histoire*, i. 441–2; *Johnston*, 139.

[20] Roger Williams, Vane's ally in the cause of toleration, had in April 1653 remarked that 'we stand as two armies ready to engage', with Hesilrig and all the Independent and Presbyterian ministers on the opposing side: *Letters of Roger Williams, 1632–1682*, ed. J. R. Bartlett, Providence, RI 1874, 255. Vane confessed himself a 'backe friend' to the clergy, and dissented from even the 'most Refined' religious forms: *Letters to Oliver Cromwell*, 84; Vane, *Meditations*, title. Hesilrig supported 'moderate Presbytery': *Burton diary*, iv. 336.

[21] There is much evidence of Hesilrig's promotion of reconciliation with the Army and professions of forgiveness in his speeches in Richard's parliament. See, for examples, *Burton diary*, iii. 26–7, 99, 258, 316.

Hesilrig's suspicious nature and abrasive manner could irritate even trusted comrades, and certainly did not inspire confidence in his ostensibly reconciled military colleagues. While Ludlow counted both men among his 'good friends', he would remember Vane as 'a polititian truely pious and a Christian truly politique', but characterise Hesilrig as 'a man of a disobliging carriage, sower and morose of temper, liable to be transported with passion and to whom liberality seemed to be a vice'.[22] Despite these defects, Hesilrig, like Vane, was a powerful orator and an astute parliamentary manager. Where he led, many MPs followed: when he served as teller, Hesilrig, unlike Vane, was never in the minority.[23] The increasing advocacy of hardline republican courses by this influential and often impetuous figure was no minor factor in the gathering crisis.

But Hesilrig's growing distrust of the grandees was more than an irrational freak of temper: it was also nourished by a series of circumstances that seemed to justify his suspicion. Doubts sown by the officers' negative initial reactions to their new commissions and the Indemnity Act were reinforced by their behaviour after the rebellion. Retrospective narratives, from the statements of Whitelocke and Rugg that the officers were 'heightened' or 'a litle flushed with that victory' to the bitter charges that they were given to 'trumpeting their own honour and the great valour they shewed at Winnington bridge', agreed that – as so often after victory – the Army's mood underwent a perceptible change.[24] Stronger evidence for the alteration may be found in its few contemporary pronouncements. Lambert's official report of the rout of Booth's forces closely resembled letters from Cromwell on similar occasions: introducing the result as a fresh manifestation of 'the good hand of Providence', he insisted that his soldiers had had their 'former courage encreased by seeing the presence of God with them'. In the petition drawn up by his officers at Derby a few weeks later, the positive implications of this new success were still more clearly spelt out: as the 'late view of his appearances as of old' extended hope that God had pardoned their 'provocations', the rejoicing petitioners called for more rapid progress towards settlement. More generous in its apportionment of the blessing, the London officers' *Humble Representation* to Parliament would express the same delighted interpretation of the victory, declaring that 'to our great encouragement the Lord hath once

---

[22] *Ludlow memoirs*, ii. 103; *Voyce*, 314; *Ludlow memoirs*, ii. 133. Contemporary evidence of Ludlow's regard for both Vane and Hesilrig is in a letter to his 'deare friend' Scot of 30 Aug.: MS Clarendon 64, fo. 109.

[23] During the restored Parliament's lifetime, Hesilrig was teller on 7 occasions, losing only once, when the two sides were equal and the Speaker's casting vote went to his opponents. Vane was four times a teller, and was decisively defeated once.

[24] Whitelocke, *Memorials*, iv. 361; *The diurnal of Thomas Rugg*, ed. W. L. Sachse (Camden 3rd ser. xci, 1961), 6; *True relation of the . . . case*, 3. On the changes that earlier victories, especially Worcester, had wrought in the Army's temper see Worden, *Rump Parliament*.

more appeared to own You and Your Army & the good old Cause'.[25] Gone was the chastened, introspective frame that had marked the public repentance of the spring; in its place had come a renewed confidence in the Army's God-given mission, and a conviction that it was necessary to improve this latest mercy by pursuing a suitably righteous settlement.[26]

Although the Army's new-found self-assertiveness was far from welcome to MPs determined to control the eventual constitution, it was not the only disquieting consequence of the rebellion. Victory had also enhanced the prestige of the officers, above all Lambert, the cleverest and most charismatic, who had commanded the expeditionary force. The officers' quest for appropriate recognition bred suspicion. Parliament was very willing to encourage its servants by acknowledging their merits: on receiving Lambert's dispatch reporting the surrender of Chester, it readily sent a letter of thanks and £1,000 to buy a jewel – a liberal sum, given the parlous state of the finances. Subsequently lesser payments were allotted to various other officers whom he had recommended.[27] It was not the principle, but the type of reward that was contentious. Bordeaux heard that the House had rejected a proposal to restore Lambert's old rank of major-general; subsequent accounts claimed that this suggestion had been put forward by Fleetwood and scotched by Hesilrig.[28] As it left no trace in the *Journal*, it is improbable that it was ever seriously entertained by the members, who had consistently declined to promote the grandees, leaving Fleetwood himself as a lieutenant-general, though commander-in-chief. Hitherto this policy, strongly advocated by hardline republicans anxious to prevent any officer from becoming too powerful, had not produced any visible discontent in the Army. Now that Lambert had once more proved his ability and loyalty, at least some of his closest subordinates expressed resentment of the refusal of promotion. Early in September, one Royalist claimed to have been present at Lady Lambert's when Major Creed 'her husbands great confidant fell foul upon the parliament for detaining him his old commissions of Major General and said he knew no reason why he should depend upon them [for] any command and much more and higher'.[29] While this story may well be exaggerated – Creed was, after all, one of the officers whom Parliament had just rewarded for their part in the campaign – the question of Lambert's rank would recur at intervals until he finally assumed the title of major-general after the dissolution, and so

---

25 Lambert's letter was printed in *Politicus*, no. 584, 18–25 Aug., 681–4; *Armies proposalls*, 1; officers' *Representation*, 3.
26 So obvious was the change in the Army's mood that Henry Reece suggests that victory 'radically altered its self-image', and draws a parallel with the situation after Worcester: 'Military presence', 250. This may be going a little too far: as the Army's enemies hastened to point out, the threat from Booth, with his fellow conspirators so effectively forestalled, was nothing like as great as the king's invasion with foreign aid.
27 *Journal*, 766, 769.
28 Guizot, *Histoire*, i. 469; *Ludlow memoirs*, ii. 115; *True relation*, 7.
29 This anonymous letter is dated 12 Sept., MS Carte 213, fo. 301.

lent credence to conjecture that he had always been eager to advance himself at the expense of Parliament's authority.

In the aftermath of the rising, Lambert's conduct did nothing to dispel such hostile surmises. Monarchists and diplomats avidly repeated rumours that Hesilrig, Fleetwood and even Vane were 'jealous of his design to make himself chief magistrate'.[30] Like Cromwell before him, Lambert was popular with the soldiers, and concerned for their material welfare, appealing to Parliament for better provision in his public letters.[31] Nor did Lambert stop at words: he reinforced his popularity by distributing his own financial reward among his underpaid troops, a generous but, from Parliament's viewpoint, scarcely a reassuring gesture.[32] The fear that Lambert, the original architect of the *Instrument of Government*, was plotting to become the next Lord Protector gained further credence from his prolonged absence in the north without a word of explanation. On 29 August the council resolved to recall both Lambert and Disbrow, who had been sent to the west; in a second letter to Lambert five days later, the council reiterated its desire for his presence.[33] Disbrow had returned by 5 September; the newsbooks and Giavarina that week represented Lambert's arrival as imminent.[34] Yet he lingered at Derby, releasing captured rebels on security – a practical rather than liberal policy that might nevertheless occasion suspicion of a 'design for himself' – and did not reach London until the 20 September.[35] Though these weeks should not be perceived as a period of ever-increasing alarm – even a Royalist admitted that a 'very great calm' had reigned for the past fortnight – the subsequent reactions of Hesilrig, and Parliament, must be seen in the light of the real anxieties fostered by what can only be understood as Lambert's imprudence.[36]

Until 22 September anxieties over Lambert's intentions could be dismissed as largely groundless. On that day, however, Hesilrig triumphantly

---

[30] Nicholas to Jones, 20 Sept., *CSPD 1659*, 234. See also ibid. 188; MS Carte 213, fo. 301; Guizot, *Histoire*, i. 473; and *CSPVen.*, 65, 71.

[31] *Politicus*, no. 584, 18–25 Aug., 684; no. 585, 24 Aug.–1 Sept., 696.

[32] After the dissolution, Lambert's enemies openly denounced this gesture as an attempt to divorce the soldiers' affections from Parliament and make them his 'Janissaries': see, for example, *The ARMIES DECLARATION Examined . . . Discovering some of their Contradictions, Lies, Calumnies, Hypocrisie and Designs*, 12. No contemporary articulation of such fears is extant.

[33] SP 25/98, fos 173, 185.

[34] Disbrow was back in council on 5 Sept., and received its thanks the following day. Lambert's impending arrival was reported in *PI*, no. 192, 29 Aug.–5 Sept., 700, and by Giavarina on 9 Sept.: *CSPVen.*, 68.

[35] On 12 Sept. a Royalist reported that Lambert's 'unwonted generosity' to defeated enemies was occasioning such suspicion: MS Carte 213, fo. 301. Several prisoners liberated by warrants from Lambert at Derby are among those reported to the council by Chester's governor, Col. Croxton, who promised to rearrest them if necessary, but defended the expediency of this policy, and urged action to settle the fate of the remaining prisoners, who gave him 'great trouble': MS Clarendon 64, fo. 70.

[36] [?] Rumbold to Hyde, 25 Sept., *CSP* iii. 568–9.

unveiled the first tangible evidence of a 'dangerous design among some in the Army' to elevate a new single person: the petition signed by fifty members of Lambert's Northern Brigade at Derby.[37] This document, in fact, expressed no treasonable ambitions. Addressing 'the Supream Authority' with all proper respect, the officers grounded their advice upon first-hand experience of both the latest providential deliverance and the remaining problems. Parliament's prerogative was, however, invaded by the specific requests for the permanent appointment of Fleetwood, Lambert, Disbrow and Monck as general officers, and the revival of the Army's *Humble Petition*, which had asked for a 'select Senate' of the most eminent and godly. While the officers sweetened this demand by recalling that Parliament had 'unanimously and cheerfully' accepted the Army's earlier address, their unequivocal insistence that this was the 'best and only expedient yet offered . . . to a happy and durable settlement' was certain to displease the many MPs who favoured alternative republican forms.[38] Other requests, including those for the investigation and removal of 'neutral magistrates', the punishment of aiders and abettors of the rebellion and the regulation of corporations to empower the 'well-affected', revealed a just appreciation of the dangers of local disaffection, but an impatient assumption that the lack of instant action implied that Parliament was ignorant or indifferent. Distance from Westminster encouraged this misapprehension. Even as the officers prepared their proposals, the House had been busy with the annulment of Chester's charter and had begun to contemplate general corporation reform.[39] To observers in London, Parliament's negative response to the Derby officers' seemingly presumptuous, and superfluous intervention was therefore quite predictable.

Given the controversial contents of the Derby petition, it is hardly surprising that it found no favour with the godly but weak-willed Fleetwood, who was deeply perturbed. Rather than recommend it to the General Council of the London officers, as its signatories had desired, Fleetwood sought advice from the stronger minds of his trusted colleagues in Parliament and council: showing the covering letter to Hesilrig, he requested further discussion with Vane and the latter's close ally, Richard Salway. Hesilrig naturally had no desire to invoke the assistance of Vane, who was already suspected of collusion with Lambert.[40] Nor did he wait to read the petition. Instead, armed with the electrifying intelligence of what Lambert had been up to during his mysterious absence, Hesilrig hastened to the House, had the

---

[37] *Journal*, 784; *A DECLARATION OF THE GENERAL COUNCIL Of The Officers . . .*, *27th Octob. 1659*, 8. The Derby petition was published after the interruption as the *Armies proposalls* to Parliament.

[38] *Armies proposalls*, 3, 2; officers' *Humble petition*, 14.

[39] *Armies proposalls*, 3–5; *Journal*, 780. These moves towards local government reform are considered in ch. 5 above.

[40] For the suspicions circulating concerning Vane's alliance with Lambert see especially *Mordaunt letter book*, 48, 65; Guizot, *Histoire*, i. 485.

doors closed, and secured orders extracting both the originals and Fleetwood's copy from Wallingford House.[41] That afternoon Johnston found the council meeting cancelled because Parliament was holding an extraordinary session in 'great heate' over the petition, which Fleetwood obediently produced. Though none of them personally witnessed the debates of 22 and 23 September, all contemporary commentators emphasised their furious character. According to Johnston, Lambert's enemies called for his confinement in the Tower, comparing the Derby petition to Adonijah's apparently innocent but actually treasonable suit to Solomon.[42] While Lambert and his supporters protested his entire ignorance, it was, and is, incredible that he could have been in the area without some knowledge of what was happening.[43]

The intensity of the distrust aroused by the Derby petition may be gauged from the fierce reaction of hardline republicans, who rushed to extend the debate into the public arena by printing. On 23 September Thomason acquired a brief pamphlet entitled A GENERAL Or, No GENERAL Over The Present Army, which Johnston accurately judged a set of 'very bitter queries', whose circulation inflamed tensions still further. Tracing all the trouble to the old complaint that Parliament had entrusted commands to Cromwellians rather than 'faithful Adherers' of the Commonwealth, these queries seized upon the new request for a general as the ultimate proof that those in 'greatest Trust' had 'so much Ambition that they [could not] be stayed Six Months from a ravenous persuite after Power and Honour'. To promote divisions within the Army, the writer declared that Fleetwood's 'Honesty and Integrity' placed him above suspicion, and heaped all the blame upon Lambert. After explaining why a general was the 'most dangerous Undertaking' possible, the pamphlet summoned the soldiers to prove their 'Commonwealth Principles' by adhering to Parliament. Indeed, it went so far

---

[41] Journal, 784–5; Armys plea, 15–16; Declaration of the General Council, 7–8; A REMON-STRANCE And DECLARATION . . . Setting Forth The . . . Grounds of the putting a stop . . . to the Sitting of the late PARLIAMENT, 5; Ludlow memoirs, ii. 134–5. As not only Ludlow but all the near-contemporary justifications of the Army recount this sequence of events, there seems no reason to follow Hutton in dismissing the 'charge that Fleetwood deliberately betrayed the documents to Hesilrig': Restoration, 311. Army sources insisted that the betrayal was not Fleetwood's disclosure but Hesilrig's instant recourse to Parliament 'contrary to expectation and all ingenuity': Declaration, 8.

[42] Johnston diary, 137–8 (the biblical reference is to I Kings ii.13–25); CSPVen., 74; Guizot, Histoire, i. 477–8, 484; MS Clarendon 65, fo. 95. Reports of such 'reproachful speeches' also reached the officers, who repeated them in their post-interruption defences; cf. Armys plea, 16–17; Remonstrance and declaration, 6.

[43] The most convincing denial of Lambert's knowledge is that of Col. Mitchell, in a letter written at Wingeworth, Derbyshire on 24 Sept., before he could have known of the storm raging at London: HMC, Leyborne-Popham MSS, 123. Yet even this is not conclusive: Mitchell admits Lambert's presence in the vicinity, and provides only a summary of the proceedings; conscious of the need for caution, he urged his correspondent to drop a 'quiet hint' to Monck. Even if Lambert, like Monck, was not officially informed, it is incredible that subordinates close to him would not have dropped some hint of their activities and obtained at least tacit countenance.

as to challenge the members to test 'their Authority' by openly confronting disloyal grandees and calling for assistance from the faithful. The conclusion commended this provocative course by exploiting Parliament's highly developed sense of its own importance, and excluding the possibility of compromise: the only alternative was to 'stoop to receive Laws from the Servants of the Commonwealth'.[44]

Extreme counsels did not, however, prevail with Parliament. To many members Lambert remained a trusted figure, who had just two days ago received the council's thanks for his 'Extraordinary service'; on the morrow he confirmed his submission by surrendering his special commission and reporting on his activities.[45] Closer scrutiny of the petition that day had convinced a narrow majority, led by Vane and Fleetwood, that it should not be declared 'unseasonable and of dangerous consequence'. Vane's eloquence, in particular, did much to restore calm: warning that conflict with the Army would bring 'complete ruin', since 'the regime had no other friends nor support abroad or at home', he argued that the grandees could not be held responsible for all the actions of their inferiors, and that Lambert deserved reward, not punishment. Parliament contented itself with a resolve that more general officers were 'needless chargeable and dangerous', and instructed Fleetwood to 'admonish' the soldiers and prevent further action in 'this irregular proceeding'. This vote affirmed Parliament's authority and tacitly reproved the officers, but was not deliberately provocative, making no radical departure from previous policy. The delegation of enforcement to Fleetwood indirectly confirmed his standing as supreme commander and trusted intermediary between his fellow MPs and the Army.[46]

On the very next day Fleetwood dutifully communicated Parliament's resolves to the officers assembled at Wallingford House. Not only the meagre contemporary reports but the positive result of this meeting disprove retrospective accounts of 'specious promises' emerging from 'debates of the utmost rage and madness'. In fact, the officers' initial reaction was as docile as any but the most extreme republicans could have wished. Far from silently encouraging insubordination among his juniors, as Ludlow's *Memoirs* alleged, Lambert himself disclaimed the Derby petition and dramatically offered to resign for the sake of peace. The London officers readily agreed to drop that divisive document, to which they had never been committed.[47] Instead, they appointed a committee to compose a new address that would assure Parliament of their 'adherence to their Authority . . . in the settlement of this Commonwealth against all disturbances'. Government newsbooks greeted

44 *Johnston diary*, 137; *A GENERAL Or, No GENERAL Over The Present Army*, 5, 6, 8, 7.
45 Council minutes, 20, 23 Sept.
46 *Journal*, 785. Vane's reasoning was reported at length by Bordeaux, who had closer contact with him than with any other republican leaders: Guizot, *Histoire*, i. 478.
47 *Ludlow memoirs*, ii. 135; *Johnston diary*, 138; Bordeaux to Mazarin, 26 Sept., Guizot, *Histoire*, i. 446.

this decision as an indisputable sign of the Army's loyalty: Nedham confidently foretold that the forthcoming address would 'serve abundantly to check the idle Reports and wicked hopes of the Adversary'. Distant officers, including those who had served under Lambert and subscribed the Derby petition, were prepared to acquiesce in its abandonment for the greater goal of Army and republican unity. Even before definite instructions arrived from the capital, Lambert's client, Robert Baynes, reported that his regiment, stationed at York, had voluntarily forborne to send up the signed petition on receiving 'hints of the parliament's displeasure . . . and some demurrers among the officers at London'. The ostensible resolution of the crisis was not lost upon foreigners: Bordeaux apprised his government that though Parliament had been in 'some danger of losing its authority', there now seemed to be neither 'alteration or diversity of opinions between these two bodies, the Army professing desire to remain firm in the interests of the Parliament'. On the surface, at least, Parliament had once more succeeded in preserving both its authority and the vital partnership with the officers.[48]

Beneath the surface, however, the republican alliance had been weakened. Anger and distrust, once voiced, were not instantly forgotten, but stimulated further suspicion. As Parliament's prestige rose with the officers' submission, so, too, did speculation regarding its intentions. In government circles Johnston encountered many who commented that 'Parliament was very high and the Airmy very low' and predicted that its policies 'would break this Airmy in peeces be tyme and keepe them from being fixed in heads and leaders that might disturb the Parliament'. Such talk, however popular with hardline republicans, was scarcely calculated to reassure the officers, who feared divisions and resented the unjust aspersions cast upon their leaders. Rumours of their discontent and the insincerity of their acquiescence ran rife. Johnston observed that 'som thinks it sticks in the stomak of sundry officers, this evening of Lambert to the Tower and uther officers to hanging', while Bordeaux noticed sceptics who dismissed the Army's submission as a 'palliative measure' temporarily adopted by the grandees to placate the 'large party' among the junior officers who favoured a 'true republic'. Royalists, as usual, repeated the most encouraging gossip, and claimed that another dissolution was imminent.[49]

In this climate of suspicion and uncertainty, the nervous MPs, awaiting the Army's promised petition, began to consider precautions. On 28 September an enacting clause making it treason to collect any taxes without Parliament's assent was read twice as an appendage to the act to continue the customs and excise. This was an obvious attempt to impede any usurping government by depriving it of legal revenue. Though the clause was withdrawn, Parliament

---

[48] *PI*, no. 195, 19–26 Sept., 748; Robert Baynes to Adam Baynes, 27 Sept., MS Add. 21425, fo. 141; Guizot, *Histoire*, i. 446.

[49] *Johnston diary*, 138; Bordeaux to Brienne, 26 Sept., Guizot, *Histoire*, i. 478. For Royalist predictions see especially *CSPD 1659*, 234; *Mordaunt letter book*, 50, 54; *CSP* iii. 568–9.

ordered the assiduous lawyer Augustine Garland to make it the subject of a separate bill. When the House was called two days later, ex-major-general Thomas Harrison, who had, next to Cromwell, played the leading role in the expulsion of 1653, was discharged as an MP and 'disabled forever' from election. This gesture had no practical consequences, since Harrison, who had lived in retirement ever since his breach with Cromwell, had never shown any interest in regaining his commission or his seat. It was, however, a clear warning to serving officers of the consequences of disloyalty: the same treatment had recently been meted out to Peter Brook for his part in Booth's rebellion.[50]

But MPs did not just resort to threats: they also sought to regain the Army's trust, offering inducements to loyalty. Contrary to the supposition of Davies, there was no 'mutual antipathy' between civilians and soldiers. Republican leaders such as Hesilrig and Scot were first committed to the efficient defence of the state, and had willingly trusted Lambert with two regiments earlier in the year. Even now, as their suspicions of the grandees grew, these members remained as willing as they had been in Richard's parliament to provide for the just concerns of a properly subordinate Army.[51] Thus the House, on 4 October, allocated revenues for the payment of arrears, and ordered a report on the needs of widows and disabled soldiers to be made on the morrow. The same day the constitutional committee reversed the previous week's rejection of a 'fundamental of Toleration', resolving that the 'Supream delegated power' was 'not intrusted to restrain' Trinitarians who accepted 'the holy Scriptures' as 'the revealed or written Word of God'. All such were to receive 'due protection and equal encouragement', unless guilty of 'civil injury . . . or disturbance of others'. This resolution mirrored the relevant clause in the Army's May Petition, to which Parliament had then agreed; the only difference was the omission of the standard exception for Catholics and episcopalians. Unlike the committee's other decisions, it was published in Politicus, to assure the widest possible audience of the falsehood of the damaging charge, formerly brought by Cromwell, and now the subject of 'many . . . Rumors', that Parliament threatened liberty of conscience.[52]

The resolve effectively excluding the future civil authority from the religious sphere was a victory for Vane, who had consistently advocated this course throughout the 1650s. Nor was this his sole success. Although the constitutional committee, chaired by Whitelocke, represented every shade of

---

[50] Journal, 788, 790, 778.
[51] Davies, Restoration, 146. For the republican assurances in Richard's parliament see, especially, Hesilrig's speeches recorded in Burton diary, iii. 26–7, 56–7. Republican concilatoriness in that assembly is analysed in Hirst, 'Concord and discord'.
[52] Journal, 791; Johnston diary, 138; Politicus, no. 590, 6–13 Oct., 792. The importance of such charges, and the limited nature of Cromwellian toleration schemes, which were much less extensive than those of Parliament's committee, are demonstrated in Blair Worden's essay, 'Toleration and the Cromwellian Protectorate', in W. J. Sheils (ed.), Persecution and toleration (Studies in Church History xxi, 1984), 199–233.

opinion in the House, it adopted several elements of Vane's 'new Model'.[53] This carefully omitted controversial specifics like the senate and extent of the electorate in order to establish agreement on vital principles. September saw gradual advances towards a limited, representative government. Successive resolutions affirmed that the 'Supream . . . Power' was 'delegated' by the people 'for their preservation, not for their Destruction', and must be restrained in exercise by 'some Fundamentals not dispensed with'. Of these, toleration was the second, the first being comprehensive rejection of 'any earthly King or single person whomsoever', together with every 'Hereditary claim', as 'destructive to the peoples Right and true Freedom, unto which by Gods blessing they are now restored'.[54] Designed to attract both secular and millennarian republicans, this fundamental incorporated the Common-wealth's original motto, devised by Marten in 1649, and now signalling not merely the recovery of mythical ancient liberties but the recent deliverance from the Protectorate. Despite formulation in neo-Leveller terms, encour-aging those of this persuasion to believe that 'we are now in a hopefull way of settling a Commonwealth', the committee's resolutions did not endorse any one brand of republicanism to the exclusion of others, except perhaps rigid Harringtonians.[55] There is no evidence of a return to the 1653 plan for 'regular, unicameral parliaments', which was also the Levellers' preferred solution. The precise composition of both 'the People' and their 'Trustees' remained undecided.[56] A preliminary report was ready by 5 October, but the

[53] So described by witnesses at Vane's trial, who accurately summarised three of the committee's four resolutions, including that against kingship, and affirmed that he gave 'Reasons to maintain them'. Vane, significantly, did not attempt to deny these allegations: *The TRYAL Of Sir Henry Vane*, 1662, 30. The resolutions were entirely consistent with his proposal for a supreme legislature restrained by certain 'fundamental . . . conditions': *Healing question*, 20.

[54] The full list of the committee's resolutions, with the dates of their adoption, was published in *The REMONSTRANCE And PROTESTATION Of the Well-affected People . . . Against Those Officers . . . Who . . . interrupted the PARLIAMENT the 13th of Octob. 1659. And against all pretended Powers . . . that is not established by Parliament*, 4. This pamphlet was not collected by Thomason, and seems to have escaped historical notice. Though Rugg condemned it as a 'false remonstrance' (*Rugg's diurnal*, 11–12), and the concluding list of 450 quality supporters of Parliament may well be spurious, the account of the committee's resolves tallies with both the one previously published on toleration and the subsequent testimony at Vane's trial. Had the truth been otherwise, the Army's apolo-gists would surely have attempted to refute this evidence of Parliament's superior care for 'all the indifferent interests'.

[55] *Grand concernments*, 29. Though this pamphlet does not directly allude to the committee, it was largely written during the period of its deliberations, which may well have contributed to its judgement that 'the good of the Nation . . . every day appeared more and more, since this Paper hath been under my pen' (p. 40).

[56] Worden speculates that there was such a return, and that the emphasis on 'delegated' power spelt defeat for Neville and Harrington: 'Oceana: origins', 136. Yet Harrington, too, opposed 'unbounded power' (p. 134), while his followers, especially Neville, had repeatedly shown themselves flexible, and were far from despairing. The resolutions conformed to their rejection of any authority not founded on the 'choyce of the People', and did not

crisis delayed its presentation – indefinitely, as it turned out. Without Parliament's approval, Vane's achievement in committee was vulnerable to challenge.[57]

The progress of constitutional compromise had not healed the rifts among MPs. Hostile observers noted Hesilrig's increasing alignment with Neville and 'Harringtons caball' against Vane and Lambert.[58] On 1 October Hesilrig made a furious attack on Vane in council, shouting 'that he would ruyne the nation, and he desyred never to come in the place wheir he was'. Shortly thereafter, Vane confided to Johnston his suspicion that schemes to widen the basis of consent to the eventual constitution by holding recruiter elections were a subtle means to 'settling the government as Sir Arthur would haive it'. Recruiting the House to eventually become the new senate was, indeed, a key aspect of Hesilrig's preferred model, which would also have affronted the Army by applying strict rotation to military as well as civil officers.[59] Whereas Hesilrig defended the 'absolute power' of Parliament, Vane advocated consultation and harmonious relations with the officers, insisting that MPs should not 'take so much offence at what the airmy did, but settle the government with their consent'.[60] Yet the outcome was still far from certain. No open breach had occurred, and many expected none. Outwardly, the republicans remained united: loyal newsbooks made much of the City's respectful invitation of MPs, councillors and officers to a banquet following the thanksgiving for the defeat of the rebellion.[61] On 4 October Johnston recorded that some, especially Vane and Salway, were predicting agreement, but darkly reflected that providence was already restraining and might 'yet agayn break Parliament by the Airmy'. Much would depend upon the content and reception of the address that the Council of Officers had just resolved upon.[62]

---

exclude the investiture of the 'supreme Legislative Authority' in a 'Senate and Representative': *Model of a democratical government*, 8, 3.

57 *Journal*, 791. On 12 Oct. the report was scheduled for the fateful 13th.

58 *Mordaunt letter book*, 48, 65. Hesilrig's *rapprochement* with Neville is also implied in Bordeaux's report of 3 Oct. that 'true republicans', reputedly Presbyterian, dominated Parliament, and opposed a saintly faction more powerful in the Army: Guizot, *Histoire*, i. 480–1. Whitelocke afterwards recalled that 'Haslerigge, Nevil and their friends . . . eagerly' promoted antimilitarist measures: *Memorials*, iv. 361–2.

59 *Johnston diary*, 139; *Model*, 4, 10. Parliament debated recruiter elections on 1 and 3 Oct., when the constitutional committee was ordered to consider the number, distribution and qualifications of the recruitees: *Journal*, 791. Bordeaux noted the opposition of the 'Army party' to recruiter elections that might fill the House with Presbyterians: Guizot, *Histoire*, i. 491.

60 *Johnston diary*, 139.

61 The invitation and its acceptance made headline news in both *WI*, no. 22, 27 Sept.–4 Oct. and its rival the *Post*, and was prominently displayed in *PI*, no. 196, 26 Sept.–3 Oct., 764.

62 *Johnston diary*, 140.

The officers, like the members, were far from united.[63] Whereas the May petition had been drawn up and agreed within five days, the committee appointed on 24 September took that long just to compose its successor.[64] When a draft was finally presented to the General Council, it sparked 'high and hott debaytes'. Johnston heard that Hesilrig, present in his capacity as colonel, had contended vehemently for Parliament's supremacy against other officers who declared that they were 'imployed against arbitrary government in whatsoever'. Several, including the influential councillor of state and Colonel James Berry, another ex-Cromwellian, expressed strong resentment of Hesilrig's response to the Derby petition, and taxed him with 'accusing the Airmye wrongouslye'.[65] Hesilrig was not, however, without high-ranking defenders: not only his fellow MP and Colonel Herbert Morley but Okey, Saunders and Alured, republicans who had remonstrated with Cromwell, and other colonels such as Moss and Hacker affirmed the duty of subjection to Parliament. Amongst the juniors, Saunders's friend Captain Clement Nedham shared Hesilrig's conviction that the officers on the committee had exceeded their instructions by seeking to 'impose and limitt the supreame authority of the Nation'; he therefore appealed to Fleetwood to stop the petition. Confronted by these heated arguments, Fleetwood signally failed to provide firm and constructive leadership, advancing the cause of moderation only by feebly exhorting everyone to 'sleepe upon the whol business'. This advice was eventually taken. Next day consensus suddenly emerged: a massive majority of the London officers accepted the new address. It is hard to believe that Fleetwood's prescription accomplished this miraculous turn-about. Rather, we must suppose that the petition had been modified to meet at least some republican objections.[66]

The Army's *Humble Representation and Petition*, presented to Parliament on 5 October, has been variously dismissed by historians as a 'very stiff' or 'very aggressive' document devoid of both 'healing assurances' and humility.[67] But even contemporary monarchists hunting for signs of rebelliousness had to resort to affirming the existence of a hidden meaning: the actual text was 'so

---

[63] Massarella estimates that the officers were more divided at this point than at any other since 1647: 'Politics of the Army', 610.

[64] That petition, dated the 12 May, must have been composed within five days of Parliament's return. Though Nedham originally predicted that the September committee would have a draft ready within three days, he did not report its completion until 1 October: *PI*, no. 195, 19–26 Sept., 748; no. 196, 26 Sept.–3 Oct., 764.

[65] *Johnston diary*, 139; *CSP* iii. 573–4; Guizot, *Histoire*, i. 484.

[66] Clement Nedham to Fleetwood, 4 Oct., MS Sloane 4165, fos 31–2; *Johnston diary*, 139–40. Johnston heard that the petition was accepted by 400:3 votes; the printed title claimed that it had been signed by 230 officers. Bordeaux, in a letter written immediately before the General Council first met, reported that the petition contained demands for reprisals against MPs who had inveighed against the Army, but predicted modifications by the 'true republicans': Guizot, *Histoire*, i. 484.

[67] Davies, *Restoration*, 149; Hutton, *Restoration*, 65; Woolrych, 'Introduction', 113, 114.

misteriously . . . penned', or 'drawne up with so much artifice that some looke upon it as a Complyance'.[68] In fact, the *Representation* was a masterpiece of moderation that skilfully promoted the 'Cordial and Affectionate Agreement and Union of the Parliament and Army' whereon the Republic's security depended. The officers identified the chief threat to that unity as the recent efforts of certain unnamed persons to 'beget mis-understanding' by misrepresenting the Army's aims and actions. Though Hutton has claimed the contrary, this address carefully refrained from criticising MPs or demanding reprisals; casting a veil of oblivion over the past, the petitioners merely asked for the punishment of anyone 'creating jealousies and casting scandalous imputations' in future.[69] To clear the air, the London officers vigorously asserted their own and the Derby petitioners' 'faithfulness and integrity to the Parliament and this Commonwealth', and explicitly denied allegations that they were plotting another 'interruption' or the 'setting up of any Single Person whatsoever'. Ardently as they protested their own innocence, the petitioners expressed deep respect for Parliament, humbly presenting themselves as its 'faithful servants', who prayed for the divine blessing upon its endeavours to construct a 'well-regulated Commonwealth', whose form they did not presume to prescribe.[70]

In keeping with this humility, the nine specific requests of the petition were not imposed as conditions of allegiance, but merely recommended as means to discourage the Republic's enemies by preserving a 'good understanding'. Most were not controversial: the pleas for provision for 'poor Souldiers', countenance for the officers, especially those who had shown their loyalty in the 'Northern Expedition' and employment for 'well-affected' locals all tallied with policies that Parliament had begun to pursue before the furore over the Derby petition. So, too, did the proposal that no new officers should be appointed without the consent of a Nomination Committee chosen by Parliament, the very method employed throughout the recent purge. Even the suggestion that MPs prevent 'Confusion' in the Army by considering the imminent expiration of its commander's commission was extremely tactful: unlike the Derby petition, the *Representation*'s request list did not even name Fleetwood, much less demand his permanent generalship.[71] More open to misconstruction was the request that officers should only be dismissed by consent or after court-martial. Though this was an attempt to ensure the future stability of the command structure, since all commissions had now been approved by Parliament, dissatisfied republicans

---

[68] These were the reactions of Brasy and Rumbold in reports to Hyde of 7 Oct., MS Clarendon 64, fos 92, 94.

[69] *Representation*, 3, 2, 6. Hutton incorrectly states that the petition demanded 'censure of MPs who had vilified the army': *Restoration*, 65.

[70] *Representation*, 1, 2, 3.

[71] Ibid. 5–9. Fleetwood's commission, by the act of 7 June, was to last for the duration of this Parliament, or till 'further order': *A&O* ii. 1283.

such as Clement Nedham read it as an infringement of prerogative designed to transform the Army into a privileged 'corporation', distinct from the national interest.[72] The officers did, however, affirm their identity with the rest of the English nation by asking freedom from discouragement in the exercise of their 'undoubted Right' as 'Freemen' to petition 'in a peaceable and submissive way'. As Parliament had readily confirmed that liberty of the people, and accepted the Army's first petition in May, this modest request was hardly contentious. The *Representation* concluded with a moving appeal to MPs to maintain a 'good opinion of your Army' and persist in the 'good work', and pledged faithful assistance despite 'all endeavours to the contrary'.[73] It is not surprising that the final version of this document, which so clearly communicated Army concerns and so eloquently pleaded for peace and a right understanding, won support from almost all the officers.[74]

The *Representation* afforded a real opportunity for the recreation of trust. It was presented by a deputation tactfully headed not by Lambert but Disbrow, who made a short speech reiterating the Army's sincere goodwill and submission to Parliament's authority. Having read the petition, a majority of MPs realised the potential for reconciliation. The Speaker returned thanks for the 'good expressions of . . . affections and faithfulness', and replied that the House was already working on the 'speedy' redress of the soldiers' material grievances, and would consider the other requests in three days' time.[75] Harmony seemed restored when MPs and officers, on the morrow, solemnly heard the thanksgiving sermons, which not only celebrated their union but praised the Army as 'excellent servants of the Commonwealth'; afterwards they 'dined altogeather very lovingly' with the City dignitaries.[76] Loyal newsbooks diligently propagated the image of unity: Nedham averred that 'this threefold cord cannot be easily broken' and dismissed 'the vain Reports of many intestine Enemies' to the contrary. The *Weekly Intelligencer* focused on the petition and the answer as a sign that the former differences in the 'Councels' of Parliament and Army were starting to 'concenter', and emphasised both the officers' wholehearted devotion and the 'great Care . . . taken' by MPs 'to content' them. Even the hostile Giavarina, who was obstinately convinced that 'hidden embers [were] waiting for an opportunity to

---

72 *Representation*, 8; Nedham to Fleetwood, 4 Oct., MS Sloane 4165, fos 31–2. Monck, of course, would later raise the same objection. Woolrych sees this proposal as a mere revival of a similar assertion of Army independence during the previous year's agitation against Richard ('Introduction', 115), but this overlooks the purge that had occurred during the interval. The officers did not question Parliament's authority to sanction appointments; they did fear the arbitrary revocation of the new commissions.

73 *Representation*, 6–7, 9.

74 A few republicans still held out: an Army newsletter of 6 Oct. lists 10 dissidents, including Hesilrig's cronies Hacker, Okey, Alured, Saunders and Moss: MS Clarke 32, fo. 5.

75 *Journal*, 792. The May petition, by contrast, had been presented by a group of officers led by both Lambert and Disbrow.

76 Holmes, *Sermon*, 42; *Rugg's diurnal*, 7.

blaze out', admitted that only 'ashes' were currently visible, since the Army's 'complete submission' on several points had quenched the flames of tension.[77]

Moderation, for the moment, had triumphed in Parliament. When the Warwickshire 'well-affected' presented a 'humble petition in all humility' that not only urged 'all due incouragment' for the Army and the 'highest Characters of . . . favour' for the 'chief Officers' but revived the Derby demands for the reformation of local government, the House responded positively, returning thanks for the 'very good affections . . . expressed in it'. Detached from the fear of military interference, there was plainly nothing unacceptable about these requests. The petition, with the answer, was found worthy of publication in the official newsbooks, as a monument to Parliament's good intentions and the loyalty of its subjects.[78] Parliament also advertised its commitment to reform by giving a first reading to a bill for the relief of creditors and poor prisoners, duly highlighted by the *Weekly Intelligencer* as the 'most memorable' event of the day.[79]

On Saturday 8 October MPs began, as they had promised, to consider the *Representation*. When debate resumed on Monday, the first request was answered with the assurance that the officers would now, as formerly, 'receive marks of the favour of the Parliament and Countenance answerable to their faithfulness and merit'. The response to the second proposal, for the punishment of future slanderers, affirmed the 'undoubted right of the Parliament to receive and debate' any 'Informations' offered by MPs or others, provided that they were pursuing their duty to promote the 'publique safety'. This answer indirectly vindicated Hesilrig, who always professed the purest motives, but did not, as some supposed, amount to a flat refusal to prevent misrepresentation; rather, it asserted Parliament's authority to evaluate the evidence, and left no reason to suppose that malicious calumniators would be encouraged.[80] Next morning Marten, as chairman of the committee for the third article, reported a carefully crafted reply. This provided the desired confirmation of the right of all soldiers, as 'freemen of England', to petition, but warned them to exercise it peacefully and cautiously, to eschew requests tending to 'the disturbance of the Commonwealth' or 'the dishonour of the Parliament', and to accept Parliament's judgement. These qualifications were not innovatory, but attempted to prevent further friction by expounding the Army's own allusion to the 'peaceable and submissive way' of proper petitioning. That afternoon MPs accorded a generous answer to the fourth proposal, on material needs: they voted two months' pay to all the forces, ordered the immediate distribution of the funds previously allocated to the

---

[77] *PI*, no. 197, 3–10 Oct., 777; *WI*, no. 23, 4–11 Oct., 177, 178; *CSPVen.*, 77.
[78] *Journal*, 793; *PI*, no. 197, 3–10 Oct., 778.
[79] *WI*, no. 23, 4–11 Oct.,183.
[80] *Journal*, 794. Giavarina was among those supposing that Parliament had absolutely rejected the second proposal: *CSPVen.*, 79.

disabled, and even established a committee to introduce a bill to secure the rights of apprentice soldiers to practise their trades on returning to civilian life, a grievance that had not been mentioned in the *Representation*. An equally gracious, if less specific, response went to the fifth request: Parliament promised 'all due encouragement' to those who had been 'faithful and active' on its behalf during the rebellion. Through these conciliatory answers, MPs sought to retain the soldiers' loyalty while safeguarding their own authority.[81]

By Tuesday afternoon, however, tensions in the House were already rising again. The *Representation* had not cured Hesilrig and his associates of their now deep-rooted distrust of the grandees. Viewed through the lens of suspicion, it was easy to discount the assurances of fidelity and focus on the failure to disown the Derby petitioners, the implicit desire for a permanent general, and the questioning of Parliament's absolute power to cashier.[82] Even as they courted the ordinary soldiers and junior officers with concessions, the militant republicans called for immediate precautions against the dangerous ambitions of the senior commanders. On Tuesday they produced the previously-ordered bill making it treason to tax without parliamentary consent, and rushed it into law, with an additional preamble nullifying all legislation during the interruption of 1653–9 unless ratified since Parliament's restoration. Although provisoes confirming the Indemnity Act and the possession of lands acquired since April 1653 offered some protection, the new law deliberately affronted Cromwellians, and threatened any usurping government with legalised insurrection.[83] Later that day Vane told Johnston that MPs were 'running to a very great height' over the officers' more controversial sixth proposal, for no dismissal without court-martial, and were preparing to refuse both that and the requested confirmation of Fleetwood's commission. At nightfall, Johnston heard that there had even been 'som motion . . . to putt Fleetwood in the Tower, and that it should be a cryme in any to insist on such proposals'. Such vociferous condemnation was typical of the hard-line republicans, yet this extreme motion, if made, commanded little support from the other members.[84] There was, after all, no definite evidence of Fleetwood's untrustworthiness or the Army's intention to insist on their proposals at swordpoint.

On the morning of Wednesday 12 October Hesilrig presented Parliament with the 'proof' of Lambert's disloyalty that he had been waiting for. It was a

---

81 *Journal*, 795. The difficulties encountered on leaving the Army by apprentice soldiers whose masters required them to complete their terms before entering upon their trades had received much attention from the Indemnity Committee in the late 1640s, but considerably less thereafter.

82 These were the points emphasised in the contemporary accounts of Bordeaux (Guizot, *Histoire*, i. 490) and Giavarina (CSPVen., 76), as well as the retrospective republican narratives. Such biassed sources usefully reveal the influence of anti-Army prejudice on interpretation.

83 *Journal*, 795. The act is printed in A&O ii. 1351–2.

84 *Johnston diary*, 142. The *Journal* contains no record of a motion to commit Fleetwood etc.

brief circular inviting Colonel Okey and his officers to subscribe the enclosed *Representation*, and signed by ten grandees, including Lambert and Disbrow.[85] Although it contained no treasonable expressions whatsoever, and was actually nothing worse than an attempt to maintain Army communications and secure the support of every regiment for the stance adopted by the Council of Officers at London, Hesilrig magnified the sinister implications and incited the members to save the civil authority by a pre-emptive strike on the signatories. The House was in no mood for calm deliberation: subsequent accounts mirrored the militants' speeches in their stress on the imminent danger of a 'New Interruption and total Extirpation', and the desperation born of the sense that Parliament was at the 'last Gasp', and must act now or never to prevent the 'exorbitant rebellious Domination of the Sword'.[86] Yet even in this panic-stricken atmosphere, the outcome hovered in the balance, as a significant minority appealed for clemency. Signing the letter did not entail the automatic forfeiture of Parliament's trust. Of the ten officers, one, Colonel Nathaniel Rich, was also an MP, who ably defended his own and his brother officers' loyalty. While Rich secured exception for himself, his pleas had no effect on the fate of the other nine, whose commissions were annulled with the assent of a substantial majority.[87] The real cause of this drastic action was less the ostensible justification, the letter, than the contagious suspicion of Lambert that its revelation had unleashed. To enforce the dismissal of Lambert and his associates, and maintain Parliament's dominion in future, an act vesting the government of the Army in seven commissioners was hastily passed. Confidence in Fleetwood's ability to control his colleagues was dead. Though his reputed integrity and popularity with the soldiers earned Fleetwood inclusion among the commissioners, legitimate authority over the English forces had effectually been transferred to Hesilrig, Morley and their faithful ally, Colonel Valentine Walton.[88]

The votes of 12 October signalled the sudden abandonment of Parliament's previous policy of partnership with the officers. Johnston deplored the decisions as a 'strange and judicial madnesse, unles they wer sure of most pairt of the Airmy, whereof they wer confident'. Confidence in the fundamental loyalty of the lower ranks of the Army was, indeed, almost as significant a factor in militant republican thinking as their near-pathological distrust of the grandees. Hesilrig and his associates were not inept or suicidal politicians who impaled themselves upon the 'sword of Damocles' to escape an intoler-

---

[85] The letter in its original and printed form survives in MS Sloane 4165, fos 33, 34.
[86] *THE PARLIAMENTS PLEA: Or XX REASONS For The UNION Of The PARLIAMENT & ARMY . . .*, 9; *THE RENDEZVOUZ OF General Monck, Upon The Confines of England*, 5–6.
[87] The exception of Rich has been overlooked by all historians of the crisis, yet is plainly recorded in the *Journal*, along with his service as teller against the motion to revoke the commissions, which passed with the support of 75% of the MPs present.
[88] *Journal*, 796. The other three commissioners, Monck, Ludlow and Overton were, of course, absent commanding the forces in Scotland, Ireland and Hull.

able situation, as Davies supposed.[89] Rather, they deliberately provoked a confrontation that they believed they could win. During the previous few days, they had been actively mustering support among the London officers by soliciting subscriptions to a counter-petition, and had received loyal guarantees from the colonels of at least four regiments, which they now summoned to their aid. Assistance was also anticipated from the militia forces in the London area. Further encouragement had come from Monck, in Scotland, who had suppressed the Derby petition and again pledged allegiance to Parliament.[90] As Fleetwood himself meekly acquiesced in the new arrangements for the government of the Army, his fellow commissioners, encamped in the House to ensure that it would remain open as usual next day, seemed set to subdue the startled officers.[91]

In the event, of course, this radical attempt to assert Parliament's power over the Army precipitated the very rebellion that it was intended to prevent. Lambert surrounded the House with regiments loyal to him, and stopped most MPs from entering. The Southwark militia mustered, but were deterred from action by Lambert's cordon; the City militia commissioners, divided between supporters of both sides and neutrals eager to mediate for the sake of peace, issued contradictory orders, and eventually declined to intervene.[92] Ordinary soldiers rallied to the commanders whom they were accustomed to obey, rejecting an attempt by the Speaker, an unknown civilian, to pronounce himself their General.[93] So popular was Lambert that he secured the defection of Parliament's entire life-guard simply by challenging its irresolute major.[94] Yet the Army was not united. Despite the desertion of some troops, the besieged commissioners retained the support of the regiments commanded by Mosse and Morley, which obdurately confronted Lambert's forces with 'their Muskets charged and their Matches lighted', and remained deaf to all his blandishments. As Lambert was as reluctant as his opponents to resort to actual bloodshed, the stalemate ended only when the Council of State interposed, ordering all soldiers in Westminster to withdraw to quarters. Next day the insurgent officers took care to guard the doors with their own

89 *Johnston diary*, 143; Davies, *Restoration*, 151.

90 For these activities, and Monck's support, see Guizot, *Histoire*, i. 491; *Clarke papers*, iv. 59–60; *Mordaunt letter book*, 59; MS Carte 30, fos 487–9. Ludlow later claimed to have provided similar assurances from Ireland, but the contemporary records do not mention them: *Ludlow memoirs*, ii. 120.

91 Fleetwood's initial acquiescence in the creation of the seven commissioners was used to reproach him by republicans, and was, significantly, never contradicted in the Army's self-justifications. See, for examples, *True relation*, 5, and *Ludlow memoirs*, ii. 137.

92 *WI*, no. 24, 11–18 Oct., 189–90; *Declaration of the proceedings*, 5–6; Royalist letters, 14 Oct., MS Clarendon 64, fos 234, 239.

93 *WI*, no. 24, 11–18 Oct., 198; *Johnston diary*, 144.

94 *Clarke papers*, iv. 64; *WI*, no. 24, 11–18 Oct., 190.

troops, who rejected the council's order to allow the members to 'return to the free exercise of the Legislative power'.[95] Parliament was again suspended.

Self-preservation, not malice aforethought, was the principal motive of the displaced officers, who were unwilling to accept their exclusion from power and profit in the Republic that they had restored, and feared that the loss of their commands might prove the prelude to severer penalties. Thus Lambert, according to Ludlow, was certain that Hesilrig 'was so enraged against him that he would be satisfied with nothing but his blood'; a contemporary letter from Wallingford House observed that the officers 'thought time to looke about them, if the Parliament intended not only their commissions but their very lives'.[96] Their resistance won the cordial backing of Fleetwood and a majority of the other officers, who were alarmed by Parliament's adoption of 'strange and violent courses . . . without any just cause, examination and trial', and determined to preserve the Army's integrity at all costs. In his explanations to Monck, Fleetwood appealed to the 'necessity of Providence', but admitted bewilderment at the 'very strange' turn of events. Denying any design to dissolve Parliament, he blamed the 'sudden resolucion' of the new commissioners to engage in warlike preparations for the 'sudden revolucion' of the officers, who had acted only to preserve peace and 'prevent blood and devision of this Army'. The official *Declaration of the General Council* placed similar emphasis on the necessity created by the unexpected and dangerous alteration in Parliament's attitude so soon after the *Representation*'s acceptance had 'renewed some hopes of a right understanding'.[97] The reality of these hopes, and the absence of a prior plot, was attested by the officers' conduct after the interruption. In 1653 Cromwell and the radicals had rapidly excused the Army's intervention by issuing condemnations of the members, who made little effort to defend their authority. In 1659 the situation was reversed: it was the officers, in marked contrast to Parliament's supporters, who were very slow to publish coherent justifications and recriminations.[98] Instead of proceeding to appoint a new Protector or institutionalise their *de facto* power, the grandees, aided by Vane and other sympathetic civil-

---

[95] *WI*, no. 24, 11–18 Oct., 190; *Johnston diary*, 144; SP 25/79, fos 253, 256. Though Johnston ascribed the credit for the council's first order to himself and Salway, it was in fact the unanimous resolution of a meeting attended by all the grandees.

[96] *Ludlow memoirs*, ii. 143; Capt. Griffith Lloyd to Montagu, 18 Oct., MS Carte 73, fo. 319. See also the account of similar language used by the officers on 13 Oct. in E. D., *COMPLAINTS And QUERIES Vpon ENGLANDS Misery Acted Octob. 13, 1659, By some OFFICERS . . . Against the Parliament*, 4. This writer was, of course, concerned to vindicate Parliament by demonstrating that such fears for life and property were groundless.

[97] *Armys plea*, 18; Fleetwood to Monck, 18, 22 Oct., *Clarke papers*, iv. 63, 71; *Declaration of the General Council*, 10.

[98] The officers' first printed defence, *The Armys plea*, was not collected by Thomason until 24 Oct., more than a week after he acquired the republicans' first attack; the *Declaration of the General Council* was not issued until 27 Oct. By the end of the month, at least twelve tracts vindicating Parliament had appeared, compared to just five for the Army, including the two official explanations.

ians, tried to construct a compromise enabling Parliament to return on suitable conditions. Only when it became clear that Hesilrig and his associates would not co-operate did the Army finally abandon Parliament and set up the Committee of Safety.[99]

More significant than the officers' actual innocence was, of course, their inadvertent success in convincing, first Hesilrig and at last a majority of MPs, that they were guilty of conspiring against Parliament. Memories of the 1653 dissolution facilitated, but did not cause, the growth of that conviction. Nor were the personal differences within the government inherently insuperable: ever since the spring, Army and Parliament had devoted much attention to the task of earning each other's trust and establishing a satisfactory union. What destroyed their achievement was, primarily, a series of misunderstandings arising from the particular circumstances following Booth's rising. Crisis escalated as each side, suspecting the other, took actions and precautions that confirmed the other's fears. Thus Parliament's vote against Harrison was intended as a warning of the consequences of disloyalty, but could be read as proof of an inveterate design to avenge the dissolution of 1653;[100] the officers' letter soliciting wider Army support for the *Representation* was, fatally, interpreted as preparation for an assault on the civil government.[101] There was, however, no linear progression towards breakdown. Efforts to defuse tensions and preserve unity persisted to the end, and even beyond; despite increasingly difficult conditions, these efforts very nearly prevailed. The Army's *Humble representation*, with Parliament's initial response, created a genuine opportunity for reassurance and reconciliation. That disaster instead ensued was due not only to the wall of distrust that now divided Hesilrig from Lambert and Vane, but to contingency. Hesilrig was certainly looking for evidence, and the disclosure of the letter to Okey, which enabled him to drive Parliament into confrontation, may or may not have been fortuitous; but the arrival of the letter from Monck, which did much to persuade him that he could win such a confrontation, certainly was. The result of this miscalculation was the shattering of the republican alliance and the ruin of the republican cause by a series of Pyrrhic victories: of Hesilrig on 12 October, Lambert on 13 October and, ultimately, Hesilrig on 26 December, when a depleted Parliament, its authority mortally weakened by the second interruption, reassembled for the last time.

---

99 For these efforts at compromise, and the implacable opposition of Hesilrig, Scot, etc., see *Johnston diary*, 145–6; *Ludlow memoirs*, ii. 144–6; [?] Samborne to Hyde, 21 Oct., *CSP* iii. 585–6; [?] Lloyd to Montagu, 18 Oct., MS Carte 73, fo. 319; and Bordeaux to Mazarin, 20 Oct., Guizot, *Histoire*, ii. 269.

100 This interpretation of the vote against Harrison was advanced in the *Armys plea*, 20, and *Remonstrance and declaration*, 6–7.

101 That the officers sent out letters indiscriminately to all regiments, including those headed by zealous republicans such as Okey, is further proof of the unconspiratorial nature of their behaviour.

10

The Absence of Authority

This Parliament is the only remaining Branch of the Peoples Authority, to whom of right belongeth the settlement of our Government: Therefore that Head is not to be severed from this Body, to wit, that legal Authority from this legal People: *The Parliament's Plea*, Oct. 1659.

I would not be absent, could I satisfie myself in the authority from whence the commission issueth . . . when I find that foundation layd, derived from good people and to them to be duelye conveyed, with that I can willinglye . . . engage . . . but truly I dare not engadge the blood of any one person in a cause I understand not: John Pyne, declining to serve the Committee of Safety, 14 Nov. 1659.

Why cannot some other number of honest men chosen to serve the present Exigency . . . be as lawfull an Authority . . . and sooner answer the desire of all good People?: Jeremiah Ives, *Eighteen QUESTIONS PROPOUNDED To Put the great Question between the Army and their dissenting Brethren out of Question*, Nov. 1659.

The story of the Commonwealth's collapse in the autumn and winter of 1659 is only too well known.[1] As a triumvirate, Fleetwood, Lambert and Disbrow notoriously lacked the prestige and political acumen which had enabled Oliver Cromwell, in 1653, to make constitutional changes without destroying Army unity or weakening central government. The Committee of Safety eventually improvised by these officers proved the least effectual of all Interregnum regimes. It assumed power amidst bitter republican infighting exacerbated by the ominous news that General Monck's army in Scotland had declared for Parliament; it dispersed ignominiously just two months later, when Fleetwood despaired of countering similar revolts by the forces in Ireland, Portsmouth and the Channel fleet. During the interval the committee failed, not only in the essential task of designing a future constitution, but in preventing such present disasters as the suspension of the judiciary, the exhaustion of public revenue and the revival of militant conservatism, especially in London, which became openly hostile to the Republic. Civil war conditions returned to many areas; elsewhere apprehensions of disorder ran high. Not surprisingly, contemporary monarchists and subsequent historians have seen in this confusion the inevitable culmination

---

[1] The course of events is thoroughly narrated by Davies, Woolrych and Hutton. The latter, in particular, accords as much space to these ten weeks as to the previous five months.

of republican politics. Yet paradoxically, the calamities which befell the Committee of Safety in fact reveal the strength of its predecessor, the Parliament's government.

Parliament had enjoyed the great advantage of some plausible claim to legitimacy, grounded in the resurrection of a ten-year-old tradition. Foreign powers, major corporations and a host of petitioners had again acknowledged it as the 'Supreme Authority of the Commonwealth'. Though this title had been hotly contested by counter-revolutionary polemicists during the spring and summer, the defeat of Booth's rising had virtually silenced their protests, and afforded those unmoved by legal arguments a fresh sign that providence endorsed the regime. By September, only a few disillusioned Fifth Monarchists and Quakers openly questioned Parliament's rule. Tacit assent from the majority, together with the professed loyalty of an active minority, had made possible both competent government and progress towards a permanent settlement. The second interruption dissipated these assets by reopening the whole debate on legitimacy. At the root of the Committee of Safety's difficulties was the lack of any comparable claim on which to construct a new order, or even maintain the existing one. Amidst the chaos of December, even a Presbyterian would see merit in restoring Parliament, the 'last remaining authority . . . twice intrusted . . . the three Nations submitting thereunto as the supreme'.[2] By then, however, it was too late to save the Commonwealth. This chapter will contend that the lapse of legitimate authority in October undermined not just the next expedient, but ultimately the entire republican experiment.

In and of itself, the coup of 13 October need not have extinguished parliamentary authority. Subsequent days saw strenuous efforts to resuscitate it in some form, and meanwhile minimise instability by preserving appearances as much as possible. Far from coveting a monopoly of power themselves, Lambert and the other Army leaders lacked any profound dissatisfaction with the management of civil affairs; driven to intervene in self-defence, they did not relish an open challenge to the *status quo*. Aided by such civilian peacemakers as Sir Henry Vane, the grandees sought a compromise that would redress their grievances yet maintain legal government by either Parliament itself, or else an executive with its sanction. The quest for a 'mutual accord . . . preventing . . . all abuses, interruptions and irregularities for the future' was not inherently unrealistic: co-operation had defused the potential for conflict until very recently, while precedents existed for the repeal of resolutions the soldiers deemed injurious.[3] As long as negotiations with MPs con-

---

2 ENGLANDS present Case Stated, In A further Remonstrance of many thousands of the Citizens, Housholders, Freemen and Apprentizes of the City of London, 11.

3 Declaration of the proceedings, 6. The author of this pamphlet must have derived his information from a high-ranking army source: on 14 Oct., the time of writing, he knew that the Council of Officers was preparing proposals for submission to the Council of State, where Fleetwood was acting as intermediary.

tinued, the officers refrained from widening the rift by publishing recriminations. Moderation also characterised the earliest printed accounts: though decidedly pro-Army, these represented the members as, at worst, 'unserviceable Patriots', whose actions were misguided rather than malicious, and attributed the crisis to a mere 'Misunderstanding', which was not expected to last.[4] John Canne went so far as to predict that Parliament would 'meet tomorrow as formerly'; another journalist insinuated that the members had voluntarily resolved to adjourn.[5] Even after relating the Army's extraordinary intervention, newsbooks emphasised the continuance of normal, civilian authority at the highest levels: the Council of State maintained its 'usual times of sitting'.[6] For such reassurance to carry more than temporary conviction, however, a speedy agreement restoring at least the semblance of harmony was necessary.

What prevented any reconciliation, and precipitated public controversy over the issue of authority, was the intransigence of Parliament's most passionate adherents. Furious and doubly distrustful since the humiliating siege of the House, Sir Arthur Hesilrig, Thomas Scot, Herbert Morley and their associates asserted 'Parliament's absolut authority' in council against suggestions that it should, in practice, be 'limited' for the good of 'the cause'. In their eyes these pacific overtures seemed disingenuous, attempts to further military ambition by substituting the semblance for the substance of parliamentary rule. To prevent such a deception of the people, Hesilrig's faction demanded an instant, unconditional restoration, failing which they withdrew from Whitehall and sponsored a spate of pamphlets denouncing the *de facto* regime as another intolerable usurpation of 'the civil and Soveraigne power'. Their case derived simply, but forcefully, from the recent consensus. All subjects, especially the newly recommissioned officers, owed obedience to Parliament, 'the only lawfull authority', without whose sanction no future government could be legitimate. Parliament's supremacy was indestructible, since inherent in its status as the last 'Relick of Civil Authority', and 'the natural, legal . . . true Magisterial Head' or 'politicall Father' of the good people. Such extravagant appellations clearly affirmed Parliament's accession to the exalted station in the body politic once occupied by the king. Anticipating accusations that it, like him, had forfeited its rights, Parliament's defenders devoted much attention to exonerating its administration from blame, so rendering rebellion inexcusable. Delays and difficulties, down to the latest interruption, sprang, in this version of events, from the struggle

---

[4] Ibid. 4. Canne, who had little reason to esteem the Parliament that had summarily ejected him from the editorship of *Politicus*, was even more respectful.
[5] The first newsbook to describe the crisis was Canne's *Particular Advice*, no. 29, 11–14 Oct., whose report is reproduced in *Occurrences*, no. 30, 11–18 Oct., 392. The first pamphlet narrative, *Declaration of the proceedings* (collected by Thomason on 17 Oct.) advanced the claim (pp. 3, 6) that MPs had freely refused to sit.
[6] *Post*, no. 24, 11–18 Oct., 196; *WI*, no. 24, 11–18 Oct., 198; *PI*, no. 198, 10–17 Oct., 796.

between Parliament's 'just authority' and the treacherous 'Design of . . . Domination of some few' officers, principally Lambert, 'the head and great engine of this great defection'. Such a bipolar paradigm left no place for neutrality or compromise. Englishmen, insisted the earliest extant pamphlet, must now choose whether to 'suffer all Authority in our old and ancient Conservators the Parliament, the great boundary of all our Liberties against Tyranny and Slavery, to be trodden under foot'. The alternative, vigorously promoted by 'that Noble Patriot of his Countries freedom', Sir Arthur Hesilrig, and his companions, was, of course, to oppose the change by any and every means.[7]

Had active opposition been confined to Hesilrig and a few vociferous malcontents, the Commonwealth might again have survived the suspension of parliamentary authority. Instead, to near-universal astonishment, their defiance soon found support from the majority of the army under General Monck, who declared his determination to 'prosecute this just Cause to the last drop of [his] Blood'. Monck's motives for this momentous decision remain obscure. Though he had gained the good graces of Hesilrig's faction by apparent loyalty before the coup, he did not share their profound reverence for this particular Parliament. He undoubtedly preferred it to an 'Arbitrary power' of Lambert's devising, and may even have sincerely seen no prospect of a 'legall foundation for a free state' without it.[8] Real or feigned, devotion to 'the Liberty and Authority of Parliament' brought Monck distinct advantages. Not only did this profession assist him to pose as the consistent champion of the 'Good Old Cause' revived that spring, and to refute suspicions that his intervention sprang from self-interest or crypto-Royalism: it also imparted 'Legal Authority' to independent initiatives that Parliament, in power, would never have countenanced, since they considerably strengthened his position.[9] Conversely, commitment to Parliament justified Monck

7 *Johnston diary*, 145; [Thomas Scot], *The Copy of a LETTER To a Countrey Collonel, or, A serious dissuasive from joyning with those Officers now in Rebellion against the PARLIAMENT*, 6, 2–3; *Parliaments plea*, 6–7; *True relation*, 10; *THE DECLARATION Of the Officers of the Army Opened, Examined & Condemned and the PARLIAMENT VINDICATED*, 28.
8 *A DECLARATION Of the Commander in Chief of the Forces in SCOTLAND . . . Together with Three LETTERS from the Lord General MONCK*, 7, 8; Monck to Owen, 29 Nov., *Clarke papers*, iv. 153. Monck's conduct astonished contemporaries ranging from his bewildered colleagues at Wallingford House to hopeful Royalist conspirators; only Hesilrig's group, encouraged by their recent correspondence, were not surprised. His motives have never been satisfactorily elucidated, despite a wealth of speculation. That he consistently intended to restore Charles, or suddenly succumbed to fear of radical groups such as the Quakers, seem the least likely explanations. It seems most probable that he genuinely disapproved of Parliament's removal, and seized this opportunity to exert his own influence in English politics with the greatest hope of support from his own army and the wider republican constituency.
9 *Declaration of the commander*, 6; *The FORM Of the New COMMISSIONS By which the Forces act, that are under the Command of CHARLES FLEETWOOD Esq.* [broadsheet]. Besides the march south, these initiatives included the purge of dissident officers, which

in disobeying commands emanating from Whitehall after the interruption. Warrants issued by the Committee of Safety he dismissed 'in regard the authority is soe we neither know of its constitution or power', and thus made nonsense of that body's claim to rule the entire Commonwealth. Even instructions from the depleted Council of State to appoint commissioners to administer justice, a necessary measure which Parliament intended, and he himself had advised, he now repudiated, predicting dangerous consequences 'if the lawes be executed from an illegal foundation'.[10] In this way Monck's stand for legality escaped the least taint of compliance with an illicit regime, yet, ironically, ensured that the laws remained unexecuted. Nor were the resultant problems purely local. Scotland was not only beyond central government control, but posed a serious threat for the first time since the conquest. Militarily, Monck was the weaker, yet his unyielding stance, skil-fully promoted in printed and personal overtures, fuelled resistance to the irresolute committee in England and Ireland. By taking up arms in defence of Parliament's lapsed authority Monck and his subordinates were, inadver-tently yet effectively, undermining the Commonwealth that Parliament had done so much to create.

While Monck's immediate resort to armed resistance was unique, dismay at the loss of parliamentary authority was widespread. In Ireland, the Council of Officers expressed 'Astonishment and Sorrow' at the 'direfull and tragicall' news that their colleagues at Wallingford House had ventured 'to treade upon the Brinke of Ruine and Desolation . . . in the unfixing of that Nationall authority which themselves . . . had but few monethes before restored'. Besides its inconsistency, this 'extraordinary and . . . unexpected transaction' distressed these officers by destroying their 'hope of . . . settlement . . . upon a lasting and righteous foundation . . . [insofar] as it . . . depended upon legall Instruments and formal Nationall Constitutions'. The Dublin officers' reac-tion, indeed, differed from Monck's only in their willingness, after 'greate thoughte and searching of heartes', to dispense with legality and believe that their brethren in London had acted from 'necessity and . . . duty', with the intention of achieving 'a more firme establishment of Peace and Righteous-ness'. This flexibility stemmed from the over-riding impulse to maintain Army unity, essential to the 'safety of these nations', rather than great faith in Lambert or disaffection to Parliament. Colonel John Jones, the MP and civil commissioner commanding this army in Ludlow's absence, indignantly

gave Monck much greater control of his army than Parliament had permitted, and the convening of a Scottish assembly which accorded qualified approval to his plans – a degree of consultation not seen since the conquest, but intended to prevent disturbances during his projected invasion of England.

10 Monck to Archibald Johnston, 3 Nov., *Clarke papers*, iv. 88. The council's letter, dated 25 Oct., is the last in its letter book, SP 25/98, fo. 218. Monck's scruples naturally did not stop him accepting a commission as commander in chief from the underground Council of State, chaired by Scot, a month later: *Clarke papers*, iv. 138.

denied his superior's charges of 'deserting the Parliament who sent me hither, by whose Authority I now Act, or . . . doeing of any Act tending to the diminution of their Honour or Authority'. His incomprehension of Ludlow's displeasure illustrates the persistence of confused loyalties despite the efforts of Parliament's partisans to reduce the issue to a simple choice between lawful and unlawful authority. Jones's comfortable conviction that compliance with Whitehall and criticism of Monck's militancy were perfectly compatible with fidelity to both Parliament and the 'publique safety which is above Parliaments' was not, however, shared by all his juniors.[11] Their growing dissatisfaction would culminate in the coup of 13 December, which overthrew Jones and resulted in a declaration condemning the interruption and re-pledging obedience to Parliament.[12]

Important as the responses of the peripheral armies were, it was in England that the sudden removal of the accepted authority most immediately affected the Commonwealth's adherents. Some welcomed the opportunities thus created: one Fifth Monarchist near Hull assured Fleetwood that the saints there were 'in a Rapture of Joye for this overturn', and offered copious advice, while Sir Henry Vane, who had done his utmost to prevent the breach, indulged the cautious hope that 'the glorious appearance of the Kingdom of God' was now approaching. But optimism was uncommon, and – in contrast to the spring – seldom illumined discourse out of doors. Even Richard Salway, Vane's closest political associate, inclined to believe the change a divine judgement.[13] Despite their disenchantment with Parliament, many Fifth Monarchists mourned 'this Gloomy, Dark, Overturning Day', or frantically tried to defer despair by reading a favourable meaning into the 'symptoms and characters of trouble and perplexity hanging over [their] heads'.[14] George

---

11 Council of Officers in Ireland to Fleetwood, 26 Oct., in *Inedited letters of Cromwell, Col. Jones, Bradshaw and other regicides*, ed. J. Mayer (Historical Society of Lancashire and Cheshire, 1861), 90–1; Jones to Ludlow, 30 Nov., ibid. 107–8. Jones's bewilderment is understandable, given Ludlow's own ambivalent stance: instead of publicly condemning the interruption, he sought a compromise, and was nominated to the committee; though he avoided active involvement there, he would sit in December's General Council of Officers.

12 *A Declaration of several Officers of the Army in Ireland . . . holding forth their stedfast resolutions to adhere to the Parliament*. On the complex events leading up to the coup see Clarke, *Prelude*, ch. iv.

13 John Turner to Fleetwood, 16 Nov., MS Sloane 4165, fo. 43. The views of Vane and Salway on 27 Oct. are in *Johnston diary*, 149–50.

14 *A Faithfull Searching HOME WORD . . . presented to the Officers . . . as another Looking-Glass wherein they may plainly see, how wofully they also have Dissembled*, title; *A REPLY To Mr William Prinne, His . . . Dangerous &c Expedient for the . . . Settlement of these Nations, by restoring the ancient Nobility . . . Together with a few Directions to the Persons now in Authority, opening a door to Peace, Righteousness and Prosperity*, 2. Somewhere between the poles represented by these texts was the *Warning-piece to the General Council*, whose authors, while unwilling to condemn the officers outright, lamented the improbability of reformation amidst 'the thickest midnight hour of MYSTERY BABYLON AND INIQUITY' (p. 6).

Wither, though personally disappointed with that assembly, celebrated the dissolution only by recommending remedies 'against the fainting of the Heart in these distracted times' of the Commonwealth's 'hazardous unsettlement'. No unthinking admirer of the 'famous, but not the blameless parliament', John Milton had nevertheless trusted to its 'wisdom and care' before the crash. He now perceived the Army's 'relapsing . . . into the same fault' of dissolving it 'without just autority' as 'most illegall and scandalous', and proposed political measures to arrest England's descent to an 'Anarchy without a counselling and governing power' – reconciliation with Parliament, or the speedy publication of 'some better cause' of its removal.[15]

Consternation at the loss of authority among the Republic's active servants had serious practical consequences. Divisions that had immobilised London's militia commissioners during the coup escalated into public strife in November, when a slender majority voted to send Monck a reproachful letter which, ironically, affirmed that Parliament had established them to 'suppress all Insurrections', including his. The minority protested against disowning their parliamentary commission by discouraging 'that Faithful and generous Assertor of the Parliaments Right'. A new commission from the Committee of Safety omitted outspoken dissenters but failed to find substitutes or secure the services of all those continued – William Allen, for example, would not act for fear of thereby 'espousing [the Army's] quarrill against those whose authority . . . they had so lately acknowledged as supreame'.[16] Thus a significant force for stability in the capital disintegrated. In the provinces, few officials openly sided with Parliament, but several retreated quietly from their responsibilities to a sorrowful neutrality. A rare insight into their motives comes from John Pyne, an MP previously prominent in the administration of Somerset, who scrupled to act without proof of an 'authoritative power' founded on the 'true interest and constitution of a commonwealth . . . derived from good people and . . . duely conveyed'.[17] Those who stayed at their posts

15 Wither, *Cordial confection*, title; Milton, 'Letter to a friend', 20 Oct., CPW vii. 324–5, 327, 329. Though gladdened by Parliament's return, Milton had previously offered advice only on ecclesiastical policy. Despite the vote to retain tithes, he evidently had not lost confidence in Parliament's ability to rule and reach a settlement.

16 The City militia commissioners' letter to Monck was published in *PI*, no. 201, 31 Oct.–7 Nov., 843–4; a narrative of the protest, listing those voting on each side, appeared in *Scout*, no. 28, 4–11 Nov., 218–19; William Allen to Baxter, 8 Nov., *Baxter correspondence*, i. 416; on 30 Dec. Allen denied serving the 'new power', despite inclusion in its commission: ibid. 422. The committee's new commissioners are listed in *PI*, no. 202, 7–14 Nov., 860; comparison with the 100 men appointed by Parliament reveals that 32 commissioners were dropped, and only 7 added, leaving a new total of 75. As various accounts of the division show that a maximum of 58 men voted on that occasion, 42 had already withdrawn.

17 John Pyne, 11 Nov., HMC, *Ninth report*, ii. 493–4. Additional evidence of the withdrawal of some of those entrusted with implementing policy in the localities and the uncertainty of others how or whether to proceed following the change exists in correspondence of sequestration commissioners for Hertfordshire, Wiltshire, Durham, Cornwall, Kent,

could accomplish little; perplexed by the change, they appealed in vain for explanations and directions. Thus Durham's sequestration commissioners requested fresh instructions because of the 'great amazement [put] upon most men' by 'these strange revolutions'.[18] Captain Cloke, in Cornwall, pleaded for 'a little light in this darke day', and warned of the probable loss of 'all taxe', since those responsible for its collection had dispersed in the belief that they lacked 'power now to act'. In South Wales Captain Price reported the reluctance of sequestration and militia commissioners to 'raise moneys, they know not for whom nor to what end'. This inertia owed less to esteem for legality or Parliament *per se* than to the uncertainty arising from the lack of any 'good account' of developments at Westminster. Silence was swiftly exploited by local adversaries to challenge the authority of Parliament's appointees. Price and his colleagues might have embraced a 'more righteous settlement'; they dared not act by an 'implicit faith', for fear of the consequences to themselves, should the Army 'repent for this [interruption] alsoe'. A similar anxiety to 'Acte safely' moved Cheshire's excise commissioners to seek guidance from London instead of coercing those who used Parliament's absence as an excuse for non-payment.[19] Pending such reassurance, paralysis set in.

To restore effective administration, regain waverers and repress resistance, the Army needed to counter the exclusive claims advanced on Parliament's behalf, and establish a strong new central authority – fast. Instead, the Council of Officers hesitated for two weeks before issuing an inadequate official statement and inaugurating the puppet Committee of Safety.[20] Though crammed with grievances and good intentions, the *Declaration* of 27 October

Gloucestershire, Hampshire and Yorkshire: *Calendar of the proceedings of the Committee for Compounding*, i, ed. M. A. E. Green, London 1889, 758, 761, 762, 764, 765, 774–5.

[18] Durham sequestration commissioners to the central sequestrators, 31 Oct., *Proceedings of the Committee for Compounding*, i. 762. The general lack of progress applied even to the few bold spirits who accorded the new regime unquestioning support. Derbyshire's sequestration commissioners, for example, were soon diverted from that business to the more urgent task of suppressing disorders and raising forces against Monck; as their zeal for Lambert ensured their disgrace in January, the hesitation of more cautious individuals was entirely justified: ibid. i. 764, 768, 771, 775.

[19] Edward Cloke to Bennet, 20 Oct., FSL, MS X.d.483, fo. 131; Richard Price to Fleetwood, 28 Oct., MS Sloane 4165, fo. 36; Timothy Reyner to Baynes, 22 Oct., MS Add. 21425, fo. 165. Those resisting the excise in Cheshire cited the act of 11 Oct. making it treason to collect taxes unauthorised by Parliament; more confident administrators would have proceeded on the basis that this act did not repeal the act of 28 Sept., which renewed the excise for three months. Their diffidence illustrates the confusion engendered by the crisis, and the fear of seeming to collaborate with an unlawful power.

[20] Hutton overestimates the Army's self-defence, using two non-polemical neutral tracts to substantiate his assertion that 'at least six statements of their case' were printed during this period, and erroneously claims that it now established the *Scout* as 'its own newspaper' (*Restoration*, 72). The *Scout* had actually existed since April, and was far from uniformly supportive of Army policies, as its reproduction of the militia commissioners' protest showed.

evaded the question of the Army's right to interfere, despite the surge of criticism directed at that crucial point. Its pages divided responsibility for recent events between Parliament's failings and the over-ruling of a 'wise and all-disposing Providence', of which the officers were merely well-meaning but fumbling agents. Thus the May invitation to MPs was depicted as the blunder of 'drowning men' desperately clutching 'any thing which carried with it but the least appearance of Civil Authority'. Such language, while belittling Parliament's grandiose pretensions, was hardly calculated to inspire confidence in either the officers' political judgement or their latest civil expedient, wrapped in a much more transparent mantle of legitimacy.[21]

Neither the *Declaration*, nor the longer *Army's Plea For Their present Practice*, to which Wallingford House also referred enquirers, directly confronted Parliament's claim to an indissolvable supremacy. The *Declaration* hinted at the existence of 'learned arguments' for a dissolution long since, but gave no details; the *Plea* expressly declined to discuss Parliament's authority. This document did, however, assert the conditional nature of allegiance, reminding readers that 'uncontroulable Power and absolute Authority' belonged to God alone, and rehearsing the now-familiar principles and precedents for the removal of magistrates who endangered the 'publike Liberties and Interest of this Nation and the people of God'. Consigning Parliament to that category strained credulity, however, since there was no concrete proof of a plot to betray the cause, only alarmist inferences from its policies, especially the cashiering of the nine officers. Such insinuations, reinforced with ancient, equally ill-founded, allegations of self-perpetuation and persecution, blackened Parliament's reputation, but did not justify the Army in expelling it by force on mere suspicion. As their public pronouncements nowhere addressed this problem, the grandees remained vulnerable to the charge of presumptuously invading the single 'Supreme Authority' to save their own careers.[22]

The Whitehall officers were not reluctant to grasp the thorny issue of authority because the case for Parliament was irrefutable. In the new climate, Royalists and Presbyterians campaigned aggressively and with impunity against Parliament's pretensions to indissolubility, despite their almost equal antipathy to military rule.[23] The Army's reluctance to compromise its

---

[21] *Declaration of the General Council*, 2, 4. The Committee of Safety derived its name from Parliament's initial executive, its seal, procedures and many members from the late Council of State. There, however, the superficial impression of legality ended.

[22] Ibid. 3; *Armys plea*, 22, 2, 19. The panic-stricken assertion that the officers could not 'suffer themselves to be Voted out of their Commands . . . and next unto the Gallows' (p. 28) illustrates the extreme interpretation put on Parliament's decisions. There was no evidence that MPs actually intended any executions; when restored they readily indemnified repentant officers as to life and property while removing their commands: *Journal*, 800.

[23] The massive revival of conservative printing is clearly illustrated by Thomason's collection: between 13 Oct. and 30 Nov. he acquired 22 pamphlets and broadsheets by Presbyterians and Royalists, as opposed to a mere 5 in September and early October.

commitment to the Commonwealth by using such monarchist material in its official statements is understandable. Some of its apologists nevertheless tried to adapt elements of these arguments, with varying results. Jeremiah Ives, for example, contended that 'Law and Custom' contradicted Parliament's claim to be a 'free Representative', and highlighted the inconsistency of condemning the use of force in 1659 but not 1648 – a favourite theme of the secluded members. Instead of advocating a return to tradition, however, Ives maintained that 'some other number of honest men chosen' by the Army must be 'as lawfull an Authority' as any parliament, and more likely to 'answer the desire of all good People'. In his hands the mixed approach was confusing, and still begged the question of the Army's right to appoint governments in the first place.[24] More successful in this respect was a pamphlet directed to Monck's soldiers, which cleverly deployed conservative reasoning to refute the notion that the remnant of the Commons possessed any intrinsic or 'new Authority', and to adduce the principle, shared by both armies, that 'defence of Peoples Liberties' had justified all former changes. The writer then proceeded to erase the distinction between civil and military manifestations of the good people's sovereignty, and reached the radical conclusion that 'power and true Authority' originated in the 'good Cause of Justice, freedome and Righteousness', which likewise warranted the officers' recent actions.[25]

Notions of authority untainted with reactionary ideas were also available. Quakers vigorously defended the dissolution because MPs had not delivered the reforms that they demanded. George Fox, Jr, and Francis Howgill in addition denounced the 'great blindness' of those 'doting on the Name of a Parliament, as though it were essential': fidelity to the divine purpose was, in their view, the only source of legitimacy, so the godly should 'wait to see' what the next regime intended.[26] But the boldest and most comprehensive rejoinder to Parliament came from the godly republican writer of *The ARMIES Vindication*, which set out to demonstrate 'the Equity, Power and Right of the Army to settle these Nations upon the Foundations of Righteousnesse and Freedome'. Strongly influenced by Vane's ideas, he argued that the 'priviledge of Rule' had reverted to 'honest men', embodied in the Army, which was not

---

Adding those printed in December, and others that he did not acquire yields a staggering total of 51 conservative tracts surviving from the second interruption. From November onwards Prynne dared to enter his pamphlets in the Stationers' Register, a clear sign of confidence.

[24] Jeremiah Ives, *Eighteen QUESTIONS PROPOUNDED To Put the great Question between the Army and their dissenting Brethren out of Question*, 2, 5, 6.

[25] *Conference between two souldiers*, 5–6, 22.

[26] George Fox, Jr, *A Few Plain Words to be considered by those . . . that would have a PARLIAMENT that is chosen by the voyces of the people . . . Wherein is shewed unto them . . . that a Parliament so chosen are not like to govern for God and the good of his People*, 4; Francis Howgill, *An INFORMATION, and also ADVICE to the Armie on both parts . . . and also to all People who seeks peace and righteousness*, 4–5. At best, the Quakers offered the Army a tepid acquiescence, together with stern admonitions against emulating Parliament's errors.

subservient but a 'distinct power raised by God' to destroy the 'former slavish Government'. With the demise of the old regime, Parliament, always the Army's inferior, proceeding only in a 'low, weak, inconsiderable way, their greatest Authority lying in the Camp', had lost any legal right to govern, and become the discreditable and dispensable symbol of the iniquitous past – a 'Worldly Constitution . . . every whit as Babylonish as Kingship it self'. To contend on its behalf was therefore as foolish – and futile – as to 'honour a dead Carcasse' or seek to 'repair a broken Idoll, that can no longer be the Interest of the kingdome of Christ' – vivid metaphors underlining Parliament's remoteness from the pedestal on which its adherents sought to enthrone it. Instead of looking back to the 'Egypt' of traditional parliaments chosen by a largely corrupt electorate, the godly should go forward to the 'Canaan of peace and truth . . . righteousness and justice', attainable only by realising that their liberties were 'wrapt up with the Armies Interests'. To understand that authority rightly belonged to an 'Army cloathed with the peace, freedom and privileges of the good people' was not only to clear the officers of treason and rebellion, but to transform the prospect of military rule from the terrifying spectre raised by their enemies into a positive good – 'an Ordinance of God . . . as rational and as just as any other . . . and much better and most suitable . . . for us at this day'. This doctrine encouraged acceptance of, even optimism concerning, the eventual constitution, and, by extension, the interim Committee of Safety. All the 'present Troubles and Perplexities' were ultimately fruits of the Army's failure to 'own that Power that God and nature hath given them, the most Superior, the most absolute'; this acknowledged, together with their true friends, and, the writer pledged, the Army could be sure of 'success and happiness'.[27]

That this comforting theory, authorising almost any form of godly rule, found so little favour at Wallingford House was due to its radicalism. Conservative by instinct, the grandees did not welcome advice to overturn 'old and rotten Customes', regardless of English law; vague promises to replace tithes and effect a 'full and thorough Reformation' notwithstanding, their strongest desire was to dispel suspicions of a 'design . . . to ravel all into confusion'. Defending the 'sober godly interest', consisting chiefly of Independents and moderate Presbyterians, against both prelatists and 'fanatical' sectarians was the great concern of John Owen, to whose gathered church Fleetwood and Disbrow belonged. In their eagerness to assure such influential mentors that

---

27 *The ARMIES Vindication of this last Change*, title, 6, 8, 5, 10–11, 15, 20–1. Though published in the Army's name, it was not printed by their official printer, Henry Hill; both internal evidence and the officers' consistent referral of the dissatisfied only to the *Armys plea* and *Declaration of the General Council*, show that it was actually written by a sympathetic civilian. Vane's influence appears not only in the doctrine of the honest party's sovereignty, but in the emphasis on unity, and the balance between millenarian enthusiasm and realistic expectation: even the 'best Government . . . from man will be mixt, having something of Christ and his Kingdome, and something of humane prudence' (p. 22).

there were no plans to 'throw down the Ministers, destroy Learning . . . [or] countenance Heresies', the senior officers shunned closer ties with those who held less conventional opinions.[28] Though the pliable Fleetwood did accept his case for a 'vast liberty of conscience', Vane found himself so mistrusted and marginalised, especially after Lambert's departure, that by late November he spoke of withdrawing northwards. Quakers lamented that he, Rich and other advocates of 'good things' were ignored, and that many of their people were reincarcerated.[29]

The corollary of the officers' conservative inclinations was wilful blindness to the radical implications of their own conduct. Dissolving Parliament, nullifying the legislation of its last days and nominating new administrators were acts appropriate only to the sovereign – yet the Army persisted in portraying itself as a disinterested subordinate. Thus the *Declaration* expressly repudiated 'Military or Arbitrary Government', even as it announced a committee entirely dependent on armed force and invalidated Parliament's last decrees. Another narrative based on the *Plea* went so far as to insist, in the teeth of the contrary evidence, that the Army's correction of civilian magistrates actually served 'to fasten the crowns of Government upon their heads'. Fleetwood rebuked soldiers who collected parliamentary taxes in Nottinghamshire for invoking the authority of the sword when questioned by affronted civilians. Vainly pursuing political respectability, the officers affirmed the representative principle at every stage, from the illusory agreement with Monck to the last, desperate, attempt to stifle simmering revolt by summoning a new parliament – despite the extreme improbability that any elected assembly would approve their deeds. Fleetwood himself admitted no contradiction between the Army's commitment to 'preserve the Ends of all Parliaments and Authority' and its dispersal of the Long Parliament.[30] By professing an unassuming attitude so inconsistent with its actions, the Army not only discouraged radical supporters without placating hostile conservatives, but confined itself to the negative role of rescuing the cause in emergencies, rather than creating alternative forms of government.

---

[28] *The ARMIES Vindication of this last Change*, 21; *Declaration of the General Council*, 18; John Owen to Monck, 22 Nov., *Clarke papers*, iv. 124, 122; *Armys plea*, 10. The value Fleetwood set on 'sober godly' support is evident from his correspondence with Monck, who liked to pose as the true defender of 'sober and judicious Christians': *Clarke papers*, iv. 71, 152.

[29] *Johnston diary*, 153, 163; Bordeaux to Mazarin, 25 Nov., Guizot, *Histoire*, ii. 294; Richard Hubberthorn to Margaret Fell, 21 Nov., FHL, MS Vol. S81 fos 400–3. It is unclear whether Vane thought of joining Lambert at Newcastle, or simply retiring to one of his northern residences. Vane's declining influence in November contrasts with the first weeks after the interruption, when Bordeaux noted the close alliance between him and Lambert, whom he saw as the 'most distinguished' government members: Guizot, *Histoire*, ii. 270, 273, 274–5.

[30] *Declaration of the General Council*, 18; *Remonstrance and declaration*, 5; Lucy Hutchinson, *Memoirs of the Life of Col. Hutchinson*, London 1822, ii. 242; *Three SPEECHES Made To the . . . Lord Maior, Aldermen and Common Council . . . November the 8th 1659*, 4.

The Army's confusion on the subject of authority subverted both the status and administrative effectiveness of its creature, the Committee of Safety. On paper, that body seemed impressive enough: twenty-three experienced administrators, mainly distinguished civilians selected for their sympathy towards the officers, were entrusted with all the powers of the late council, together with responsibility for the militia, diplomacy, granting indemnity, suppressing rebellion, appointing officials and disposing of delinquents and their estates.[31] In practice, doubts concerning the validity of its commission divided and diminished the committee from the first. Even those members most satisfied with their own inclusion had little faith in its legitimacy. Thus Whitelocke, addressing the City, defended the committee on pragmatic rather than principled grounds, presenting it as the bulwark of peace and order. He subsequently excused his involvement by asserting that this government, derived from the Army, the only 'visible authority', was preferable to naked military rule or a radical new form – hardly a resounding endorsement, but no more than might be expected of such a timeserver. Archibald Johnston congratulated himself on his appointment at the time, and accepted for Scotland's sake, despite premonitions of divine judgement; after the committee's collapse, however, he secretly confessed his lack of any 'real conviction that they wer the lawful authority'.[32] Other nominees without such convictions quietly refused to participate.[33] In all, seven of the sixteen civilians never seem to have sat; four more scrupled to commit themselves by signing any official documents.[34] Most prominent among the latter

---

[31] The committee included 15 men with conciliar experience, under Parliament, the Protector or both, 3 City magistrates, and 6 high ranking officers of the Army in England. Steele and Bennet, the only two outside these categories, both had substantial administrative experience, the former in Ireland, the latter in Cornwall. The names and powers of the committee are listed in *Politicus*, no. 592, 20–7 Oct., 827–8.

[32] Whitelocke to the City, *Three speeches*, 1–2 (the other speeches, by Disbrow and Fleetwood, were similarly devoid of principled argument); Whitelocke, *Memorials*, iv. 368; *Johnston diary*, 147–8, 150, 166. Johnston, as its president, and Whitelocke, as keeper of the great seal after Bradshaw's death, and judge in Chancery, were the civilians most active on the committee.

[33] These included Ludlow, who declined out of loyalty to Parliament, and continued to promote a reconciliation; his recent colleague in Ireland, William Steel (*Ludlow memoirs*, ii. 153, 156); and Bennet, who would not believe himself in danger from the restored Parliament in January because he knew he had 'never medled . . . nor acted in the Committee of Safety so called': FSL, MS X.d.483, fo. 133. This statement is not incompatible with Berners's evidence that he went out to welcome Monck's commissioners to London, a peacemaking mission that did not necessarily entail approbation of the committee.

[34] I have classed as civilians all those who held no regular commands in England, even if they still used military titles. As the committee's minutes were deliberately destroyed upon its collapse, attendance can only be inferred from other sources, which provide an incomplete picture. The seven were Ludlow, Steel, Brandrith, Thompson, Harrington, Laurence and Bennet. Tichborne and Sydenham also avoided signing any of the committee's warrants (recorded in MS Rawlinson A259, fos 138–59), but are among the ten sitting

group were Vane and Salway, who withdrew from the main sessions in protest at the appropriation of legislative powers pertaining to Parliament alone, though they did attend the subcommittee debating the constitution.[35] Conscientious absenteeism not only removed the services of able men – Vane's diplomatic talents were sorely missed – but reduced respect for the remnant, in which the military element necessarily became more conspicuous.[36]

The fact that its own members, whether soldiers or civilians, had no assurance of its authority, goes far to explain the feebleness of the Committee of Safety. Previous councils, secure in serving Parliament or Protector, had outfaced opposition with comparative confidence.[37] The Army's committee, reluctant to earn its reputation for arbitrariness, took diffidence to self-destructive lengths. Instead of deploying its power to prosecute monarchist conspirators imprisoned since Booth's rising, the committee released them on security.[38] Republican dissidents whom Oliver Cromwell[39] would have clapped into preventive custody upon far less provocation were left at liberty to plot its overthrow, and duly did.[40] Nor would this executive defend

members listed in late November by Berners, an ex-councillor who supported Parliament: MS Tanner 51, fo. 161.

[35] Bordeaux described Vane's protest on 1 Nov.; with typical cynicism, he interpreted it as insurance against prosecution by Parliament for 'meddling in a government without a legitimate title': Guizot, *Histoire*, ii. 283. Self-preservation may have been a motive, but Salway endorsed his summons to the committee with the words 'I utterly refuse to act', indicating principled opposition: HMC, *Tenth report*, pt ii, app. iv, 411. A hostile newsletter of 3 Nov. confirms his and Vane's aloofness (*Clarke papers*, iv. 93); there is ample evidence in Johnston's diary of their participation in the constitutional debates. They also remained active admiralty commissioners, an office to which Parliament had appointed them. Vane would confidently challenge his prosecutors to prove that he had acted for the committee; they could only produce an admiralty warrant for sending arms to Lambert: *Tryal*, 33.

[36] Bordeaux commented that Vane's withdrawal left the committee sadly short of able men. The inference that even skilful politicians sympathetic to the dissolution doubted its permanence further diminished the standing of the new regime in foreign eyes. Hostile domestic commentators, such as Berners and the newswriter quoted above, also used low attendance as a sign of the committee's parlous position. Of the six most active members of the committee, measured by the numbers of warrants signed, three were soldiers: in order, Johnston, Berry, Disbrow, Holland, Whitelocke and Fleetwood.

[37] See, for example, the recent, energetic response of Parliament's council to the summer conspiracy.

[38] The committee issued 14 warrants for the release of Royalists and Presbyterians, including Booth himself, and authorised only 6 arrests.

[39] Though Cromwell had evinced reluctance to arrest godly ex-allies who had become opponents, he had found the requisite firmness when necessary – for example, his imprisonment of Vane in 1656 for writing the *Healing question*, and participating in opposition activities far less immediately dangerous than most of those directed against the Army and its committee.

[40] Despite their outspoken opposition, the Army's parliamentarian enemies were only pursued in extreme cases: after appearing in arms, or attempting to seize the Tower. Thus Hesilrig, according to Berners, left London at the end of November in response to

itself against the torrent of vituperation pouring from the presses by reviving censorship or projecting a positive counter-image. Few printers or writers complained of harrassment; a proclamation for the suppression of 'unlicensed, dangerous, seditious . . . and scandalous Pamphlets' was drafted but never implemented.[41] Loath to admit dependence on the opprobrious sword, the committee made little effort to vindicate its power. Orders despatched to local authorities omitted any demonstration of its right to rule, in the hope of harnessing habitual obedience to the centre. The absence of any request for allegiance suggests that the lessons of the Engagement controversy may have been learnt. Even the committee's public declarations merely pleaded a providential call and patriotic duty to use 'all endeavours' to preserve peace.[42]

That plea would not withstand critical scrutiny, and its makers knew it. Challenged to prove an 'authority established by Parliament or derived from the good people', the committee could produce no arguments.[43] The only way to conserve the illusion of order was to disguise the regime's illegitimacy by avoiding or minimising confrontation as much as possible. Thus the committee's response to the judges' refusal to sit once their parliamentary commissions expired in November was simply to forestall a public walkout by adjourning all cases until the next legal term.[44] When the lord mayor and

Fleetwood's warning that he would be arrested if he stayed; he proceeded to persuade Portsmouth's governor to declare for Parliament, an event precipitating the committee's collapse.

41 The draft proclamation survives among the committee's warrants: MS Rawlinson A259, fos 145–6. According to Rugg, the committee did identify and imprison the printer of the militantly republican *Remonstrance and protestation: Rugg's diurnal*, 12. The only printer who has left complaints of interference was John Clowes, who blamed the delayed appearance of two works vigorously asserting Parliament's authority on their confiscation by the committee's agents. See his notes to William Bray's *PLEA FOR THE Peoples Fundamentall Liberties and Parliaments*, 19, and the broadsheet *No Parliament but the Old, or a NEW YEARS GIFT for the late interrupted PARLIAMENT*. The story of a raid in late December, within days of the committee's collapse, seems improbable; even if true, the proliferation of both monarchist and parliamentarian attacks throughout the committee's life suggests no serious attempts at censorship.

42 *By the Committee of Safety . . . A PROCLAMATION Inhibiting all Meetings for the Raising or drawing together of Forces without order of the said Committee or the Lord Fleetwood*, 5 Nov. The earlier proclamation continuing JPs similarly defined the committee's aims in terms of 'preservation of the publick Peace, and the better carrying on of the Affairs of the Commonwealth'. Surviving committee orders, silent on the subject of its authority, include the menacing letter sent to Monck (*Clarke papers*, iv. 80) and a command to Gloucester's magistrates to provide for the soldiers there: GRO, GBR H 2/3, fo. 261. Similar orders went to Exeter: Devon Record Office, Exeter, Exeter chamber act book 10, 126.

43 Monck to Johnston (who as president had signed the committee's letter), 5 Nov., *Clarke papers*, iv. 100. The committee did not attempt to persuade him, but retreated, leaving negotiations to the Army. Gloucester's magistrates, though not openly disrespectful, protested at the burden on their city, and cited an act of parliament against the committee's orders, obliging it to write a second letter explaining the 'good and warrantable grounds' for its request: GBR H 2/3 fos 262–3, 264–5.

44 The judges' commissions were due to expire on 20 Nov.; on 17 Nov. committee writs

aldermen rejected a summons to attend it after the apprentice riots of December, the committee meekly swallowed the affront, and subsequently accepted its exclusion from negotiations with the City.[45] Though faced with the imminent exhaustion of revenue, the committee dared not defy Parliament's edict by imposing further taxes on its own account, at the risk of provoking the rebellion so zealously promoted by its enemies. Rather, its financial wizards resorted to unpopular but technically legal devices, such as republication of a 1649 act requiring inhabitants to advance money for the soldiers' keep in lieu of free quarter, and a declaration justifying collection of customs and excise until June 1660 by ingenious exploitation of a loophole in Parliament's law continuing them till January.[46] In light of this self-effacing style of government, it is not surprising that the 'Tirannical Committee of Safety' failed to win respect from either its nominal subjects, foreign powers, whom it never notified of its existence, or even its creators, the officers, who bypassed it whenever expedient, and eventually discarded it altogether. Its tyranny was, ironically, by usurpation alone, not practice.[47]

The problem of authority not only enfeebled the temporary Committee of Safety, but blocked all prospect of a satisfactory permanent settlement. There was, at first, no shortage of ideas. Far from exemplifying the 'constitutional bankruptcy of radical Puritanism', as Worden has alleged, the second interruption saw fresh proposals from the formidable intellects of Vane, Milton and Henry Stubbe, besides input from lovers of the Commonwealth in

adjourning cases in Upper Bench, Common Bench and the Exchequer until Hilary term were entered in the Chancery clerks' docket book: PRO, C231/6, fo. 444.
[45] The City's refusal is recorded in the minutes for 6 Dec., CLRO, Rep. 67, fos 21–2. The next day Johnston noted the City's proposal to negotiate directly with Fleetwood 'waiveing the Committee of Safety', and expressed his personal support for 'al peaceable overtures and prevention of blood': Johnston diary, 155–6. In November, the aldermen had had no qualms about soliciting favours from the committee (for examples see Rep. 67, fo. 9). The City's new-found reluctance to negotiate was a response to the committee's decreasing ability to maintain order, and the mounting pressure for resistance from below. The best analysis of that pressure, and the apprentice riots which it produced, is T. Harris, London crowds in the reign of Charles II: propaganda and politics from the Restoration until the Exclusion Crisis, Cambridge 1987, ch. iii.
[46] An ACT for The more certain and constant Supply of the SOLDIERY with PAY, reprinted by committee order, 24 Nov.; A DECLARATION By the Committee of Safety . . . Touching the Payment of the Duties of Customs and Excise, 9 Dec. It was to the 1649 act that the committee referred Gloucester's government; this promised repayment from the first moneys received on the assessment. There was little more, however, to be expected from that source: since Parliament had accelerated collection, most of the whole year's tax had been paid by December.
[47] Remonstrance and protestation, 3 (one of many works condemning the committee as illegitimate, and urging resistance). Diplomats' correspondence shows that, though they had some informal meetings with individuals, the committee as a body neglected to institute official relations. Disregard for the committee increased as the situation deteriorated: by 10 Dec. its president was 'troubled . . . to find almost al bodyes to slight us of the Committee of Safety': Johnston diary, 156.

Hampshire, Baptist churches of Berkshire, Presbyterian zealot Archibald Johnston and humble Fifth Monarchist John Turner, to name only a few groups and individuals concerned.[48] Meanwhile Harrington, not content merely to continue advertising his model in print, established the famous Rota Club to debate its provisions. That none of the proffered solutions got beyond discussion was due not, primarily, to their diversity, but to the absence of an authoritative arbiter between them once Parliament was removed. After the committee failed to secure recognition, the General Council of Officers, supposed to represent the entire Army, took over this role, and made visible progress towards drafting a constitution.[49] Both theocratic and neo-Leveller elements of the republican alliance, however, followed Parliament's supporters in rejecting the council's resolves, for seemingly opposite reasons arising from perceived deficiencies in its authority. Regarded by extremists on the one hand as 'another Horn of the fourth Beast', obstructing Christ's kingdom, and on the other as usurper of the people's fundamental right to representative rule,[50] committee or council could rely only on those either convinced of Army supremacy or less troubled by its dubious credentials than by the dangers of disunity.[51] The latter constituency, dominated by the gathered churches, was too narrow a base on which to build a new government depending, as virtually every model did, on consent and co-

48 Worden, 'Oceana: origins', 136. Stubbe, Letter . . . concerning a select senate (26 Oct.); Milton, 'Proposals of certaine expedients for the preventing of a civil war now feard & the settling of a firme government', CPW vii. 336–9; England's Standard . . . Or, A REMON-STRANCE Of The Lovers of the COMMONWEALTH, Inhabitants of HAMPSHIRE. Delivered to The Council of the Officers . . . , November 21, 1659. Like Milton, Vane and Johnston did not publish their schemes, but debated them in committee (Johnston diary, 150–2); Turner outlined his model on 16 Nov. (MS Sloane 4165, fo. 43), while the advice of Berkshire's Baptists appears amongst other letters in Warning-piece, 11–13. Republican creativity, measured by the number of proposals published, did decline during these months, as energies were diverted elsewhere.

49 Ten points were published in THE AGREEMENT Of the General Council of Officers of the Armies of England, Scotland and Ireland . . . (22 Dec.); the council had previously agreed to summon a new parliament, limited by 'seven fundamentals', which 21 'Conservators of Liberties' were to enforce: A Particular Advice, no. 47, 9–16 Dec., 527–8. The council contained no members from Scotland, the navy or Lambert's forces, so was not truly representative.

50 Edward Burrough, A MESSAGE to the Present Rulers of England whether Committee of Safety, (so called), Councell of Officers, or Others, 8. Hostile Fifth Monarchists attacked the Army/committee in similar language. Unlike these groups, who condemned all previous governments, the Army's neo-Leveller critics often expressed support for Parliament; their milder pronouncements include To The GENERAL COUNCIL . . . The Representation of divers Citizens of LONDON, and others Well-affected, and John Streater, A LETTER Sent to . . . THE Lord Fleetwood . . . On December the 15th.

51 This was the reasoning of John Owen and the Congregational churches in their letters to Monck: Clarke papers, iv. 121–4, 184–5. Baptists William Kiffin and Samuel Moyer were also prominent among the Army's supporters. William Allen, another Baptist, confirms that many of the 'so called sectarian party' inclined to 'the Army, as their onely visible security': Baxter correspondence, i. 416.

operation from a majority of the Commonwealth's now divided and largely disheartened adherents.[52] Without so much as the conviction of their own authority which had sustained them in 1653, the London officers abandoned the attempt to impose a settlement on dissenting fellow soldiers and civilian republicans, and surrendered unconditionally to the Long Parliament.

Hesilrig had seemed to triumph, but ten weeks without a credible authority had sown the seeds of the Commonwealth's final collapse. That practical consensus in Parliament's favour among the 'good party', which had enabled efficient administration until the October crisis, disintegrated rapidly thereafter. Factionalism erupted in the republican camp for the first time that year. It exposed differences, and drove lasting wedges, between rigid parliamentary supremacists, those whose support for Parliament had sprung from expediency, and those who vainly sought to steer a non-committal middle course. Try as the Committee of Safety would to paper over the cracks, an ever more discernible vacuum developed at the centre. The unmistakable deterioration of government greatly assisted monarchists in affirming the time-tested excellence of the one truly legal 'Supreme Authority' over every alternative model, and in transforming latent popular hostility to the Republic into growing agitation for a 'free Parliament'. Thanks to the ambiguity of this slogan, an uneasy alliance against the military threat to English laws and liberties developed between disgruntled MPs and moderate Presbyterians; this emboldened the latter while undermining the exclusive claims of the former. By December it was too late to turn back the clock. After Parliament's second restoration, moderate Baptist William Allen observed that 'we seeme on every side under as great and in reference to many under farr greater difficulties than before'. Vane and Salway lamented that 'al was going wrong and looking towards the King agayne in House, City and Army'. Ensuing months would vindicate Vane's forebodings rather than Hesilrig's 'very jocund and high' demeanour.[53]

Hesilrig's miscalculation was to assume that parliamentary authority would emerge intact from the fragmentation of its former adherents and the example, even encouragement, of sedition that he and his associates had given. But the genie of popular unrest could not be bottled again so easily: instead of reverting to passivity, county after county joined the capital in campaigning for a 'free and full Parliament'.[54] The depleted House, itself

---

[52] The main exception to this general rule was, of course, Harrington, who opposed the rule of a 'refined party' backed by a 'perpetual Army', and proposed instead a Commonwealth based on the 'whole People ... without exception, or with exception for a time of so few as may be': *Valerius and Publicola*, 17–18, 27.

[53] Allen to Baxter, 30 Dec., *Baxter correspondence*, i. 421; *Johnston diary*, 165, entry for 30 Dec.; Whitelocke, *Memorials*, iv. 385, recalling Hesilrig's re-entry to the House on 29 Dec. The events following Parliament's second restoration are described in detail by the narrative histories.

[54] Newsbooks of Jan.–Feb. 1660 reported the promotion of addresses to this effect in Suffolk, Norfolk, Buckinghamshire, Leicestershire, Devon, Northamptonshire, Kent,

divided on this issue, tried in vain to recover, promising recruiter elections, proclaiming the superior dedication to Protestantism, prosperity and the 'public Interest' of republics, and pledging support for the law, trade, a learned ministry and 'due Liberty of Conscience'. Disillusioned sectaries compared this decidedly unrevolutionary declaration unfavourably with those of 1649 and 1651.[55] Secluded Presbyterians, unappeased, intensified their struggle for readmission, while equally irreconcilable Royalists flooded the presses with ever more repulsive satires of the 'Rump' and its leaders.[56] Republican demoralisation continued. From Milton's warnings against 'returning to old bondage' in the *Readie and Easie Way* to the petition of well-affected Londoners, led by Praisegod Barebone, against 'the present confidence and bold attempts of the Promoters of Regal Interest', a defensive, increasingly desperate note pervades the final publications of the Commonwealth's advocates.[57] Barebone's was one of only three loyal addresses presented by civilians.[58] Scarcely any pamphleteers now sought to justify Parliament's government or offer constructive advice.[59] Unable to repress the resurgent reactionaries, the Republic's rulers further discouraged erstwhile supporters by removing the MPs, officers and administrators who had been active in the interruption, and employing 'Rigid, Royal, Neutral Spirits' with little or no record of commitment to the 'Good Old Cause'.[60] Foremost among these was Monck himself.

Devon, Dorset, Lincolnshire and Yorkshire. Monck himself transmitted this request of 'most Counties' to Parliament in a speech at his reception, reported in *Politicus*, no. 606, 2–9 Feb., 1082.

[55] Parliament's declaration was printed ibid. no. 604, 19–26 Jan., 1037–8; radical disappointment was expressed in *A COFFIN For the Good Old Cause; Or A Sober Word by way of Caution to the Parliament and Army*, 3.

[56] Presbyterian implacability manifested itself in such attacks on the sitting MPs as *SIX IMPORTANT Q U A E R E S, Propounded To the Re-sitting Rump*; *The CURTAINE DRAWNE; Or the Parliament exposed to view*, and Prynne's latest works, *Conscientous, Serious theological and legal quaeres*, and *A Legal Vindication Of the Liberties of ENGLAND Against ILLEGAL TAXES And pretended Acts of Parliament*. At least 15 ballads, broadsheets and pamphlets produced in the first months of 1660 execrated 'the Rump' in their titles.

[57] Milton, *Readie and easie way*, 1; 'The Representation . . . of the Well-affected Persons, Inhabitants of . . . London and Westminster', presented by Barebone on 9 Feb., was reproduced in *An Exact Accompt*, no. 65, 3–10 Feb., 654–5.

[58] The others were the watermen's petition, subscribed by dubious methods, and an address from Leicester dissociating the town from the county's petition for a free Parliament: *Politicus*, no. 605, 26 Jan.–2 Feb., 1066; no. 607, 9–16 Feb., 1095–6. Petitions from Norfolk and Exeter supporting the secluded can hardly be classed as loyal. Most addresses to the re-restored Parliament came from penitent officers; several examples survive in the Nalson papers.

[59] Thomason collected less than half a dozen republican tracts between the end of December and the beginning of March. These excluded the few defences of Parliament that did appear; the latter, however, were all delayed publications from the autumn controversy rather than new writings. Among the few constructive texts were S. E., *Toutch-stone of mony*, and H[awke], *History of the union*, which carried a fulsome dedication to Speaker Lenthall.

[60] *Coffin*, 2, 4; cf. the dismay of Baynes's relatives at the promotion of individuals formerly

As undisputed commander of the purged Army, he attained a position of greater power than Fleetwood or Lambert had ever aspired to, and used it to conciliate the 'sober Gentry' by promoting 'moderate' conservative counsels.[61] Conflict between City and Parliament in February exposed the essentially opportunistic nature of Monck's professed republicanism; once he agreed to reinstate the secluded members, a return to monarchy became certain. Lambert's last, feeblest, effort to prevent this outcome foundered on the same rock as his first: the lack of any credible alternative authority.[62]

'layd aside for being soe hott for a kingly government', and hence likely to 'Act coldly for [Parliament's] interest': MS Add. 21425, fos 195, 201.

[61] This was the keynote of his speech to Parliament: *Politicus*, no. 606, 2–9 Feb., 1082.

[62] Ludlow refused to participate in Lambert's abortive rising in April for want of positive agreement on its objectives, a refusal contrasting with his earlier readiness to advocate precipitate action to 'recover all' when 'the lawfull authority was on our side': *Voyce*, 112–13, 90.

Conclusion

1659 constitutes a major challenge to interpretations of the 1650s as a steady retreat from revolution to tradition, from idealism to disillusion or a 'cynical pragmatism' associated with 'the Rump'.[1] Much more than a negative reaction to the increasingly monarchical Protectorate, the remarkable outpouring of ideas reveals the confidence, the maturation of radical thought. This year was the Machiavellian 'occasione' *par excellence*, witnessing the fullest flowering of English republicanism, under conditions of maximum freedom. From an expedient reluctantly adopted in the aftermath of regicide, the Commonwealth had become the object of passionate ideological commitment, inspiring sophisticated vindications of its authority and visions of its future constitution. The most influential individual theorist, Harrington, was by no means the only 'creative and innovative thinker'.[2] Of equal importance was the godly republicans' novel blend of biblical, classical and contemporary wisdom, and the nationalist, historically driven attention to detailed reform that distinguished the resurgent Levellers. Diversity flourished within a substantial consensus on basic principles, which encouraged respectful communication rather than internecine conflict. Hopes of achieving a lasting republic centred in Parliament, the authoritative arbiter accepted by all the differing parties.

Reliance on the restored Parliament was realistic. Its second session not only supplied further proof that kingless government was feasible, with active assistance from loyal citizens, but also demonstrated the members' capacity to look beyond immediate emergencies to the future form of the commonwealth. Vane, in particular, was a statesman who transcended the gulf between constitutional theory and practice, comprehended all the various political languages, and used them to constructive effect. Progress towards settlement did occur. Despite the absence of any direct record of the debates in the House and its committees, there are tantalising clues to what might have been: a unified British republic, religiously tolerant, politically based on the solidarity of the 'well-affected' constituency, incorporating the best of their different ideas, and closely allied with the United Provinces. Such a commonwealth could well have proved as powerful and prosperous as its neighbour. If enforced with sufficient firmness for a sufficient period, the most revolutionary changes may become internalised, as the eventual success of the initially unwelcome Protestant Reformation in England and Scotland

---

1 Underdown, *Freeborn people*, 87–8.
2 Worden, 'English republicanism', 474.

showed. Given time to re-educate the majority in the principles of popular government, the republicans might have reduced monarchists, demoralised by repeated defeats, to a dissident element no more, and perhaps much less, disruptive than the Roman Catholics, or the Dutch Orangists.

Time was, of course, the commodity that the Commonwealth conspicuously lacked. What ruined its promising recommencement was the sudden crisis of the autumn. In this contingency played the greatest, though not the only, part. Strenuous efforts to avert or resolve a breach came very close to succeeding. If there was a moment that sealed their failure, it was Hesilrig's exit from negotiations with the officers on 15 October. The devastating impact of the second expulsion on republican morale owed much to the apparent solidity of the reconciliation between Army and Parliament. One neo-Leveller pamphlet, begun before the interruption, but finished soon afterwards, neatly encapsulates the transition from optimism to dismay, symbiosis to separation. The main sections confidently refute counter-revolutionary arguments, enunciate principles for settlement, and incidentally defend the officers' devotion to the 'Publique Spirit'. But instead of the planned peroration exhorting all groups to submit to Parliament's decision, the writer concludes with 'smart rebukes' to the soldiers:

> You have broken this Parliament, you have broken your selves and us too, yea have turned all topsie turvie . . . you have made England, Scotland & Ireland *a Chaos without form and void* . . . We who . . . encouraged you in the day of your straights, and told every body . . . how honest the Army would be, now they understood themselves; that they would stand by the Parliament while they did settle the Nation upon the foundation of righteousness and truth: We, even we, are laughed to scorn . . . You were and are as necessary . . . to defend us as their Counsell to give forth such Orders as may make us happy . . . Do you overturn, overturn, overturn and take no care for the Nation, nor your selves? . . . The Ship of the Commonwealth is now launched out into the Ocean of Confusion . . . though but the other day we deemed that we drew nigh to some Countrey, to some Settlement.[3]

Embarrassment and anger, disillusion and disappointment, amounting almost to desolation, at the snatching away of a significant opportunity pervade this vehement jeremiad. Such sentiments were widespread among the 'well-affected', who either withdrew from politics to ineffectual neutralism or else consumed their energies in undermining each other. Without the unifying focus that parliamentary authority had provided, government gradually disintegrated. Meanwhile monarchists, emboldened by the confusion, began to mobilise public opinion against the Commonwealth. Hesilrig's victory in the war of attrition was won at the cost of severely weakening his own side. In its third and shortest session Parliament could neither subdue reactionaries,

[3] *Grand concernments*, 7, 55, 57, 59, 69. The rebukes were also published separately as *A parliamenters petition*.

arrest the republican decline nor heal the divisions now raging both indoors and out. The initiative had passed to its enemies, and the instinctively conservative General Monck, whose promotion, another unintended consequence of the second interruption, led to the demise of this Parliament, and with it the Republic.

Despite the disarray of the winter, the spring of 1659 had shown the resilience, the remarkable regenerative capacity of English republicanism. Hopes, still cherished by many, that the sun would rise once more upon the 'Good Old Cause', after another 'Night of Tyrannie', were far from groundless.[4] The Commonwealth represented a compelling alternative to kingship, and failed to establish itself by the narrowest of margins. It left an enduring legacy of political and religious dissent, which perpetuated instability and provoked fierce repression. The very intensity with which Royalists denounced the futility, and sought to eradicate the memory, of republic and republicanism testifies to their powerful appeal, and the fears for traditional order that they aroused. The restored monarchy was vulnerable. When Charles II resolved to execute the defiant Vane, as 'too dangerous a man to let live', he was not just indulging personal vindictiveness, but responding to the actual possibility that this charismatic republican leader might again become a centre of radical opposition.[5] Vane's performance in 1659 amply supports such suspicion. The crisis of that year indicates that England was by no means as inherently monarchical as some have supposed. Historiography rooted in the perceptions of the victors has too long obscured the fluidity, the creative possibilities of this moment. Discarding such hindsight discloses the Commonwealth's real potential, and the true significance of this turning point in Britain's history.

---

[4] This metaphor, so often used of the Protectorate in the spring (see, for examples, Morris, *To the supream authoritie*, 3–4; Milton, *Considerations*, 274) could equally be applied to the restored monarchy. In 1662 Vane would interpret the 'dark night and black shade, which God hath drawn over his work' since 1659 as the prelude to 'some beautiful Piece', and confidently anticipate 'resurrection' of the 'glorious Cause': *Tryal*, 77, 79–80.

[5] Charles II to Clarendon, 7 June 1662, in *The letters, speeches and declarations of King Charles II*, ed. Arthur Bryant, London 1935, 128. Though malice was certainly present, Hutton seems mistaken in representing Charles's action as sheer 'vindictiveness' against an 'expendable' victim: *Restoration*, 162, 204. Vane was far from helpless, and his death was, as he had hoped, a propaganda defeat for the monarchy.

Bibliography

Unpublished primary sources

GREAT BRITAIN

Bristol Record Office
MS Ashton Court C/C64 Correspondence of Hugh Smyth

Chester, Cheshire Record Office
DSS/Drawer 5 Diary of Somerford Oldfield

Exeter, Devon Record Office
Exeter Chamber act book 10

Gloucester, Gloucestershire Record Office
GBR H 2/3 Gloucester Letter Book

Hull Corporation Archives
Letters

Hull, Humberside Record Office
BC II/7/4/1 Beverley Corporation minutes

Lewes, East Sussex Record Office
Rye MS 47/161 Rye correspondence

Maidstone, Kent Record Office
'Miscellaneous letters to Sandwich'
Quarter Session order books, East Kent 1, West Kent 2

Matlock, Derbyshire Record Office
MS 1232 m/o fos 80–103 Correspondence of Thomas Saunders

London, British Library
MS Add. 11411 Correspondence of Thomas Povey
MS Add. 11597 Financial reports
MS Add. 21425 Correspondence of Adam Baynes
MS Egerton 1048 Scottish commissioners' instructions
     Buckinghamshire petition
MS Egerton 2395 Proposals for West India company
MSS Harley 1929, 2125 Randall Holme's Cheshire compilation
MS Sloane 4158 Diplomatic correspondence
MS Sloane 4159 Secret instruction to Sound commissioners

MS Sloane 4165 Correspondence of Charles Fleetwood
MS Stowe 185 Post-Restoration lists of the Commonwealth's active servants
 Irish commissioners' instructions to Ludlow

London, Corporation of London Record Office
Common Council Journal, vol. 41
Common Hall minutes 1659
Repertories of the court of aldermen, 66–7
Sessions files 1659

London, Dr Williams' Library
'Copy of Yarmouth Congregational Church Record, 1642–1855'

London, Friends House Library
MS Great Book of Sufferings
MS Portfolio I
MS vol. S81 William Caton manuscripts III
MS vol. 316 Ellwood manuscripts II
MS vol. 356 Swarthmore manuscripts IV
MS vol. 359 Swarthmore manuscripts VII

London, House of Lords Record Office
MS Journal of the House of Commons, 1659

London, Public Record Office, Kew
ASSI 1/2 Oxford circuit
ASSI 35/100 Home circuit
C181/6 Lists of JPs, judges etc.
C193/13/5 JPs, 1657–8
C231/6 Chancery clerks' docket book
SP 25/79 Council minutes, 11 Aug.–25 Oct.
SP 25/98 Council letter book
SP 28/334 Accounts for Cornwall, Middlesex, London
SP 28/335 Accounts for Shropshire
 Sussex militia commissioners
SP 78/114 Diplomatic correspondence

Oxford, Bodleian Library
MSS Carte 30, 213, 73 Ormonde and Montagu papers
MSS Clarendon 60–6 Clarendon papers, 1659
MS Dep. C. 159 Nalson papers
MS Rawlinson A65 Dunkirk commissioners' papers
MS Rawlinson A259 Committee of Safety warrants
MS Rawlinson C79 Council minutes, 19 May–10 Aug.
MS Rawlinson D397 Quaker manuscripts
MS Tanner 51 Lenthall papers
MS J Walker C11 Leicestershire militia commissioners' proceedings

Oxford, Worcester College
MS Clarke 31–2, 267/1 Army newsletters
Monck's correspondence

Preston, Lancashire Record Office
QSO/2/32 Quarter sessions order book

Trowbridge, Wiltshire Record Office
A1/160/2 Quarter sessions order book
G23/1/4 Ledger D Salisbury Common Council minutes

York, City Archives
Corporation Assembly minute book

UNITED STATES

New Haven, Folger Shakespeare Library, Yale University
MS X.d.483, fos 123–33 Correspondence of Robert Bennet, 1659.

Published primary sources

Official publications
Acts and ordinances of the Interregnum, ed. C. H. Firth and R. S. Rait, London 1911
Calendar of the proceedings of the Committee for Compounding, i, ed. M. A. E. Green, London 1889
Calendar of state papers, colonial America & West Indies, 1574–1660, ed. W. N. Sainsbury, London 1860
Calendar of state papers, domestic series, 1658–9, 1659, ed. M. A. E. Green, London 1867–95
Calendar of state papers and manuscripts, relating to English affairs, existing in the archives and collections of Venice and in other libraries of northern Italy, xxxii (1659–61), ed. A. B. Hinds, London 1931
A collection of the state papers of John Thurloe, ed. J. T. Birch, London 1742
Journals of the House of Commons, vii, London 1802
State papers collected by Edward earl of Clarendon, commencing from the year 1621, ed. R. Scrope and T. Monkhouse, Oxford 1767–86

Historical Manuscripts Commission
Leyborne-Popham MSS
Third report, appendix
Ninth report, appendix ii
Tenth report, pt ii, appendix iv

Memoirs, collected papers, letters etc
Aubrey's brief lives, ed. A. Powell, London 1949
The autobiography of Henry Newcome, ed. R. Parkinson (Chetham Society xxvi, 1852)
Calendar of the correspondence of Richard Baxter, ed. N. H. Keeble and G. Nuttall, Oxford 1991

The Clarke papers: selections from the papers of Sir William Clarke, ed. C. H. Firth (Camden n.s. lxi, lxii, 1894–1901)

Coke, R., *A detection of the court and state of England*, London 1691

Complete prose works of John Milton, VII: *1659–1660*, ed. R. W. Ayers, New Haven, Conn. 1980

The diary of Andrew Hay of Craignethan, 1659–1660, ed. A. Reid (Scottish History Society 1st ser. xxxix, 1901)

The diary of Sir Archibald Johnston of Wariston, ed. J. D. Ogilvie (Scottish History Society xxxiv, 1940)

The diary of the Revd Ralph Josselin, ed. E. Hockliffe (Camden 3rd ser. xv, 1908)

The diary of Samuel Pepys, from 1659–1669, ed. Richard, Lord Braybrooke, London 1879

The diary of Thomas Burton Esq., ed. J. T. Rutt, London 1828

The diurnal of Thomas Rugg, ed. W. L. Sachse (Camden 3rd ser. xci, 1961)

Extracts from the records of the burgh of Edinburgh, 1655–1665, ed. M. Wood, Edinburgh 1940

Guizot, F., *Histoire du protectorat de Richard Cromwell et du retablissement des Stuart*, Paris 1856, appendices (correspondence of Ambassador Bordeaux)

Hutchinson, L., *Memoirs of the life of Col. Hutchinson*, London 1822

Inedited letters of Cromwell, Col. Jones, Bradshaw and other regicides, ed. J. Mayer (Historical Society of Lancashire and Cheshire, 1861)

The journal of Edward Mountagu first earl of Sandwich, 1659–1665, ed. R. C. Anderson, London 1929

The journal of George Fox, ed. J. L. Nickalls, Cambridge 1952

The letter book of John, Viscount Mordaunt, 1658–1660, ed. M. Coate (Camden 3rd ser. lxix, 1945)

Letters of early Friends, ed. J. Barclay, London 1811

The letters and journals of Robert Baillie, ed. D. Laing, Edinburgh 1842

Letters of Roger Williams, 1632–1682, ed. J. R. Bartlett, Providence, RI 1874

The letters, speeches and declarations of King Charles II, ed. A. Bryant, London 1935

The life of Adam Martindale, written by himself, ed. R. Parkinson (Chetham Society, 1845)

The life of Robert Blair, minister of St Andrews . . . with continuation of the history of the times to 1680, by his son-in-law, Mr William Row, minister of Ceres, ed. T. McCrie, Edinburgh 1848

Ludlow, Edmund, *A voyce from the watchtower: part five, 1660–62*, ed. A. B. Worden (Camden 4th ser. xxi, 1978)

The memoirs of Edmund Ludlow . . . 1625–1672, ed. C. H. Firth, Oxford 1894

The Nicholas papers, ed. G. F. Warner (Camden 3rd ser. xxxi, 1920) iv

Nicoll, John, *A diary of public transactions and other occurrences chiefly in Scotland, 1650–1667*, Edinburgh 1836

North Riding quarter session minutes & orders, ed. J. C. Atkinson (North Riding Record Society vi, 1888)

Orders made by the court of quarter sessions for Shropshire, i, ed. R. L. Kenyon, Shrewsbury 1901

Original letters and papers of state addressed to Oliver Cromwell, ed. J. Nickolls, London 1743

The pyramid and the urn: the life in letters of a Restoration squire: William Lawrence of Shurdington, 1636–97, ed. I. Sinclair, Stroud 1994

The Rawdon papers, ed. E. Berwick, London 1819

Records of the borough of Leicester, ed. H. Stocks, Cambridge 1923

Register of the consultations of the ministers of Edinburgh, ed. W. Stephen (Scottish History Society, 1930)

Somerset quarter sessions records, ed. E. H. Bates (Somerset Record Society, 1907)

Sydney papers, ed. R. W. Blencowe, London 1825

Vertue, G., Medals, coins, great seals and other works of Thomas Simon, London 1780

Whitelocke, B., Memorials of the English affairs, Oxford 1853

Contemporary periodicals

An EXACT ACCOMPT Of the daily Proceedings in PARLIAMENT. With Occurrences from Foreign Parts

The Faithful [then National, then Loyal] Scout: Impartially Communicating The most remarkable Intelligence, From all Christian Kings, Princes, States and Common-Wealths: With the chief Affairs and Transactions of the Parliament of England

Mercurius Democritus or a Perfect NOCTURNAL Communicating many strange Wonders Out of the World in the Moon . . . Published for the right understanding of all the Mad-merry People of Great Bedlam

Mercurius Politicus Comprising The sum of Foreign Intelligence, with the Affairs now on foot in the Three Nations . . . Published by Order of Parliament

Mercurius Pragmaticus

The Moderate Informer Communicating The most remarkable Transactions both Civil and Military in the Commonwealth of England Together with A Faithfull Account of the Actions and Affairs from all other Nations

Occurrences from Forraigne Parts also a Particular Advice from The Office of Intelligence

A Particular Advice FROM The Office of Intelligence Neer the Old Exchange in Cornhil And also Weekly Occurrences from Forraigne Parts . . .

The Publick Intelligencer Communicating the Chief Occurrences and PROCEEDINGS Within The Dominions of England, Scotland and Ireland. Together with an Account of Affairs from severall Parts of Europe. Published by Order of Parliament

The Weekly Account. Faithfully Representing, The most Remarkable Passages in Parliament; And proceedings of the Armies, in England, Scotland and Ireland. Together with other Foreign Intelligence . . .

The Weekly INTELLIGENCER of the COMMON-WEALTH: Faithfully communicating the Affairs of these three Nations. As also the most remarkable Transactions . . . of all other Nations

The Weekly Post: Truly Communicating The Chief Occurences and Proceedings, within the Commonwealth of England, Scotland and Ireland: And an Account of Affairs from several Christian Princes and Commonwealths in EUROPE

Contemporary books, pamphlets, and broadsheets

[all printed in London, and in 1659 unless otherwise stated]

An ACT for The more certain and constant Supply of the SOLDIERY with PAY; And the preventing of any further Oppression . . . to the People by Free-quarter or Billet, 1649, repr. Nov. 1659

An Alarum to the City and Souldiery

Ambitious TYRANNY, Clearly Demonstrated in ENGLANDS Unhappy and confused Government . . .

[Annesley, Arthur], ENGLAND'S CONFUSION Or A True and Impartial Relation of the late Traverses of State in England

AN ANSWER To A PROPOSITION In order to the proposing of A Commonwealth or Democracy. Proposed by friends to the Commonwealth by Mr. Harringtons consent

AN ANSWER of some if not all the CITIZENS of London & Freemen of ENGLAND, To a Paper entituled An Express from the Knights and Gentlemen now Engaged with Sir George Booth

The ARMIES DECLARATION Examined and Compared with Their Declaration May 6, Their Petition and Addresse May 12 And their Petition & Representation

The ARMIES DECLARATION Examined . . . Discovering some of their Contradicitons, Lies, Calumnies, Hypocrisie and Designs

THE ARMIES DUTIE; Or Faithfull Advice to the Souldiers

The Armies Proposalls to the PARLIAMENT . . . [Derby petition]

The ARMIES Vindication of this last Change. Wherein Is plainly Demonstrated, the Equity, Power and Right of the Army to settle these Nations upon the Foundations of Righteousnesse and Freedome

The Army Mastered, OR GREAT BRITTAINS JOY: Briefly Presented to those true Patriots . . . now assembled in Parliament . . .

THE ARMY'S PLEA For Their present Practice

Articles of Impeachment of Transcendent Crimes, Injuries, Misdemeanours, Oppressions and high Breach of TRUST Committed by Col. Philip Jones . . . read in PARLIAMENT the 18th of May 1659. Together with . . . Jones' Answer

Ascham, Anthony, Of the Confusions and Revolutions of Government, 1649

Bache, Humphrey, A Few Words in true love written to the old long sitting PARLIAMENT who Are yet left alive, and do sit there now . . .

A BAKERS-DOZEN OF Plain Down-right QUERIES

Baker, Daniel, The PROPHET APPROVED By the WORDS Of his Prophesie coming to passe . . .

Ball, William, LAW and STATE PROPOSALS Humbly Presented to the Supream Authority, the Parliament

Baxter, Richard, A Holy Commonwealth, or Political Aphorisms, Opening The true Principles of Government

———— A Key for Catholicks

[Bethel, Slingsby], A Second NARRATIVE Of The Late Parliament (so called)

BIBLIOTHECA MILITUM: Or the SOULDIERS Publick LIBRARY

Bibliotheca regia or, The Royal Library containing such papers of His late Maiesty King Charls, the second monarch of Great Britain, as have escaped the ruines of these times

B[illing], E[dward], A MITE OF AFFECTION, Manifested in 31. PROPOSALS, Offered to all the Sober and Free-born People, Tending and tendred unto them for a Settlement in this the day of the Worlds Distraction

Bishop, George, MENE TEKEL, Or The Council of Officers of the Army Against The Declarations &c. of the Army

Bland, John, Trade Revived, or, A way proposed to restore, increase, inrich and preserve the decayed and even dying trade of this our English nation, in its

282

manufactories, coin, shiping and revenue whereby taxes may be lessened if not totally taken away . . .

A Bloudy FIGHT Between the Parliaments Forces and Sir GEORGE BOOTH'S

[Brathwait, Richard], Panthalia: or the Royal Romance. A Discourse stored with infinite variety in relation to State-Government And Passages of matchless affection . . .

Bray, William, A BRIEF ADMONITION of Some of the Inconveniences Of all the three most Famous GOVERNMENTS known to the World: With their Comparisons together

———— A PLEA FOR THE Peoples Fundamentall Liberties and Parliaments. Or, Eighteen QUESTIONS Questioned & Answered, Which QUESTIONS were lately propounded by Mr. Jeremy Jves . . .

———— A Plea for the Peoples Good Old Cause, Or The Fundamental Lawes and Liberties of England Asserted . . . to be our RIGHT before the CONQUEST . . . By way of Answer to Mr JAMES HARRINGTON his cxx Political Aphorisms

Burrough, Edward, A DECLARATION To all the WORLD of our FAITH: And what we believe who are called QUAKERS

———— A MESSAGE to the Present Rulers of England whether Committee of Safety, (so called), Councell of Officers, or Others whatsoever by an Ambassadour from the only Right Heire of the Government, whose Right alone it is to Rule . . .

———— To the PARLIAMENT of the Common-wealth of ENGLAND who are in place of Authority to do Justice, and in present power to ease the oppressed Nation from its Bonds. Councel and Advice. . . .

———— To the PARLIAMENT. . . . A Presentation, by a faithful Friend to the Nations, in the Name . . . of Jesus Christ . . . That you may take off oppression . . . that Truth, justice and Righteousness may come nigh unto us . . .

———— A Visitation & Warning PROCLAMED And An Alarm Sounded in the Popes Borders . . . Being the Account of a Journey to Dunkirk

By the Committee of Safety . . . A PROCLAMATION Inhibiting all Meetings for the Raising or drawing together of Forces without order of the said Committee or the Lord Fleetwood

Canne, John, A Seasonable Word to the Parliament-Men, To take with them when they go into the HOUSE . . .

The CASE of Colonel MATTHEW ALURED

A CATALOGUE of the NAMES of this Present Parliament

Chamberlen, Peter, A SCOURGE For A DENN Of THIEVES

CHAOS: Or, A DISCOURSE, Wherein Is presented . . . a Frame of Government by way of a Republique . . .

The CHARACTER or EAR-MARK of Mr. WILLIAM PRINNE

The Character of the Parliament, commonly called the Rump, &c., begun November 23, in the year 1640 with a short account of some of their proceedings, 1660

A COFFIN For the Good Old Cause; Or A Sober Word by way of Caution to the Parliament and Army, 1660

Cole, William, A ROD FOR THE LAWYERS

———— Severall PROPOSALS Humbly tendered to the CONSIDERATION Of those in Authority, for the Ease, Security, & Prosperity of this Common-wealth

A COMMONWEALTH, And Commonwealths-men Asserted and Vindicated . . . And PEACE and UNITY Commended . . .

A Common-wealth or NOTHING Or, Monarchy and Oligarchy Prov'd Parallel in Tyranny

A CONFERENCE BETWEEN *Two Souldiers Meeting on the Roade. the one being of the Army in ENGLAND, The other of the Army in SCOTLAND* . . .

CONSIDERATIONS AND PROPOSALS *Presented to his late Highness Oliver Lord Protector* . . . *Touching the not Warring with SPAIN*

CONSIDERATIONS *Upon the late transactions* . . . *of the ARMY, In reference to the DISSOLUTION of the PARLIAMENT*

The CURTAINE DRAWNE; *Or the Parliament exposed to view. The Names of the Members yet living of both Houses of Parliament forceably secluded* . . . , 1660

A DECLARATION *Of the Christian-Free-Born Subjects of the once Flourishing Kingdom of ENGLAND*

A DECLARATION *Of the Commander in Chief of the Forces in SCOTLAND, Also another DECLARATION Of the Officers* . . . *in SCOTLAND To the Churches of Christ* . . . *Together with Three LETTERS from the Lord General MONCK* . . .

A DECLARATION *By the Committee of Safety* . . . *Touching the Payment of* . . . *Customs and Excise*

A *Declaration of the English Army* . . . *to the People of Scotland* . . . *Aug. 1 1650*

A DECLARATION OF THE GENERAL COUNCIL *Of The Officers of the Army: Agreed upon at Wallingford house, 27th Octob. 1659*

A DECLARATION OF THE OFFICERS OF THE ARMY, *Inviting the Members of the Long PARLIAMENT, Who Continued Sitting till the 20th April 1653 to return to* . . . *their TRUST. Friday May 6 1659*

THE DECLARATION *Of the Officers of the Army Opened, Examined & Condemned and the PARLIAMENT VINDICATED* . . .

A *Declaration of several Officers of the Army in Ireland* . . . *holding forth their stedfast resolutions to adhere to the Parliament* . . . *and the just Rights and Libertyes of the People* . . .

The DECLARATION *and PROCLAMATION of the ARMY of GOD Owned by the Lord of Hosts in many Victories. To all the good People*

A DECLARATION *Of The PARLIAMENT Assembled at Westminster*

A DECLARATION *Of the Parliament* . . . *July 7*

A DECLARATION OF THE PROCEEDINGS *Of the Parliament & Army And The Resolution of the Souldiery: With The Remonstrance, Grounds & Reasons, of these unexpected Changes and sudden Interruptions* . . .

A DECLARATION *Of the Well-affected to THE GOOD OLD CAUSE In the Cities of London, Westminster, and Borough of Southwark* . . . *for the Return* . . . *of The Long PARLIAMENT*

DEMOCRITUS *Turned STATES-MAN: Or Twenty QUAERIES Between Jest and Earnest* . . .

A *Dialogue betwixt an EXCISE-MAN and DEATH*

The Dispersed United: *Or, Twelve Healing QUESTIONS propounded To Persons of ingenious Principles and Tempers* . . .

Duncon, Samuel, SEVERAL PROPOSALS *Offered by a Friend to Peace & Truth to The Serious Consideration of the Keepers of the Liberties of The People of England, In Reference to a SETTLEMENT Of Peace and Truth* . . .

[Dury, John], *The Interest of ENGLAND IN THE Protestant Cause*

Eccles, Solomon, *In the year 59, in the fourth month* . . .

E.D., COMPLAINTS *And QUERIES Vpon ENGLANDS Misery Acted Octob. 13, 1659, By some OFFICERS* . . . *Against the Parliament* . . .

Eight and Thirty QUERIES Propounded By One that is setting forth Sail, and desires to steer his Course aright, that escaping the Gulphs he may arrive at SAFETY. . . .

Eliot, John, *The Christian COMMONWEALTH: Or, The Civil Policy of The Rising Kingdom of Jesus Christ*

England ANATOMIZED: Her Disease discovered, and the Remedy prescribed . . .

ENGLAND'S CHANGELING . . . A clear Discovery of the New Cheat of the Thing called the Good Old Cause

ENGLANDS present Case Stated, In A further Remonstrance of many thousands of the Citizens, Housholders, Freemen and Apprentizes of the City of London . . .

ENGLANDS REMEMBRANCES

ENGLANDS SAFETY in the LAWS Supremacy

ENGLANDS SETTLEMENT, upon the Two solid foundations of The Peoples Civil and Religious LIBERTIES . . .

England's Standard . . . Or, A REMONSTRANCE Of The Lovers of the COMMONWEALTH, Inhabitants of HAMPSHIRE. Delivered to The Council of the Officers . . . , November 21, 1659

An Essay towards Settlement upon a sure Foundation being an humble Testimony for God in this perilous time by a few, who have been bewailing their own and others Abominations, and would not be comforted, until their Redeemer . . . be exalted in Righteousness . . .

Evans, Aris, *A Rule from Heaven, OR, VVholsom COUNSEL To A Distracted STATE Wherein is discovered The onely Way for settling The GOOD OLD CAUSE* . . .

[Evelyn, John], *An APOLOGY for the ROYAL PARTY*

EXCISE ANOTOMIZD, AND TRADE EPITOMIZD: Declaring, that unequall Imposition of Excise, to be the only cause of the ruine of Trade, and universall impoverishment . . .

An EXPRESS from the KNIGHTS and GENTLEMEN now engaged with Sir GEORGE BOOTH; To the City and Citizens of London, And all other Free-men . . .

A Faithfull Searching HOME WORD . . . presented to the Officers . . . as another Looking-Glass wherein they may plainly see, how wofully they also have Dissembled . . . Together with another Seasonable Word by way of Counsel and Proposal . . . All which, is also to be . . . read of all men loving Righteousness that thereby they may . . . rightly steer their Course . . . for the Exaltation of Christ . . . against all the Apostacy . . . that may further appear in this Gloomy, Dark, Overturning Day

Feake, Christopher, *A BEAM OF LIGHT Shining In the midst of much Darknes & Confusion: Being . . . An ESSAY toward the . . . fixing upon its true and proper basis The Best Cause under Heaven: viz. The Cause of God, of Christ, of his People* . . .

The Fifth Monarchy, or Kingdom of Christ, In opposition to the BEAST'S, Asserted . . . wherein the Old Cause is Stated . . . and some brief Proposals grounded upon Scripture, in order to a lasting Settlement

The First & Second Parts of Invisible JOHN made Visible: Or A Grand Pimp of Tyranny portrayed in BARKSTEADS ARRAIGNMENT . . .

Fisher, Samuel, *To the Parliament of England*

Five PROPOSALS Presented To the General Council of the OFFICERS . . .

Forraign and Domestick PROPHESIES . . . Foretelling . . . His Highness arrival to the . . . Government of Great Britain . . .

Fox, George, Jr, *A Few Plain Words to be considered by those . . . that would have a PARLIAMENT that is chosen by the voyces of the people . . . Wherein is shewed unto them . . . that a Parliament so chosen are not like to govern for God and the good of his People . . .*

FRANCE No Friend to ENGLAND. Or, The Resentments of the French upon the Success of the ENGLISH . . .

Freeze, James, *The OUT-CRY and Just Appeale of the Inslaved People of England, Made To the Right Honourable the PARLIAMENT . . .*

A Friendly LETTER of ADVICE To the SOULDIERS . . .

A FURTHER EVIDENCE Of . . . THOMAS HEWET His DISAFFECTION To the PRESENT AUTHORITY . . . And his perfect enmity against the people of God . . .

A GENERAL Or, No GENERAL Over The Present Army . . .

The Good Old Cause Explained, Revived, & Asserted and the Long-Parliament Vindicated

The Grand Concernments of ENGLAND ENSURED . . . By a constant Succession of Free Parliaments, the only possible Expedient to preserve us from Ruine or Slavery . . . With a Sad EXPOSTULATION, and some smart Rebukes to the ARMY

Hall, Thomas, *Samaria's Downfall: OR, A COMMENTARY . . . on the Five last Verses of the Thirteenth Chapter of H O S E A . . . Very suitable to . . . these present Times . . .*, 1660

Harrington, James, APHORISMS POLITICAL

—— *A DISCOURSE Shewing That the Spirit of Parliaments, With a Council in the Intervals, Is not to be trusted for a Settlement: Lest it introduce MONARCHY, and Persecution . . .*

—— *A DISCOURSE upon This Saying: The Spirit of the Nation is not yet to be trusted with Liberty; lest it introduce Monarchy, or invade the Liberty of Conscience*

—— *Pour enclouer le Canon*

—— *Valerius and Publicola: Or, the true FORM Of a Popular Commonwealth . . .*

Harris, John, *PEACE and not WARRE: Or The MODERATOR. Truly but yet Plainly, STATING the CASE Of The COMMON-WEALTH . . .*

H[awke?], M[ichael], *The History of the Union of the four famous kingdoms of England, Wales, Scotland and Ireland, wherein is demonstrated that by the prowess and prudence of the English, those four . . . nations have . . . been entirely united . . . into one Commonwealth. . . .*, 1660

H. N., *An OBSERVATION and COMPARISON Between the Idolatrous Israelites and Judges of England. A Word to the ARMY. A Memorandum . . . to the Parliament; and an Encouragement to all faithful hearts . . .*

Hodgson, J., *Love, Kindness and due Respect, By way of Warning to the PARLIAMENT, That they may not neglect the great opportunity . . . for the redemption and freedom of these Oppressed Nations*

Holmes, Nathaniel, *A SERMON Preached before the Parliament, the Councill of State, the Lord Major, Aldermen & Common Councill of the City of London, and the Officers . . . Oct. the 6th. A.D. 1659. Being the Publick day of Thanksgiving . . .*

The Honest Patriot. A short DISCOURSE Touching the POLEMICAL SWORD, And of the command in chief of The Militia

Howgill, Francis, *An INFORMATION, and also ADVICE to the Armie on both parts: and this present Committee of safety Newly erected, and to the late Parlia-*

ment : and also to all People who seeks peace and righteousness, and are for the Good Old Cause . . .

———— The MOUTH Of the Pit Stopped And The Smoke that hath arisen out of it scattered by the breath of TRUTH

Hubberthorn, Richard, An ANSWER To a DECLARATION Put forth by . . . the People called ANABAPTISTS In and about the City of LONDON

———— The REAL CAUSE Of The NATIONS Bondage . . . Demonstrated And the Way of their Freedome . . . Asserted. Presented unto the PARLIAMENT . . . Who have a Power and Oportunity to do good and to fulfil the expected ends of many . . .

The Humble ADDRESSE of the Lord Maior, Aldermen and Common-Council of the City. . . . , on the 9th of this instant August to the Council of State . . . with the Lord Whitlock's SPEECH in Answer . . .

The Humble PETITION And ADDRESSE of the Officers of the Army to the PARLIAMENT . . . Thursday May 12

THE HUMBLE PETITION Of Divers Well-affected Persons, Delivered The 6th day of July 1659 To the SUPREME AUTHORITY, The PARLIAMENT of the Common-wealth of England. With the Parliaments Answer thereunto & Sense thereupon

The Humble Petition of the Marchants Trading to the Dominions of the King of SPAIN

The Humble REMONSTRANCE Of the Non-Commission Officers and Private Soldiers of Major General GOFFS Regiment (so called) of Foot . . .

The Humble Representation and desires of divers Freeholders and others well affected to the Commonwealth . . . , inhabiting within the County of Bedford

The Humble Representation of divers well-affected Persons of the City of Westminster . . .

The Humble Representation and Petition of the Field Officers & Captains of the . . . Trained-bands of the City . . .

The Humble REPRESENTATION And PETITION Of the Officers of the Army, To the Parliament . . . Weds. the 5th of Oct 1659 . . .

AN INDICTMENT Against TYTHES: By John Osborne . . . Likewise a QUERY to William Prynne. By JOHN CANNE

The Interest of England stated: or A faithful . . . Account of the Aims of all Parties . . . Offering an Expedient . . . to the bringing solid, lasting Peace . . .

IRELANDS Ambition taxed, The PARLIAMENTS Authority vindicated, in A Discourse humbly proposed unto the supreme judicature . . .

Ives, Jeremiah, Eighteen QUESTIONS PROPOUNDED To Put the great Question between the Army and their dissenting Brethren out of Question

Johnson, Edward, AN EXAMINATION OF THE ESSAY: OR, AN ANSWER to the Fifth Monarchy

Le White, Thomas, AN ANSWER To A LETTER Sent To a Gentleman of the Middle-Temple. Concerning the late various and strange changes . . .

Let me Speake too? Or, Eleven QUERIES Humbly Proposed to the Officers . . . Concerning The late Alteration of Government . . .

A LETTER of Addresse from the Officers of the Army in SCOTLAND

A Letter from Sir George Booth . . . shewing the Reasons of his present Engagement in Defence of his Countries Liberties

LILBURNS GHOST, With a Whip in one hand, to scourge Tyrants out of Authority; And Balme in the other, to heal the Sores of our as yet Corrupt STATE . . .

A LIVELY CHARACTER of some Pretending Grandees of SCOTLAND To the good old cause

THE LONDONERS LAST WARNING

Long Parliament-Work, (if they will please to do't) For the Good of the COMMON-WEALTH: Or, The Humble Desires of the Well-affected, Revived . . .

Margery Good-Cow . . . Or, a short DISCOURSE, Shewing That there is not a Farthing due from this Nation to old Oliver . . .

Milton, John, *Considerations Touching The Likeliest Means to Remove Hirelings out of the Church*

————— 'Letter to a Friend Concerning the Ruptures of the Commonwealth', unpubl. manuscript, repr. CWPM vii. 324–32

————— 'Proposals of certaine expedients for the preventing of a civil war now feard & the settling of a firme government', unpubl. manuscript, CWPM vii. 336–9.

————— *The Readie and Easie Way to Establish a Free Commonwealth, 1660*

A MODEL Of a Democraticall GOVERNMENT, Humbly tendered to Consideration, by a Friend . . . to this COMMON-WEALTH

Morris, William, *To the Supream Authoritie Under God of the COMMON-WEALTH . . . The Commons in Parliament Assembled . . .*

Naylor, James, *Having heard that some have wronged my words which I spoke before the committee of Parliament . . . I shall speak a few words which may satisfie such as loves the truth . . .*

[Nedham, Marchamont], *Interest will not Lie. Or, a view of England's True Interest: In reference to the Papist, Royalist, Presbyterian, Baptised, Neuter, Army, Parliament, City of London: In refutation of a treasonable Pamphlet, entituled, The interest of England stated*

————— *The Case of the Commonwealth Stated, 1650*

The New LETANY

The New Lords Winding-Sheet; or, AN ARROW Shot at Randome . . .

No Parliament but the Old, or, A NEW-YEARS GIFT For the late Interrupted PARLIAMENT, Now Restored . . ., 1660

No RETURN To MONARCHY; & Liberty of Conscience SECURED, Without a Senate . . . in a way most agreeable to a COMMONWEALTH . . .

The Northern QVERIES From The Lord General Monck His QVARTERS, Sounding An Allarum, to all Loyal Hearts and Free-born English men . . . Against the Tyrannical Power, & Domination of the Sword

One SHEET, Or, if you will A Winding Sheet for the Good Old Cause

Overton, Robert, *Humble and Healing Advice . . . to Charles Lord Fleetwood and General Monck and all other inferior officers of both armies . . .*

————— *A LETTER From Ma. Gen. OVERTON, Governour of Hull, And the Officers under his Command . . . for the Honourable Lieut. General Fleetwood . . .*

O[wen], J[ohn], *Two Questions concerning the Power of the Supream magistrate about Religion, and the Worship of God with one about Tythes . . .*

A Pair of SPECTACLES For this Purblinde NATION with which They may see the Army and Parliament like Simeon & Levi Brethren in Iniquity walk hand in hand together . . .

Panarmonia, Or, The AGREEMENT Of The PEOPLE Revived, and Recommended to the Great Patrons of the Commonwealth and to the Sober-minded people . . . with an APOLOGY For Christian Liberty

A PARLIAMENTER'S PETITION TO THE ARMY *The present Supreme Authority . . .*

THE PARLIAMENTS PLEA: *Or XX REASONS For The UNION Of The PARLIAMENT & ARMY . . .*

PAUL'S CHURCHYARD. *Libri Theologici, Politici, Historici, Nundinuis Paulinis una cum Templo prostant venales Done into English for the Assembly of Divines*

The PEACE-MAKER: *Or Christian Reconciler. Being The Breathings of a Troubled Spirit, sadly considering the woful Calamities, grievous Confusions, unnatural Enmity, and impendent Ruine, of the People . . .*

Pennington, Isaac, *To the Parliament, the Army, and all the Wel-affected in the Nation, who have been faithful to the Good Old Cause*

A Perfect Description of the people and countrey of Scotland.

Pittilloh, Robert, THE HAMMER of PERSECUTION: *Or, the Mystery of Iniquity, in the PERSECUTION Of many Good People in SCOTLAND Under the GOVERNMENT Of OLIVER . . . Disclosed with the Remedies thereof*

THE POOR MAN'S MITE, *Unto the more large CONTRIBUTIONS of the LIBERAL . . . in Testimony of that respect which is born unto the faithful, and their interest as it's . . . hid in Jesus*

Prynne, William, A Brief Necessary VINDICATION *Of the Old & New SECLUDED MEMBERS, from . . . Calumnies; And Of the Fundamental Rights, Liberties . . . Interest of the . . . Parliaments, People of England, from the late avowed Subversions, 1. Of John Rogers . . . 2.Of M: Nedham . . .*

—————— *Concordia Discors, or the Dissonant Harmony of sacred publique oaths . . . lately taken by many Time-Serving Saints*

—————— *Conscientous, Serious* THEOLOGICAL *And* LEGAL QUAERES, *Propounded to the twice-dissipated, self-created Anti-Parliamentary Westminster Juncto . . ., 1660*

—————— *A Legal Vindication Of the Liberties of* ENGLAND *Against* ILLEGAL TAXES *And pretended Acts of Parliament, 1660*

—————— Loyalty Banished: *Or* ENGLAND in MOURNING. *Being A perfect Narrative of the . . . Proceedings, between divers Members of Parliament and Mr. Wil. Prynne, neer the Lobby at Westminster*

—————— *[?]* MOLA ASINARIA: *Or, The Unreasonable and Insupportable* BURTHEN *now press'd upon . . . this groaning* NATION: *By the headless Head, and unruly Rulers, that usurp upon the Liberties and Priviledges of the oppressed People . . .*

—————— *The New Cheaters forgeries, detected, disclaimed*

—————— *The* RE-PUBLICANS *and others spurious Good Old Cause, briefly and truly Anatomized . . .*

—————— *Ten Considerable Quaeries concerning* TITHES, *The Present Petitioners and Petitions for their total Abolition . . . excited . . . by disguised Jesuits . . . to . . . extirpate our Protestant Ministers, Church, Religion*

—————— *The true Good Old Cause rightly stated, and the False un-cased*

—————— *A true and perfect Narrative of what was done, spoken by and between Mr Prynne . . . the Army Officers and those now sitting . . . with the true Reasons . . . inducing Mr Prynne . . . to press for entry . . . And what proposals he intended there to make . . . .*

A *Publick PLEA Opposed to A Private Proposal, or Eight necessary QUERIES Presented to the Parliament. and Armies consideration, in this morning of Freedom, after a short, but sharp, night of Tyranny and oppression*

QUESTIONS Propounded to George Whitehead and George Fox, who disputed by turns against one University-Man in Cambr. Aug. 29 1659, 1660

A *RELATION Of The CRUELTIES And Barbarous Murthers . . . committed by some Foot-Souldiers and others . . . upon some of the Inhabitants of Enfield . . .*

A *RELATION Of the Riotous Insurrection of divers Inhabitants of Enfield, and Places Adjacent; Humbly offered to the Consideration of the MEMBERS of PARLIAMENT*

A *REMONSTRANCE And DECLARATION . . . Setting Forth The Grounds . . . of the putting a stop . . . to the Sitting of the late PARLIAMENT*

The *REMONSTRANCE And PROTESTATION Of the Well-affected People . . . Against Those Officers . . . Who . . . interrupted the PARLIAMENT the 13th of Octob. 1659. And against all pretended Powers . . . that is not established by Parliament*

THE *RENDEZVOUZ OF General Monck, Upon The Confines of England . . . A Declaration of the LORDS, Knights, Ministers & Gentry in the Northern parts; and their adhering to Gen.Monck . . . And Proposals to the Free-born people of ENGLAND*

A *REPLY To Mr William Prinne, His . . . Dangerous &c. Expedient for the . . . Settlement of these Nations, by restoring the ancient Nobility . . . Together With a few Directions to the Persons now in Authority, opening a door to Peace, Righteousness and Prosperity . . .*

R. H., *The Good Old Cause Briefly demonstrated With ADVERTISEMENTS To AUTHORITY . . . to the end, All persons may see the Cause of their Bondage, and way of deliverance*

Rigg, Ambrose, *OH YE HEADS Of The NATION Who are set in the SUPREAM AUTHORITY Thereof, and at this time Assembled in PARLIAMENT . . .*

Rogers, John, *Diapoliteia. A Christian Concertation With Mr.Prin, Mr.Baxter, Mr.Harrington, for the True Cause of the COMMONWEALTH . . .*

―――― *Mr Harrington's Parallel Unparallel'd . . . Wherein it appears, Neither the Spirit of the People, nor the Spirit of men like Mr.R but the Spirit of God, of Christ, of his People in Parliament and Adherents to the Cause, is the fittest for the Government of the Commonwealth*

―――― *Mr. PRYN'S Good Old Cause Stated and Stunted 10 years ago . . .*

Rous, Francis, *The lawfulnes of obeying the present government,* 1649

[Scot, Thomas], *The Copy of a LETTER To a Countrey Collonel, or, A serious dissuasive from joyning with those Officers now in Rebellion against the PARLIAMENT*

S. E., *The Toutch-Stone of MONY and COMMERCE: Or an Expedient For increase of Trade, Mony, and Shiping in England . . .*

A *Seasonable ADVERTISEMENT To the People of England. Whether a Monarchy, or Free State, be better; in this juncture of time?*

A *Seasonable QUESTION Soberly Proposed, ARGUED AND RESOLVED*

A *Secret Word to the WISE: or Seventeen QUERIES, Humbly proposed to the Well-affected People of the Good Old Cause*

Seven Additional Quaeres in behalf of the secluded Members, propounded to the twice-broken Rump now sitting . . . and all English Freemen . . ., 1660

Several New Cheats brought to Publique View; or the Good Old Cause Turn'd to a NEW CHEAT

Several REASONS why some Officers of the Army with Many other good People, did heretofore . . . subject to Oliver Cromwel as the Supreme Magistrate . . . Likewise, Why they have rejected the said Government, and earnestly desire the Long Parliament to sit . . .

A Short DISCOURSE concerning The Work of God in this NATION, and The Duty of all good People, both Governors and Governed, in This their DAY

SIR GEORGE BOOTH'S LETTER Of the 2nd of August, 1659. Shewing the Reasons of his present Engagement. Together with An Answer . . . invalidating the said Reasons

SIX IMPORTANT Q U A E R E S, Propounded To the Re-sitting Rump

Six New Queries

Some REASONS Humbly Proposed to the Officers . . . for the speedy Re-admission of the Long Parliament Who setled the GOVERNMENT In the way of a FREE STATE

Some Sober ANIMADVERSIONS . . . Upon A Testimony and Warning, emitted by the Presbytery of Edenburgh

The SOVLDIERS Alarum Bell, To awaken all such Who are lull'd asleep in the supposed security of a Parliamentary Conventicle unlawfully sitting . . .

Speculum Libertatis Angliae Re restitutae: Or, The Looking-Glasse of Englands Libertie Really Restored. Being the Representation of the Just & Equitable constitution of a real Commonwealth

[Sprigge, William], *A Modest Plea For An Equal Common-wealth Against Monarchy In which the Genuine Nature and true Interest of a Free-State is briefly stated . . . and humbly tendered to the Parliament*

S[treater], J[ohn], *The Continuation of this Session of Parliament, Justified; and the ACTION of the ARMY . . . Defended . . .*

——— *Government Described: Viz: What Monarchie, Aristocracie, Oligarcie, And Democracie is Together with . . . the GOVERNMENT of the . . . Free-State of RAGOUSE . . .*

——— *A LETTER Sent to . . . THE Lord Fleetwood . . . On December the 15th*

——— *A SHIELD Against the Parthian Dart . . . in Defence of the present Actions of State here in England, that produced the late Change of GOVERNMENT*

S[tubbe], H[enry], *The Common-wealth of ISRAEL, or a brief Account of Mr Prynne's Anatomy of the Good Old Cause*

——— *An ESSAY In Defence of the GOOD OLD CAUSE, Or A Discourse concerning the Rise and Extent of the power of the Civil Magistrate in reference to Spiritual Affairs . . .*

——— *A LETTER To An OFFICER of the ARMY Concerning a SELECT SENATE . . .*

——— *MALICE REBUKED, Or A CHARACTER Of Mr. Richard Baxters Abilities. And A VINDICATION Of The Honourable Sr. HENRY VANE . . .*

A Testimony to truth, agreeing with an ESSAY for Settlement

A Testimony and Warning of the Presbyterie of Edinburgh against a late petition tending. . . . to the overturning of the ordinances and truth of Christ in this Church, Octob. 5. Anno. Dom. 1659

These several PAPERS Was sent to the PARLIAMENT The twentieth day of the fifth

Moneth, 1659 Being above seven thousand of the Names of the HAND-MAIDS
And DAUGHTERS Of the LORD, And such as feels the oppression of Tithes . . .

Three PROPOSITIONS from the CASE of our Three Nations: Viz. I. That
Monarchie . . . is the best way of Government . . . Ergo, neither Parliamentarie nor
Militarie Government is best. II That it is very dangerous . . . to change the antient
Government . . . Ergo, till our antient Government be resumed . . ., the Nation
lieth exposed to many dangers . . . III. That Hereditarie Succession is the onely way
for preservation of Peace in Nations. Ergo, till the Stuarts return Princes . . . no
hope of Peace

Three SPEECHES Made To . . . the Lord Maior, Aldermen and Common Council
. . . By The Lord Whitlock, Lord Fleetwood, Lord Disbrowe. At Guildhall on
Tuesday November the 8th 1659

Timely Advice, from the Major part of the old Souldiers in the ARMY, To all the rest of
our fellow Souldiers, wherein is held forth the Politically intended Destruction of the
whole Souldiery By our new Masters

To his Excellencie the Lord Charls Fleetwood, and the rest of the Officers of the ARMY

To The GENERAL COUNCIL . . . The Representation of divers Citizens of
LONDON, and others Well-affected . . .

To the Officers and Souldiers . . . The humble Petiton and Advice of divers well affected
to the Good old Cause, Inhabitants in and about . . . Southwark

To the PARLIAMENT . . . The Humble Petition and Representation of divers
well-affected of the County of South-hampton

To the PARLIAMENT . . . A Representation of the Outrages and Cruelties acted
upon the servants of Christ, at two Meetings at Sabridgworth in Hartfordshire

To the Right Honourable, the Supreme Court of Parliament. The humble Petition of the
Sentinels in the Regiment formerly belonging to Major General Goffe

To the Supreme Authority the PARLIAMENT . . . The hearty Congratulations and
humble Petition of thousands of well-affected Gentlemen, Freeholders and Inhabitants of the County of Kent, and City of Canterbury

To the Supreme Authority the Parliament . . . The humble Petition of divers
well-affected inhabitants of the County of Wilts.

Trades Destruction is Englands Ruine, or Excise Decryed

A True Catalogue, Or An Account of the several Places and most Eminent Persons . . .
where and by whom RICHARD CROMWELL was Proclaimed Lord Protector . . .

A TRUE RELATION OF THE STATE of the CASE Between the ever Honourable
PARLIAMENT And the OFFICERS . . . , That fell out on the 11th and 12th of
October 1659

TRUTH Seeks no CORNERS: or, Seven Cases of Conscience Humbly presented to
the Army and Parliament

The TRYAL Of Sir Henry Vane, Knight, At the Kings Bench, Westminster, June the
2nd & 6th 1662, 1662

Twelve Plain PROPOSALS Offered to the Honest and Faithful OFFICERS and
SOULDIERS of our English ARMY

Twelve QUERIES Humbly Proposed to . . . the Parliament & Army, For the better
Security of . . . the Present Government; and Publique Satisfaction of the Good
People . . .

Twenty Four QUERIES Touching the Parliament & Army, and The Interest of the
Royal-Party, and Others . . .: Tending to Settlement, on the Basis of Justice &
Honour

Twenty seven QUERIES Relating to the General Good . . . Which will neither please Mad-Men nor displease Rational Men

Underhill, Thomas, *Hell broke loose: Or An HISTORY of the QUAKERS . . .*

The Unhappy Marks-man: or, Twenty three QUERIES Offered To the CONSIDER-ATION of the PEOPLE of These Nations

University QUERIES, In a Gentle Touch by the By

[Vane, Henry], *A Healing Question propounded and resolved upon the occasion of the late . . . call to HUMILIATION, in order to the Love and Union of the Honest Party . . .*, 1656, reprinted 1659

———— *A Needful CORRECTIVE Or BALLANCE In Popular Government, Expressed in a Letter to James Harrington, Esquire . . .*

———— *The Retired Mans Meditations, Or The Mysterie and Power of GODLINESS Shining forth in the Living Word, to the unmasking the Mysterie of Iniquity in the most Refined and Purest Forms*, 1655

———— *Zeal Examined: Or, A Discourse for Liberty of Conscience . . .*, 1652

A VINDICATION of That Prudent and Honourable Knight, Sir Henry Vane, from the LYES and CALUMNIES of Mr. Richard Baxter . . .

Violet, Thomas, *A TRUE NARRATIVE Of The PROCEEDINGS In the Court of Admiraltie . . . Together with several Humble Proposals, for the Profit and Honour of this Common-wealth, in saving them many score of thousand pounds*

Vox vere ANGLORUM: or Englands Loud Cry for their KING . . .

A WARNING-PIECE To The General Council of the ARMY, Being sundrey Concurrent ESSAIES, Towards a Righteous Settlement

WHITE-HALLS PETITION To The PARLIAMENT: That he may enjoy his former Priviledges

Wither, George, *A Cordial Confection against the fainting of the Heart in these distracted times . . .*

———— *Epistolium-Vagum-Prosa-Metricum: or, An Epistle at Random, in Prose and Metre . . . first intended only, for . . . the Authors Friends in Authority . . . to meditate in Parliament, the Redress of his destructive Grievances . . .*

A WORD to Purpose: Or, A Parthian Dart, Shot back to 1642, and from thence shot back again to 1659 . . . in two Substantial QUERIES, 1.Concerning The Legality of the Second Meeting of some of the Long-Parliament-Members. ALSO, A Fools Bolt shot into Wallingford House . . . concerning A Free State

A WORD OF SETTLEMENT In these Unsettled Times. Containing Some Necessary Encouragements for the Well-affected and godly People . . . in the time of present danger . . .

A Word To the Twenty Essayes towards a Settlement &c. Who under a pretence of a Testimony for God either ignorantly . . . or voluntarily, give forth a perillous one

Secondary sources

Armitage, D., 'The Cromwellian Protectorate and the languages of empire', *HJ* xxxv (1992), 532–55

———— 'John Milton: poet against empire', in Armitage, Himy and Skinner, *Milton and republicanism*, 206–25

———— A. Himy and Q. R. D. Skinner (eds), *Milton and republicanism*, Cambridge 1995

Ashley, M., *John Wildman, plotter and postmaster: a study of the English republican movement in the seventeenth century*, London 1947

Aylmer, G. E., *The state's servants: the civil service of the English Republic, 1649–1660*, London 1973

———— *Rebellion or revolution? England, 1640–1660*, Oxford 1986

Barber, S., *Regicide and republicanism: politics and ethics in the English Revolution, 1646–1659*, Edinburgh 1998

Barnard, T. C., *Cromwellian Ireland: English government and reform in Ireland, 1649–1660*, Oxford 1975

Bliss, R., *Revolution and empire: English politics and the American colonies in the seventeenth century*, Manchester 1990

Bradshaw, B. I. and J. S. Morrill (eds), *The British problem, c. 1534–1707: state formation in the Atlantic archipelago*, London 1996

Brailsford, H. N., *The Levellers and the English Revolution*, London 1961

Brenner, R., *Merchants and revolution: commercial change, political conflict and London's overseas traders, 1550–1653*, Princeton 1993

Burgess, G. (ed.), *The new British history: founding a modern state, 1603–1715*, London 1999

Capp, B. S., *The Fifth Monarchy men: a study in seventeenth-century English millenarianism*, London 1972

Clarke, A., *Prelude to Restoration in Ireland: the end of the Commonwealth, 1659–60*, Cambridge 1999

Condren, C., 'Radicals, conservatives and moderates in early modern political thought: a case of Sandwich Islands syndrome?', *Journal of Political Thought* x (1989), 525–42

Damrosch, L., *The sorrows of the Quaker Jesus: James Naylor and the Puritan crackdown on the free spirit*, Cambridge, Mass. 1996

Davies, G., *The Restoration of Charles II, 1658–1660*, San Marino 1955

Davis, J. C., 'Religion and the struggle for freedom in the English Revolution', *HJ* xxxv (1992), 507–30

Dobranski, S. B., ' "Where men of differing judgements croud": Milton and the culture of the coffee houses', *Seventeenth Century* ix (1994), 35–56

Dow, F. D., *Cromwellian Scotland, 1651–1660*, Edinburgh 1979

Fletcher, A., *A county community in peace and war: Sussex, 1600–1660*, London 1975

Goldsmith, M., 'Levelling by sword, spade and word: radical egalitarianism in the English Revolution', in C. Jones, M. Newitt and S. Roberts (eds), *Politics and people in revolutionary England: essays in honour of Ivan Roots*, Oxford 1986, 65–80

Greaves, R. and R. Zaller (eds), *Biographical dictionary of the British radicals in the seventeenth century*, Brighton 1982

Harris, T., *London crowds in the reign of Charles II: propaganda and politics from the Restoration until the Exclusion Crisis*, Cambridge 1987

Hill, C., *The experience of defeat: Milton and some contemporaries*, London 1984

Hirst, D., 'Concord and discord in Richard Cromwell's House of Commons', *EHR* ciii (1988), 339–58

———— 'The fracturing of the Cromwellian alliance: Leeds and Adam Baynes', *EHR* cviii (1993), 868–94.

—— 'The English Republic and the meaning of Britain', *Journal of Modern History* lxvi (1994), 451–86

Holmes, C., *Seventeenth century Lincolnshire*, Lincoln 1980

Hughes, A., *Politics, society and civil war in Warwickshire, 1620–1660*, Cambridge 1987

Hutton, R., *The Restoration: a political history of England and Wales, 1658–1667*, Oxford 1985

Kelsey, S., *Inventing a republic: the political culture of the English Commonwealth, 1649–1653*, Manchester 1997

Lindley, K., *Fenland riots and the English Revolution*, London 1982

Mayers, R. E., ' "Real and practicable, not imaginary and notional": Sir Henry Vane, *A healing question*, and the problems of the Protectorate', *Albion* xxviii (1996), 37–72.

Morrill, J. S., *Cheshire, 1630–1660: county government and society during the English Revolution*, Oxford 1974

—— 'The Scottish National Covenant in its British context', in *Nature of the English Revolution*, 91–117

—— *The nature of the English Revolution*, London 1993

—— 'Three kindoms and one commonwealth? The enigma of mid-seventeenth century Britain and Ireland', in A. Grant and K. Stringer (eds), *Uniting the kingdom?*, London 1995, 170–90

—— (ed.), *Revolution and Restoration*, London 1992

Norbrook, D., *Writing the English Republic: poetry, rhetoric and politics, 1627–1660*, Cambridge 1999

Pincus, S., 'England and the world in the 1650s', in Morrill, *Revolution and Restoration*, 129–47

—— 'Coffee politicians does create – coffeehouses and Restoration political-culture', *Journal of Modern History* lxvii (1995), 807–34

—— *Protestantism and patriotism: ideologies and the making of English foreign policy, 1650–1668*, Cambridge 1996

—— '"Neither Machiavellian moment nor possessive individualism": commercial society and the defenders of the English Commonwealth', *American Historical Review* ciii (1998), 702–36

Pocock, J. G. A., 'Introduction', to *The political works of James Harrington*, Cambridge 1977

—— 'The Atlantic archipelago and the war of the three kingdoms', in Bradshaw and Morrill, *The British problem*, 172–92

Raymond, J., *Making the news: an anthology of the newsbooks of revolutionary England, 1641–1660*, Moreton-in-the-Marsh 1993

—— *The invention of the newspaper: English newsbooks, 1641–1649*, Oxford 1996

Reay, B., 'The Quakers, 1659 and the restoration of the monarchy', *History* lxiii (1978), 193–213

—— *The Quakers and the English Revolution*, London 1985

Roberts, S. K., *Recovery and Restoration in an English county: Devon local administration, 1646–70*, Exeter 1985

Rostvig, M.-S., *The happy man: studies in the metamorphoses of a classical ideal*, I: 1600–1700, Oslo 1962

Round, J. H., 'Colchester and the Commonwealth', *EHR* xv (1900), 641–64

Scott, J., *Algernon Sidney and the English Republic, 1623–1677*, Cambridge 1988
———— *Algernon Sidney and the Restoration crisis, 1677–1683*, Cambridge 1991
———— 'The English republican imagination', in Morrill, *Revolution and Restoration*, 35–54
———— *England's troubles: seventeenth-century English political instability in European context*, Cambridge 2000
Sharpe, K., ' "An image doting rabble": the failure of republican culture in seventeenth century England', in K. Sharpe and S. Zwicker (eds), *Refiguring revolutions*, Berkeley, Ca. 1998, 25–55
Skerpan, E., *The rhetoric of politics in the English Revolution, 1642–60*, Columbia 1992
Skinner, Q. R. D., 'Conquest and consent: Thomas Hobbes and the Engagement controversy', in G. E. Aylmer (ed.), *The Interregnum: the quest for settlement*, London 1972, 79–98
Smith, N., 'Popular republicanism in the 1650s: John Streater's "heroic mechanicks" ', in Armitage, Himy and Skinner, *Milton and republicanism*, 137–55
———— *Literature and revolution*, Yale 1994
Stevenson, D., 'The Early Covenanters and the federal union of Britain', in R. Mason (ed.), *Scotland and England, 1286–1815*, Edinburgh 1987, 163–81
———— 'Cromwell, Scotland and Ireland', in J. S. Morrill (ed.), *Oliver Cromwell and the English Revolution*, London 1990, 149–80
Taft, B., ' "They that pursew perfection on earth . . .": the political progress of Robert Overton', in I. Gentles, J. S. Morrill and A. B. Worden (eds), *Soldiers, writers and statesmen of the English revolution*, Cambridge 1998, 286–303
Underdown, D., *Royalist conspiracy in England, 1649–1660*, New Haven 1960
———— *Somerset in the civil war and Interregnum*, Newton Abbot 1973
———— *A freeborn people: politics and the nation in seventeenth century England*, Oxford 1996
Wallace, J. M., *Destiny his choice: the loyalism of Andrew Marvell*, Cambridge 1968
Walter, J. and J. S. Morrill, 'Order and disorder in the English Revolution', repr. in Morrill, *Nature of the English Revolution*, 359–91
Warmington, A. R., *Civil war, Interregnum and Restoration in Gloucestershire, 1640–1672*, Woodbridge 1997
Wheeler, J. S., 'Navy finance, 1649–1660', *HJ* xxxix (1996), 457–66
———— *The making of a world power*, Sutton 1999
White, B. R., *The English Baptists of the seventeenth century*, London 1983
Williamson, A. H., 'Union with England traditional, union with England radical: Sir James Hope and the mid-seventeenth-century British state', *EHR* cx (1995), 303–22
Woolrych, A. H., 'The Good Old Cause and the fall of the Protectorate', *Cambridge Historical Journal* xiii (1957), 133–67
———— 'Introduction', to *CPWM* vii
———— *England without a king, 1649–1660*, London 1983
Wootton, D. (ed.), *Republicanism, liberty and commercial society, 1649–1776*, Stanford 1994
Worden, A. B., *The Rump Parliament, 1648–1653*, Cambridge 1974
———— 'Classical republicanism and the Puritan Revolution', in V. Pearl, H.

Lloyd-Jones and A. B. Worden (eds), *History and imagination: essays in honour of Hugh Trevor-Roper*, London 1981, 182–200

———— 'Toleration and the Cromwellian Protectorate', in W. J. Sheils (ed.), *Persecution and toleration* (Studies in Church History xxi, 1984), 199–233

———— 'Oliver Cromwell and the sin of Achan', in D. E. D. Beales and G. Best (eds), *History, society and the Churches*, Cambridge 1985, 125–45

———— 'Providence and politics in Cromwellian England', *Past and Present* cix (1985) 55–99

———— 'Milton's republicanism and the tyranny of heaven', in G. Bock, Q. R. D. Skinner and M. Viroli (eds), *Machiavelli and republicanism*, Cambridge 1990, 225–45

———— 'English republicanism', in J. H. Burns and M. Goldie (eds), *The Cambridge history of political thought, 1450–1700*, Cambridge 1991, 443–75

———— 'Harrington's *Oceana*: origins and aftermath, 1651–1660', in Wootton, *Republicanism*, 111–38

———— 'James Harrington and *The Commonwealth of Oceana*, 1656', in Wootton, *Republicanism*, 82–110

———— 'Marchamont Nedham and English republicanism', in Wootton, *Republicanism*, 46–81

———— 'Milton and Marchamont Nedham', in Armitage, Himy and Skinner, *Milton and republicanism*, 156–80

Zagorin, P., *A history of political thought in the English Revolution*, London 1954

Unpublished theses etc.

Black, S. F., 'The judges at Westminster Hall during the Interregnum', BLitt. diss. Oxford 1970

Chivers, G. V., 'The City of London and the state, 1658–64: a study in political and financial relations', PhD diss. Manchester 1961

Massarella, D., 'The politics of the Army, 1647–1660', PhD diss. York 1977

Reece, H. M., 'The military presence in England, 1649–60', DPhil. diss. Oxford 1981

Weinstock, M., 'The position of London in national affairs, 1658–1660', MA diss. London 1934

Index

Allen, Thomas, 90
Allen, William, 70 n. 100, 84, 259, 270
Alsop, Colonel Roger, 155, 156, 157, 159, 160
Alured, Colonel Matthew, 29 n. 5, 55, 244, 246 n. 74
American colonies, 150, 152–5. *See also* Barbados, New England, Maryland, Virginia
ancient fundamentalists, *see* Levellers
Annesley, Arthur, 13
Archer, John, 36
Argyll, Archibald Campbell, marquis of, 173
Armitage, David (historian), 114, 115
Army: alleged authority of, 13, 203–4, 262–4; conservative attitude to, 22–3; criticises Parliament (1653), 13–14, 203 (1659) 28, 29, 148, 251, 255, 260–1; differences within, 7, 244, 250, 253, 256–7; expels Parliament (Oct.), 229, 250–1, 264; material needs/pay of, 19, 23, 28, 43, 59–60, 236, 241, 247–8; recruitment of, 43; relations with Parliament, 6, 18, 22, 47, 48, 55–63, 71–2, 107, 230, 235, 237, 238–41, 244–50, 252, 274; restores Parliament (May), 1, 5, 185, 261; stationed abroad: in Dunkirk, 156–9; in Ireland, 161, 164–6, 181, 253, 257–8; in Jamaica, 154; in Scotland, 161, 162–4, 168, 176, 181, 250, 253, 256. *See also* officers
Ascham, Anthony, 199
Ashfield, Colonel Richard, 158
Ashley-Cooper, Sir Anthony, 31, 34, 46 n. 2
Aspinwall, Alexander, 188–9
assessment, assessment commissions/commissioners, 82, 102
Atkins, Richard, 36
Atkins, Thomas, 81
Aylmer, Gerald (historian), 28, 44, 182

Backhouse, Captain Edward, 99
Baker, Daniel, 91 n. 68
Baltimore, Cecilus Calvert, Lord, 153
Baptists, 21, 65, 69, 70, 84, 165, 172, 193,

219, 227, 269. *See also* Allen (William), Kiffin
Barbados/Barbadians, 152, 153
Barber, Sarah (historian), 4
Barebone, Praise-God, 84, 271
Barkstead, John, 55
Baxter, Richard, 9, 70 n. 100, 202, 205 n. 82, 207–8, 210, 221
Baynes, Adam, 98, 104
Baynes, John, 163 n. 53, 164 n. 55
Baynes, Captain Robert, 164 n. 55, 240
Bedfordshire, 63
Bennet, Robert, 54, 100, 101, 104, 106, 265 n. 33
Berkshire, 269
Berners, Josias, 34, 265 n. 33
Berry, Colonel James, 33, 56, 57, 58, 244
Berwick, 97 n. 15
Bethel, Slingsby, 84
Beverley (Yorkshire), 97 n. 15
Billing, Edward, 151, 219 n. 134
Bishop, George, 52, 54, 211
Bland, John, 40
Boone, Thomas, 124, 126
Booth, Sir George, 96; rebellion of, 20, 21–2, 38–9, 85, 94, 160, 166, 234, 241; refutation of, 199–200
Bordeaux-Neufville, Antoine de, French ambassador: diplomacy of, 134, 135–6, 137, 190–1, 231; and English fleet's return from Sound, 127, 128, 132; observations of: on Army, 163, 232, 235, 240; on London, 78, 79; on republicans, 53, 55, 62, 119, 121, 139, 230
Boston (Massachusetts), 153
Boteler, ex-Major-General William, 55
Bourne, Major Nehemiah, 1, 99–100, 129, 163
Bradshaw, John, 33
Brathwait, Richard, 188
Bray, William, 211, 224
Brenner, Robert, 147
Brentford, 109
Brewster, Thomas, 50
Bristol, 52, 94, 98 n. 19
Britain, idea of, 149, 150